BIG APPLE

Safari

for families

BIG APPLE
Safari
for families

THE URBAN PARK RANGERS' GUIDE
TO NATURE IN NEW YORK CITY

Sharon Seitz

The Countryman Press
Woodstock, Vermont

We welcome your comments and suggestions.
Please contact: Editor, The Countryman Press, P.O. Box 748, Woodstock, VT 05091, or e-mail
countrymanpress@wwnorton.com.

First Edition

Library of Congress Cataloging-in-Publication Data
has been applied for.

ISBN 0-88150-621-4

Cover and text design by Melanie Jolicoeur
Cover photographs courtesy of the author, Robertstock.com, and Photos.com
Interior photographs by the author unless otherwise specified
Maps by Paul Woodward, © The Countryman Press
Illustration on page 180 by Jeff Goodwin

Published by The Countryman Press, P.O. Box 748, Woodstock, Vermont 05091

Distributed by W. W. Norton & Company, Inc.,
500 Fifth Avenue, New York, NY 10110

Printed in the United States of America

10 9 8 7 6 5 4 3 2 1

For my Junior Rangers,

Caleb and Lucas

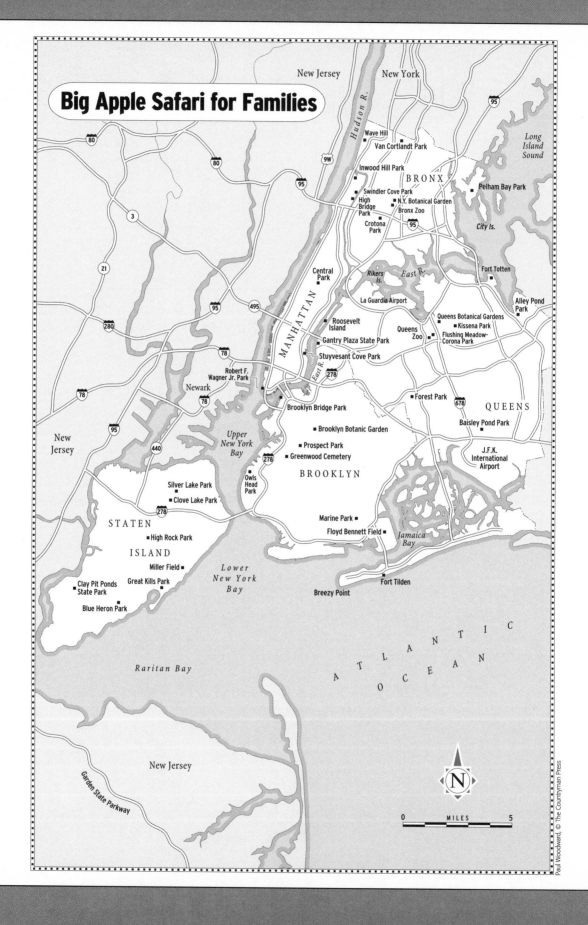

Big Apple Safari for Families

New Jersey   New York

Hudson R.

Long Island Sound

Wave Hill
Van Cortlandt Park

9W

Inwood Hill Park

B R O N X

Pelham Bay Park

Swindler Cove Park
High Bridge Park
N.Y. Botanical Garden
Bronx Zoo

City Is.

Crotona Park

Fort Totten

Central Park

Rikers Is.

East R.

La Guardia Airport

Alley Pond Park

M A N H A T T A N

Roosevelt Island

Queens Botanical Gardens
Kissena Park
Flushing Meadow-Corona Park

Queens Zoo

Gantry Plaza State Park

Stuyvesant Cove Park

East R.

278

Newark

Robert F. Wagner Jr. Park

Forest Park

Q U E E N S

Baisley Pond Park

Brooklyn Bridge Park

Brooklyn Botanic Garden

J.F.K. International Airport

Upper New York Bay

Prospect Park
Greenwood Cemetery

B R O O K L Y N

Owls Head Park

Silver Lake Park
Clove Lake Park

Marine Park

Floyd Bennett Field

Jamaica Bay

S T A T E N

High Rock Park

Lower New York Bay

I S L A N D

Miller Field

Clay Pit Ponds State Park

Great Kills Park

Blue Heron Park

Fort Tilden

Breezy Point

New Jersey

A T L A N T I C   O C E A N

Raritan Bay

New Jersey

Garden State Parkway

N

0   M I L E S   5

CONTENTS

Five-Borough Map vi

Acknowledgments viii

Foreword by Adrian Benepe, Commissioner of the New York City
Department of Parks and Recreation ix

Preface by Sara Hobel, Director, Urban Park Rangers x

Introduction xi

1. Nature and Environmental Centers 2

2. Nature Walks 30

3. Birding with Children 76

4. Nights on the Town 110

5. Paddling with Kids 132

6. Exploring the Shore 148

7. Gardens Grow Children 164

8. Bicycling 190

9. Goin' Fishing 212

10. Museums, Zoos, and Farms 228

Getting There 248

Additional Resources 270

Index 274

ACKNOWLEDGMENTS

When I began researching this book, I immediately went to the Urban Park Rangers (a division of the New York City Department of Parks & Recreation) for help in getting to know the city's wild places and about how families may enjoy them. Director Sara Hobel was intrigued with my idea and offered the division's assistance and support as well as a point person who would accompany me on some outings, field my emails and phone requests, and provide answers to my questions—or, at the very least, point me in the right direction and, finally, read my manuscript. No matter how busy he was—and he is a busy man—Deputy Director Matt Symons never let me down; and to him I am forever grateful.

I am also thankful for the help of all the Urban Park Rangers with whom I have had contact during my research. We should all be thankful for their hard work and commitment to educating the public about New York City's natural treasures. Short staffed and low paid, these dedicated individuals not only shared with me their insights and knowledge, but do so with others every working day to make sure that city kids develop a relationship with nature. I especially appreciate all those Rangers who stayed up practically around the clock to make sure that campers under their watch, including my family and me, were always safe, comfortable, and well fed with s'mores.

I would also like to thank all the naturalists and experts who took the time to be interviewed, including Zenobia Barlow, Joseph Cornell, Dave Taft, Leslie Day, and Regina McCarthy. Their commitment to the natural world and its importance in one's life, particularly children's lives, inspires me.

Thanks also to Mickey Cohen for teaching me how to seine, Don Riepe for sharing his beautiful photographs and being my own personal reference desk when it came to birds, and the unknown fishermen at the 69th Street Pier who loaned me their rods and turned me on to some great snapper fishing.

When I first proposed this book, it was Ann Kraybill who embraced the project and brought it to the attention of The Countryman Press and editor Kermit Hummel. I thank them both for their support and enthusiasm. Thanks also go out to Assistant Production Manager Jennifer Thompson, who oversaw the project and kept it on track. I am especially grateful to my editor, Hal Hager, whose friendly professionalism, keen eye, and superb organization were invaluable to me in shaping the final manuscript.

Finally, I would like to thank my children, Caleb and Lucas, for willingly accompanying me up hills, through mudflats, along beaches, and on hikes in the dark. Even when Mommy was too busy jotting down notes to appreciate their discoveries, they remained cheerful and enthusiastic. These two tireless little boys provided me with constant inspiration and are the best companions an outdoor Mommy could ever have.

There is, however, a third guy in my life who supported me and cheered me on the whole time—my husband, Stuart Miller. Thank you for generously giving me the time I needed to get this right, listening to my impassioned ramblings on praying mantises, helping me flip over beached horseshoe crabs, and being open to doing just about anything I proposed. Thank you for putting yourself aside for me.

FOREWORD

by Adrian Benepe, *Commissioner of the New York City Department of Parks & Recreation*

Dear Readers,

Little did I know when I joined Parks & Recreation in 1979 that I would still be here a quarter century later, now serving as Commissioner. I could not have anticipated that by becoming an Urban Park Ranger, I would rediscover New York City's parks and fall in love with them all over again, with the fresh perspective of a child. During my early years with the agency, I trekked off the beaten path, acquiring a new understanding of familiar landscapes. I found that the more one truly explores parks, the more one discovers the unusual, the unexpected, and the beautiful. Parks may serve as City ballfields, basketball courts, and gardens; but they also contain some of the City's most precious natural secrets.

Most people don't know it, but there are areas in our parks that are virtually untouched. The north end of Central Park, from the Harlem Meer south to 102nd Street, is much the same as it was 400 years ago. One need only venture 20 feet into the forests of Inwood Hill Park to be confronted by the massive blocks of toppled schist, which provided Native Americans thousands of years of seasonal shelter, along with 120-foot-tall tulip trees.

And then there's the wildlife. As a Ranger, I began to notice the animals that make their homes in New York City parks; what most captivated me were the birds. I learned to identify red-tailed hawks, great blue and black-crowned night herons, woodpeckers, chickadees, long-eared owls, red-bellied woodpeckers, and canvasback ducks.

I learned to appreciate the diversity of our urban canopy. Parks & Recreation cares for 2.5 million trees, from London plane trees and tulip trees, to majestic American elms, white oaks, mulberry trees, horse chestnuts, and honey locusts, Norway maples, sycamores . . . the trees are as variegated as their names are colorful.

But, one doesn't need to be an Urban Park Ranger to see all of this. There is no better place to start discovering New York City's nearly 29,000 acres of parkland than with this guide. Soon you, too, will be birding at dawn in Prospect Park, paddling softly down the Bronx River, and camping out under the stars in Alley Pond Park.

As Commissioner, I have the privilege of protecting New York City's natural resources. I also have the honor of supporting people like Sharon, who, like Parks & Recreation, are committed to spreading the word about our natural wonders.

PREFACE

Preface by Sara Hobel, *Director, Urban Park Rangers*

We are all born with specific talents. Mine included finding bugs, birds, stray dogs, and tiny motherless kittens.

It drove my mother crazy. Jackie Kennedy was in the White House, setting the style for elegant women of merit—the behind-the-scenes partners of powerful men—women who could decorate their homes, entertain their husbands' colleagues, and look appropriate at all times in a short strand of pearls. My mother was fighting a losing battle in raising me to be such a lady.

There is, in particular, one photograph of the two of us. She in an empire-waist pink satin dress, hair buoyed by a "lift" and lengthened by a "fall." Me in a teal velvet A-line dress with a white satin collar, with a velvet headband, posed and poised, at the bottom of a graceful flight of stairs in the center hall of my childhood home. It is a frozen statement that belies the truth. In truth, I was always, in ragtag pigtails and dirty clothes, tagging after my brothers or venturing off to explore the woods or fields on my own. My room was filled with mice, lizards, recuperating injured wild birds, bottle-nursing kittens, lost dogs, salamanders . . . whatever I could sneak in when my mother was out. As long as they stayed in my room, she gave me the liberty to keep them; but if they dared to cross the threshold into the main part of the house . . .!

I just did not fit into my family, the times, and the trends—nor, as I entered my teen years, even with my friends. But I was lucky in that I could head outdoors, make my way to my world, and develop the skills that are now the foundation of my well-being: hiking, caring for animals, canoeing, camping, and exploring nature.

When I became the Director of the Urban Park Rangers, I asked myself this question: "Can children here in New York City make their own way into the natural world, as I had done in the suburbs? " The answer was "no." In this city, as in all cities, children need significant help to explore the outdoors . . . from parents, teachers, mentors . . . and the Urban Park Rangers.

Perhaps the Rangers' core mission reflects my own: to provide education and recreation opportunities for children to experience the natural world. But it also reflects the heart and soul of the Department of Parks & Recreation, with more than 8,000 of its 29,000 acres designated as "Forever Wild" preserves, filled with the natural resources of plants, rivers, lakes, kettle ponds, trails, and wildlife—together with 14 nature centers and a staff of Rangers dedicated to connecting people and parks. And perhaps, despite the times, the trends, and even your own interests, your child may be like me and so many others and need nature to help sustain her or him and create a sense of well-being.

Thank you, Sharon Seitz, for writing this book and helping to spread the word to so many New York parents that our parks, the Urban Park Rangers, and many other wonderful organizations are here to open the door for you and your children to explore the natural world.

INTRODUCTION

"The best place to observe nature is where you are."
—John Burroughs, New York–born Naturalist (1837–1921)

Experiencing nature with my children, and thereby fostering a love for and responsibility to it, is nearly as important to me as breath. While this may sound a bit extreme, consider that our very survival is linked to the vitality and health of the land and its creatures. Exploring nature with my kids, however, goes way beyond selfish concerns and philosophical dictums. On a basic level, it is simply fun to skip rocks, spot salamanders, and blow seeds from a stem. Indeed, there is much to be gained from making nature part of your family life.

I want my sons to love even the seemingly ugly and unreasonable things. So after it rains, we look for lumpy mushrooms that have sprouted from the ground and earthworms that have wriggled their ways to the top of the soil. In spring, we watch squirrels wantonly steal birdseed put out for cardinals and sparrows; and come autumn, these pesky guys tear into our beautifully painted jack-o'-lanterns. Even though they're ripping us off, it's fun to watch unbridled nature at work.

When presented with an insect opportunity, I encourage my kids to gently hold a monarch butterfly plucked from a butterfly bush or allow a praying mantis to walk across their pant's leg. Sometimes we go on scavenger hunts for pill bugs, turning over rocks to see how many we can find. Then we gently tap them on the back to see how quickly they roll up into a ball.

I want my sons to appreciate flowers right down to the pollen and pistil and to understand that gardening means planning for the future. I want them to hold dear the taste of home-grown raspberries and cherry tomatoes picked from the few plants in our yard or sold by farmers at neighborhood greenmarkets. I want them to recall the year when a wayward seed —one not yet broken down in our compost — gave way to a wily squash plant that stretched across our yard, yielding four tremendous and tasty butternut squashes.

Most of all, I want my city kids to understand that nature can be enjoyed right where we live—in New York City, a place too often thought of as devoid of anything organic. Nature isn't a theme park that exists someplace else, visited during family vacations or long weekends away. Nature lives, even thrives, in New York City, which has more open space than Los Angeles, Chicago, and Philadelphia combined—nearly 53,000 acres of city, state, and national park land, according to the Trust for Public Land, a nonprofit organization that has done its part to preserve some of New York's more beautiful places. Within this mix is a diversity of ecosystems—wetlands, woodlands, and meadows—home to hundreds of animals and plants—from flying squirrels and screech owls to 300-year-old trees and edible wildflowers. And it's all waiting to be discovered by you and your children.

"Once you start to value our parks as a home for birds and other animals, and the plants these animals depend on, you develop a sense of stewardship which leads to an environmental awareness that results in your becoming an advocate and protector of our parks," says local environmental educator Leslie Day. "You begin to realize that if a particular lake becomes polluted, the waterfowl that depend on returning to it each spring in order to nest, raise their young, and feed, will stop coming. You start to realize that if trees on a hillside die and are not replaced, the songbirds that nest in them and use them for protection will no longer be able to return."

Unfortunately, modern kids are increasingly lured indoors by television and computers and overscheduled with soccer practice, karate classes, and other pressing activities. And this withdrawal from nature doesn't apply only to kids. America is less rural than it used to be, with four out of five Americans living in cities and suburbs. As a species, we spend, on average, 95 percent of our time and 99.9 percent of our thinking disconnected from nature, according to one researcher.

"The natural world is perceived as peripheral, if it is acknowledged at all," says Zenobia Barlow, executive director and founding director of the California-based Center for Ecoliteracy, which uses the natural world and local ecosystems as its classroom.

Indeed, when it comes to environmental education, kids are often taught (and at too young an age) more about the destruction of Amazon rainforests than the importance of local habitats. They "are asked to heal the world's wounds without ever having bonded with nature, a huge responsibility for young hearts and minds," writes Richard Louv in his book, Childhood's Future.

"Knowledge without love will not stick," wrote naturalist John Burroughs. "But if love comes first, knowledge is sure to follow." In other words, children need to get close to nature, make friends with it, and feel comfortable in it, before we ask them to protect and fix it.

Moreover, experts assure us that estrangement from nature can have lasting implications, from breeding fear of and contempt for it (and therefore apathy for the environment) to even fostering violence. "If you want to create violence, remove people from the cycles of light and life and put them into denatured settings, away from a green and natural context, and into manmade materials," says Barlow. "That's what we do with prisons."

On the other hand, engaging in nature can have lasting benefits. "It is restorative to people individually and to families as units," says New York City Parks Commissioner and New York native Adrian Benepe. "There's something nice about just hiking in the woods with your family and staring at a 120-foot tree. Kids remember these things."

In her book, The Sense of Wonder, the late naturalist and environmentalist Rachel Carson urges adults—parents, aunts, uncles, grandparents, friends—to nourish children's instinctive appetites for nature discovery, something that is essential to their development and happiness and the future of our planet, not to mention the wonderful family memories that will ensue. "If a child is to keep alive his inborn sense of wonder," Carson wrote, "he needs the companionship of a least one adult who can share it, rediscovering with him the joy, excitement, and mystery of the world we live in."

Let that person be you, even if you can't tell a grasshopper from a cicada, an oak tree from an elm. Does the tree have thorns? Is its bark smooth? Are the leaves big or small? The names aren't that important at first. What matters is that you've discovered something and observed it together. You may even find that your family's affinity with nature may come in handy during trying times.

The emerging field of ecopsychology recognizes, among other things, the healing benefits of nature, encouraging people in therapy to turn to nature when stressed or disturbed, much like Sophie in the children's book, When Sophie Gets Angry, who calms herself by retreating to her favorite tree. Some researchers even believe that people have an inherent biological need for nature, and by abandoning that need we create a powerful discontentment that is hard to explain or understand.

"You can type in 'frog' on a computer and find out about frogs," says Dave Taft, District Ranger, Jamaica Bay Wildlife Refuge, in Queens. "But to truly understand 'frog' in your life, somehow you need to catch one, hold one, look into its watery eyes. And with that, have wet, muddy feet, smell the pond edge, and wade with the other things growing and swimming in the pond."

Nature close to home begs to be explored, and for some people that may mean altering their perception of nature. This is probably more difficult for parents than for their children. New York City is not the Adirondacks and there are no black bears or breathtaking gorges here. But as naturalist and author Joseph Cornell explains, "Children don't need exotic places. To children, everything is new. It's all a matter of how you see things anyway."

So instead of lumping pigeons together, focus on their different colors and the iridescence of their wings. Consider the wildness in a simple handful of soil—ants, mites, worms, centipedes, spiders, millipedes, and grubs all working together—as well as nature's resilience, as seen in plants bursting through sidewalk cracks. Community gardens offer a wealth of nature exploration, from beehives and fish ponds to vegetable gardens where Brussels sprouts grow on tall nubby stalks—something you'll never see in the supermarket. Vivid songbirds, and even predators like hawks and owls, bed down in city trees, while bats roam the night skies.

New York City has had, and continues to have, a symbiotic relationship with nature that goes back to the ancient bedrock upon which our skyscrapers stand and the harbor along which the city was founded. New York is not simply about hallowed halls of money and power and cultural destinations, it includes many natural wonders, from centuries-old tulip trees to wild surprises like coyotes.

When kids learn to see beyond the streets and buildings, they will notice things they passed by before—Canada geese flying in their signature V, migrating monarch butterflies, tree galls, stinkbugs, and holes dug by chipmunks in the park's grounds.

Blurring the boundaries of nature and city also creates a more realistic sense of place. Senses are heightened. Kids learn patience in waiting for a red-tailed hawk to appear in a tree, teamwork in observing ants helping one another carry a huge cookie crumb, responsibility in caring for a plant, and resourcefulness in witnessing squirrels storing acorns for the winter. By watching millipedes, mites, flatworms, and beetles creating compost, kids discover the earth's natural laws of give and take—and renewal.

Seasons are acknowledged and experienced, while respect and compassion for all living things is nurtured, leading to a kind of paternal desire to protect the future. As a byproduct of their children's interest and concern, parents may also catch the bug—so to speak—becoming environmental advocates more inclined to pressure government officials to increase spending for the city's severely underfinanced and understaffed parks.

It's a great time to explore nature with your kids in New York City. "It's right here, right now, on your balcony," says Zenobia Barlow.

In the last few years, several new nature centers have opened in the city's five boroughs—from the Audubon Center at Prospect Park in Brooklyn to the Greenbelt Nature Center on Staten Island. New waterfront parks like the Hudson River Park and Brooklyn Bridge Park bring families closer to the shoreline. Fishing and hiking opportunities abound in the city, with the Urban Park Rangers' Explorer Programs expanded to include free camping and canoeing in parks around the city. Cyclists can enjoy an ever-growing network of greenways, while budding gardeners can adopt plots in any of city's many community gardens or participate in programs at the city's renowned botanical gardens.

It's never too soon to explore nature with your kids. Even an infant carried in a front carrier or backpack will benefit from the stimulation provided by nature, the sounds of birds, the rush of waves, the smell of a forest, the tickling sensation of grasses and leaves. When they become toddlers, children begin to more actively interact with nature, observing and making connections. Older kids develop a more complex understanding of the world around them.

Kids are born naturalists. They love to turn over rocks or kick up leaves to discover what's hidden beneath them. They relish the rhythm of a stone skipped on the surface of a pond and are drawn to the sight of a mother duck leading her fuzzy ducklings on a swim. Pinecones, acorns, and autumn leaves—all readily available in city parks—are the stuff of childhood collections.

"They are attuned to beauty and still own a sense of wonder," Leslie Day says of children. "They love animals and flowers. They are closer to the ground and have their senses wide open."

How to Use This Book

This book includes ten chapters. Some focus on activities that families may undertake to explore nature in New York City—such as fishing and camping—while others spotlight nature centers, nature-related museums, zoos, and farms (with suggestions on how best to enjoy them), as well as organizations that welcome kids on their field trips. Where pertinent, I suggest appropriate ages for specific activities and exhibits.

There is information on how to get started in your chosen outdoor activity and, where necessary, suggestions for appropriate gear. Most of the recommended outings are free; but if there is a charge—usually minimal—I've indicated so.

Spread throughout the book are fun and informative sidebars on subjects ranging from monarch butterfly migration and rescuing baby birds to building a sea scope and poking fun at nature. Travel directions to every destination—including both car and public transportation—may be found at the back of the book, after chapter 10. And there is also a bibliography of age-appropriate books for further reading, as well as a list of additional kid- and family-friendly Web sites.

BIG APPLE

Safari

for families

1 NATURE AND ENVIRONMENTAL CENTERS

Ask most New Yorkers for directions to the nearest nature center and you'll likely get blank stares. That's because many urbanites still think that nature exists someplace else, outside the city, and can only be experienced during weekend trips to the Catskills or vicariously on the Discovery Channel and Internet.

But nature is literally breaking through the cracks of city sidewalks and happily nesting in our parks' leafy trees, not to mention some of our high-rises. Reflecting on all this nature and educating the public are more than two-dozen nature centers that provide an often free passport to the city's natural world.

Nature centers in New York City are a relatively new concept, although a handful of them, such as the Alley Pond Environmental Center in Queens, were established during environmentalism's early years in the 1970s. Most of the nature centers, particularly those under the auspices of the New York City Department of Parks & Recreation, were created within the last decade. They've even gotten better in recent years. Some of the most impressive, like the Greenbelt Nature Center on Staten Island and the Prospect Park Audubon Center in Brooklyn, are 21st-century creations.

As with all nature centers and their programs, New York City's are only as good as the people who run them, from parks employees to dedicated volunteers. Some are housed in tiny, converted comfort stations and storage sheds, have limited hours, and often serve as little more than a starting point for walks and events. Others are fully outfitted with hands-on exhibits, animals, frequent programming, and educational opportunities. Budget cuts have forced some city-run nature centers to rely on "friends groups" and nonprofit organizations to help staff programs and host activities. Almost always, the centers with strong links to these outside sources are most successful at what they do.

Programs, tours, and activities offered by city, state, and federally managed nature centers are usually free. The New York City Department of Parks & Recreation's Urban Park Rangers oversee 14 nature centers. These centers—there's at least one in each borough—usually focus on the ecosystem in which the center resides, illustrating how the habitat works within the city's larger, diverse environment. In recent years, and thanks to financial help from the National Geographic Society, the Rangers' outdoors menu has exploded with numerous Explorer Programs, designed to get kids into the thick of nature through free fishing, camping, canoeing, and challenging activities.

The nature centers also offer such informational material as trail maps and a calendar of seasonal events, which is the best way to find out about Ranger-led walks, tours, programs, and special events. You may also read the calendar online, at www.nycgovparks.org/sub_about/parks_divisions/urban_park_rangers/pd_ur.html; or subscribe for free, by dialing 311 and asking for the Urban Park Rangers.

The National Park Service operates the 26,644-acre Gateway National Recreation Area, created in 1972 as the nation's first urban national park, linking it with such existing greats as Yellowstone and Yosemite. A collection of waterfront natural areas, open spaces, and recreational spaces, Gateway is named for the two arms of land—Sandy Hook and Breezy Point—that bend toward each other to create a gateway to New York Harbor. Most of the property (24,981 acres) is within the Jamaica Bay/Breezy Point Unit in Brooklyn and Queens and the Staten Island Unit on the island's south shore. (The rest is in New Jersey's Sandy Hook Unit).

The closest thing the Gateway has to a nature center is the visitor's center at the Jamaica Bay Wildlife Refuge (now undergoing an extensive renovation), although some of Gateway's other buildings, mostly Ranger or contact stations, have small exhibits. They provide trail information and issue permits and serve as starting points for free walks and, sometimes, classrooms for free nature programs. The best way to find out about activities is to call the individual site or pick up a copy of Gateway's quarterly calendar at any of the parks. Events are also listed at www.nps.gov/gate/pphtml/events.html.

The New York State Office of Parks, Recreation and Historic Preservation manages one park preserve in the city, the 260-acre Clay Pit Ponds State Park Preserve on Staten Island. The preserve supports ecologically fragile plant and animal communities that, by law, must be protected. Most of the preserve's programs and tours are free, provided by a dedicated troop of knowledgeable volunteers, many of them Staten Island naturalists. Some nonprofit nature centers also operate in conjunction with the city's Parks Department and usually charge a fee for programs and activities, with members receiving discounts. Private nature centers generally charge an admission fee. Most of the nature centers keep regular hours, but the parks and trails are open from dawn to dusk.

Many of New York's nature centers resulted from local pressure placed on developers and government agencies that would have otherwise bulldozed these important green spaces. People can make a difference; so as you watch your child kick his or her way through autumn leaves, marvel at butterflies, and soak up exhibits at the nature centers, remember that you are not only nurturing your child's heart and creating memories, but influencing his or her conscience and creating future environmental stewards.

Crotona Park Nature Center

**Charlotte Street and
Crotona Park East
718-378-2061**
www.nycgovparks.org/sub_about/parks_divisions/urban_park_rangers/pd_ur_nature_centers.html

Ranger-led walks and nature programs; canoeing; fishing; bilingual (English and Spanish) exhibits on local wildlife; nature videos; library; community garden; picnic tables; restrooms.

This 127-acre site took on new life in 1996 with the creation of the Friends of Crotona Park, who later triumphed with the reopening of the park's nature center in 2001. The center is housed inside a former boathouse that faces 3-acre Indian Lake, which often hosts canoeing. Bilingual exhibits (serving the local Latino community) highlight local birds, such as the northern mockingbird and northern flicker, and illustrate how nest designs vary from species to species. There's even a huge squirrel nest, called a drey, made from twigs and heaps of leaves. Squirrels build their dreys high up in the tangle of tree branches, so they can be safe from predators; and they can be easily spotted during winter, when taking a nature walk with your children.

While Crotona Park may not appeal to those looking for a truly natural experience, it has more to offer than meets the eye, starting with chunks of Fordham gneiss (the city's oldest rock) bulging out of the lawn and two red-tailed hawks who call the park home. Look for them high atop the trees, or, once inside the nature center, ask to see the beautiful, short hawk video made and donated by local photographer, Steve Nunez. That alone is worth the trip. It documents the hawks building nests and dining on squirrels, rats, and pigeons. It's a bit gory, but only briefly, and provides urban kids with a window into the real lives of seemingly exotic animals living right in the neighborhood.

Open—Tuesday-Saturday, 9 AM-4 PM. Free.

Pelham Bay Ranger Station

Wilkinson Avenue and Bruckner Expressway (I-95 North) 718-885-3467

www.nycgovparks.org/sub_about/parks_divisions/urban_park_rangers/pd_ur_nature centers.html

Ranger-led walks and programs; nature trails; bridle paths (contact: Bronx Equestrian Center,

9 Shore Road, 718-885-0551; www.bronxequestrian center.com); picnic tables; restrooms.

Aside from scheduled programs, trail maps, and restrooms, there's little reason to visit this ranger station. It is, however, a good starting point from which to explore the southern portion of Pelham Bay Park.

At 2,766 acres, Pelham Bay Park is the city's largest park and is incredibly diverse, with 782 acres of forest, 83 acres of meadow, 51 acres of mixed scrub, 195 acres of salt marsh, 3 acres of freshwater marshes, 161 acres of salt flats, and a 13-mile stretch of saltwater coastline—all shared with two golf courses and other recreational facilities. Within the park is the

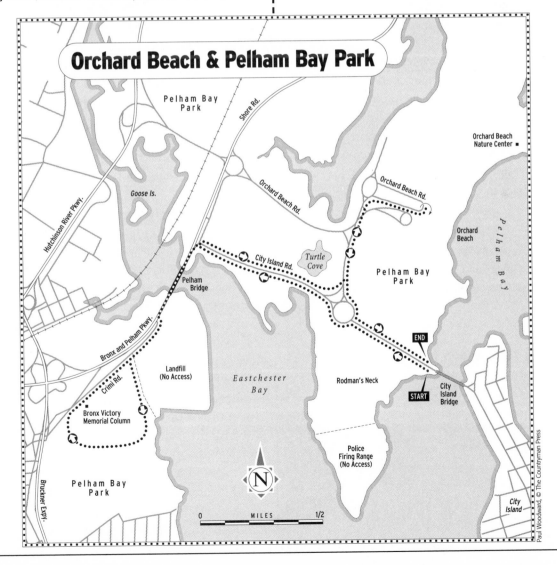

Orchard Beach & Pelham Bay Park

Thomas Pell Wildlife Sanctuary, named for the English physician who originally purchased much of the area from the Siwanoy Indians in 1654. This environmentally sensitive, 489-acre mix of wetlands and forest, north of the ranger station, was preserved in 1967 after local citizens, headed by Dr. Theodore Kazimiroff, pressured the city to stop illegal dumping here. East of the sanctuary are beautiful gardens, part of the historic Bartow-Pell Mansion (open to the public), built in 1842 and replacing the original manor house that had been destroyed during the American Revolution.

In addition to the park's natural beauty, migrating songbirds like the wood thrush and eastern towhee love it here. Eastern coyotes have also been spotted in the park; and egrets and herons are common in the marsh, which may be viewed via the 1.5-mile Split Rock Trail, north of the Pell sanctuary and beginning at the Bartow traffic circle. (See chapter 2, Nature Walks.) A huge erratic rock (for which the trail is named) at the intersection of the Hutchinson River Parkway and the New England Thruway is said to be the place where Siwanoys killed Anne Hutchinson in 1642, just three years after she had fled Puritan Massachusetts and built her new home on Indian land, at what is today the northwest corner of the park.

Open–September–May: Sunday-Thursday, 10 AM-4 PM; for summer hours, see Orchard Beach Nature Center, below.

Paddling the Lagoon in Pelham Bay Park

Orchard Beach Nature Center

Pelham Bay Park, Section 2 of Orchard Beach
718-885-3466
www.nycgovparks.org/sub_about/parks_divisions/urban_park_rangers/pd_ur_naturecenters.html

Ranger-led nature and bird walks; nature crafts; exhibits on marine ecology and Pelham Bay Park history; nature trail and maps; free nature kits with binoculars; canoe and kayak launch (permit required); public beach; picnicking; restrooms.

The Orchard Beach Nature Center serves the eastern section of Pelham Bay Park and is designed to get kids excited about saltwater and tidal ecosystems. Aquariums and touch tanks let kids see and feel live animals from the area. Microscopes and stereoscopes help them view tiny creatures up close. Marine specimens include dissected squids, dogfish skeletons, a turtle skeleton, and a replica dolphin skull. Kids accompanied by an adult may borrow nature guides, maps, and equipment to explore nearby mud flats, salt marsh, the beach, and woodlands.

The center itself is on the Orchard Beach boardwalk, near Hunter and Twin Island. Facing Long Island Sound, Twin Island features the city's only rocky coastline, the southernmost extension of a sheet of bedrock that runs straight up to Maine. Fishermen enjoy angling from the rocks. (The nature center occasionally offers saltwater fishing workshops for children.) There are also glacial erratics (rocks formed someplace else and pushed here by glaciers) scattered about—including one called Mishow (near the nature center), a ceremonial rock once used by the local Siwanoys, and Sphinx Boulder (on the island's northeast side), also said to have been sacred to native people.

Hunter Island features the 1.5-mile Kazimiroff Nature Trail (see chapter 2, Nature Walks), which snakes through a 166-acre native forest that includes a stand of white pine where saw-whet owls frequently perch. The trail is named for Theodore Kazimiroff (1915–1980), a dentist, naturalist, and founder of the Bronx Historical Society who, in the 1960s, led the fight to preserve this area and the nearby 489-acre Thomas Pell Wildlife Sanctuary.

Today, Twin and Hunter Islands are "islands" in name only; during the 1930s and 1940s, Parks Commissioner Robert Moses joined them with landfill to the Bronx to create Orchard Beach. Worlds away from the often boisterous beach, the islands are havens for migrating birds, woodland creatures and wildflowers, and such edibles as wild strawberries and asparagus. Those lucky enough to own a canoe or kayak can launch them from the park's public boat slip on the lagoon, right behind the parking lot. (See chapter 5, Paddling with Kids.)

Open—Memorial Day–Labor Day, only: daily, 10 AM–4 PM. Free

Van Cortlandt Park Nature Center

**246th Street and Broadway
718-548-0912**
www.nycgovparks.org/sub_about/parks
_divisions/urban_park_rangers/pd_ur_
nature_centers.html
www.vancortlandt.org

Ranger-led hikes; nature trails and maps; woodland cross-country running course; exhibits on urban-forest ecology; nature stories and crafts at park playgrounds; annual Earth Day celebration; Junior Naturalist program; bridle paths (contact Riverdale Equestrian Center, West 254th Street and Broadway, at 718-548-4848); butterfly and woodland plants garden; library; restrooms.

The focus of this nature center (a restored comfort station at the south end of the Parade Grounds) is the urban forest—what's in it, how it works, and ways to preserve it. That's

Van Cortlandt Park's 16-acre lake is the largest freshwater lake in the Bronx.

because half of 1,146-acre Van Cortlandt Park is wooded; active recreation is relegated to the southern end, while three forested tracts with trails comprise the park's northern section.

Exhibits help kids identify the individual trees that make up an urban forest, from the black cherry with its crinkly hide to the hickory with its smooth bark. A great seed collection showcases a variety of little kernels, from the sugar maple's winged seed (open one and paste it on your nose) to the sweet gum's itchy ball. Another exhibit highlights the amazing sizes, shapes, and colors of bird eggs, from tiny black-capped chickadee and white-breasted nuthatch eggs to larger, speckled red-tailed hawk eggs and rounded great horned owl eggs. Nests range from the intricately constructed pouch of the northern oriole to the cupped, unkempt home of the blue jay.

The park surrounding the nature center is hilly, its topography the result of millions of years of geologic activity; ancient Fordham gneiss outcroppings stand testament to the last ice age, while the park's steep ridges are the result of glacial movement. The park has centuries-old oak and tulip trees, particularly in its Northwest Forest.

Like many urban parks, Van Cortlandt Park's vast acreage is crisscrossed by highways, breaking the forest into three sections: Northwest Forest (188 acres), Croton Woods (127.5 acres), and Northeast Forest (117 acres). Several trails meander through forests and wetlands, offering a chance to explore the northwestern Bronx. (See chapter 2, Nature Walks.) Look for Eastern screech and great horned owls, wild turkeys, rabbits, woodpeckers, and even flying squirrels. You may even see a white-tailed deer or coyote that has wandered into the park from nearby Westchester County.

The park's 16-acre lake—the largest freshwater lake in the Bronx—is a perfect place to see dragonflies, as well as egrets and herons. The lake was created in the early 1700s when Jacobus Van Cortlandt (later mayor of New York) dammed Tibbetts Brook to power his mills. In 1748 his son built what today survives in the park as the Van Cortlandt Mansion, a fieldstone farmhouse turned museum, the oldest building in the Bronx. The family donated the house and property to the city in 1888. An old stone wall surrounds the Van Cortlandt family cemetery on Vault Hill, although the remains have been re-interred at nearby Woodlawn

Eastern tiger swallowtails like to extract salt and drink water from moist soil.

Cemetery. Butterfly experts say that in June and early July, Vault Hill is a good place to see spicebush swallowtails, eastern tiger swallowtails, American coppers, great spangled fritillaries, and various hairstreaks. And don't be surprised if you see a pack of runners darting past; Vault Hill is on the park's famous cross-county running trail, one of the country's best, where college championship races are frequently held.

Open—Summer: daily, 9 AM-5 PM; Winter: Wednesday-Sunday, 10 AM-4 PM. Free.

Brooklyn

Prospect Park Audubon Center

**Prospect Park Boathouse, off Ocean Avenue at Lincoln Road
718-287-3400**
www.prospectpark.org

Guided nature and bird walks; nature and bird-watching cruises; self-guided trail maps; binocular kits to borrow; nature and interactive wildlife exhibits; nature crafts (pre-registration and fees sometimes required); family programming; environmentally themed music, dance, and theater programs; book club for kids; annual raptor event; annual nature-film series; pedal-boat rentals; electric-boat tours; gift shop; café; restrooms.

This is one of the city's most beautiful nature-center settings, overlooking Prospect Park's picturesque Lullwater. And the center, itself, is one of the city's most gorgeous, occupying a historic, two-story Beaux Arts boathouse (1905), lovingly restored in 2002 by the nonprofit Prospect Park Alliance and the national Audubon Society. It is Audubon's first urban nature center, one of 1,000 Audubon plans to open around the country by 2020—all with the idea making environmental stewards out of city kids.

Prospect Park is a good place to start. It contains Brooklyn's last remaining forest (150 acres), the borough's only freshwater lake (60 acres, with catch-and-release fishing), and Lookout Hill (enter at 16th Street and Prospect Park Southwest), the highest point in Brooklyn. The park's 526 acres are also essential habitat for more than 200 bird species that are year-round residents or pass through during spring and fall migrations. Outdoor seating at the nature center provides the perfect vantage point from which to view some of these winged wonders—from blue herons and ducks to swans and red-winged blackbirds—and offers a perfect place to help kids hone their binocular skills. Smooth-sailing electric boat rides provide additional intimate views of the shoreline and its birds, with the areas surrounding the center serving as an outdoor classroom for educating kids about the park's nature. There are big trees, dragonflies flitting about, and fish swimming in the park's lake and Lullwater, butterflies sipping from wildflowers, and other wildlife that call the park home.

Inside the Audubon Center are exhibits perfect for children. Model birds of various species found in Brooklyn are perched into corners and above doorways and staircases. As kids pass by, sensors pick up their presence, and the models emit recorded bird calls specific to the species. Kids can peer through the eyes of a child-size cardinal, squirrel, or hawk model to experience how the animals see the park's landscape. For example, chipmunks see low to the ground, while hawk eyes—focusing from high above—are eight times more powerful than human eyes. There are also science stations and video installations throughout the building that give kids a high-tech look at nature. A favorite spot to sit is in the giant oriole's nest (with equally large eggs) from which youngsters may view a short video on local birds. They can also step outside on the second-floor balcony to watch real-life birds at the feeder or get something of a bird's-eye view of the Lullwater and surrounding trees in search of critters. In fact, a red-tailed hawk often perches on the top of a tree straight across from the nature center.

Kids are encouraged to join their parents on Citizen Science explorations, looking for and counting different species of butterflies or birds in the park and then handing their findings over to naturalists, to be shared with the Audubon Society. Or they can enjoy one of the naturalist-led lake cruises aboard the 15-seat electric boat *Independence* or walk along the nearby Lullwater Nature Trail. The center also offers drop-in nature crafts that may include leaf rubbings or nest making, as well as storytelling and dozens of wildlife puppets with which kids are encouraged to play. Children may also read the many nature-inspired books from the center's wonderful library. There are age-appropriate nature clubs for kids, as well as a free Friday-afternoon nature program for children ages 3–5 (with an adult). Annual events include a September raptor festival with visits from real-life owls and hawks and a film festival (usually during winter break) featuring environmental and nature films for kids of all ages.

The center also serves as a visitor center and introduction to the 587-acre park, which was designed by Frederick Law Olmsted and Calvert Vaux and opened as a country retreat for Brooklynites in 1867.

While at the center, be sure to visit the historic Camperdown Elm with its long, outstretched, weeping branches, just southeast of the center, on the west side of the Cleft Ridge Span. It's the one with the protective iron fence around it. This treasured freak of nature, planted in 1872, resulted from the grafting of a limb of a mutated Scotch elm (with drooping branches)—first discovered in 1843, in Scotland, by the Earl of Camperdown—with a normal Scotch elm. The tree can never self-reproduce, but must always be created by grafting these two specific types of trees.

Open–Thursday-Sunday & holidays, 12-5 PM; July 1-September 6: until 6 PM. Free.

Brooklyn Center for the Urban Environment

**Prospect Park at 9th Street–
inside the Tennis House
718-788-8500**
www.bcue.org

Walking tours (fee); environmental education programs; nature, cultural, and historic exhibits; restroom.

Founded in 1978 by a descendent of naturalist John Muir to preserve and explore both the city's built and natural environments, the Brooklyn Center for the Urban Environment sponsors unique outdoor tours, including boat excursions of the city's myriad islands, as well as star gazing and sunset walks in natural areas. Children are usually welcomed, but most tours are geared toward adults. Housed in a historic 1910 building in Prospect Park, designed by Frederick Law Olmsted, the center's exhibits have included displays of bug and butterfly collections as well as landscape photography and paintings.

Open–Weekdays, 9 AM-5 PM; weekends 12-5 PM. Free, but fee for tours.

Magnolia Tree Earth Center

**677 Lafayette Avenue (between Marcy and Tompkins Avenues)
718-387-2116**

Horticultural and environmental education programs; rotating exhibits; community garden and tours; restrooms.

Founded in a brownstone by local activist Hattie Carthan (1902–1984) in 1972, the Magnolia Tree Earth Center is a Bedford–Stuyvesant institution that offers workshops and support to its neighbors, fostering environmental stewardship and community beautification. Its huge community garden at the corner of Marcy and Lafayette Avenues grows organic

produce (see chapter 7, Gardens Grow Children), while the center's gallery showcases environmentally themed art. But it's the building's towering 40-foot *Magnolia grandiflora* that draws visitors from far and wide.

The tree is of a southern species and the only one growing north of Philadelphia. It came to Brooklyn in 1885 as a seedling from North Carolina. In the 1960s, a developer threatened to chop it down, but Carthan—who had cultivated a reputation as the "tree lady" after beautifying her downtrodden block with new trees—saved the magnolia by having it declared a living landmark in 1970. The all-season tree is taller than the three-story center. In summer it blooms with tremendous, fragrant, saucerlike flowers; in fall it has red conelike fruit and seeds; and in winter its leathery leaves remain green.

Carthan's story provides the perfect opportunity to teach your children how one's passion can turn into an activism that leaves a lasting impact on an entire community. It also shows how important neighborhood trees are to a city's quality of life and how vulnerable they are if neglected and undefended. The Magnolia Tree Earth Center's Urban Tree Corps teaches local young people how to maintain street trees and then puts them to work in the neighborhood. Perhaps you and your children could adopt a tree or two on your own block. Trees New York, a nonprofit organization, offers 12-hour care and maintenance courses throughout the year for a fee. For information, call 212-227-1887, or see their schedule at www.treesny.com.

Open–Monday-Friday, 9 AM-5 PM. Free.

Ryan Visitor Center, Floyd Bennett Field

**Flatbush Avenue, just before the Marine Parkway Bridge
718-338-3799**
www.nps.gov/gate

Ranger-led walks; nature trails; surf fishing; bicycle paths; community garden; camping: boat launch;

Junior Ranger program; picnic tables; restrooms in Ryan Center, visitor contact station (at the park entrance) and near Tamarack campsite.

You'd be hard pressed to call the Ryan Visitor Center a nature center. But Ranger-led nature tours periodically depart from this empty, cavernous, old control tower to explore the 800-acre park—a former marshland packed with landfill in the 1920s, opened as the city's first municipal airport in the 1930s, and then preserved as part of the 28,000-acre Gateway National Recreation Area in the 1970s. There are self-guided maps of the park; and Junior Ranger quiz booklets encourage kids from 7 to 12 to explore Gateway's history, flora, and fauna, talk to Rangers, and participate in Gateway programs in order to answer questions in the 16-page guide. Upon completion, kids are awarded a certificate and badge.

Concrete runways and abandoned hangers surround the center, but there are also pockets of shoreline beauty and tranquility here that are rare in the city. Kids can enjoy fishing (permit required; see chapter 9, Goin' Fishing), biking and skating on miles of open runways (see chapter 8, Bicycling), or walking sandy trails and spotting birds, hawks, and maybe even an

Watching for herons and ducks at Return-a-Gift Pond, Floyd Bennett Field.

owl or peregrine falcon (see chapter 2, Nature Walks). A 140-acre native grassland (unique in New York City) is mowed annually to stop natural succession and keep the area free from trees and shrubs. The wildflowers and grasses attract such butterflies as the swarthy skipper and the common buckeye, and grassland bird species such as grasshopper sparrows and eastern meadowlarks.

From late May to early June, a large area near Ecology Village on the park's eastern side is bright with golden coreopsis flowers. Visit the park's huge community garden (see chapter 7, Gardens Grow Children), the city's largest, with 587 plots and a unique calendar garden planted with 12 flower beds designed to bloom consecutively through the months of the year.

Open—Daily, 8:30 AM–5 PM. Free.

Salt Marsh Nature Center, Marine Park

**3302 Avenue U
(at East 33rd Street)
718-421-2021**
www.nycgovparks.org/sub_about/parks_
divisions/urban_park_rangers/pd_ur_
nature_center.html

Ranger-led nature, ecology, and bird walks; interpretive nature trail; trail maps; salt-marsh and local history exhibits; canoeing; camping; beehives; nocturnal events; Junior Ranger program; lectures; library; picnic tables; restrooms.

This 5,000-square-foot nature center, with a modern sky-lit rotunda, overlooks Gerritsen Creek, which supports herons, cormorants, marsh hawks, fiddler crabs, and other wetland creatures, and is part of 798-acre Marine Park. It is a fabulous place for kids to learn how salt marshes work and why they're not just soggy pieces of land, but rather, productive, vital components in the estuarine food web. Almost every living creature in some way depends on the salt marsh for survival. Tiny animals like shrimp, snails, and mussels at the bottom of the food chain eat organic matter (often decaying salt-marsh cord grass), then fish and birds eat them, and so on and so on.

After entering the nature center, show your children the rotunda floor, colorfully decorated with a huge dragonfly, a gull, a bee, a flounder, and other local wildlife, as well as the names of great environmentalists Edward Abbey, John Muir, and Rachel Carson. In the middle of the floor design is Earth and the four compass points. Now have the kids look up at what's flying overhead—an osprey, a great blue heron, a mallard, and other birds (taxidermy), all of them species that live in or pass though the area.

Kids can touch specimens, like horseshoe crabs, which have lived locally for 450 million years, and run their fingers along bird and animal tracks preserved in sand. They can study slide specimens under a microscope, examine a real beehive, or visit the library with its marsh view and borrow field guides to take on the trail. One exhibit explains how the tidal ebb and flow affects the salt marsh, twice a day submerging it and then retreating, combining salt water with fresh water to create a brackish environment with varying degrees of salinity. Another exhibit depicts the marsh before and after restoration. At one time, junked cars and garbage were more common at the marsh than birds. In the 1990s, local citizens began removing the debris and pressured government officials to help restore this priceless habitat, one of the last salt marshes in Brooklyn.

Outside, look for butterflies—eastern tiger and black swallowtails, as well as monarchs—on summer-blooming buddleias planted near the nature center. Or take a butterfly walk along the 1-mile trail (see chapter 2, Nature Walks). Hardcore butterfly lovers particularly like scanning the salt marsh for such special species as the American snout and the tawny emperor, which breed on the marsh's hackberry trees, and the salt-marsh skipper, which breeds on the spartina grass. Three kinds of bats, including brown bats, flutter around the salt marsh at night while meadow crickets sing.

At the rear of the center is Gerritsen Creek, which empties into Jamaica Bay and on into the Atlantic Ocean. The creek once powered the city's first tidal gristmill, operating continuously from about 1645 until 1889. Vandals burned down the mill in 1935, but at low tide, you can still see pilings that supported the boardwalk that led to the mill.

Open—Summer: daily, 10:30 AM–5:30 PM; Winter: daily, 9:30 AM–4:30 PM. Closed Wednesdays. Free.

Manhattan

Charles A. Dana Discovery Center

Central Park near 110th Street and Lenox Avenue
212-860-1370
**www.nycgovparks.org/sub_about/parks_
divisions/urban_park_rangers/pd_ur_
nature_center.html**

Ranger-led walks; nature trails; nature programs and exhibits; free fishing (April–October); free fishing kit (Tuesday–Sunday, 10 AM–4 PM, last pole loaned at 3 PM); annual fishing contest; bilingual (English and Spanish) exhibits on local flora and fauna; restrooms.

The Dana Discovery Center, located on the idyllic 11-acre Harlem Meer (*lake*, in Dutch) in the park's northeastern corner, features bilingual English-Spanish nature exhibits that explore the wildlife found at the Meer, such as great egrets, cormorants, black-crowned night herons, and bullfrogs. An insightful exhibit that goes beyond what can be seen with the naked eye features a cross section of the Meer, depicting life at its various levels, from bottom-feeding snails and crayfish to surface-riding ducks like mallards and buffleheads. Rotating exhibits have included such topics as the journey of a single drop of water from the Catskills watershed to city faucets. An aquarium showcases fish and turtles found in the Meer. The exhibit room's huge picture window provides a rainy-day vantage point from which to view the Meer, beautifully ringed with bald cypress, weeping willow, and red maples. Listen in early summer for the male bullfrog's deep-toned mating call. In October, hundreds of candlelit jack-o'-lanterns are sailed on the Meer in a captivating nocturnal Halloween display.

The nature center is the perfect starting point from which to explore Central Park's rugged northern section, especially the 97-acre North Woods (mid-Park from 102nd to 106th Streets). Watch butterflies at the Wildflower Meadow (near 102nd Street) with its joe-pye weed, milkweed, goldenrod, asters, and black-eyed Susans. The nearby 6-acre Conservatory Garden, downhill from the meadow and across the East Drive at 105th Street and Fifth Avenue, is a more formal place for butterfly viewing. Or drop a line into the Meer and catch a bluegill or large-mouthed bass (catch and release only). The nature center lends kids 12 and under accompanied by an adult free bamboo poles with non-barbed hooks and corn bait (photo identification required). You may also bring your own fishing pole. (See chapter 9, Goin' Fishing.)

The nonprofit Central Park Conservancy, which maintains Central Park's two nature centers (the other is in Belvedere Castle) in partnership with the New York City Department of Parks & Recreation, was founded in 1980 and is often credited with cleaning up and beautifying the park. In the late 1980s the Conservancy restored the Meer and its landscape, planting native flora and wonderful trees, and created a strolling path along the perimeter. It also built the picturesque neo-Victorian nature center in 1993 on the site of an old, burnt-out boathouse.

When visiting the nature center, take a look at the bald cypress tree to the left of the entrance. In the fall, this conifer does some-

thing strange—it loses its needles, much as deciduous maples and oaks lose their leaves. Usually conifers retain their needles throughout the seasons. Bald cypresses also have odd fruit—wrinkly, 1-inch, brainlike cones that turn from green to brown and then very hard (like wood), making it tough for even the most determined bird to get at the seeds.

Open—Tuesday-Sunday, 10 AM-5 PM (closes at 4 PM in winter).

The Henry Luce Nature Observatory at Belvedere Castle

Central Park (Mid-park at 79th Street) 212-772-0210
www.nycgovparks.org/sub_about/parks_divisions/urban_park_rangers/pd_ur_nature_center.html

Ranger-led nature and bird walks; nature trails and maps; nature programs; free bird-watching kits (12 and under, accompanied by an adult; photo identification required); free Experimental Science and Nature Fun family program (Tuesday-Sunday, 10 AM-4 PM; call to register); historical and environmental exhibits; weather-recording equipment; restrooms.

Belvedere Castle was built in 1867 as a magical fortress crowning Central Park's highest natural elevation, Vista Rock, which tops out at 135 feet. It was meant to be a decorative, picturesque palace around which to wander and from which to view the park. During the 1960s and 1970s, the castle was neglected and vandalized, becoming a medieval ghost town. The Central Park Conservancy later restored the castle, reopening it in 1996 as a nature center, offering hands-on exhibits and lookouts from which to view migrating hawks and monarch butterflies.

A gargoyle over the main entrance greets you and your kids. Inside, windowsill telescopes and microscopes will pique your children's curiosity. Plants and animals found at Turtle Pond (just below the castle) and the Ramble (38 acres of woodlands south of the castle) are featured in the first floor's Woods and Water Discovery Room, where kids are encouraged to identify trees and invertebrates by process of elimination, indirectly learning the procedures used by real scientists in their quests to identify specimens. There is also a native-rock exhibit, and a cross section of some healthy forest soil—rich in organic material at top, slowly broken down by insects and worms below.

Climbing the castle's narrow spiral staircase is fun in itself. On the second floor, youngsters will come upon papier-mâché sculptures of some of the 200 bird species seen inside the park and hear bird-song recordings. Outside, on the north terrace, they can experience a bird's-eye view of the east and west sides of Manhattan, as well as Turtle Pond, the Great Lawn, Delacorte Theater, and the fluffy tops of so many trees. On the south terrace, they can also obtain an up-to-date weather report where weather-gathering equipment has provided the official weather of record for the city since 1919. The instruments, which record everything from temperature to barometric pressure, were automated in the 1960s.

After your tour through the center, take advantage of the free backpacks with binoculars, guidebook, maps, and sketching paper that are loaned to budding naturalists. Then scramble to the Ramble, one of the country's top 15 birding sites, according to the Audubon Society (see chapter 3, Birding with Children). It's a sculpted woodland with rocky areas, thickets, and secluded glades that may look natural, but were totally contrived by landscape kingpin Frederick Law Olmsted to look and feel like the Adirondacks. Even the stream that runs through the Ramble is turned on and off by a tap. Be careful not to get lost, because the Ramble's many intersecting paths can be confusing.

Another good place to see birds, butterflies, and flowers is the Shakespeare Garden, west of the nature center, on the slope of Vista Rock. This rustic-designed, 4-acre cottage garden features herbs and flowers mentioned in Shakespeare's plays. Look for a large black mulberry tree, said to have originated from a cutting taken from one planted by Shakespeare in his front lawn. The fruit ripens in July and is yummy sweet.

You can also take your borrowed backpack kits down to Turtle Pond (man made and a remnant of the old Croton reservoir), just below Belvedere Castle, and study aquatic life, particularly dragonflies and damselflies, which mate and lay their eggs here. Look for the male blue dasher, with green eyes, white face, and powder-blue abdomen—the most common dragonfly in Central Park. And remember—dragonflies may look a bit scary, but contrary to popular belief they don't have stingers and are harmless to humans. They are, however, hungry predators in the insect world. A welcomed exterminator in the age of the West Nile virus, they particularly like mosquitoes.

Look for the pond's namesakes, including red-eared sliders, eastern painted, and—more frequently—snapping turtles. Shoreline plants like lizard's tail, bulrush, turtlehead, and blue-flag iris provide habitat for birds, insects, amphibians, and reptiles. Kids will love the dock and nature blind that extends into the pond, a place from which to view wildlife. A

Dragonflies abound at Central Park's Turtle Pond, just below Belvedere Castle.

man-made island provides sandy spots for turtles to lay their eggs and nesting and foraging sites for birds.

Open–Tuesday-Sunday, 11 AM-5 PM; October-February: closes at 4 PM. Free.

Inwood Hill Park Nature Center

218th Street and Indian Road
212-304-2365
www.nycgovparks.org/sub_about/parks_
divisions/urban_park_rangers/pd_ur_
nature_center.html

Nature trails and maps; Ranger-led hikes and bird walks; canoeing; camping; exhibits on the park's cultural, geologic, and natural history; nature activities (ages 4 and older; first Saturday of each month, 10 AM-noon); aquariums; library; native plant garden; restrooms.

The nature center at Inwood Hill Park—a 196-acre, largely wooded wonderland with steep hills at the north end of Manhattan—features a variety of exhibits and hands-on activities that get kids excited about the outdoors. There are aquariums with local fish, including striped bass, white perch, and mummichog—small "killifish" that travel in schools along the shore of the park's salt marsh, hence the name mummichog, a Native American word for "going in crowds."

There are also exhibits on the park's history, as well as local plants, trees, and animals. Huge rock specimens include Manhattan schist, sparkling with mica; sugarlike Inwood marble; and Fordham gneiss, with bands of light and dark minerals—as well as a huge erratic rock, formed elsewhere and pushed all the way from the New Jersey Palisades to the New York side of the Hudson River by glaciers millions of years ago.

The white-and-turquoise-tiled nature center was originally constructed as a boathouse in 1937 as part a grand design to improve the park under the auspices of the Works Progress Administration. It remained open until the 1950s, then became a storage building, before its reincarnation as a nature center in 1995. The building faces Manhattan's last remaining salt marsh (12 acres), where waders and waterfowl congregate. At one time, marshes like this ran all along Manhattan's perimeter.

Inwood Hill Park hosts Manhattan's last natural forest, about 140 second-growth acres, last cut during the American Revolution. (Recreational facilities are relegated to the park's fringes.) There are also natural rock formations carved by glaciers and used by Native Americans as sanctuary, a large erratic rock where Europeans are said to have bought Manhattan from Native Americans, copious wildlife, and gorgeous views of the Hudson River—all in Manhattan, but a world away from its bright lights and manic energy.

To the north is Spuyten Duyvil Creek, or the Harlem River Ship Canal, separating northern Manhattan from the Bronx. On the west, craggy bluffs overlook the Hudson River. Explain to your kids that this is what much of Manhattan looked like before landfill and development changed its natural topography, which was sculpted by glaciers, the most recent about 10,000 years ago.

Kids will find plenty to explore (see chapter 2, Nature Walks) and may even see an American bald eagle. After more than 100 years of extinction in the area, eaglets have been released annually into the park as part of a five-year plan (commencing in 2002) to reintroduce this federally endangered species and have bald eagles nest here in the near future. In addition to the new eagles, Inwood hosts 150 bird species, its woods filled with inviting oak, beech, and very tall, very straight tulip trees—a native species, some of which are more than 200 years·old. Native Americans once carved tulip tree trunks into canoes. The tree is named for its showy orange, yellow, and chartreuse tulip-shaped flowers. Rather than craning their necks to see the blooms growing at the top of trees that can reach 100 feet tall, have your kids look for fallen flowers scattered on the ground.

And those cute black squirrels frolicking about the park? They're simply a pigmentation variation on the everyday eastern gray squirrel and are inexplicably seen in only certain areas of the city, including Inwood Hill Park and my Brooklyn backyard.

Open—Wednesday-Sunday, 11 AM–4 PM. Free.

The River Project

Pier 26, off West Street
212-431-5787
www.riverproject.org

Aquariums; free guided tours, upon request or by appointment; waterfront lectures and programs; marine biology internship programs; reference library; picnic tables; restroom (outdoor Port-o-San).

Beneath the surface of New York Harbor is an entire world most of us never get to see. The River Project—housed since 1997 in an old shipping warehouse—offers a peek at this diverse underwater ecosystem through a 3,000-gallon aquarium system, or estuarium, filled with various fish and invertebrates (even seahorses!) plucked directly from the city portion of the river.

In addition to the free exhibits and the nonprofit marine biology field station, whose various projects include restoring oyster beds in the Hudson River and assessing the biodiversity of life in the river, the River Project sponsors educational programs and champions the protection and restoration of the city's urban ecology. There are plans to upgrade the center and its pier as part of the new Hudson River Park.

Open—Daily, 11 AM–5 PM. Free.

Queens

Alley Pond Environmental Center

228-06 Northern Boulevard
718-229-4000
www.alleypond.com

Guided nature walks; nature trails and maps; nature exhibits; mini-zoo and aquarium; animal, science, and nature programs for families; nature club (pre-K kids); astronomy program (ages 8 and older); children's nature writers' club; library; gift shop; picnic area; restrooms.

One of the city's first nature centers when it opened in the 1970s, the Alley Pond Environmental Center in northeastern Queens is a private, nonprofit operation that works in partnership with the New York City Department of Parks & Recreation. Within its 5,000-square-foot space is a mini-zoo with plenty of animals to see

The Douglaston Estate Windmill, a replica of a mill built around 1870.

and touch, including box turtles, painted turtles, diamondback terrapins, rabbits, nesting finches, corn snakes, and a giant marine toad. Parents may also explore nature with their toddlers through one of the center's daytime programs or take part in stargazing workshops and nature walks with older kids. There is often a charge for programs.

The center—tucked inside 654-acre Alley Pond Park, with its several spring-fed ponds, tidal creek, glacial formations, fresh- and salt-water wetlands, meadows and old woods with tall oaks and tulip trees—maintains a bird registry, where visitors jot down what they've seen along the park's nine trails. (See chapter 2, Nature Walks.) The Alley Pond Nature Trail is the city's oldest, blazed in 1935, when the park itself opened.

While you can access this trail from the center, others begin in other parts of the park, which is broken up into sections by the Long Island Expressway and Cross Island Parkway. It was the proposed construction of these highways that threatened the area's diverse ecosystems and prompted the city to create the park. Then, in 1972, a group of educators concerned over the lack of environmental education in the public schools went one step further, founding the Alley Pond Environmental Center.

While at the nature center, go around back to see the Douglaston Estate Windmill, a replica of a mill built around 1870 on nearby Arleigh Road. The mill pumped water from the ground for use by farmers in irrigation. The mill building was modernized and became a residence in the early 20th century. In the 1980s, it was threatened with demolition until some residents decided to move and restore it. Unfortunately, arsonists destroyed the mill, prompting preservationists to build this reproduction.

Open—September-June: Monday-Saturday, 9 AM-4:30 PM; Sunday, 9 AM-3:30 PM. Closed Sundays in July and August and on some major holidays. Nature center is free; fee for some programs.

Urban Park Rangers Adventure Center, Alley Pond Park

**Winchester Boulevard, under the Grand Central Parkway
718-217-6043 or 718-846-2731**
www.nycgovparks.org/sub_about/parks_divisions/urban_park_rangers/pd_ur_nature_center.html

Ranger-led nature walks and programs; nature trails; small library; pamphlets on trails and wildlife; picnic tables; restrooms in nearby comfort station.

During the week, from May through October, the Urban Park Ranger Adventure Center offers outdoor adventure and camping programs to schools and youth groups. But on weekends and during special events, the center focuses on families, hosting campouts, orienteering and nature walks, and night hikes, and offers programs on entomology and pond ecology, among other activities.

The nature center is also a good starting point to explore the woodsy side of Alley Pond Park, with trails wending past kettle ponds and

Petting a toad at Alley Pond Park

tall trees and such forest creatures as chipmunks and Fowler's toads. A great horned owl recently staked out territory near the nature center and may be seen atop a tree in broad daylight. Kids who like to cycle may enjoy biking through the woods along the former Long Island Motor Parkway, a privately funded road built in 1908 by William K. Vanderbilt Jr., who used it for a short time to promote automobile racing. A National Register of Historic Places landmark, it was transferred to the New York City Parks Department in 1937 and turned into a 2.5-mile jogging and bicycling path. (See chapter 8, Bicycling.) Or take the Tulip Tree Trail in the park's Oaks Section (a narrow swath of woods next to the Cross Island Parkway) to see a 250-year-old tulip tree that is taller than the Statue of Liberty.

Open—For scheduled events; call for information. Free.

Fort Tilden Ranger Contact Station and Breezy Point

Gateway National Recreation Area
718-318-4300
www.nps.org/gate

Ranger-guided walks; nature trails and maps; scavenger hunts; bike tours; surf fishing; kids' fishing clinics (ages 10 and older); hawk observation tower; community garden; picnic tables; restrooms.

Fort Tilden is a 317-acre hodgepodge of abandoned concrete bunkers, batteries, and radar stations, all reclaimed by nature—much like its neighbor, Floyd Bennett Field. Every autumn, birdwatchers stand atop Battery Harris East (which once had a 70-foot cannon that could fire a one-ton shell 30 miles) to watch the hawk migration.

The contact station has a few nature exhibits, including one about the narrow, 11-mile-long Rockaway Peninsula, the barrier beach on which Fort Tilden and Breezy Point are located. This barrier beach serves as a buffer between the ocean and the mainland, and supports diverse habitats, including a natural dune system on its ocean side, a salt marsh on its bay side, and a maritime forest in the middle. A big display map of the peninsula will help you get your bearings.

There are also photographs of Gateway National Recreation Area wildlife, including black skimmers, common terns, least terns, and tree swallows. From October to May, Brant geese (an arctic species that breeds in Alaska and Canada) vacation in the area. And don't forget to visit the huge, 13-year-old snapping turtle in the Marine Ecology Room.

Kids will love beachcombing for shells and polished stones (some may even have fossils!) deposited by tides. A good time to search is after a high tide or a huge storm. Keep in mind, however, that visitors are prohibited from keeping their finds; so return them to the sand for others to see.

The area's sand dunes, some of them 20 feet tall, comprise one of the last natural dune systems in the city. While these mounds will likely appeal to the climber in every kid, please make sure that children stay on designated paths—explaining to them that, while sand is usually all fun and games, this sand and its construction is a valuable part of nature. Walking on dunes not only destroys their natural beauty, it kills their delicate plant system, which includes sea-beach amaranth, a federally protected species. You'll recognize it by its spinach-green leaves, red stems, and creeping growth habit. The dunes also protect this barrier island and its maritime forest of gnarled pines, cottonwood trees, quaking aspens, autumn olive, and bayberry from destructive winds, waves, storms, and natural beach erosion. This area can be accessed from the 2.5-mile Back Fort Trail. Watch for ticks and poison ivy.

Nearby, at the western tip of the Rockaway Peninsula, is Breezy Point, part private community, with another section part of the Gateway

National Recreation Area. The parking lot at the tip of Breezy is reserved for fishermen with permits; but if you are going birding, you can stop at Fort Tilden beforehand for a free day pass. (Don't forget the binoculars to prove you are birding.) It's best to call the day before and notify the Rangers of your visit, because if a permit-issuing Ranger is not around when you spontaneously show up, you may not be able to secure a pass.

What makes Breezy Point special are the very cute, but very shy, piping plovers, a threatened shore bird that nests on the beach from March through August. (See chapter 3, Birding with Children.) Other wonderful shore birds, as well as winter ducks, also frequent Breezy Point.

Open—Spring and summer: daily, 9 AM–4 PM; Fall and winter: 10 AM–2 PM. Free.

Forest Park Nature/Visitor Center

Corner of Woodhaven Boulevard and Forest Park Drive
718-846-2731
www.nycgovparks.org/sub_about/parks_divisions/urban_park_rangers/pd_ur_nature_centers.html

Ranger-led walks; nature trails and maps; car-free cycling path; bridle paths (contact D&D Stables, 88-11 70th Road, 718-263-3500, or Lynn's Riding School, 88-03 70th Road, 718-251-7699); children's nature crafts (free, Sunday, 2:30–3:30 PM; pre-registration required); rotating nature and local-history exhibits; library; picnicking; restrooms across the street at Victory Field and, in summer, at the center.

This former ranger station was converted into a small nature and visitor center in 2001. Located in the middle of Forest Park (bisected

A real find on the beach at Fort Tilden.

by busy, six-lane Woodhaven Boulevard), it offers a growing number of activities and exhibits and is the starting point for many Ranger-led nature programs. Originally called Brooklyn Forest Park, the park was created in 1895 after officials in the nearby City of Brooklyn purchased the land as a recreational respite for its residents.

A short distance from the nature center on Forest Park Drive is a recently restored kettle pond fringed with native plants and home to tadpoles, frogs, long-legged waders, and other birds. This deep basin created by glaciers some 20,000 years ago was long misused for baseball fields that were always soggy and unusable. After decades of abandonment, the wetland was reclaimed in 2004 and returned to a pristine pond, ringed with a nature trail.

The park also offers great nature walks via several trails, all on the park's eastern, wilder side. (See chapter 2, Nature Walks.) In fact, 413 of the park's 538 acres are wooded and include the 165-acre Northern Forest, a secondary old-growth forest. The original forest was cut down during the American Revolution by British and Hessian troops stationed in Queens. Among the large native oak, hickory, and tulip trees you may see chipmunks, rabbits, songbirds (particularly migrating warblers in May), and even a mole or a shrew. In late summer, a wide variety of mushrooms dot the forest floor.

The park's hills and high ridge are the result of ancient glaciers that stopped here and the terminal moraine they left behind. Big boulders strewn around the park are erratics, rocks formed elsewhere and deposited here by retreating glaciers. A 1.4-mile bicycle and walking path (East Main Drive, part of the Brooklyn/Queens Greenway and closed to traffic) runs through an old pine grove, whose beginnings date back to 1914. (See chapter 8, Bicycling.)

While athletic fields and other recreational pursuits, including a 1903 wooden carousel (behind the nature center) and the 3,500-seat Seuffert Bandshell (free Sunday afternoon concerts), dominate the park's western side—a stupendous view—at least for Queens, can be had on a clear day from the top of Forest Parkway. From Park Lane South, follow the hill up Forest Parkway to a clearing on your left and enjoy the sight of distant Jamaica Bay.

**Open—Sunday, 9 AM–4 PM,
Tuesday–Thursday, 1–4 PM.
Call for additional summer hours. Free.**

Jamaica Bay Wildlife Refuge Visitor Center

**Gateway National Recreation Area
Crossbay Boulevard
718-318-4304**
www.nps.gov/gate

Ranger-led nature and wildlife walks; nature trails (free permit required); self-guided maps; nocturnal programs and walks; exhibits on the natural history of the area and creation of the refuge; lectures; bookstore; restrooms.

The 9,155-acre Jamaica Bay Wildlife Refuge is a diverse habitat with marshes, sandy beaches, channels, freshwater and brackish ponds, upland fields and woods, and islands. At this

Jamaica Bay Wildlife Refuge is most active during spring and fall migrations.

internationally renowned bird sanctuary (see chapter 3, Birding with Children), kids will get a look at some of the more than 325 water-, land-, and shore-bird species that have been seen here. The refuge is most active during spring and fall migrations; your family can scout out American oystercatchers, marbled godwits, black-bellied plovers, warblers, scarlet tanagers, woodcocks, egrets, short-billed dowagers, and more. In winter, look for snow geese and snowy owls.

Every season, the small visitor center (which is undergoing an expansion to include more lecture and exhibit space, as well as solar-powered panels) features specimen wildflowers picked fresh from the refuge and labeled, from butterfly weed to bouncing bet. Information on the park's history as well as its flora and fauna may be retrieved from the center's computer station. Rotating exhibits feature mostly nature photography and art.

The center also has a ringed binder detailing the history of the refuge, complete with old newspaper articles. The city, and more notably the park's first manager, Herbert Johnson, created the refuge from barren land in 1953; it was all transferred to the federal government in 1972. The East Pond (100 acres) and West Pond (45 acres) are man-made—the result of a deal made between Parks Commissioner Robert Moses and the Transit Authority; the Authority dug the ponds in exchange for the right to dredge Jamaica Bay and build a subway embankment.

In 1983, the half-acre Big John's Pond was also created along the East Pond Trail and named for the bulldozer operator who dug it. It is a breeding site for spring peepers (listen for their call in April) as well as other frogs and turtles that kids can spy on from behind a bird blind.

The refuge offers plenty of natured-themed programs and walks that always welcome children. Pick up a calendar of events; then ask for a permit to walk the grounds. It's free, you get it on the spot, and it's good forever. It's the National Park Service's way of unscientifically tracking who comes into and out of the refuge.

Outside the nature center is a bird log (look and see what has been spotted recently), bird-feeding station, and butterfly bushes (buddleia) planted specifically to attract butterflies. (Seventy species have been recorded at the refuge.) Rangers often spread mung (a mixture of fermenting fruit and beer) on trees to attract species such as angelwings and emperors. In early summer, tall, pink-blooming milkweed planted along the entrance to the center attracts monarch butterflies. In autumn, the flowers yield to fascinating long seedpods that split open, sending seeds into the air like fuzzy

The diamondback terrapin, its shell intricately patterned, its head and neck spotted.

parachutes. Kids will also marvel at the seemingly misplaced prickly pear cactus growing along the West Pond Trail, its large flowers bright yellow in summer. Actually a native to the area, it thrives in the refuge's dry, sandy earth.

During early summer, look for saltwater-loving diamondback terrapins crossing the West Pond Trail (see chapter 2, Nature Walks) en route to nesting sites along a sandy spur known as the terrapin trail. This is your best chance at a peek, because the terrapin trail is closed to the public during the June and July nesting periods. If you see a terrapin—just one of six turtle species at the refuge—look with your binoculars from about 150 feet away so as to give it a little privacy. During the winter, the terrapins hibernate in the mud.

Open—Daily, 8:30 AM-5 PM. Free.

Staten Island

Greenbelt Nature Center

**Intersection of Rockland and Brielle Avenues
718-351-3450 or 718-667-2165**
www.sigreenbelt.org

Naturalist-led weekend hikes, 11 AM and 2 PM; trails and maps; gardens; family nature programs and workshops (some requiring a fee); hands-on natural history and ecology exhibits; restrooms.

You enter the grounds of the city's newest nature center through dramatic iron gates designed with tree silhouettes. Opened in 2004, this earthy, Frank Lloyd Wright–inspired creation constructed of stone and wood, and with a slate roof, is framed by a spectacular woodland backdrop. Inside, the 5,400-square-foot space introduces families to Staten Island's beloved Greenbelt, 2,800 contiguous acres of protected parkland and natural areas that run through the center of the island.

The Greenbelt was assembled over the years in chunks, beginning in the 1960s when local environmentalists successfully fought then-Parks Commissioner Robert Moses's attempt to run a highway through the middle of Staten Island and urged the city to protect the island's natural areas, which were increasingly threatened by urbanization arriving via the Verrazano-Narrows Bridge. Before the bridge opened in 1964, easily connecting Brooklyn (and therefore the rest of the city) to Staten Island, the island was accessible only by ferry. A 200-foot-high hill in High Rock Park, created with boulders and soil excavated to build the ultimately thwarted highway is sarcastically named Moses Mountain. It provides 360-degree views: and on a clear day, you can see for 16 miles.

Inside the center, operated by the nonprofit Greenbelt Conservancy in partnership with the city's Parks Department, is an exhibit that shows kids how Staten Island's topography was initially sculpted by three or four ice sheets that moved across the land beginning about 4.6 million years ago. And the high ridge that runs through the island is where the last glacier stopped about 10,000 to 12,000 years ago, leaving behind piles of rocks and debris. A large, contoured map gives a bird's-eye view of the island, with the virtually undeveloped Greenbelt rising green and proud.

One of Staten Island's most interesting features is the exposed ridge of serpentinite, a dense waxy, greenish metamorphic rock that runs along the island from northeast to southwest. (You can see exposed cliffs of it near Exit 13 on the Staten Island Expressway.) Land formation is a difficult concept for anyone to grasp, but you might make this interesting for your kids by explaining that long, long ago this bedrock was part of the ocean floor. When geological forces caused continents to shift, collide, and buckle, the rock was squeezed to the top, much like Play-Doh being compressed between clenched fists until it is forced to emerge.

The center also provides practical information about the Greenbelt's 35-mile trail system, which wends through mature stands of forest, wetlands, meadows, and fields, and past ponds and streams—with starting points right behind the nature center. Kids may use a computer mouse to stop at points along a virtual hike projected on a large screen and learn about specific plants and animals found along the trail. Touch screens feature nature quizzes designed to teach youngsters a bit about Greenbelt flora, fauna, and ecosystems, while telephones held to the ear amplify nature sounds that kids can try to identify—a great way to hone outdoor listening skills.

Displays include birds' nests, tree barks, seeds and seedpods, and a regurgitated owl pellet opened to reveal the bones of an ingested rodent. Another exhibit highlights the work of the Greenbelt Native Plant Propagation Garden, which collects and germinates seeds from more than 60 Greenbelt plant species, helping to restore native habitats around the city. Its Native Plant Demonstration Garden (see chapter 7, Gardens Grow Children) showcases native plants and how families can use them in their own gardens.

Outside and behind the nature center is a tranquil bluestone terrace that backs up to the forest. Kids love the whimsical frog fountain spurting water from its mouth. There are also plenty of benches scattered around the grounds, which are beautifully landscaped with flowers and cobblestones.

Open–April-October: Tuesday-Sunday, 10 AM-4 PM; November-March: Wednesday-Sunday, 10 AM-4 PM. Free.

High Rock Park Environmental Education Center

**200 Nevada Avenue
(off Rockland Avenue)
718-667-7475**

Nature trails and maps; family workshops and walks; Young Naturalists Club ($15 annual fee, ages 5-12);

summer volunteer program (ages 13 and older); native-plant garden; picnic tables; restrooms (just outside nature center); fees charged for some programs.

While the new Greenbelt Nature Center has pretty much supplanted the High Rock Park Environmental Education Center as the starting point for exploring the Greenbelt, the older center still offers some family programs (in addition to its huge menu of school programs) and is a great place from which to hike to a series of Greenbelt ponds or explore 90-acre High Rock Park. Considered the Greenbelt's crown jewel, this park is a pristine habitat and food source for migratory birds (particularly warblers) and year-round birds

Enjoy a huge menu of ranger-led programs at Staten Island's High Rock Park.

(such as chickadees and woodpeckers), as well as moles, possums, and chipmunks. Nature-based art classes are sometimes held at the center's cozy art studio. A short interpretive nature loop, which is paved and wheelchair accessible, begins at the art studio and has 11 gorgeous watercolor panels explaining the Greenbelt's ecosystems, flora, and fauna.

Open—Daily, 9 AM-5 PM. Fees charged for some programs

High Rock Park Ranger Station

200 Nevada Avenue
718-667-6042 or 718-967-3542
www.nycgovparks.org/sub_about/parks_divisions/urban_park_rangers/pd_ur_nature_centers.html

Nature trails; Ranger-led walks and programs.

This Rangers outpost, operated by the city's Department of Parks & Recreation, is open only by chance and serves as the starting point for various Ranger programs and guided hikes. Maps and schedules are available outside the door.

**Open—Daily, 9 AM–4:30 PM.
Free programs and walks.**

Blue Heron Nature Center

**222 Poillon Avenue (between Amboy Road and Hylan Boulevard)
718-967-3542**
www.nycgovparks.org/sub_about/parks_divisions/urban_park_rangers/pd_ur_nature_centers.html
www.preserve2.org/blueheron/

Naturalist-led walks; nature programs and trails; bird-feeding station; free discovery kits; wildflower and perennial gardens; Saturday afternoon bird banding (in season); Mama & Me nature program (ages 3–4, with parent); natural-science club (ages 8–12); Junior Audubon Nature Club (ages 9 and older); slide shows and lectures; nature and composting exhibits; library; picnic tables; restrooms.

In the 1970s local Annandale residents protested the bulldozing of some forested wetlands, grassy meadows, ponds, and streams to make way for a 244-unit housing development. Today that tract is part of 222-acre Blue Heron Park, its namesake celebrated on an 11-foot, hand-forged gate leading to the nature center. The park features trails that kids can easily navigate and where they'll perhaps encounter a blue heron themselves.

Unlike some centers that have sporadic programming, Blue Heron Nature Center offers a full calendar of activities for all ages. In addition to Urban Park Ranger events, the Friends of Blue Heron—one of the most successful groups of its kind—offers regular programs ranging from winter woodcock walks and weekend bird banding to toddler programs and a natural-science club for older kids. Jack and Lois Baird, local residents

Above: Turtles bask in the sun at many of the city's ponds.

Below: At Blue Heron Nature Center, young naturalists can lead their parents on nature walks.

who sounded the alarm when development threatened, founded the group and still head it.

The contemporary, 5,000-square-foot brick and bluestone building built in 1998 is surrounded by wildflowers and butterfly-attracting plants and stands on the site of an old farmhouse, part of an area once belonging to one of Staten Island's original French-Huguenot families. Its rear windows look out onto woods and a bird-feeding station where youngsters can watch woodpeckers and chickadees fill their bellies. Bird banding takes place here on select weekends. Aquariums showcase red-eared sliders, nonnative turtles most likely abandoned as pets and now pushing out the area's native painted turtle population. A touch box lets kids identify things found in nature—pinecones, acorns, feathers, and galls, for example—with their hands. Young naturalists can borrow free discovery kits with binoculars and a field guide and lead their parents on nature walks.

Just a stone's throw from the center is 1.75-acre Spring Pond, full of hovering dragonflies, sun-basking turtles, and—in summer—majestic blooms of hundreds of water lilies. It's not exactly wilderness—suburbia sometimes infringes on the woods—but the pond offers a visual and audible serenity not found on a typical city street. Across the road is 1.4-acre Blue Heron Pond, where swamp loosestrife blooms pink in summer. These ponds, as well as the park's streams and wetlands, may be beautiful, but they also serve a practical purpose; as part of the island's Bluebelt system—managed by the New York City Department of Environmental Protection—they are used to collect stormwater runoff (rather than build costly sewers), providing flood protection and water-pollution control and, in so doing, preserving freshwater wetlands in southern Staten Island.

Open—Daily 11 AM–4 PM; closed Mondays. Free.

Clay Pit Ponds State Park Preserve

83 Nielsen Avenue
718-967-1976
http://nysparks.state.ny.us/cgi-bin/cgi wrap/nysparks/parks.cgi?p+24

Guided nature walks; nature trails and maps; bridle paths (no horse rental; horses must be boarded nearby); nature programs, including bird watching, pond ecology, tree and wildflower identification, and evening campfires; exhibits on composting and local archaeology, history and ecosystems; live animals; picnic tables; restrooms.

The Clay Pit Ponds Nature Center stands at the end of a dead-end road, snug against a 260-acre state park preserve—the only state park preserve in New York City. The preserve is intended for passive recreation only, thereby protecting its fragile ecology and giving it the feeling of a remote outpost. Some areas are closed to the general public to preserve rare plants like the spring-blooming pink lady's slipper. In addition to the center's Native American artifacts—projectiles, arrowheads, clay pipe bowls, and other objects found at the preserve—there are exhibits on local history, including the Staten Island clay industry. Clay was mined locally during the 19th and early 20th centuries and used for making brick. (Operations ended in 1927.) Rainwater and natural spring water eventually filled the cavities, creating clay pit ponds.

Before setting out on your walk, take your kids to the bathroom, even if they don't have to go, because this is one of the city's more memorable restrooms—an environmentally friendly, waterless system. Rather than sit on a toilet and flush, children sit on a big can and send their waste into a compost pit to become fertilizer.

Outside the center are a few animals to visit, including hens and roosters, two goats, and silver pheasants.

Sharrotts Pond is one of several ponds formed from old clay-mine cavities.

The preserve features an area unique in New York City, the Mason–Dixon line of the plant world. Both northern and southern species call this the end (or the beginning) of their ranges, a place where a mixed hardwood forest meets a sandy, pine-oak habitat similar to that of the New Jersey Pine Barrens. Tough-to-spot northern fence lizards frequent the sandy barrens. These shy creatures use an interesting scare tactic—to defend themselves, they dislodge their tails, leaving the squirmy things to frighten predators. Not to worry; they later grow new, although smaller tails.

Birders have recorded eight species of hawks, including red-tails and falcons, and four species of owls at Clay Pit Ponds; and you may see a muskrat at Sharrotts Pond or turtles at

Ellis Swamp. There are also red-backed salamanders, eastern box turtles, and bullfrogs. More rare are spotted turtles, once the most populous turtle in New York City, and mud turtles—both threatened by over development and poor water quality. But new creatures are always being found here, including a dragonfly species not seen on Staten Island since 1898, and two rare plants—the short-leaf pine and St. John's cross—thought to be extinct in the city.

This living laboratory probably would have been bulldozed if not for two Brooklynites, Ed Milanese and Joe Furnicolla, who often explored what was then a remote area in the 1970s, looking for reptiles and amphibians. Taking advantage of a state bond act designed to preserve unique areas, they lobbied the government to save the area, which became a state preserve in 1980, and helped found what is today Staten Island's largest environmental organization, Protectors of Pine Oak Woods.

Open—Tuesday–Saturday, 9 AM–5 PM. Free.

Great Kills Park Field Station, Gateway National Recreation Area

Hylan Boulevard at Buffalo Street
718-987-6790
www.nps.gov/gate

Ranger-led nature walks and activities, including seining and evening campfires; nature trails; Junior Ranger program; beach (10 AM–5:45 PM, with life-guards during summer); fishing; boating; marina; boat launch (closed early December–late March/early April); free boat-safety program; picnic tables throughout the park; education field station; restrooms.

Pretty much unknown outside of Staten Island, 1,000-acre Great Kills Park occupies a barrier peninsula jutting out into Lower New York Bay, with a protected harbor on its western side. Rangers offer free, seasonal nature programs at the field station and walks and explorations around the park. Some programs include an annual horseshoe-crab walk in May and June, when these prehistoric creatures lay their eggs under a full moon, and night prowls to hear the mating calls of spring peepers and to view the bizarre mating dance of male woodcocks.

Most visitors frequent the park's small beach, marina, or 2-mile multipurpose path (used by joggers, in-line skaters, and cyclists), but there's a charming nature preserve at the tip of the peninsula, Crooke's Point, with unimpeded views of both bay and sky. (A yearly $50 nature-study permit allows you to park there; otherwise walk .3 miles from the nearest free parking at the beach.) This beach is also a good place for saltwater fishing.

The point is named for John Jeremy Crooke, a wealthy inventor and naturalist who, in 1860, bought what was then an island and built a cabin there. The island was connected to Staten Island by landfill in the 1940s and allowed to return to its wild state. It is now a wonderful place where city kids can consider the horizon and watch the sun set, comb for jingleshells, razor clams, and slipper shells along the sandy coastline, and see real sand dunes tufted with beach grass. (See chapter 6, Exploring the Shore.) In autumn, monarch butterflies fuel up on the nectar of seaside goldenrod before heading south. (See chapter 7, Gardens Grow Children.)

Crooke's Point also has three short nature trails that wind through a shrubby forest lush with bayberry (look for yellow-rumped warblers eating the frosted berries in winter), winged sumac (not poisonous), and black cherry, plants that tolerate salt, wind, and sun. It's a good place to look for birds during spring migration (look for woodpeckers in winter), but watch for poison ivy and ticks.

On the other side of the peninsula is Great Kills Harbor, featuring a public marina where quietly bobbing sailboats are a welcome respite for busy city eyes. If you're lucky enough to own a boat, canoe, or kayak, you may launch it from the ramp in the middle of the park—but no Jet Skis please; they are banned. You may borrow a child's life jacket at the ranger station—just present your driver's license and phone number.

A small beach on the bay side of the park is filled with locals, mostly Italian–American transplants from Brooklyn. Don't expect white sand. This sand is reddish because it contains naturally occurring iron oxides and some clay particles deposited by the last glacial advance.

There's also a little-visited salt marsh at the end of a short path that leads from the northeastern end of Parking Lot A, a quiet place for kids to see fiddler crabs skitter into their holes and mud snails slither across the sand, as well as shore birds such as sanderlings, oyster catchers, and black skimmers. (See chapter 3, Birding with Children.) This is also a good place to go seining. (See chapter 6, Exploring the Shore.)

The city bought what is today Great Kills Park in the late 1920s, to create a park, but didn't start filling in the wetlands until the 1940s. The park opened in the summer of 1949 and was transferred to the federal government as part of the Gateway National Recreation Area in 1973. Stop in at the ranger station and ask for your free copy of the new "Family Field Guide to the Natural Areas of Great Kills Park."

Open—Friday-Monday, 9 AM-4:30 PM. Free.

Miller Field Ranger Station

26 Miller Field
718-351-6970
www.nps.gov/gate

Ranger-led walks and nature programs; nature trail; evening campfires; community garden; unprotected beach; fishing; picnic tables (by reservation only); restrooms.

Miller Field—flat, well worn, and fringed with aged aircraft hangers—is a popular recreational venue, with one-third of its 187 acres taken up by sports fields. But closer inspection reveals that nature resides in small doses—from a swamp-oak forest hidden in the park's northwest corner to a bountiful community garden and uncombed shoreline. The Rangers host free nature programs and periodic evening campfires, a rare treat for most city kids.

While the ranger station is little more than an information office, the Rangers, if asked, will guide you to the 9-acre swamp white-oak forest, which has many types of trees, most notably its namesake, a wetland species whose leaves are dark green on top and whitish on the bottom and whose dark brown bark flakes and peels in papery curls. The tree is locally unique, but likely will not continue to proliferate in these woods because the creek that once kept the forest ground moist for them was diverted a couple of decades ago. This has left the forest dryer and created a habitat that better supports red maples and other species that like things drier. Look for identification labels on some of the trees.

One of the park's memorable trees was a large elm that stood in the southeast corner, a landmark to colonial Dutch mariners. In 1852, a lighthouse named for the tree was built in its place. It was replaced in 1939 by an unromantic concrete slab of a lighthouse, which still stands—although decommissioned in 1964. On a clear day, the park's shoreline is a great place to view other harbor lighthouses, including the Fort Wadsworth Light under the Verrazano-Narrows Bridge as well as Romer Shoal Light, Sandy Hook Light, and even the Coney Island Light Station.

Before there was a Miller Field, the property belonged to generations of wealthy Vanderbilts, who sold it to the federal government in 1919. An airfield and army base were built and named for Captain James Ely Miller (1883–1918), a New York banker and the first American pilot killed in aerial combat during World War I. The field was deactivated in 1969. In 1999, the park was officially renamed World War Veterans Park at Miller Field.

Open—Daily, 9 AM-4:30 PM. Free.

2 NATURE WALKS

When heading out with children, take your time wandering through Mother Nature. It's not about the destination, it's about the journey; and kids, particularly toddlers, love picking up sticks and acorns, splashing in water, and basically feeling their way along the trail—because everything out there is just so endlessly fascinating. Bigger kids will love finding the perfect fallen branch to use as a walking stick, looking inside tree holes for critters, and turning over logs and rocks to see what's hiding underneath. (Be sure they turn them back over when they're done.) By going at your children's pace, stopping to smell things or just to watch and listen, you too will see things you've perhaps never noticed before, like birds snatching insects in mid-air, chipmunks digging through the leaf litter, and maybe even a muskrat swimming in a stream.

With this approach in mind, all of the following walks are suitable for toddlers on up and I've indicated walks that work best for younger kids. Infants may be carried in a backpack as long as they can hold their heads up, while hiking with toddlers will be slow and riddled with questions. If you don't know the answer to a question, tell them the two of you will find the answer together when you go home. Older kids experience a sense of freedom not often found on city streets, so they will probably want to run ahead. Let them be the leaders but remind them to stay within your sight.

Kids 2 through 5 can generally handle an hour-long walk. Older children can obviously manage more, but keep in mind that only you know your child—and every child is different. If your youngster wants to turn back, do so; it's no fun walking with or carrying a cranky kid. You also don't want your children to get turned off to field walks. If you finish just a fraction of the route, it's okay as long as your children have had fun. The idea is to get outside, explore nature, and have an adventure.

If you're concerned about ticks, insect bites, or poison ivy, you may want to dress yourself and your children in light-colored, long-sleeved shirts, and long pants. Afterward, check for ticks, picking them off your kids' clothes if necessary. To remove a tick from skin, grab the insect at its mouthparts with tweezers and pull gently but firmly, careful not to twist the insect and making sure it's removed in one piece.

In colder weather, layers of clothing work nicely, because they may be added and removed as needed. If there's the threat of rain, consider carrying a change of clothes and a waterproof poncho or rain jacket. And always wear a wide-brimmed hat, although a baseball cap will do.

There are, however, some things you should never leave behind: water, snacks, sunscreen, insect repellent, and tweezers for picking off ticks, if necessary. You may even want to invest in a Swiss army knife equipped with all sorts of gizmos that can be handy out in the field. Band-Aids—or a small first-aid kit—are a good idea; and if you have a map, bring that along, too. If traveling with a baby, bring extra diapers and a plastic bag to carry them out. Personally, I consider a camera a necessity.

More optional items include field guides, a nature journal for sketching and writing, and binoculars and a magnifying glass for each person. Pedometers are fun because invariably your children will want to know how far they've walked. Little children also like wearing a compass around their necks because it makes the outing feel official; while older kids will actually use the compass and report on what direction the trail is heading. Some parents feel assured bringing a cell phone. Pack it all up in a daypack, and off you go!

BRONX

John Kieran Nature Trail, Van Cortlandt Park

Easy 1.25-mile loop
Ages: Infants and Older
Best: Spring, late summer, autumn, winter

The John Kieran Nature Trail winds through woods and marshes and along the western shore of Van Cortlandt Lake, the largest freshwater body in the Bronx. The trail is not blazed, meaning there are no markers here, but it is difficult to get lost if you follow this guide and map. Portions of the trail follow the Old Putnam Trail, which is also used by bicyclists.

The trail is named for Bronx resident John Kieran (1892–1981), the first by-lined columnist for the New York Times and author of the highly regarded Natural History of New York City (1959).

Begin your walk on an asphalt path behind the Van Cortlandt Nature Center. On your left is an iron fence decorated with leaves. The trail soon becomes pebbly dirt and is bordered by invasive garlic mustard, which has white blooms in spring. Crushed leaves smell like garlic.

On the right, you come to a swampy area with native cattails, a member of the grass family. While admiring their singular appearance, explain to your youngsters that Native Americans found in this one plant an astonishing array of uses. The flower starts off green and is hidden by a grassy husk, like corn. Native Americans used these husks in weaving. The flower later reveals itself as a velvet-brown, cigar-shaped bloom before growing fuzzy and going to seed. Native Americans dried the starchy central part of the root and lower stalk and ground it into meal. Flowers were roasted

and eaten or used as torches, while the absorbent fuzz padded baby diapers and insulated moccasins in winter.

Turn left onto a wood-chip path at Tibbetts Brook dam. Van Cortlandt Lake and the golf-course clubhouse (1895) are in front of you. People like fishing here; and if your children are lucky, they may see a great blue heron. Explain to your kids that the dam was built in 1699 and holds water back on one side, creating Van Cortlandt Lake. On the other side of the dam, the flow of water was controlled to turn the waterwheels that powered the mechanisms in grist and saw mills. Before the dam was built, Tibbetts Brook, called *Mosholu* by Native Americans, ran unimpeded from Yonkers through what is today Van Cortlandt Park and Broadway, before joining Spuyten Duyvil Creek, which flows into the Hudson River.

Cross the old railroad bridge over the brook and turn left onto a wide gravel path. Tell your kids that trains used to run on this path, a remnant of the northbound track of the Putnam Division of the New York Central Railroad. Watch for cyclists. The Putnam once ran from Highbridge in the Bronx to Brewster, New York, where travelers could connect with trains to Boston—the city's first such link. The line carried passengers from 1881 to 1958 and freight until 1981.

Ask your children if they hear anything other than bird song and ducks. The highway din is the Major Deegan Expressway (1956), one of three highways (the others being Mosholu Parkway and Henry Hudson Parkway) that crisscross the park, forever altering the park's natural terrain. Then focus their attention on Van Cortlandt Lake, a great place to see swans and ducks as well as cormorants drying their outstretched wings. Explain that this is the way cormorants keep dry because they lack the natural water-repelling oils of other waterfowl. Notice the pretty aquatic plants called spatterdocks, native water lilies with vibrant yellow flowers in summer. Point out their heart-shaped leaves, both food and shelter to lots of tiny pond creatures. Look for the hanging orange blooms of jewelweed; juice crushed from its stems is said to relieve poison ivy itch when spread on the rash. Kids love touching the plant's thin, beanlike seed pods in late summer because they burst open upon the slightest contact, shooting tiny seeds everywhere—hence its other name: "touch-me-not."

You will soon see 13 giant stone slabs on the left side of the trail, an unintentional tribute to the building of Grand Central Terminal. According to the City Parks Department, they were placed here at the turn of the 19th century by the New York Central Railroad (of Commodore Cornelius Vanderbilt fame) to see which rock would best stand the test of time and, therefore, be best suited for the façade of the new station. In the end, Indiana limestone, a fine-grained, light-colored stone was selected, mostly because it could be brought in on the railroad's own tracks and, consequently, was cheapest to transport. This is a good entry to a little earth science for older youngsters. Millions and millions of years ago, a shallow inland sea covered large parts of North America, particularly the Midwest. The tons of fossilized remains of many sea creatures were eventually compressed into limestone. While the slabs along the trail have been painted over the years to cover graffiti, you may see some bits of fossil at the back of the slabs or where paint has peeled.

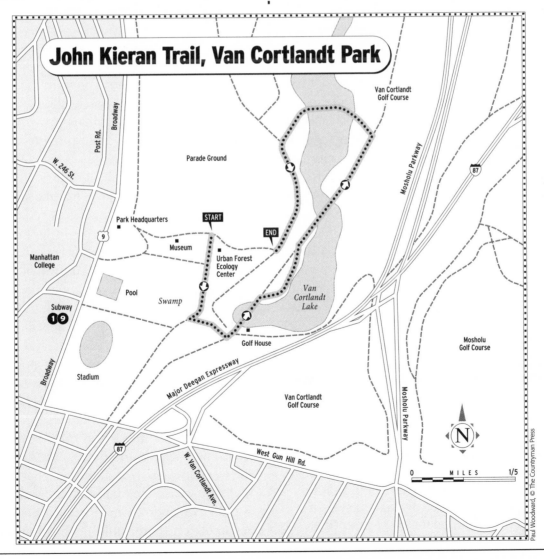

Paul Woodward, © The Countryman Press

Return to the trail. Across from the stones is a gap in the fence. Walk through and onto a mulch path that parallels the lake shore. In late spring, two types of Solomon's seal wildflowers bloom here—the "false" and more common variety has a plume of white flowers at the tip and speckled red berries in autumn; while the light-green flowers of the "true" variety dangle consecutively along the stem and produce blue-black berries in autumn. If your children are familiar with the Star of David, you may want to explain that when the stem of the true variety dies and falls from the rhizome root, the scar that is left is said to resemble the Seal of King Solomon, which is the Star of David.

Along the walk you'll also encounter Lady's Thumb, its lance-shaped leaves smudged with a dark splotch, resembling a polished fingernail. Native Americans rubbed the leaves on their horses to keep flies away. Introduced from Europe, probably in colonial times, the plant has tightly packed, beadlike pink flowers on spikes in summer and is a member of the smartweed family. Many of the ferns growing along the trail are New York ferns, not specific to the city but rather an East Coast species. The fronds are tapered at both ends, just like New Yorkers burning the proverbial candle at both ends. If it's mid- to late summer and your kids smell something sweet, it's likely sweet pepperbush, a large shrub with white elongated flowers and a favorite of butterflies. The path is also surrounded by many species of beautiful trees, perhaps

Deadly Graffiti

As you and your children walk the woods, you may notice autographs on trees with smooth, gray bark. The trees are beech, and as the tree grows, these signatures spread and enlarge; and the carved initials and sentiments not only mar their beauty but expose the trees to disease, just as a break in our skin exposes us to infection.

the most striking being the red maple, which leaves a crimson carpet on the trail in autumn.

Ask your children to be wildlife detectives, always keeping their eyes open for raccoons, chipmunks, even deer and wild turkey that walk down from nearby Westchester County. (The Bronx is the only borough connected to the mainland United States; the other four boroughs are islands.) In spring, look around for migrating birds like black and orange Baltimore orioles, vireos, song sparrows, and all kinds of warblers. Brown-headed cowbirds are also numerous, with the females acting just like the mother bird in the Dr. Seuss classic, Horton Hatches an Egg. Like that mama, cowbirds lay their eggs in other birds' nests, duping them into rearing the cowbirds' young.

Kids may also see galls—strange growths on tree branches, twigs, and leaves—and learn a little about entomology. Galls are a tree's way of responding to insect or mite eggs laid on them. After the grubs hatch, the tree is stimulated into forming a gall or growth from its own tissue, which in turn, provides food and shelter to the developing insect. When the insect becomes an adult, it drills a little hole in the gall and comes out. The tree doesn't get anything in return for its generosity, but in most cases is unaffected by the little freeloaders. There are many different galls, with specific insects choosing specific species of trees for their eggs. Some galls are about the size of a brown golf ball and found on oak trees and are called oak galls, while others appear as yellow and orange spots on oak leaves, and are called spangled galls. Cherry trees get pouch galls, which look like blisters on leaves.

The trail soon turns back through the fence and onto the main trail, which leads to a bridge. On the left is a marsh and on the right is the lake. This is a pleasant place to sit. At one time, the wetlands were part of the lake; but over time highway runoff, sewage output from Yonkers, and silt carried downstream from Tibbett's Brook accumulated here, filling the bottom and increasing nutrient levels. Aquatic plants such as water lilies, phragmites, and buttonbush—to name only a few—found a place to grow. The marsh may eventually become a meadow, which may in turn become a forest, over a very long period of time—in a natural process called succession. The tall, wheatlike reeds are phragmites, an invasive plant that quickly takes over moist, sunny areas. This habitat is also favored by red-winged blackbirds and muskrats.

Turn left. You are facing a twisted black willow tree, with the golf course on your right and Tibbetts Brook on your left. On the bridge, near marker 12, is a good place to linger with your children. A pair of binoculars is helpful. Have your children scan the marsh for nesting swans, large snapping turtles, and bullfrogs peering above the surface of the water and have them listen for the male's "Ahoohm, Ahoohm" mating call in spring.

The plant with glossy, arrowhead-shaped leaves growing in the water is arrow arum; the seeds are enjoyed by wood ducks, so keep your eyes open for the colorful males. During the spring, pretty sky-blue forget-me-nots grow close to the ground along the marsh edges. Tell your kids that the green stuff growing on the water's surface is duckweed, a word that brings a giggle to young children; and yes, ducks like to eat it. To the right of the trail, look for the bright yellow flowers of marsh marigold in spring.

You will soon reach a knotty, bent-over, sprawling mulberry tree that beckons you and your kids to climb; so take the time to gently inch along its very long, horizontal branches and think of it as nature's playground.

Return to the trail and continue on until you reach a huge London plane tree smack in the middle of the path and on the fringe of the park's parade grounds. It takes about three adults and two children to wrap their arms around this mammoth. Try it. Then turn left, keeping the parade grounds on your right. The trail is no longer wild, the quiet now interrupt-

ed by athletes playing cricket and baseball on land that was once the growing fields of local Native Americans. At the end of the trail, on the left, is the old Kingsbridge Burial Grounds, the final resting place of some early, prominent Bronx residents, although there are no tombstones left to see. Continue until you reach the nature center and the end of the trail.

Twin Island Nature Trail, Pelham Bay Park

Easy .75-mile loop along salt marsh and rocky coastline
Ages: 4 and Older
Best: Low tide in late summer and autumn

In Pelham Bay Park's eastern end is 19-acre Twin Island, with a rocky coast that will appeal to kids eager to scramble over its boulders flecked with sparkling mica and banded with wide veins of quartz. It's a bit of Maine in New York City, a rock-strewn shoreline deposited by glaciers thousands of years ago and the southernmost end of the same sheet of bedrock that runs up to the Pine Tree State.

As you walk around the island you may notice that it's really not an island, but a peninsula. Before Orchard Beach was built in the 1930s, there were two islands here—East and West Twin—but the watery areas between them were filled in to create one big land mass and the crescent-shaped beach.

The Twin Island Nature Trail begins just west of the nature center, where you'll find a path with a sign that says "Twin Island Preserve." Mention to your kids that many stone tools and tool-making items have been found in the area, evidence that Native Americans once lived here. Many of the large erratics or "wandering boulders" left behind by the glaciers were revered by Native Americans and used as gathering places for rituals and ceremonies.

A bit of Maine in New York City: The rock-strewn shoreline of Twin Island was deposited by glaciers thousands of years ago.

Continue along the path until you reach a "T." Turn left (the path may be weedy in summer) and continue to the end of a broken stone bridge, which once connected neighboring Hunter Island (166 acres, now attached to the mainland) to Twin Island. Watch out for thick stands of poison ivy on the left side of the path.

The soggy beach below the path is a great place to explore at low tide, because children can turn over rocks and find dozens of Asian shore crabs hiding underneath, waiting for high tide. These crabs have lots of babies and you'll probably find various sizes, although none are larger than an Oreo cookie. These

Asian imports were first sighted in New Jersey in 1988 and probably arrived in ship's ballast water; but now they have proliferated, becoming a potential threat to native crabs. There are lots of sea lettuce and snails on the shore, as well. Kids will also see herons, egrets, gulls, ducks, and cormorants, mostly in summer, although wintering ducks arrive when it's cold farther north. In spring, hundreds of horseshoe crabs appear on the beach—particularly at night—in their annual mating ritual.

Turn around and retrace your steps, keeping the shoreline on your left and passing the "T." Once you are out of the woods, cross some rocks, and turn left, now keeping the salt marsh on your left. This is a transitional zone between land and sea that is affected by the tides—submerged and exposed, submerged and exposed. The smell is that of decaying organic matter, which provides nutrient-rich food to animals, including microscopic creatures invisible to unaided eyes.

If you notice quick, scurrying movements on the sand during spring and summer, it's probably fiddler crabs running from you and your children and retreating into their sandy holes. Stand quietly for a while and wait for them to come out or at least peek out from the mouths of their tunnels. Explain to your kids that male fiddlers have one claw larger than the other, which they use to impress females and ward off other males. It looks like they're playing some hoe-down music as they wave their big claw in front of them.

You may see a jimsonweed growing on the right side of the trail. The plant is beautiful, with long, trumpet-shaped lavender flowers and spiky, round seed pods; but it smells bad and is very poisonous. You may not, therefore, want to point it out to your kids—although it is an interesting plant that for centuries has been used as a mind-altering drug. You will see kinder plants, especially one with lots of very tiny, pale lavender flowers that create a kind of purple haze. This is sea lavender, which is often dried and used in flower arrangements. Glasswort has slim, tender, segmented stems that are pretty tasty—crunchy and salty. If you accidentally step on some, you'll see where this plant gets its name.

Straight ahead is Two Trees Island, named for the man said to have been the last Native American to live in the wilds of Pelham Bay

Tidal pools often contain crabs, fish, and other creatures stranded when the high tide retreats.

Park. According to Theodore Kazimiroff's *The Last Algonquin*, Joe Two Trees (born 1840) befriended Kazimiroff's father, then a young boy scout, and instructed him in the ways of his people so that their traditions wouldn't die with Joe.

Today, the island has its beauty and its drawbacks. It is often occupied by a handful of skimpily attired men who like to lie around on the island's rock outcroppings; and there's some trash. Children are not frequent visitors here; but it's perfectly safe to wander around and, on a clear day, enjoy the breathtaking views of Long Island Sound and beyond to Westchester.

After exploring Two Trees Island, return to the trail, now keeping the salt marsh on your right. Then turn left onto the rocky coastline, instead of taking the path into the woods. The massive rocks—complete blankets of stone— are far more interesting to kids, who love

climbing and walking across them. They're visually interesting, too, because many of them are embedded with colorful swirls (folds in the rock) and striations that are kind of psychedelic. Some also have thick ribbons of quartz running through them. These rocks are Hartland schist, exposed about 15,000 years ago during the time of the Wisconsin Glacier; but youngsters will simply consider them nature's jungle gym. The coastline eventually loops back to the nature center, so don't worry about getting lost. And don't be afraid to ask the fishermen what's biting. Your kids may get to see a bluefish, summer fluke, or striped bass.

If it's low tide, kids can investigate puddles in the rocks' depressions. These are tidal pools and they often contain crabs, fish, and other creatures stranded when the high tide retreats. Tell your kids that these tiny pools are like little outdoor aquariums, only the inhabitants won't survive unless the tide returns in time to replenish the pools with oxygen and food.

You will eventually come to a huge, dark-colored erratic boulder on the right-hand side known as Lion Rock or The Sphinx. It has been here for more than 10,000 years. There used to be another boulder balanced on top of it, but that one toppled and now lies on the ground to the right. This boulder, as with other erratics, was revered by Native Americans.

When you reach the end of the rocky trail, you'll find a narrow, sandy path leading back to the beachfront promenade, just to the right of the fence. Check out the "Pools and Sea Creatures" interpretive sign and see how many you and your kids have encountered during your walk around Twin Island.

Other Bronx Trails to Explore

Split Rock Trail, Pelham Bay Park

This 1.5-mile trail winds through the Thomas Pell Wildlife Refuge and Sanctuary, with its rare saltwater marshland. It begins at the northern part of the Bartow traffic circle on Shore Road, runs north along the Pell Sanctuary's western edge, and ends at historic Split Rock.

Kazimiroff Trail, Pelham Bay Park

This 1.5-mile trail explores parts of 166-acre Hunter Island, dense with pine, birch, black locust, oak, and flowering crab apple trees. Flora include violets, lilies, strawberries, asparagus, and wild geraniums. Popular with birders, the area often has great horned owls, northern saw-whets owls, wood thrushes, brown thrashers, orioles, and others. The trail begins just west of the Orchard Beach Nature Center.

John Muir Nature Trail, Van Cortlandt Park

This 1.7-mile trail is the only trail that crosses the park from east to west, passing through forests with 100-foot trees, wetlands with frogs and salamanders, and grasslands filled with songbirds. It is named after the great Scottish American conservationist John Muir, the founder of Yosemite National Park and the Sierra Club.

Old Croton Aqueduct Trail, Van Cortlandt Park

This 1.1-mile trail runs through the center of Croton Woods, with both moist and dry woodlands. Sugar maple, oak, and hickory trees predominate in dry areas in the north, while black walnut, American sycamore, and American elm trees are most common at the moist southern end. The trail follows part of the 41-mile-long aqueduct that was used to deliver water from Westchester to New York City in the 19th century. The New Croton Aqueduct replaced it in 1897. Access to the trail is from the southern entrance to Van Cortlandt Park at the intersection of Mosholu Parkway. Follow an unpaved path north to the Major Deegan Expressway, then switch to a paved path that runs under the expressway and connects with the Old Croton Aqueduct Trail.

While you won't encounter bear and moose in New York City, there are plenty of furry friends parading around our forests and fields. The best way to encounter these creatures is by remaining quiet, because the slightest sound will send them scurrying for cover. Even if you don't see any mammals, it's fun searching for evidence of their presence. Look for tracks in mud, snow, and sand. Raccoon prints, for example, are paired, with a rear foot beside a front foot. The detail of their five claws is also clearly discernable. Cottontail rabbits, on the other hand, make round front tracks and long hind tracks, with the hind tracks in front of the front tracks—because rabbits hop. Also look for upturned areas of ground, indicating tunnels made by burrowing animals like moles, and matted vegetation, where animals may have bedded down. Scan the ground for chewed acorns, leaves, and twigs as well as feathers and scat. Every animal has its own distinctive excrement, from the small, pelletlike droppings of cottontail rabbits to tubular, blunt-ended feces of raccoons.

And always be on the lookout for anything that moves. Here are some mammals you may encounter on your walks:

• **Eastern chipmunk**–Active during the day; these small, reddish, squirrel-like mammals have a white stripe bordered by black on each side. You may hear their "chip-chip-chip" before seeing them. They sleep, store food, and nest in extensive burrows.

• **Eastern cottontail**–These grayish-brown rabbits with reddish-brown necks and shoulders and white tails mainly come out at dusk and are a mealtime favorite of red-tailed hawks. Designed for speed, their hind legs longer than their front legs, they are able to run at speeds up to 15 miles per hour.

• **Eastern gray squirrel**–These agile creatures are nature's tightrope walkers and acrobats, using their big bushy tails for balance. Those tails also come in handy as blankets in winter, canopies to block out the summer sun, and fluffed-up warning signals to repel aggressors. They build messy nests 40 feet high in the trees and hoard acorns. The city's black squirrels are really gray squirrels with greater amounts of pigment.

• **Harbor seal**–These plump aquatic mammals have been making a comeback in New York City waters in recent years and are often seen basking on small islands in late winter. Gray, tan, and brown, with spots or blotches, these true seals are great swimmers and can dive as deep as 1,500 feet for food.

• **Muskrat**–These glossy reddish-brown rodents (up to 12 inches long) can be seen swimming in marshes and streams, steering with their long tails stretched out behind them. Aquatic mammals, they build lodges near shore and enter through underwater doorways that keep predators out.

• **Raccoon**–Beautifully patterned with black face masks and long bushy ringed tails, raccoons are nocturnal animals whose paws are more like hands. These dexterous critters have been known to turn doorknobs and untie knots. They like to curl up in trees, and they'll eat almost anything.

• **Woodchuck**–These chunky brown rodents, also called groundhogs, are said to predict the weather, calling for six weeks more of winter if they see their shadows on February 2. They like to standing on their hind legs to check things out and often run to the nearest hole when alarmed. Growing to as much as 17 inches, they hibernate in winter in large underground dens.

Brooklyn

North Forty Nature Trail, Floyd Bennett Field

Easy 1.5-mile loop
Ages: 4 and Older; although a baby backpack and jogger will work here
Best: Late spring, late summer and early fall

The North Forty Natural Area is tucked into a quiet corner of this former airfield, with trails that wend through different stages of young coastal forest, including grassland and stands of phragmites (perennial reeds), shrubbery and bayberry thickets, and woodlands containing ring-necked pheasants and cottontail rabbits. The walk described here features a stop at a 2-acre manmade lake where turtles, migrating birds, muskrats, and wading birds congregate. The pond is best viewed in the spring when it is full of water and dotted with white water lilies.

The term "North Forty" harkens back to the Homestead Act of 1862, when pioneers were given 160 acres of fallow public land to settle and farm. These plots were divided into four 40-acre sections, with the North Forty parcel the northernmost block of land—and

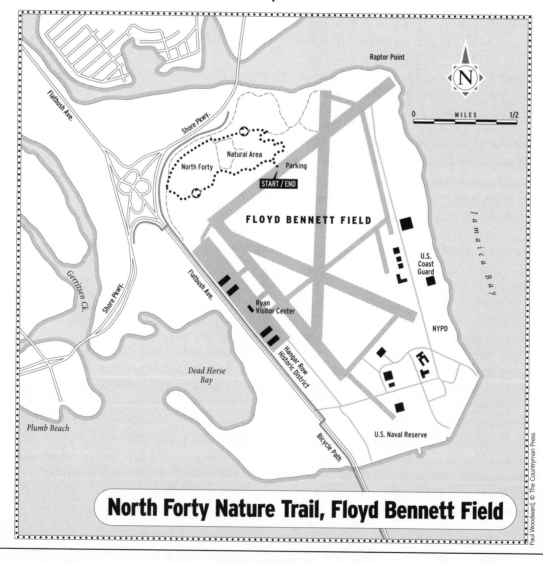

North Forty Nature Trail, Floyd Bennett Field

Paul Woodward, © The Countryman Press

the North Forty Natural Area is the northern-most area of Floyd Bennett Field.

There are three trails: Yellow, Blue, and Red. The map at the trailhead is good, but the trails are not well marked, so follow these instructions. Start off on the Yellow trail, turn onto the Blue trail, and return to the Yellow trail. If you get lost, listen for the hum of model airplanes piercing the otherwise perfect calm and head in that direction—to the model air-plane field and the main road. Mosquitoes are out even in late spring, so pack insect repellent. At trail's end, also check yourself and your chil-dren for ticks.

The trail begins west of the model airplane field and is marked by a sign describing the area. You'll find an outdoor water tank filled with drinking water (bring your own canteen). Winged sumac grows here and along the trail as either a shrub or small tree and gets its name from the foliage that grows on either side of its leafstalk. More noticeable, however, are the tightly clustered red berries that hang from the tree throughout winter, providing resident birds with a last-resort kind of meal, because they really don't taste very good. Tell your kids it's sort of like eating Brussels sprouts when there's nothing else left in the refrigerator.

There are many black cherry trees along the trail. In late spring, look for long, white clusters of fragrant blooms and conspicuous silken nests between the branches. Explain to your kids that these are the homes of hundreds of black tent caterpillars wiggling beneath the threads. They're harmless, so have your chil-dren hold one or pet the nest to see them squirm around even more. Eventually, they'll leave the nest, spin cocoons, and reinvent themselves as reddish-brown moths with pale stripes running diagonally across each forewing. As caterpillars, they feast on the tree's foliage; but the tree rebounds by putting out new growth.

Another common plant is little bluestem, a heat-loving grass that changes with the seasons.

In spring, it is a short, compact tuft of pointy blue-gray blades, like a sea urchin on land. By late summer, it has grown tall and dark with pur-plish-bronze flowers on long racemes. In fall, the blades turn burgundy red with fluffy, white seeds heads that last into winter and feed birds.

Summer wildflowers include such butterfly magnets as delicate Queen Anne's lace with its tiny nestlike seed heads, vivid goldenrod, and milkweed (with clusters of mauve flowers). In late summer, milkweeds exhibit long, fat pods shaped like jalapeno peppers. These pods are filled with neatly arranged seeds resembling the pattern of scales on a fish. When it's time to spread their seeds, milkweed pods pop open and send the seeds, attached to silky para-chutes, into the wind so that they can settle down and grow someplace else. Kids may also scan the plant for black and orange milkweed beetles trying to pierce the pod and get at the seeds themselves. Like the similarly colored monarch butterfly, these beetles have vivid coats that fend off hungry predators. Neither butterflies nor beetles taste very good because both dine on milkweed, acquiring its toxic juice, which is harmless to them but poisonous to their enemies. The milky sap that may often be seen oozing from the plants' stems and leaves illustrates the genesis of the plant's name.

Late summer isn't the only time for wild-flowers. During spring, kids may scour the ground for wood sorrel, which has three heart-shaped leaves and tiny yellow flowers. Since my kids experienced its lemony taste, they gobble it up every chance they get, even from the cracks of city sidewalks, which I discourage. You'll also see hawkweed—a tall, dandelion-like flower—and multiflora rose, an aggressive, yet attractive climbing shrub with pinkish-white flowers with fuzzy, yellow centers. The hips it produces in late summer look like, but taste nothing like, cherry tomatoes. Tell your chil-dren that birds love them nonetheless and inad-vertently plant more and more of this invasive plant when they poop out the seeds.

This might be a good time to explain to your children what makes a plant invasive. On their home turf, plants are kept in check (and diversity preserved) by insects, diseases, and other plants. But when a foreign plant is introduced into the landscape, it may run wild because there is nothing naturally in the ecosystem to stop it. As it becomes more and more widespread, the native community dwindles. There are numerous efforts citywide to rip out nonnative species and replace them with indigenous ones.

Continue on the path lined with fragrant bayberry, a scent familiar to any youngster who has ever bought his dad aftershave lotion for Father's Day. Tell your kids that colonists made candles from the berries' wax coating, a time-consuming affair that meant boiling many thousands of berries and skimming off the wax from the water to produce a single candle. Imagine having to harvest all those berries! Remind your kids that colonial children often did this labor-intensive work. Native Americans also brewed the bark for tea to ease coughs, colds, flu, fevers, headache, and sore throats.

Autumn is a great time to see berry-producing plants like Oriental bittersweet, a twining vine that climbs all over trees and shrubs and sports red berries encapsulated by yellow shells. Ask your children if they think this plant is a native or nonnative; and explain that since it's growing amok, they can bet this Asian import is an invasive.

After walking .2 mile, you will reach a "T." Turn left. There will be phragmites (common reeds), another invasive, on both your left and right. After about 100 yards, you'll come to another "T". Make another left, onto a grassy path. You are now on the Blue Trail.

At the .4-mile mark, there is a bird blind on your left. Turn in and have your children look at the oddly named "Return a Gift Pond," created in 1989 and paid for by you if you checked off the "Return-a-gift-to-wildlife" box on your New York State tax return. Explain to your kids that humans aren't designed to camouflage them-

"Ok. Now which way do we go?"

selves in the wild, so the bird blind provides a place in which to hide and spy on pond inhabitants. It's a wonderful place to linger, especially in spring, when it's common to see egrets, herons, and other long-legged waders along the shores or up in trees, where they build large stick nests. Have the youngsters look for painted turtles and red-eared sliders sunning themselves on exposed rocks and logs and swimming muskrats that like to nibble on the leaves and roots of fragrant white water lilies.

Return to the trail, soon turning left into another bird blind, which provides a different vantage point on the same pond. Have your children look for dragonflies hovering close to the pond's surface and listen for bullfrogs. If your kids have a nature journal, this is a good time to do a little sketching. Stay awhile and watch the pond life, with birds and other creatures coming and going. Explain to your children that a little patience goes a long way toward revealing the wonders of nature and, as any parent knows, comes in handy in everyday life.

Return to the trail. At this point, you have walked a half mile. If your kids are tired, turn around and retrace your steps back to the trailhead. If you'd like to continue, do so and soon turn right. There is a big stake in the middle of the trail, indicating the Blue Trail. This area is more wooded and shadier than the beginning of the walk and among the trees are red mulberries, which drip sweet, reddish-black fruit in early summer, delicious to both people and wildlife.

At the next fork (sometimes there is an orange utility cone here that reads "Pond Loop"), bear right. There are more mulberry and black cherry trees here. Listen for the "drink-your-tea" call of the eastern towhee and "meow" of the gray catbird.

At the next "T" bear right onto the combination Blue/Yellow Trail. In 100 yards or so, turn left onto the Yellow Trail, where you may see cottontail bunnies and other creatures. In summer, look for the wrinkled rose, with its 2-inch-wide white or pink flowers. Ask your children if they can figure out why it's called wrinkled rose, and then point out the crinkly leaves. In fall, the plant produces large orange hips that contain more Vitamin C than oranges and are often used for rose-hip tea.

Continue straight ahead. You'll come to some Japanese pine trees and, strangely enough, a tall yellow pole with a red top, as well as a yellow fire hydrant. Turn right, keeping the hydrant on your left. The path becomes narrow and twisted, more shaded still, and sheltered. In summer, tons of sweet blackberries drip from thorny branches. You will soon see little bluestem again, a sign that the trailhead is close at hand. You may even hear model airplanes buzzing overhead; the flying field is to your left. When you reach a "T" and a big black cherry tree, turn left and you are right back where you started!

Gerritsen Creek Nature Trail, Salt Marsh Nature Center

Easy 1-mile loop on gravel path
Ages: 4 and Older, although joggers and carriers work well
Best: Low tide in spring and autumn. Dusk is beautiful any time of the year, but summers can be buggy.

This 1-mile loop is one of the most picturesque locations in the city, with nary a building to be seen. The trail meanders through a salt-marsh habitat, a critical ecosystem existing between land and sea that provides refuge to a diverse group of organisms and animals, including migratory shore birds and ducks, waders, fiddler crabs, and little brown bats. Most of the walk follows the eastern edge of Gerritsen Creek, which flows into 250,000-acre Jamaica Bay, a federally protected area that itself empties into the Atlantic Ocean. There's also an uplands area, where tropical monk parakeets are often heard squawking.

The gravel trail begins behind the nature center. If it is low tide, your children can look in the creek for old wooden pilings. They're what's left of a 1645 gristmill that turned grain into flour, the first tidewater gristmill built in North America, which operated until 1889.

This is also a good place for youngsters to hone their binocular skills, looking for ducks in winter, including buffleheads and northern shovelers, and in summer, long-legged waders such as great and snowy egrets. Summer also brings laughing gulls and oystercatchers with their oversized orange bills, as well as a few clapper rails—long-billed, brownish, chicken-sized critters who love to forage in the marsh. Fall and spring are the best seasons for migratory shore birds.

Sit and wait a while and your children may see a black-crowned night heron gulp down a fish. A Ranger told me he once saw a skimmer eating a fish that was abruptly stolen by an aggressive gull; so there's always a bit of drama in the salt marsh.

You will soon cross the Marsh Bridge, the best place to see two grasses that make the salt marsh a productive and valuable ecosystem. Have your kids look to both the left and right sides of the bridge and report any differences they notice in the grasses. The grass on the right, with the flat, smooth blades and growing closest to the creek, is salt marsh cordgrass and twice a day it's submerged by high tides. Tell your children that this plant has a novel way of regulating its salt intake (something grandpa with his high blood pressure might heed). When the tide rolls in, a membrane on the grass's roots sucks up the water, while glands on its leaves expel the salt. Its stems also trap sediments and decaying organic matter (detritus) that accumulate to enrich the mud. These, in turn, feed and support marsh life, from the tiniest zooplankton to fiddler crabs that, in their turn, aerate the mud while poking around for food, helping the cordgrass to grow.

The short, matted, funny-looking grass on the left is salt-meadow cordgrass. Talk about cowlick city! Back in the old days, colonists let their livestock graze on it. It's a little less tolerant of salt water, but luckily it is submerged by high tides only twice a month, during what are called the spring tides (especially high tides when the moon is full or new).

Along the trail, you and your kids will see yet another, very tall grass called phragmite, or common reed. Although quite attractive in late summer when its wheatlike flowers are in full bloom, the common reed is invasive, meaning it runs amok and is less valuable to the salt marsh community. When the often misunderstood salt marsh was filled in and disturbed years ago, this provided an in for the phragmites, which like big bullies push out much-needed cordgrass. The

Parks Department hopes to remove much of the phragmites and replace them with native plants.

As you continue on the trail, ask your children what it feels like to walk here. Not very Brooklyn-like, huh? There are virtually no buildings, streetlights, or billboards to mar the scenery. It's just pure sky, particularly spectacular at sunset. Keep your eyes peeled for redwinged blackbirds and cottontail rabbits that drop raisinlike scat on the trail. In summer, skimmers—their beaks' bottom mandibles longer than the tops—quickly graze the creek for food, winged Pac-Men with bright orange bills. If you're visiting after a storm, you may want to go on a snail rescue, since many of them will be washed up on the path. Your kids may gently pick them up, briefly investigate them—waiting for them to stretch their heads out and take a look-see—then place them into the grass.

In late summer, the trail is particularly vibrant with seaside golden rod, purple coneflower, butterfly weed, and Queen Anne's lace in bloom. But it can also be pretty buggy, so bring mosquito repellent.

Continue to the Marsh Platform, sit down, and have the kids remain as quiet as possible—because out there in the sand in front of the platform are one of nature's great crowd pleasers, fiddler crabs. These guys, however, are small and quick and easily startled, so chances are they felt the vibrations of your approach and scuttled down into their holes. When they think the coast is clear, they'll resurface, the males waving their one huge claw (the other is smaller), like playing fiddles to mark their territories and attract mates. Tell your children that just as people can be right- or left-handed, fiddlers can be either right- or left-clawed.

You and your youngsters can also sit silently on the sand and wait for the fiddlers to crawl out of their shelters, with the hope of catching one to examine up close. If you do so, just keep clear of the pinchers. Then gently return the fiddler to the sand and watch it skitter from side-to-side before escaping into its hole. At high tide, fiddlers plug their holes with mud so they don't get flooded out.

Return to the trail. You will come to a beach on the right. At low tide, this is a great place to walk among ribbed mussels, all clustered together like bananas, and seaweed, particularly bladder wrack, which has air bubbles on its leaves that are fun for children to pop. If you see tidal pools, check them for periwinkles and tiny fish. The beach is also strewn with horseshoe crab shells and mollusks. Look for beached moon jellies, round, translucent jellyfish with four pinkish circles (their reproductive organs) in the center. But don't let your children touch them, because they sting. Your kids can, however, push them back into the water with a twig.

Return to the trail, which now loops around, leaving Gerritsen Creek and entering an upland area with trees, including black cherry and cottonwood. The small island ahead of you is White Island, named for Alfred T. White, who, together with Frederick B. Pratt, donated this land to the city in 1917 so that it would be protected. The island didn't exist then. Tell your kids that the city created the island when it dumped garbage on the marshes there in the 1950s, something not done anymore. After several decades as a dump, it was capped and restored in the 1990s, after local residents pressured the city to clean it up.

You will soon reach Lookout Hill. There are two mulberry trees here, one red and the other white. At dusk during the summer, you and your children can watch the sun slip beneath the horizon, turning the sky pink and purple, and see silhouetted barn swallows swooping through the air to catch insects, as crickets sing a background harmony. As night draws near, bats come out to do a little insect eating of their own—a welcome, and harmless, sight, especially on summer nights, when they

In late summer, milkweeds exhibit long, fat pods shaped like jalapeno peppers, which attract milkweed beetles.

feast on tons of pesky mosquitoes and other insects. And assure your kids that bats will not fly into their hair. Bats just don't do that.

As you near the end of the trail, and before you return to the Marsh Bridge, you may hear loud raucous calls coming from the trees. Don't worry; it's only some monk parakeets, a bit of the tropics right in Brooklyn. Have your children look in the direction of the sound and they may see these chartreuse-colored parakeets with gray faces (some say they look like they're peering out from inside a monk's hood) that are native to South America, but ended up here by accident. The first monk parakeets arrived in the 1960s, after escaping from a broken crate at Kennedy Airport, and have since found year-round niches throughout the East Coast. Because they come from a mountainous part of South America, they can withstand our winters in their heavily insulated stick nests. They also eat large seeds, which are available when it's cold, while most of the birds at the marsh eat insects.

Continue on to the nature center and the trail's end.

A pond is home to many creatures, especially in spring when it is bursting with life. Dragonfly nymphs, tadpoles, fish, diving beetles, water striders, crayfish, salamanders, toads, and turtles all thrive in or around ponds. Some animals stay at the top of the water, some at mid-depth, others at the bottom, and still others along the shore. By the end of summer, fewer creatures are around; some have left, while others have buried themselves in the mud for winter.

If your walk takes you past a pond, make sure your kids have a hand lens (10X should do), tweezers, an eyedropper, a long-handled fine-mesh net, small containers or petri dishes, and a portable microscope (if you have one)—because some of the creatures you find will be miniscule. A field guide to pond life is helpful in identifying the tiniest animals, which can look like a whole lot of moving squiggles under the lens. Larger pond creatures that youngsters may encounter include the following.

Frogs, Toads, and Salamanders—although all of them amphibians—are set apart by a few distinct characteristics. Frogs have smooth, wet skin and long hind legs, and they live in or near the water. Toads have dry, bumpy skin, which is usually brown, and short hind legs; and they live on land. They won't give you warts but do secrete a chemical toxic to humans, so it is important to wash hands after handling a toad. Salamanders retain their tails as adults. All three of these amphibians begin their lives in the water as tadpoles hatched from eggs—except for red-backed salamanders, which are terrestrial.

Some common amphibians around the city are **bullfrogs**, big and green with bulging eyes that peer above the pond's surface. They make a deep "jug-a-rum" call. **Spring peepers** are tiny tree frogs about an inch long that you may never see; but you'll surely hear their high-pitched peeps in early spring. **Fowler's toads** are covered in brown splotches and can be distinguished from **American toads** by their unspotted chests and bellies and the light colored stripe down the middle of their backs. **Spotted salamanders** (black, with yellow spots) and **red-backed salamanders** hide under stones and logs.

Turtles are shy reptiles that retreat into their hard shells at the slightest provocation. There are freshwater, saltwater, and terrestrial varieties. Common turtles include large **snapping turtles**, with massive heads, long saw-toothed tails, sharp beaks, and claws. They will bite if provoked. **Eastern box turtles** go into the water only when they're hot and dry. A movable hinge on their plastron (bottom shell) allows it to tilt up and close off all openings after the turtle has hidden inside. Our most common native species is the

Eastern painted turtle, often seen basking in large numbers on logs and stumps. Their heads are streaked yellow, the bottoms of their shells are bright yellow, and the carapaces (top shells) are dark and edged in red. **Red-eared sliders** are the most numerous of our nonnatives, the result of tossed pets that have adapted to the wild. They have red patches behind their eyes and yellow stripes on their dark shells.

You may also encounter **common garter snakes**, harmless reptiles that slither along the banks of water sources looking for worms and amphibians to eat. They are often black with yellow stripes down their backs. **Northern water snakes** spend much of their time in the water, but during the day hunt along the shorelines for frogs, salamanders, and tadpoles. They are typically dark with black blotches and cross-bands and a light belly, sometimes orange, with half-moon patterns.

Insects also abound at ponds. Dragonflies start their lives in the water, hatching from eggs into nymphs that eventually climb out of the water, shed their skins, and become airborne adults. Almost as common are water striders, small cigar-shaped insects with two short front legs (used for eating) and four very long, spread-out middle (used for swimming) and back legs (used for steering). They constantly move on the water surface, gliding so efficiently that they don't break the surface tension. Whirligigs are small black beetles that often travel in groups, quickly spinning around on the water. Their eyes are divided into two parts—one part sees above the water, the other, below.

Another Brooklyn Trail to Explore

Lullwater Nature Trail, Prospect Park

When the Prospect Park Audubon Center opened in 2002, it began blazing a series of trails in the park, in cooperation with the Prospect Park Alliance and New York City Department of Parks & Recreation. The Lullwater Nature Trail is the first to be completed, a 1.1-mile walk along the banks of the Lullwater, a manmade but very naturalistic watercourse home to many birds, turtles, frogs, crayfish, and other wildlife. In addition to posting interpretative signs along the trail, the Audubon Center lends visitors a self-guided audio tour and printed map detailing what you'll see along the way. A refundable deposit is required.

Manhattan

North Woods and Its Environs, Central Park

**Moderate .65-mile loop,
with some climbing
Ages: 4 and Older
Best time: Any time**

Most people who think they know Central Park seldom venture into the northern part of the park, unless they're avid birders or naturalists. They don't know what they're missing. Known for its dense woodlands, slopes, tranquil streams, and scenic cascades, the North Woods and its environs are Manhattan's own little wilderness. That's exactly what designers Frederick Law Olmsted and Calvert Vaux intended when they replicated a bit of the Adirondacks here so that urbanites wouldn't completely lose touch with nature.

At the beginning of the walk, you'll bump into plenty of people along the paths. At other times, especially in the woods, you may find yourself completely alone with your children. Then you'll turn out of the woods and again find yourself in an area populated by folks jogging or reading the newspaper.

In typical Manhattan fashion, this walk offers something new at every turn—terrific trees and soothing streams, wonderful wildflowers and crusty crayfish, great egrets, and huge boulders. For the most part, you won't see any city skyscrapers or hear honking taxis, and there's nothing fancy to buy. This is nature pure and simple, a wonderful place to explore with your children and share the beauty of nature coexisting with one of the world's busiest cities. If you've packed a lunch, the Great Hill provides a perfect picnic spot.

Enter the park at 100th Street and Central Park West, walking through what is called Boys' Gate. Turn left, where you and your youngsters will see an Osage orange, a tree with strange orange-sized, crinkly green fruits that look like the human brain. This is a "girl tree." Osage oranges are either male or female and only females produce fruit. If there is fruit on the ground (usually in late summer and early fall), scratch the surface and smell. Citrus, right? Researchers and locals agree that the fruits contain an essential oil that repels cockroaches. Native Americans also knew the value of the Osage, which is native to the Great Plains. There, the Osage Indians made much-sought-after bows from the wood and traded them with other Native American tribes.

Walk down the stairs leading to The Pool, a 1.5-acre, manmade pond that is one of the most idyllic spots in Central Park. Surrounded by weeping willows, native wildflowers and shrubs, and, in the spring, a huge display of daffodils and crocuses, The Pool attracts painters as well as cormorants, herons, and egrets to its shores.

When you reach The Pool, you will see a rustic bench and a lamppost numbered 01-01. To the right is a mulched path that leads to the east side of The Pool. In August, bright red cardinal flowers brighten the landscape, joe-pye weed grows tall, and duckweed gives The Pool a green coating, something ducks enjoy nibbling on. Follow the path as it turns right and ascends.

At the next rustic bench, turn left onto a paved path, keeping The Pool on your left. You'll come to an area where water pours over some huge boulders. It may look natural, but explain to your kids that this beautiful site is manufactured. The water is piped in from the park's Jacqueline Kennedy Onassis Reservoir—which also feeds The Pool, Loch, and Harlem Meer—and cascades throughout the park, including the 14-foot-high waterfall near the northeast corner of The Pool.

Even in New York City, freshwater lobsters, or crayfish, are important within the food chain.

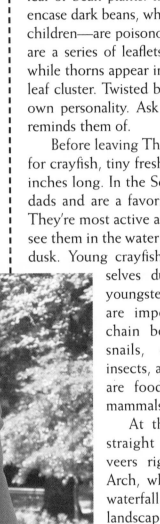

Continue on until you reach a peninsula jutting out into The Pool. To the right is a black locust with a 30-inch girth. Related to the common garden pea, black locusts produce lovely, fragrant, white pendulous flowers in spring, typical of bean plants. In late summer, long pods encase dark beans, which—you should tell your children—are poisonous to humans. The leaves are a series of leaflets that turn yellow in fall, while thorns appear in pairs at the base of each leaf cluster. Twisted branches give each tree its own personality. Ask your kids what this one reminds them of.

Before leaving The Pool, scan the shoreline for crayfish, tiny freshwater lobsters about 3–4 inches long. In the South, they're called crawdads and are a favorite of Louisiana cooking. They're most active at night, but your kids will see them in the water a couple of hours prior to dusk. Young crayfish may even show themselves during the day. Tell the youngsters that these crustaceans are important within the food chain because they eat plants, snails, dead aquatic animals, insects, and algae, and—in turn—are food for fish, reptiles, and mammals.

At the intersection, continue straight ahead. The path then veers right through Glen Span Arch, where there is a miniature waterfall. You have left the perfect landscape behind and are entering a more woodsy part of the park with oaks, elms, and maples. This is the Ravine, the park's only stream valley, with the Loch on the left. During the park's early years, the Loch, which means "lake" in Scottish, was much wider, but accumulated silt and thickets have made it more a stream. Ask your children if they hear or see any signs of the city. Chances are they won't, because the neighborhood's high-rises and city sounds are screened and muffled by trees and watery cascades. Virginia knotweed grows throughout the woods, its tiny seeds attached along tall stems in late summer. Have your kids run their fingers along the stem to watch the seeds pop off—hence the plant's other name, jumpseed.

You will soon reach a circle with two 100-year-old red oak trees. Unlike white-oak leaves, which have rounded lobes, the lobes of red oaks are pointed. On the trunk above the 30-foot mark you and your children may see telltale "ski trails." stripes on the bark that set these trees apart from another oak with pointed leaves, the black oak.

Stay to the right around the circle. You will soon reach a rustic bridge. Cross it and walk

Even in Central Park, there are huge boulders left behind by retreating glaciers.

straight ahead, up some log steps and into the woods. There are few people but plenty of birdsong because of the area's ample supply of water and shelter.

The isolation is interrupted when you reach Dead Road, a paved road where people like to jog and cycle. Turn left here. On your left is the Wildflower Meadow. Rather than staying on the path, walk onto the grass and around the meadow, and look for butterflies, bees, and maybe even a hummingbird in late summer, when gorgeous wildflowers are in bloom, including Queen Anne's lace, monarda, coneflower, goldenrod, and native grasses like little bluestem and switch grass. A particularly interesting flower is the cup plant, which grows very tall, with flowers that look like all-yellow sunflowers. Tell your kids that the plant's huge leaves form a "cup" near the stem that holds water for birds and butterflies to sip. Birds, particularly goldfinches, also love the seeds.

Return to Dead Road and before you reach its intersection with East Drive turn left onto a path, staying left at the fork, and keeping the Wildflower Meadow on your left. You have reentered the Ravine. Follow the path to the bottom of the steps. The path curves left, and then right to Huddlestone Arch. Prior to the 1960s, you could look through this magnificent stone edifice to a rustic bridge and the Harlem Meer. Then Lasker Pool was built in 1966, forever changing the landscape. The view is softened in early spring, when a curtain of yellow forsythia hangs down from the top of the arch.

Walk inside the arch and experience how shady and cool it feels. Tell your children that the arch's stones are more than 500 million years old and were found in the park when the arch was built in 1866. Then explain that nothing is holding the stones together—no screws, mortar, or Crazy Glue. Rather, the gravity and friction, and the careful placement of the huge boulders, keep the arch from falling down.

Come out of the arch and retrace your steps until you reach a rocky bridge over the Loch. Walk across the rocks, up some steps, and bear left. There is a large, labeled tulip tree on the left, growing straight and tall, as tulip trees do. In late spring, have your youngsters check the ground for wonderful chartreuse, yellow, and orange flowers, some of the prettiest blooms produced by a tree.

Climb the stairs to your right and enter a mulch path that will lead you and your children through the dense North Woods. (There is a labeled red oak on your right.) You will see few people, but the area is fairly safe, especially for people traveling with children. Look on the ground for maple seeds, known to kids as polynoses. Break one in half so that you have two wings and then peel open the seed end, which is sticky enough to keep the seed on a child's nose. You'll also see amid the leaf litter some itchy balls produced by sweet gum trees.

It's somewhat hilly here, so take it easy with young children, focusing their attention on passing butterflies and birds. In late summer, look for pokeweed, a large native plant with long clusters of berries that change from green to purplish-black. Young leaves and shoots can be eaten like spinach and are sold canned in the South. But once the plant matures, it and its berries become poisonous, though the juice of the berries makes a fine printing dye or ink.

The trail ascends, with Lasker Rink on the right. Follow the path for about .1 mile to a paved path and turn left. There's a huge boulder on the left. Continue until you reach the West Drive, where you'll see a sign for the Great Hill, the third highest point in the park. Cross the drive, keeping the sign on your left, and walk along a path edged with cobblestones to the hilltop meadow. At the second fork (take note of a tree encircled by cobblestones), walk right, on to the grass, which has picnic tables and is the perfect place to eat lunch. There are also restrooms.

After lunch, return to the tree and take the path down the hill. The West Drive will now be on your left. After going down two sets of stairs, you'll see The Pool straight ahead. You have come full circle, returning to the cardinal flowers, weeping willows, and landscaped beauty.

At the intersection, bear right, keeping The Pool on your left. Keep following the path around The Pool until you see woody formations protruding from the ground, right near the water's edge. These are called "knees," a natural phenomenon produced by the bald cypress trees growing here. Some say the knees help anchor the trees to swampy ground, while others say the knees bring oxygen to the trees' soggy roots. What is certain is that cypress knees come in many shapes and sizes and are often used by sculptors in the South, where cypresses are plentiful. Tell your kids, too, that this tree is called a bald cypress because, although it is an evergreen, it loses its needles in winter.

Return to the stairs, passing the Osage orange, and exiting through Boys' Gate, having completed your walk.

Please Don't Touch!

Some friendly warnings to anyone walking in the woods: "Leaves of three, let it be!"–"Hairy rope, don't be a dope!"–"Berries white, run in fright!" These quirky sayings remind nature lovers to stay away from poison ivy, the oily, highly toxic plant that causes rashes and persistent itching in most people who come in contact with it. If you were a squirrel, however, you could brush up against it all you wanted. Animals do not react to poison ivy and, in fact, some like to eat it.

So, beware of plants that climb trees, sprawl on the ground, or even grow like a shrub and have three pointed leaves, the middle one with a longer stalk than the two side leaves. The leaves range in size and are reddish when they emerge in spring, turning green in summer, and various shades of yellow, orange, or red in autumn. In late spring, the ivy produces clusters of green flowers that develop into poisonous berries, which in turn become white as they ripen.

Some people are unaffected by contact with poison ivy, but sensitivity may develop at any time. (The first poison ivy rash was recorded by Captain John Smith in 1609, but Native Americans were familiar with the plant's effects long before that.) If you do come in contact with poison ivy, don't touch any other part of your body; the plant's oil is extremely potent. Clean your hands immediately with soap and water and if blistering develops, apply calamine lotion, Epsom salts, or bicarbonate of soda. Some say sap from jewelweed eases the irritation. Look for jewelweed in moist woods, near the edges of streams, and–strangely and conveniently enough–often growing near poison ivy.

Inwood Hill Nature Trail, Inwood Hill Park

**Moderate 1.6-mile loop
with some hilly terrain
Ages: 5 and Older**

This 196-acre park is the city's most natural, with much of its landscape left the way Mother Nature intended it. A full 140 acres is wooded and includes Manhattan's last stand of primeval forest, many of its trees more than 200 years old. There are wondrous geological curiosities here, as well, including glacial potholes and mammoth outcroppings of Manhattan schist, as well as the borough's last remaining bit of natural salt marsh. And the park's hilly topography leads to spectacular views of the Hudson River and New Jersey Palisades.

As you walk through the park, explain to your kids that the area was of great significance to Native Americans, who relied on both the Hudson and Harlem Rivers as sources for food. Evidence of their communities has been found near the park's rock shelters. Later, colonists lived and farmed the area, but left during the American Revolution, when a small fort was built here. After the war, people returned, some of them prominent figures who built summer homes. The city bought the land for a park in 1916, with Works Progress Administration workers blazing many of the park's trails and paths during the Great Depression.

Enter the park at 218th Street and Indian Road, and walk toward the nature center, a white and blue waterfront building. Take in the center's exhibits for a brief lesson on the park's geology and terrain. (See chapter 1, Nature and Environmental Centers.) When you return to the path, cross a footbridge. On your right are about 12 acres of natural salt marsh, all that's left of an ecosystem that once completely ringed Manhattan. Explain that people in the old days didn't understand the ecological value of salt marshes. As the city grew, they were filled in to make land habitable for people, forever changing the borough's natural contours.

More importantly, we eliminated one of nature's most productive habitats, a food source and spawning ground for a wide variety of creatures. Also explain to your children that unlike a lake, a salt marsh is dynamic, meaning that it's always changing because it is affected by tides—at low tide, you'll see mudflats because the water is sucked into the nearby Hudson River; while at high tide, the marsh is flooded.

Continue on the path. When you reach a soccer field, an interpretive sign, and a London plane tree, turn left, keeping the soccer field to your right. Notice how the London plane tree's bark flakes off in pieces, revealing big, yellow patches. Some kids call them camouflage trees for this reason.

Follow the path around the soccer fields. You will come to an area with three oak trees, which provide a good opportunity to show your children how trees may differ within a single species. First is the red oak on your left, which has pointed leaves with bristly tips. Its acorns are oval and taste bitter because of the tannic acid naturally produced by the tree. This didn't stop Native Americans from using the red-oak acorns for food. They removed the tannin by mashing the acorns and soaking the mash in nets in a stream for a couple of weeks. They also used the tannin to "tan" animal hides.

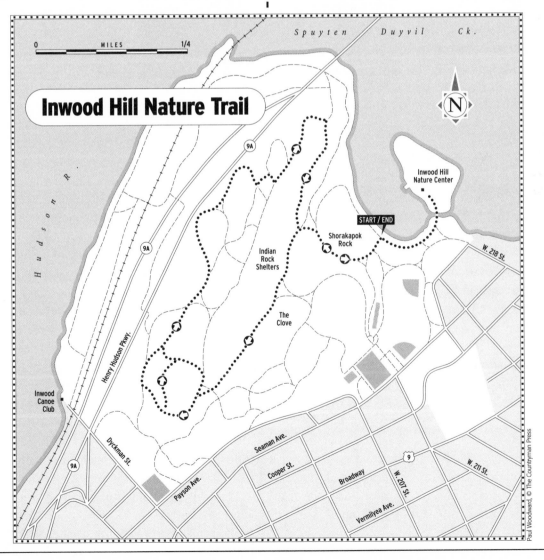

The pin oak on the opposite side of the path is in the red-oak group, so it also has bristle-tipped, pointed lobes; but the lobes are more deeply incised. Its acorn is small and kind of squat, wider than it is tall.

Next to the red oak is a white oak whose leaves have rounded lobes. When it comes to tasty acorns, squirrels are fine restaurant critics and choose this tree's sweeties before any other acorns. Behind the white oak is a tree worth pointing out for no other reason than its nickname is "muscle wood"—reflecting the texture and shape of its bark, which looks like the sinews of a flexed muscle.

Continue on the path to Shorakkopoch Rock, which according to legend commemorates the historic 1626 Dutch purchase of Manhattan from Native Americans. Explain to your children that Native Americans marked the occasion by planting a tulip tree, which grew here for 300 years, reaching final dimensions of 165 feet in height and 6.5 feet in diameter before it fell in a storm in the 1930s. The circle around the rock measures the girth of the giant tree—20 feet around.

During winter, chickadees and nuthatches are likely to greet you and your youngsters here in the mornings, especially if you bring sunflower seeds. Also, if you and your kids look up, you may see a huge red-tailed hawk nest high in the trees. Both males and females begin building their new nest or fixing up an old nest in January or February. The nests are about 2.5–3 feet across and are constructed with branches, bark, and leaves.

More often found in the South, this bald cypress stands along The Pond in Central Park, its tell-tale "knees" protruding from the ground.

From the rock, veer left into the forest, which includes many species of oak, 100-foot-tall tulip trees, and other trees. Tulip trees are easy to spot because they are perfectly straight, which is why Native Americans used them to carve out canoes. In late summer, glistening jewelweed grows along the edges of the forest, its nodding orange flowers attracting hummingbirds. By fall, tiny beanlike seedpods spring open at your child's slightest touch. Heed caution, however, because jewelweed often grows near poison ivy—and is considered a remedy for the itch. In late summer, you'll also see the bright blue flowers of the Asiatic dayflower, the two most prominent petals sometimes referred to as "mouse ears." A third, smaller, whitish petal looks like a beard. Have your kids take a good look at these flowers, because as the name implies they last only a day.

In fall, you and your kids will see both gray and black squirrels gathering acorns amid blooming goldenrods and woodland asters in full bloom.

You will soon arrive at some natural rock formations on the right, which were used by local Native Americans as shelters to keep them cool in the summer and protect them from the cold in winter.

Explain to your children that the shelters were created by a huge ice mass that began moving toward New York about 100,000 years ago, its handiwork not completed until about 10,000 years ago. The ice was hundreds of feet thick, breaking up rocks and pushing them along its path. When the glacier was done, it left stacks of boulders here.

You'll reach a "V" in the path. Turn right, following the path up a small hill. You will come to an interesting hole in a rock wall to your right. Tell your kids that this is a glacial pothole created when the glaciers started to thaw. The massive melt created a kind of tornado effect, with swirls of turbulent water containing rocks and pebbles drilling holes into the rock. Walk up to the pothole with your children and peer inside to see how deep it is.

Return to the path and continue on until you come to a "T," marked by a huge rock embedded in the ground. The Rangers call this

According to legend, this rock in Inwood Hill Park commemorates the 1626 purchase of Manhattan from Native Americans.

rock "whale back," but it is actually a chunk of striated Manhattan schist, its deep grooves created as the glacier scraped across it.

All this focus on glaciers brings fresh meaning to the phrase "moving at a glacial pace," which—you may want to explain to your kids—is really, really, really slow. So slow, in fact, that it may be incomprehensible to many children. Tell them that glaciers move more slowly than a snail's pace or buds opening to blooms, and that it would take many, many, many lifetimes to record even the slightly progress. Yet scientific evidence shows that over thousands of years these masses of icy terrain did in fact move.

Turn right. At the next "V," bear right. In early summer, you may see wineberries, which are edible and look like large raspberries growing along red, bristly stems. This Asian import is plentiful throughout the park, and some people resent its long, thorny canes growing out into the path. Wild sunflowers and Asiatic dayflowers are in bloom on the left side of the trail in

late summer. In early spring, you'll find garlic mustard everywhere, identified by white flowers atop tall stems and by heart-shaped leaves with undulating edges. As its name implies, this invasive plant does indeed smell like garlic.

If you're walking during late spring, have your kids investigate trailside plants for blobs of suds. These aren't the rude saliva of some passing hiker, but the homes of immature spittlebugs. Your children might wipe away the foam to reveal a tiny, light green nymph with red eyes that's about the size of a sesame seed. The nymphs create the foam and it keeps them cool and moist and protected from predators.

At the next "V," turn left. The path descends. At the next "V," turn right as the path veers right. The trail will not ascend. At the next "V," turn left, noticing the white blooms of woodland aster during late summer. In a moment, you will reach the scenic overlook, 200 feet high, from which you can view the leafy New Jersey Palisades and mighty Hudson River. During the fall migration, this is a wonderful place to sit and wait for passing hawks. The meadow behind the overlook, brilliant with goldenrod, chicory, milkweed, red clover, and butter-and-eggs wildflowers, is a great place to watch birds and butterflies.

After leaving the overlook, continue on the trail, passing a snag (a dead tree) on your right. Explain to your kids that, while this tree is dead, it is as valuable as a living tree. Among other things, its cavities provide wildlife with nesting and shelter sites. Even after the tree rots and falls to the ground, as a decaying log it greatly benefits insects, salamanders, and other creatures attracted to its security and dampness.

Continue straight on the path, passing some pokeweed on your right, which is most noticeable in late summer with its hanging clusters of purple berries. When you reach the confluence of three trails, turn left. At the "T," turn right and at the next "T," turn left. Stones edge the right-hand side of the trail. Have your children look among the stones and leaf litter

for ball-like soil. Explain to them that this is worm excrement, or castings, that contain nutrients that make the soil healthy. Gardeners actually buy bags of this at the store, or make their own by composting.

As you walk along this path, notice that you are walking along a high ridge, with the topography descending on your right. Notice the Virginia knotweed along the path, its tiny seeds standing out along its erect stems in late summer. Have your kids run two fingers along the stem and watch the seeds jump off, nature's unique way of ensuring a new generation of knotweeds. Another wildflower you may see all summer long that also ejects its seeds is herb Robert. It has fuzzy stems, fernlike leaves, and small pink flowers with five petals and grows close to the ground.

At the "V," veer right. The path now descends from the ridge. Kind of arrogantly, the Henry Hudson tollbooth appears on your left, a bizarre juxtaposition as you walk through the woods. But you'll soon leave it behind as you turn right and walk down a hill under the Henry Hudson Bridge, named for the 17th-century English explorer who in searching for a northwest passage happened upon the river that now bears his name.

As you walk along the path, look at the water to your left. This is the Harlem River Ship Canal, a 1-mile waterway that connects the Hudson and Harlem Rivers, separates Manhattan from the mainland, and marks the northernmost tip of Manhattan.

As you walk along the trail, your children may notice some thick, hairy ropes on the elevated portion of the park on your right-hand side. These are not poison ivy ("Hairy rope, don't be a dope.") but rather are used to control hillside erosion. During spring, these woods teem with spring migrants, while year round you can hear the "tat-a-tat-tat" of downy woodpeckers hammering on trees in search of insects. The trail soon returns to Shorakkopoch Rock and civilization.

Other Manhattan Trails to Explore

Old Croton Aqueduct Trail, Highbridge Park

This tree-lined path high atop Highbridge Park offers stupendous views, rock outcroppings, and historic sites. It's a little less than a mile long, starting at West 158th Street and Edgecomb Avenue and ending at the historic Highbridge Tower. The trail is along the top of an aqueduct that delivered water 41 miles from Westchester to the city during the 19th century, the city's first reliable source of water. The water was then stored in a reservoir at 42nd Street, where the New York Public Library now stands. The 138-foot-tall Highbridge Tower had a tank on top, which allowed folks in elevated Northern Manhattan also to be served. The tower is open to the public on weekends in July and August. The New York City chapter of the Sierra Club recently put out a map of Highbridge Park. For a free copy, call 212-539-4588, or email highbridge@igc.org.

Queens

Alley Pond Wetlands Trail, Alley Pond Park

Easy .25-mile loop
Ages: 3 and Older
Best: Spring or fall. Mosquitoes are a huge problem in summer

Alley Pond Park in northeastern Queens is about half wetlands and half woodlands and is one of the city's most diverse parks, with 10 trails crisscrossing 654 acres. This walk explores the park's freshwater and saltwater areas, an environmentally sensitive ecosystem rich in fish and wildlife that includes ospreys, muskrats, turtles, and herons. There's also an observation deck that overlooks Alley Creek.

At low tide, kids can look for bird tracks and fiddler cabs in the mudflats of Alley Pond Park.

The walk begins behind the Alley Pond Environmental Center at a sign that reads "Trail Starts Here." During late spring, the trailhead is brimming with white-flowered garlic mustard, an invasive weed probably introduced by Europeans during colonial times. It provides little nourishment to wildlife, but humans like it. While picking anything in the wild is discouraged, the New York Invasive Plants Council actually implores people to indulge in Garlic Mustard salads and pestos, because it is among the state's most invasive species.

Also at the trailhead is tiny Cattail Pond, a spring-fed freshwater pond. It is often covered with shamrock-green duckweed, our smallest flowering plant, although the flower is so small you can't see it. It's not only good for the water, filtering out unwanted matter and improving water quality, it's tasty to ducks and provides shelter for fish and frogs. Let your children pick up a piece to see how the tiny roots of this aquatic plant never touch soil.

Continue on the trail, much of it via a boardwalk, which keeps your and your kids' feet from getting sucked into the muck—although some parts of the trail do not have a boardwalk and may be wet, especially in spring or after a rain. Poison ivy grows along the sides of the trail, but is easily avoided by staying on the trail.

During late summer, jewelweed blooms everywhere, enticing hummingbirds to drink from its orange cups. In autumn, the flowers are replaced by tiny pealike seed pods which, when touched by your children, will pop open, spraying tiny seeds everywhere—hence the plant's other name, "touch-me-not." This natu-

ral mechanism allows the plants to spread the next generation of seeds.

When you reach a dead end (at the wooden platform and wetlands sign), turn left. The path goes through stands of towering phragmites, also called common reed. Phragmites grow in disturbed wet areas and, once established, elbow out more beneficial native plants like salt-marsh cord grass, which—unlike phragmites—helps feed and shelter the salt-marsh community.

At the "T," turn left to the observation deck overlooking Alley Creek, a tidal creek affected by nearby Long Island Sound. Twice a day, salt water from the Sound mixes with fresh water from streams and runoff, making the creek brackish. At low tide, look for bird tracks and

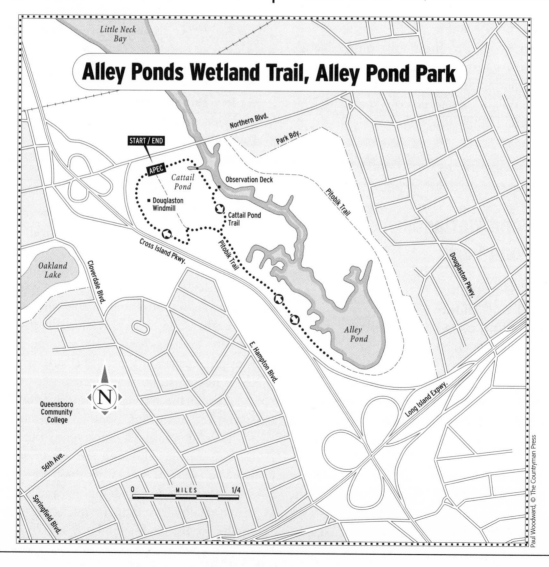

Alley Ponds Wetland Trail, Alley Pond Park

Little Neck Bay

Northern Blvd.

Park Bdy.

START / END

APEC

Cattail Pond

Observation Deck

Douglaston Windmill

Pitobik Trail

Cattail Pond Trail

Cross Island Pkwy.

Pitobik Trail

Douglaston Pkwy.

Oakland Lake

Cloverdale Blvd.

E. Hampton Blvd.

Alley Pond

Long Island Expwy.

N

Queensboro Community College

56th Ave.

0   MILES   1/4

Springfield Blvd.

Paul Woodward, © The Countryman Press

fiddler crabs on the surrounding mudflats. This is a lovely spot to sit and view the marsh, because except for the swath of Northern Boulevard to the northwest, the vista is nicely open, with the creek seemingly meandering forever. Look for egrets and herons and red-winged blackbirds. In late spring, tree swallows with their white bellies and iridescent blue wings fly and dip above the creek, sometimes stopping long enough for you to get a closer look.

Retrace your steps, then veer left. You'll soon see a sign for the Douglass Mackay Wetland Nature Trail. Step onto this trail for a while. During spring, wild strawberries grow on the left side of the trail, with tufts of white-blooming garlic mustard and yellow rockets sprouting up here and there. In summer, look for dogbane, yarrow, Queen Anne's lace, and black-eyed Susans, which attract butterflies. Walk as far as the small, wooden bridge that crosses Alley Creek and look for muskrats swimming here. In spring, migrant songbirds are plentiful and osprey soar in the sky.

Retrace your steps to the Wetland Nature Trail sign and turn left onto the boardwalk. You'll come to a huge tulip tree lying to the left of the path. The sound of the Cross Island Parkway is an unfortunate intrusion into this otherwise idyllic place. There is a huge mulber-

Phragmites may be beautiful but, once established, these invasive plants crowd out native vegetation.

ry tree on the right-hand side of the trail that simply drips with sweet ripe fruit in June.

On the right is Windmill Pond, a good place for kids to see dragonflies, Canada geese, ducks, red-winged blackbirds, and turtles sunning themselves on rocks. In summer, purple loosestrife takes over the pond. Look for monarchs alighting on milkweed plants. Without milkweeds, monarch butterflies would not exist. Adults love the nectar and lay eggs on the leaves, the only food its larvae will eat. In fall, purple flowers are replaced by unusually long and plump pods that split open, sending thousands of fuzz-covered seeds into the world.

The path turns right at a huge black willow tree. In summer, there's also a giant thistle in bloom. At the "V," turn right to the Douglaston Windmill, a replica of a 19th-century mill that once stood on nearby Arleigh Road in Douglaston. Tell your kids that wind powered the mill, which was then used to pump water from the ground to irrigate farms. After its life as a windmill ended, it was converted into a tiny two-room house. In the 1980s, it was threatened by development, so local supporters banded together to save it and move it to Alley Pond Park. Unfortunately, arson destroyed the windmill, but its supporters persevered by having this working replica built.

Your children will probably notice birds flying into and out of tree swallow nesting boxes near the windmill. In June, get close to the boxes and listen for the peepings of baby birds. Behind the windmill is a meditation garden, a peaceful place to rest for a while on a bench or big rock. The youngsters may also check out the park's summer garden of corn, tomatoes, and squash.

After enjoying the garden, proceed back to the nature center. If visiting in late spring or early summer, you may see Canada geese and their fuzzy goslings nibbling the grass. Canada geese are very protective of their young; so if one starts hissing at you, keep your distance or you might get chased or nipped.

Have you and your kids ever thanked a tree for all it does? From giving shade and growing fruits and nuts to cleaning the air and providing a source of wood, trees are generous and dependable. On a more spiritual level, their sheer size and stature can be awe-inspiring. More simply, kids love to climb them, hide behind them, and sometimes even hug them. In a nutshell, trees make the world a better place.

Trees come in many varieties, with differently textured barks and shaped leaves, a rainbow of flowers, and an assortment of seeds, and they change with the weather—naked in winter, flowery in spring, leafy in summer, and fruity and nutty in fall. Deciduous trees lose their leaves in winter, while evergreens (coniferous trees) hold onto their needles (or leaves) year round. A tree's roots not only keep it anchored in place but also absorb water mixed with nutrients from the soil. Trees even make their own everyday carbohydrates in their leaves, through a process called photosynthesis.

We have something of a symbiotic relationship with trees. Through their leaves, they "exhale" unneeded oxygen, which we breathe in; while we breathe out unwanted carbon dioxide that trees need to survive. Tree sap is blood to the tree, helping to circulate food throughout its woody body, while bark is the tree's skin, protecting it from disease. And trees grow from the top up.

Once you and your children familiarize yourselves with the conditions that appeal to different tree species, you can start trying to identify them. Summer is a good time to study trees because leaves provide excellent clues. Autumn fruits, nuts, and seeds also provide indicators of their identities. The hardest season in which to study trees is winter, when they are completely bare—except, of course, for most evergreens.

• **American elm**—Despite the many American elms that began dying in the 1930s from Dutch Elm Disease (which remains a threat today), some of the city's venerable elms have escaped infection. Growing as tall as 100 feet, these trees have thick foliage and wide-spreading canopies. The seeds are deeply notched samaras and the oval, serrated leaves turn yellow in autumn. One side of the leaf feels like sandpaper; the other side is smooth.

• **American sycamore**—Easily identified by mottled, camouflage-colored bark, these trees are long-lived and tall, and can have enormous trunks. Leaves are maplelike, and the fruits are round balls of tightly packed brown seeds that dangle from a long stem. The hybrid **London plane tree**, a popular street tree that resists pollution, is similar looking but usually has two seed balls hanging from each stem, fruits that kids like to call itchy balls.

• **Eastern white pine**—This tall, magnificent evergreen has long, soft needles, five to a bundle and slightly curved, and 5-to-8-inch cones often sticky with sap. These pines live to an average of about 200 years (sometimes up to 450 years); and you can tell an individual tree's age by counting the whorls of branches around its trunk.

• **Gingko**—Best identified by its beautiful fan-like leaves (yellow in fall) that are notched in the middle, this street tree is an Asian species about 150 million years old. In the fall, the female trees produce oval, tan-colored fruits that smell bad but are harvested around the city by local Asian New Yorkers, who cook and eat the interior nut.

• **Maples**—In general, maple trees have winged seeds, or samaras, that kids call helicopters because they spin as they fall to the ground. When split and stuck onto children's noses, they're called polynoses. Maple leaves have three or five lobes spreading out from the stem. The trees have foliage, quite colorful in fall, and are of medium height. They also produce sap, with the **sugar maple**, New

York's state tree, especially revered for the syrup made from boiling its sweet sap. In autumn, this tree's five-lobed leaves turn combinations of red, orange, and yellow. When it comes to the **red maple,** everything is red—the buds, flowers, seeds, and leafstalks. The three-lobed leaves start off green but change to a wine red in the fall. **Silver-maple** leaves turn yellow in fall, but in summer they are pale green on top and silvery on the bottom. The leaves are also the most deeply indented of all the maple species.

• **Oaks**—These are the mighty trees of the forest, growing large and old. All oaks produce acorns, and fall into either the red oak group (leaves with pointed lobes) or the white oak group (leaves with round lobes). Oak wood is strong and beautifully grained, and is used for floors, furniture, and house and bridge construction. A fun time to distinguish between species is in the fall, by collecting acorns (with their caps still on), which vary in shape and size. The sweetest acorns fall from **white oaks** and are an important food source for wildlife, particularly squirrels. Native Americans ground them for flour. Look for 1-inch-long acorns with bumpy caps. **Red oak** acorns contain tannin and are bitter. They are about an inch long, egg-shaped, and with shallow, scaly caps. The caps of **black oak** acorns (in the red-oak family) cover half the fruit, which can be covered in light fuzz. **Pin oak** acorns (also in the red-oak family) are small—about 3/8 inch—and round, with dark striations.

• **Paper birch**—If you've ever used chopsticks, toothpicks, or ice-cream sticks, chances are you touched the wood of a paper birch. Its rot-resistant bark was used by Native Americans to build birch-bark canoes. Look for a tree with white bark marked with fine black horizontal lines and that peels off in layers, and with oval, pointed, toothed leaves that turn yellow in fall.

• **Quaking aspen**—Seek this tree out just to see its leaves quiver. Shiny green above and silvery below, the heart-shaped leaves hang loosely from flattened leaf stems and flap en masse even in the slightest breeze. In autumn, they turn golden yellow.

• **Sassafras**—Kids love this tree because it bears three different leaves: one is football-shaped, another mitten-shaped, and the last resembes a ghost. Its roots were the original source of root beer extract. In fall, the leaves turn red, orange, and yellow; and the trees don't often grow very tall, maintaining a shrublike appearance.

• **Sweet gum**—The thick, gummy sap that oozes from any broken spot on one of these trees looks like liquid amber and can be chewed like gum. They have star-shaped leaves that turn red in autumn. They're often found in moist woods and swampy areas and can grow up to 120 feet.

• **Tulip tree**—This tree has the most beautiful flowers in spring—chartreuse and yellow and orange, and tulip shaped—best seen on the ground, because they grow way at the top of this very tall, very straight tree. The tallest species in the city, tulip trees grow to about 150 feet. They like moist woods, and their leaves turn yellow in the fall.

• **White Ash**—Most Major League baseball bats are made from the wood of this tree, because it is tough, yet pliant, and can withstand repeated whacks. The leaves are compound, with 7 to 12 leaflets making up one leaf. Unlike maples, the seeds are single-winged and form in clusters. In autumn, the leaves range in color from yellow to purplish.

West Pond Trail, Jamaica Bay Wildlife Refuge

Easy 1.25 mile gravel loop
Ages: 4 and Older. Strollers are permitted, but wide-wheeled joggers work best
Best: Spring and fall migration; although early summer offers the chance to see diamondback terrapin turtles, while winter brings snow geese and wintering ducks

The Jamaica Bay Wildlife Refuge is an Eden managed exclusively for wildlife. Humans simply pass through, doing so quietly, so as not to intrude on this rare city sanctuary where huge ospreys tend their young and glossy ibises poke through the mud for food. Gorgeous wildflowers, including milkweed and gaillardia, color the trail, with one of the best surprises being the yellow-flowering prickly pear cactus. And a total of 325 species of birds and 70 butterfly species, as well as other creatures, have been spotted here.

The refuge has two paths. Both can be bug-intensive in summer, including ticks, so don't forget the repellent and post-walk checking. The trails also offer little shade, so wear a hat or carry an umbrella. Visitors may eat a bagged lunch at picnic tables outside the visitors center or pop into nearby Howard Beach for food. The refuge also offers outstanding nature programs throughout the year, including walks that focus on butterflies, wildflowers, bird migration, and horseshoe crabs.

This is a good place to show your kids how humankind can positively affect the environment. As nature lovers, we may feel that controlling nature is a bad thing, but there are some instances, and the refuge is an example, in which management of a natural area is good for everyone and everything—the plants, the birds, the animals, and people. Without nesting boxes for birds, without strategically placed logs under which reptiles can rest and cool their bodies, without artificially created ponds and the right flora, the refuge would be less attractive to wildlife, and the numbers would dwindle. Instead, birds refuel here for their long journeys north and south, terrapins and owls nest and raise their young, plants provide food for butterflies and moths, trees cool the earth, and families thrill at the wonder of it all.

This walk focuses on the West Pond Trail, which begins behind the visitor center. The center is being expanded and made into an energy-efficient interpretive and education center. Upon your first visit, sign up for a free visitor's card (which allows the refuge to gauge how many people use the refuge), then show your children the fresh wildflower display in the auditorium. The rangers (National Park Service Rangers) gather specimens every day and label them to help visitors identify what they will see in bloom along the trail—everything from daisy fleabane (a tiny, daisylike flower) to brilliant orange butterfly weed (a butterfly favorite). Periodically, nature-themed exhibits are also on display.

Exit from the back door and stop to see what birds are feasting at the feeders. Look for house finches, cardinals, starlings, and others, including brown-headed cowbirds—a strange and lazy bird that likes to sneak its eggs into other birds' nests, fly off, and let the adoptive parent rear its young. Across from the feeders show your kids the butterfly bushes that always have guests, including monarchs, swallowtails, and skippers, during summer.

Set off on the gravel trail, almost immediately passing guided trail marker #1 on your left. The shrub with light-green leaves that are silvery underneath is autumn olive, a drought- and salt-tolerant Asian shrub that thrives in sandy soil and keeps it from eroding. Some people make jam from its red berries, which appear in the fall.

The South Garden Trail soon comes in on the right, but stay straight ahead on the gravel trail, passing a brush-pile clearing on your left. Have your youngsters look around for a thorny shrub with rumpled leaves, sometimes called wrinkled rose. If you're visiting in late spring, it will be bright with pink and white flowers. In early summer, the blooms are replaced by marble-sized green hips (or fruits), which gradually turn from orange to red and look like cherry tomatoes, and which birds love.

You will come to a bat box on your right, placed here to supplement the lack of natural tree cavities in which bats like to nest The refuge has both brown bats and red bats. One April afternoon, I stumbled upon a pair of red bats roosting along a path in the North Garden—so look around when you get to this uplands area.

Bench #1 on your left offers a first look at the salt marsh, an important and extremely productive ecosystem where only the best-adapted plants and animals survive. It is a harsh environment, baked by the sun and flooded twice a day by the salty high tide. It supports a diversity of creatures and provides a nursery for young fish and crustaceans.

A little farther up the trail, you will see a tall structure out in the marsh on your left. This is an osprey platform—built by the rangers and upon which you will likely see nesting osprey and, if it's summer, chicks on the nest. Binoculars help out here. Tell your children that this high-rise gives these large hawks a commanding view of the water, from which they seize fish with their sharp talons.

These predators are endangered in New York State, their survival once threatened by the use of the pesticide DDT. After DDT was outlawed in 1971, osprey populations

First-year mullein plants are low-growing rosettes with wooly leaves.

rebounded along the Atlantic coast, and this specific nesting platform has been occupied every year since 1994.

Along the trail you'll notice a strange low-growing plant—prickly pear cactus; in winter, its oval pads lying on top of one another like so many old socks. When the weather grows warmer, they plump up. Tell your kids that this plant is actually a native, well adapted to the refuge's desertlike conditions—hot, sandy, and dry. In early summer it boasts gorgeous yellow flowers that give way to pear-shaped red fruits. Both the fruit and pads are edible. Some say the fruit tastes like watermelon, while the pads taste like string beans.

When you reach Bench #2 on your right, you'll see a tree swallow box and, if it's June, some gorgeous red and yellow gaillardia flowers in bloom. Tree swallows are tiny birds, with white chests and iridescent blue backs, that arrive in droves in April. These perky fellows are often seen atop the flowering or dried stalks of mullein plants, also called velvet plants because their large, grayish-green leaves are so fuzzy.

Youngsters will love watching the tiny birds squeeze into and out of the box's small holes.

You can also see the 40-acre West Pond, an artificial freshwater pond dug out when the refuge was created by the city in 1951. (The refuge was transferred to the federal government in 1972). Have your children scan the pond for Canada geese and their chicks in late spring, as well as great egrets, snowy egrets, ibises, and other long-legged waders in summer. Tell your kids that during winter, these herons and egrets fly south to places like Florida, just like a lot of New York City grandmas and grandpas. In winter, many ducks that breed farther north relocate to the pond for the winter, because it's warmer here than there, where the ponds freeze. Lots of shore birds also migrate through here, especially in mid-August, although there are plenty of summer residents too.

Winter is particularly spectacular, with hundreds of snow geese leaving their Arctic homes and settling onto the pond. Tell your children that these geese fly about 3,000 miles to be here. It is truly wonderful is see them quietly swimming around, then—unannounced—suddenly bursting into the sky, honking up a storm (which

Butterflyweed, a member of the milkweed family, has showy, orange flowers that attract a wide range of butterflies.

gets louder and louder as they come into your field of vision), and looking just majestic in flight: pure white, with pink bills and a dab of black on their wingtips.

One of the biggest surprises for me one recent June occurred near Bench #5, when I heard some rustling in the shrubs and discovered a diamondback terrapin, its shell intricately patterned, its head and neck spotted. The thrill was only heightened when farther down the path, I found a female laying eggs in a small hole she had scooped out of the sand with her hind legs. I watched from a respectable distance as the small, white eggs dropped one by one into the sandy cup, the terrapin's thick black legs then working like shovels to cover her progeny. This is the only place in New York City where terrapins nest and they are up against the odds—raccoon predation and loss of habitat, to name just two of the perils. If you and your older youngsters are interested in getting close to a terrapin, consider volunteering during the summer at Jamaica Bay by contacting Dr. Russell Burke of Hofstra University at 516-463-5521 or biorlb@hofstra.edu. These unique marsh creatures were brought to near extinction in the 19th century when they were prized for their meat. Ever hear of turtle soup?

Continue along the path, and when you reach Bench #7 you'll see two plants that adapt well to this environment, yucca and mullein. Yucca has long, hard, pointed leaves with little white fibers curling out from the edges. A long, multibranched stalk grows out of the middle of the leaf cluster and is covered with large, white, bell-shaped flowers in early summer. Oddly enough the yucca is the state flower of New Mexico; but it grows happily here in the desert-like refuge, its long taproots reaching deep down for water. Mullein is fuzzy, so let your kids touch it. It has a long stalk thick with yellow flowers in summer.

If you now look to the left of the West Pond, where some tall trees grow, you may see egrets and herons in the tree tops, where they build their nests to discourage predators. This nesting technique is a challenge for these top-heavy birds with long legs. Look skyward for common terns sporting black caps and forked tails, as well as laughing gulls (appearing in late spring)—the only gulls in the area with black heads—and glossy ibises, mythical-looking birds whose long, skinny bills curve downward.

Continue on the path and, after passing the kestrel nesting box on your right and the barn owl nesting box on your left, the path will veer right, leaving the West Pond and entering a shadier area, where you are more likely to encounter a chipmunk than a sandpiper.

You'll soon come to the North Garden on your right, marked by trail marker #19 (which refers to a self-guided tour that the refuge sells) and, more to the point, a willow oak. This area is managed mainly for woodland songbirds, both year-round residents and migrants such as warblers, scarlet tanagers, and ovenbirds.

You can wend through the woods on a series of grassy paths that, no matter how you turn, ultimately lead you back to the main trail—although you may go in small circles a few times before figuring it out. Or you can stay on the main gravel trail, which will bring you back to the visitors center. It's a treat to dip into the garden, though, where there are a couple of trees worth a look, including an eastern cottonwood (#18). It's particularly enjoyable in spring, when it produces clumps of fuzz that cloud the air, floating this way and that, before finally coming to rest and padding the ground. Tell the kids that this is how the tree disperses its seeds. Later, compare the cottonwood seeds with the helicopter-like maple seeds (samaras) and oak corns, often propagated by squirrels.

Another tree amusing to children is the Sassafras (#13), which produces three differently shaped leaves on the same tree—the single-lobe, the mitten, and the ghost, or triple-lobed. Have the youngsters scan the tree and see if they can spot all three leaves on their own.

Getting out in nature is not only good for you, it's fun.

Along the main trail, you'll eventually come to a bird blind overlooking a pond on your right. This is a good place for children to watch aerodynamic dragonflies cruising for a meal and birds bathing. In early spring, listen for spring peepers, tiny tree frogs that breed here. As the summer progresses the pond will dry out, so spring offers the most water and a better chance of seeing wildlife.

Return to the main path and look for a red-mulberry tree on your right. In late June/early July, it's easy to spot because tons of dark fruit will be smashed on the path. This is a good place to scan the trees for birds that are attracted to the fruit, which is tasty sweet. Continue on for about 400 feet, until you reach the visitor center and trail's end.

In every season, nature dresses itself with wonderful wildflowers; even in winter gorgeous, purple-streaked skunk cabbage hoods push their way through the snow. It would be impossible to list all the wildflowers you may encounter during a nature walk, so I've collected some of my favorites, simply because they're beautiful or amazing. While many are not native flowers, having been introduced here from Europe or Asia, they have made a place for themselves in our city. See how many you can find with your kids, and search for others by consulting a field guide to wildflowers.

- **Bittersweet nightshade**—You can't help noticing this showy vine from Europe, with its purple and orange flowers shaped like a tomato plant's flowers. That's because they're in the same family. But rather than produce beefsteaks, these flowers beget clusters of shiny, red berries that are poisonous to us but not to birds.

- **Bladder campion**—Kids love picking the balloonlike calyxes and white flowers of this medium-sized plant introduced from Europe, pinching closed the top of the calyx, and then smacking the calyx between their hands to hear a loud pop. Limit this experiment to one pop per child, and enjoy the rest of the flowers with your eyes.

- **Butter-and-eggs**—This wildflower is pretty and worth pointing out for its funny name. Snapdragon-like, it is mostly butter yellow with an egg-yolk colored lip. A European import, it has become naturalized in many very sunny places.

- **Chicory**—You've probably seen this nonnative weed growing at curbs, its stem awkwardly bent but displaying cheerful blue, raylike flowers. Its root has long been roasted and used as a coffee substitute or additive.

- **Common yarrow**—Ferny leaves and flat white clusters of flowers characterize this 1- to 2-foot tall plant, seen in places as varied as forests and vacant lots. A perennial herb, this summertime bloomer has a strong scent. Rubbing its flowers on the skin or burning the dry plant as incense is said to repel mosquitoes. It's also great for activating compost.

- **Evening primrose**—These lemon-scented yellow flowers grow on long spikes, with each flower taking a turn at exhibiting its beauty. The flowers bloom late in the day and stay open all night to be pollinated by moths, then wither the next day.

- **Goldenrod**—There are many goldenrod species, from seaside goldenrod (with succulent leaves) to sweet goldenrod (with leaves that have an anise scent when crushed). All of them love the sun and have large, clustered, often plumelike, bright yellow flowers that begin to bloom in late summer. Kids will love looking at these natives for the huge variety of insects they attract—nectar lovers and predators alike.

• **Pokeweed**–In autumn, much of this tall, branching, native plant is poisonous; but when it first sprouts in spring, it is edible. A magenta-colored ink may be made by crushing the berries, straining the skins, and reducing the liquid; but the toxic seeds should be quickly disposed of.

• **Queen Anne's lace**–In summer, look for a single dark flower in the middle of each white flower cluster. A relative of the carrot, it is named for Queen Anne, a past English monarch, who is said to have once pricked her finger while working on some lace. Even in death this nonnative flower intrigues, curling up into the shape of a bird's nest.

• **Solomon's seal**–There's a so-called "true" variety and "false" variety of this plant. The former sports dangling green-ish flowers and the latter sends up a feathery white plume in spring, which many people find the more beautiful of the two. In summer, the true has dark, dangling, blue berries, while the false has clustered, red, speckled berries. The leaves look similar—long, lance shaped, and alternating on a long, curving steam. The false variety lacks the round root scars said to resemble the seal of King Solomon.

• **Spring beauty**–A spring ephemeral, meaning that it blooms in earliest spring and disappears quickly, this tiny, light pink flower with dark pink veins and five petals grows in lush colonies in woodlands. Early colonists ate its underground tubers for their sweet chestnut flavor.

• **Trout lily**–Look for groups of these short plants, with their nodding, yellow, lilylike flowers, in the forest in April. So named because their mottled leaves resemble the underside of a trout, these spring ephemerals are pollinated by ants and gone by May.

• **White water lily**–This aquatic flower floats on ponds and lakes in summer. Native American legend describes it as a star that fell to earth, changing into a beautiful flower when it hit the water.

• **White wood aster**–This native wildflower blooms in shady woodlands in late summer, its 6-10 white rays in irregular intervals around a yellow center that turns purplish as it ages.

Other Queens Trails to Explore

Blue Trail, Forest Park

This 1.75-mile trail is gorgeous in autumn when the leaves on birches and hickories turn yellow, while oaks turn red and bronze, and maples become red and orange. In late fall, look for American goldfinches feeding on seed heads. The trail passes an area called The Gully, which contains a series of depressions called kettles formed by glaciers thousands of years ago, and is a favorite bird-watching spot. The trail begins just north of the intersection of East Main Drive and Freedom Drive. Although marked with blue blazes the trail can be confusing at times, because old blue blazes are interspersed with new blue blazes, each representing different routes. Contact the Forest Park Nature/Visitor Center for guidance before setting out. While at the nature center, visit the nearby Strack Memorial Pond, which is fringed by a short loop trail.

Woodlands Trails, Alley Pond Park

There are several trails that take explorers through Alley Pond Park's woodlands and past its kettle ponds, including the Turtle Pond Trail (.5 mile), the Yellow Dot Trail (1 mile), and the Red Oak Trail (.5 mile), all of them close to the Alley Pond/Urban Park Ranger Adventure Center. Look for spotted salamanders and Fowler's toads, listen for spring peepers and cardinals, and you may even see a great horned owl or baby raccoon in a tree. If you want to see a huge tulip tree believed to be the city's oldest tree—about 400 years old—go to East Hampton Boulevard and the Horace Harding Expressway (a service road of the Long Island Expressway) in Bayside and look for a trail into the woods. Walk for about 5 minutes. You will find the 134-foot-tall tree (with 19-foot circumference) surrounded by a small fence; this is the city's tallest tree.

Staten Island

Mount Loretto Nature Walk, Mount Loretto Unique Area

Moderate 1.25-mile trail with some hills
Ages: 4 and Older
Best Time: Spring, summer, autumn

Until recently, this beautiful area, with its five unique ecosystems—grasslands, forest, tidal wetlands, freshwater wetlands, and beachfront (with views of Raritan Bay), as well as the only natural red-clay cliff bluffs in the city—was owned by the Catholic Archdiocese of New York and closed to the public. The archdiocese had operated an orphanage, among other charitable organizations here, since the 19th century.

When the archdiocese announced that it was selling off some of its land, the national, nonprofit Trust for Public Land brokered a deal in 1998 to purchase 194 of the most environmentally important acreage for $25 million. The property was then sold in three installments to the State of New York. (The archdiocese still owns about 200 acres on the north side of Hylan Boulevard). The Mount Loretto Unique Area is now a preserve, open to the public from dawn to dusk for passive recreation.

This walk meanders through grasslands and wetlands and along the Princes Bay and Raritan Bay coast. If you drive here, there's a small lot at the entrance to the preserve, as well as a portable toilet and information kiosk just outside the lot. Check the bulletin board for free upcoming natural-history and children's walks offered by the state's Department of Environmental Conservation, which manages the property. Staten Island's own Protectors of Pine Oak Woods also hosts free walks. For schedule information, check their website at www.siprotectors.org.

Begin at the kiosk. Walk about 80 yards and turn right onto a mowed-grass path labeled "Grasslands Trail." This area is critical for nesting grassland bird species and is mowed once a year to keep it as a meadow. If not mowed, it would eventually turn to forest, eliminating an ecosystem rare in the city. Overhead, you and your children may see passing ospreys, turkey vultures, and tree and barn swallows, the latter feeding on insects that in turn are feeding on wildflower nectar. This area is so green and pastoral you and your kids may just want to belt out: *The Hills Are Alive with the Sound of Music.*

When you reach an asphalt path, turn right. There will be two freshwater, vernal ponds on either side of the path, a good place to do a little exploring for insect larvae, tadpoles, and fish eggs. Vernal ponds or pools are landlocked bodies of water that fill up from rainfall and runoff. They may be dry near the end of summer. Lots of birds and insects love these pools, including great egrets, red-winged blackbirds, and dragonflies. They are also good places to see shore birds and wintering ducks.

Now turn around and walk south, away from Hylan Boulevard and toward the water. The path runs through a huge meadow flecked with wildflowers, including summer-blooming milkweed, crucial to the life cycle of the orange-and-black monarch butterfly. Explain to your children that once monarchs emerge from their chrysalises, they sip the flower's nectar

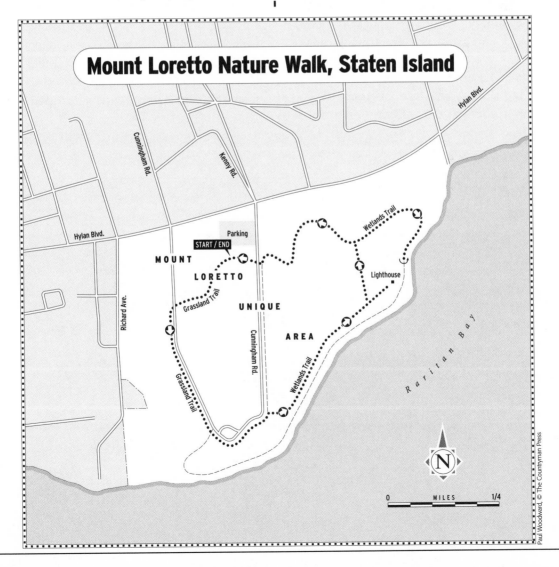

Mount Loretto Nature Walk, Staten Island

Paul Woodward, © The Countryman Press

and the females eventually lay eggs on the plant's leaves. When the monarch caterpillars hatch, they immediately begin feasting on the milkweed leaves, growing nice and fat until finally forming chrysalises in which they metamorphose into adult butterflies—and so the cycle continues.

In late summer, the milkweed plants produce interesting long, fat pods that eventually split open to expose a plethora of seeds covered in white fuzz. Colonists used the plants' sticky, white juice—hence the name milkweed—as glue. This is the same juice that makes monarchs taste bad to birds and helps them survive. In autumn, look for crowds of monarchs recharging their batteries on this plant, fueling up for their long migration south.

Another summer wildflower that you should point out to your kids is the low-growing bird's-

The 75-foot tall bluffs at Mount Loretto were created during the late Cretaceous Period(135 million to 65 million years ago).

foot trefoil, whose pretty yellow flowers later develop into curved black seed pods clawed at the end and, some say, resembling a bird's foot.

The path bends left, passing a vernal pond on the left, and then continues to wind, until arriving at an area of old trees, many of them planted during the Catholic orphanage's early days—a silver maple on the left that's more than 100 years old, a couple of London plane trees on the right, and a Norway maple on the left are among them. On the right is a stone grotto where lilacs bloom in spring.

Continue on the path, taking note of beautiful Raritan Bay on your right. Tell your children that the bay is mostly enclosed by land, but has a wide opening that leads into the mighty Atlantic Ocean.

The path soon leads to the Princes Bay Lighthouse (1864), which was deactivated in 1922 and is now closed to the public. The gate is usually locked; but if the state forester who lives there is home, it may be open, allowing

you and your children to see the lighthouse up close. Otherwise, check it out from the beach below, especially during fall when the surrounding trees are at their Technicolor best.

Turn around and retrace your steps briefly, then walk down the hill, keeping the lighthouse on your right. This is a great snow hill in winter. As you walk down the hill, notice how the meadow on the left meets the salt marsh on your right. The marsh is a transitional zone between land and sea, fed by an inlet of Raritan Bay. Explain to your youngsters that these wetlands are very important to migratory birds, which feed here—while shellfish and finfish use it as a nursery for their young. Wetlands like this also help control flooding and filter out pollutants that would otherwise flow into the bay.

The grass path veers right to a post numbered 3. There's is a freshwater pond here, so look for frogs, dragonflies, and other water-loving creatures. The wet area on your left is part of the salt marsh. In late summer, enjoy joe-pye weed, a tall native plant with wine-red flowers that grow in huge clusters. According to legend, this plant was named for a Native American doctor who cured typhus with it during colonial times. Butterflies and bees love it!

The path narrows and becomes tree lined. Continue on this now-dirt trail through the woods down to the beach. You will likely encounter a few fishermen (striped bass, winter flounder, and bluefish are plentiful here) and lots of shells and stones, and some trash. The little stream that cuts across your path is the inlet that connects the salt marsh with Raritan Bay. If it's filled with water, simply slosh through it (the kids won't mind!) or look for the wooden plank that often serves as a primitive bridge.

Walk along the shore until red clay cliffs come into view on your right. They were created during the late Cretaceous Period (135 million to 65 million years ago) and are about 75 feet tall.

Farther along the beach is an unexpected sight, a kind of primitive sculpture garden created by a Staten Island Zoo keeper who arranges and precariously balances large rocks into curious, mostly vertical, configurations. He has even constructed a stone-lined path to deliberately guide visitors past every one of his pieces.

After viewing these totemlike spires, turn around and return to the shady path into the woods and out onto the meadow again. The mowed-grass trail veers to the right and then left, eventually leading back to the asphalt trail where you started. In summer, the meadow here is dotted with black-eyed Susan, yarrow, and dogbane, which looks a little like white milkweed and has a sweet fragrance. Once at the asphalt trail, turn right and return to the preserve entrance.

Yellow and Blue Trails, Clay Pit Ponds State Park Preserve

Easy 1.5-mile loop, with some slight up-and-down elevations (Extended trail 2.5 miles)
Ages: 4 and Older
Best Time: Early spring, early autumn

Clay Pit Ponds State Park Preserve is unique in New York City because—along with its woodlands, wetlands, spring-fed streams, and ponds—it has environmentally sensitive sandy, pine-oak barrens, something like the pine barrens of Long Island and New Jersey. It also has clay deposits, which were formed 135 million years ago and mined about 100 years ago to make bricks and architectural terracotta. The depressions left in the earth filled with rainwater over time, forming clay-pit ponds.

To see one of these remarkable excavation sites, walk behind the nature center to the wooden pavilion overlooking a steep drop in the terrain. Explain to your children that hundreds of thousands of cubic yards of clay were dug out of here during the 19th and early 20th centuries and then fired into brick and terracotta ornamentation. It was hard work; and early on, immigrants with pick axes and shovels did all the digging. By the late 19th century, steam-powered equipment was used and the clay was then transported out in mule-drawn carts to the nearby Arthur Kill.

After the pits were abandoned in the 1920s, nature slowly transformed them into ponds that attracted wildlife. When the area was threatened with development in the 1970s, an intense citizen campaign saved it, creating this 260-acre nature preserve.

Walk to the left of the pavilion and enter the Ellis Swamp Trail—also known as the Yellow Trail—keeping the pit on your right. You will soon see a stream and a spread of skunk cabbage on your right. Skunk cabbage leaves are bright green and showy in summer and lots of them together look like a big cabbage patch. This swamp-loving plant smells pretty stinky when the leaves are crushed or bruised.

This plant is probably most beautiful in late winter, when mottled, purplish, curled leaf spathes push through the snow. These are often the first flowers of the season. Tell your kids that the snow doesn't kill the plant because it does something incredible—it generates heat 20 degrees above the actual ground temperature and melts its way through the snow.

Turn left onto a wooden boardwalk and point out the reddish color of the soil, which contains clay.

When you arrive at the junction with the Blue Trail, stay straight on the Yellow Trail. Youngsters will love how the terrain here gently rises and falls. Point out all the velvety moss growing on the bottoms of trees and on the ground. Explain to your children that moss is a rootless evergreen plant that absorbs water through its pores, like a sponge. Have your kids touch it; it feels like carpet or a washcloth. Then let them pick through it to see that it is made of many single plants all clumped together.

New England Asters are one of the city's fall bloomers.

Other plants that like to grow in this wet area are ferns, sweet gums, and sassafras trees. Look for round, prickly sweet gum balls scattered among the leaf litter. The leaves are star shaped. Sassafras is an under-story tree, meaning it doesn't grow really tall, and can be easily identified because it has three different leaves on the same tree. One leaf looks like a football (one lobe), another a mitten (two lobes), and the third a ghost (three lobes). See if your kids can find all three.

The thorny stuff on the sides of the trail is catbrier, a native, woody, green-stemmed vine whose tendrils allow it to climb over everything in its path. Tell your children that while catbrier barbs may prick us, birds and other creatures that seek cover here don't mind it at all. In spring, catbrier has tiny, green flowers and in autumn, bluish-black berries that, although inedible to us, provide food for catbirds, cedar waxwings, brown thrashers, and other birds and small mammals.

When you reach a set of stairs on the right, turn right and cross the wooden boardwalk. Notice the skunk cabbage on both sides of the walk, as well as some wild lily of the valley, or Canada mayflower, a low-growing native with two leaves and a spike of white flowers in May.

In summer, the flowers are replaced by brown-speckled green berries that turn red in autumn.

After crossing the bridge, turn right to a small waterfall fringed with jewelweed, whose dangling orange flowers attract hummingbirds. It's a fun place to stop with children so that they can listen to the waterfall, pop jewelweed seedpods (in late summer), and look around for snapping turtles. If you find one, don't touch it, because they really bite.

Retrace your steps, but instead of crossing the boardwalk again, go straight on the Yellow Trail, which will eventually loop around and bring you back to the top of the stairs that you just came down.

You are now walking across Ellis Swamp via a series of wooden boardwalks, which may be slippery after a rain. Tiny drops of water on spider webs look like an outdoor jewelry store. In July, high-bush blueberries appear on your right.

The path turns left and loops around. You'll notice a pretty fern whose uppermost leaflets, or pinnae, are not distinctly separate and which

Indian pipes feed on decaying matter and don't produce chlorophyll, which makes other plants green.

lacks the feathery look of many other ferns. This is sensitive fern, so named because it dies back at the first frost. The kids will get a kick out of a dead tree, or snag, also on the right, that looks like it has big, spooky eyes. If you are walking during summer, you may even see some odd, white plants growing out of the leaf litter. These are Indian pipes, which feed on decaying matter and don't produce chlorophyll, the chemical that makes other plants green.

Pass the stairs you walked down earlier and continue to the intersection of the Blue and Yellow Trails. Before turning left and crossing the bridge, let the youngsters look for water striders and other aquatic insects in this natural stream.

The trail wends right and continues up a small incline. You will come to Abraham's Pond on the left, which is really more marsh than pond. Listen for spring peepers—a kind of tree frog—in spring. Named for a 19th-century clay miner, the pond—like all natural areas—is always evolving; and this pond has become more marsh over time, as plants and organic matter have accumulated. Explain to your children that, if left alone, more plants will grow here, so that hundreds of years from now the pond may even become a forest.

Continue on the path until you reach an open, sandy area marked by a black birch tree with exposed roots. Tell your kids that Native Americans distilled the twigs and inner bark of these trees to obtain wintergreen oil, which they used for brushing their teeth. The leaves turn a beautiful yellow in autumn.

This area marks the transition from an oak and hickory forest, with wet, clay soil, to the more unusual and extreme sandy, pine and oak woods, the only place in New York City where you will find this habitat, notable for its post, scrub, and blackjack oaks and a smattering of pitch pines. Explain to your children that this habitat is more typical of the south and that this is its northernmost range. Some of the plant and animal species here are not found anywhere else in New York City, including the threatened fence lizard, a shy, spiny-scaled reptile introduced here in the 1940s by the Staten Island Zoo. To defend itself, it drops its squirming tail, leaving it behind to distract predators, then eventually grows another, smaller, tail. While you probably won't see one, you will come across some delicious low-bush blueberries.

A larger swath of pine-oak woods, about 80 acres, survives in the northern part of the park, but is off limits to the general public because it is so fragile.

Turn right. There's usually a trail sign leaning up against a sassafras tree. Keep an eye out for cottontail rabbits darting across the path. You will soon reach a meadow with a bench. This is a good place for kids to sit and watch

Mariners Marsh is dotted with picturesque ponds that attract everything from turtles to wintering ducks.

for butterflies among the swamp milkweed and other wildflowers, or simply to float some leaves on the nearby stream.

To return to the nature center, turn right, keeping the meadow on your left, and follow the Blue Trail markers. When you reach the nature center, visit some of the animal coops out back, which contain chickens, pheasants, and goats. You'll have gone 1.5 miles.

If your child is eager to continue, adding another mile or so to your outing, do not turn right; rather walk straight, keeping the meadow on your right, and turn left onto the new Green Trail, also called the Gericke Farm Trail. There is usually a heap of mulch at the trailhead.

This trail crosses two bridle paths on its way to Sharrotts Pond, just across Sharrotts Road. The trail sometimes dead-ends before you actually reach Sharrotts Road, so tell someone at the nature center office that you

would like to continue beyond the "No Trespassing" sign to the pond. They are usually accommodating.

This is a pretty path with butterflies and groundhogs, ferns, and wildflowers such as Queen Anne's lace, daisy fleabane, New England aster, and black-eyed Susan. When you reached the "No Trespassing" barrier walk around it and continue to a fork, where you'll see some maintenance buildings. Turn right and continue on until you reach Sharrotts Road, looking for deer tracks in the mud. (The deer actually swim over from New Jersey, via Raritan Bay, at low tide).

Cross the street, being careful to watch for traffic, and continue along the grassy path to the pond, which is dotted with fragrant water lilies and crowded with dragonflies. Relax here with your children on the viewing platform (you'll most likely be the only ones there) and look around for egrets and red-winged blackbirds. When you're done, return to the nature center, simply retracing your steps back to the meadow and then turning left onto the Blue Trail. Or, walk along fairly quiet Sharrotts Road back to the nature center; but keep in mind that there are no sidewalks and you'll be wise to stick to the sides of the road. At Carlin Street turn right into the park.

Other Staten Island Trails to Explore

Red Trail, Mariners Marsh Park

This 1.5-mile loop is one of four easy trails that traverse this 100-acre freshwater wetland, dotted with ponds and home to lots of animals, including Fowler's toads, spring peepers, and such large birds as waders, egrets, and hawks. It's a tranquil place for a walk in winter, when all kinds of ducks arrive, including canvasback and ring-necked ducks, as well as pie-billed grebes.

The park is also a great place to experience nature's resilience. Along the Red Trail you'll see the remains of a shipyard that occupied the site

from 1907 to 1931. There were once also an iron foundry and sand-mining operations. In fact, the mining created the depressions that later formed the park's 14 ponds, some of them with names recalling their industrial past—like Downey Pond, for the Downey Shipyard, and Monument Pond, which still contains some ruins. The northern part of the park is bordered by the remains of the Arlington Rail Yards. On all these remnants of the past, nature grows, twining its way among and around steel and stone and rearing its wonderfully green abundance.

The trailhead is located just off the corner of Holland Avenue and Richmond Terrace. The Mariner's Marsh Conservancy offers free tours of the area—call 718-720-0251.

Moses Mountain, High Rock Park

If you and your children want to experience the rare treat of a 360-degree view from one of the highest spots in New York City, take this 20-minute, moderate climb to the top of Moses Mountain, which is especially beautiful at sunset. Because the trip is so quick, it's fine for kids as young as three.

The easiest way to get to Moses Mountain is via the Yellow Trail in High Rock Park. The trail may be muddy if there has been a lot of rain, so it's a good idea to wear boots. Watch for poison ivy, which grows among the sweet white clover and the goldenrod.

Each month, Protectors of Pine Oak Woods (Staten Island's oldest and largest environmental group) offers free sunset trips to the top, led by founder Dick Buegler, who describes a few geologic and floral treats along the way. The walk back down the hill is in complete darkness, so keep this in mind if you plan to go with wee ones. Some youngsters are afraid of the dark, but most will relish the idea of lighting their path through the forest with flashlights, a rare nocturnal treat in the big city of big lights. For a schedule of Protectors sunset walks, go to www.siprotectors.org.

3 BIRDING WITH CHILDREN

Don Riepe

If you want your children to appreciate and be interested in birds, there's a little imprinting you can do early on to ensure that birds will hold a special place in their hearts. First off, be interested yourself, and make birds—and other creatures—part of your family culture.

With little ones, incorporating birds into your daily wanderings can accomplish this fairly easily. When you walk your children to school, notice the neighborhood pigeons and sparrows, and say, "Hello, Pigeon," and "Good morning, Sparrow"—and soon these birds will be conspicuous to your kids, too. It may sound silly, but silly is a real kid grabber!

And instead of proclaiming, "We will now learn about birds," casually read a book about birds or a bird story like *Albert*, by Donna Jo Napoli, and just savor the tale (and Jim La Marche's illustrations). Afterward, you might ask some fun questions: "What do you think it feels like to fly?" or "If you could fly, where would you go and what would you see?" Listen to your children's answers and encourage more questions. "Why do you think birds sing?" "How come boy birds are prettier than girl birds?"

Instead of giving your kids coloring books featuring super heroes and ballerinas, buy books and stickers depicting birds; and kids as young as three may soon be able to tell a cardinal from a house finch. Feed backyard birds, or bring some seed to the park so that youngsters may observe the behaviors of various birds and the resourceful tools they use to eat. You may even want to make a birdhouse together. Or walk in the woods and simply listen to bird songs; and, guaranteed, kids of all ages will start mimicking the tunes that they hear. You can reinforce these songs by investing in a "Birdsong Identiflyer." Just place a song card into the handy portable device and let your child push the button next to a bird illustration to hear that bird's song. An outstanding resource is the National Audubon Society's five-part *Audubon VideoGuide to the Birds of North America* (also available as a two-DVD set).

Older kids may develop an interest in birds if lured in by larger-than-life creatures like raptors—eagles, owls, hawks, and, falcons—which are usually large and fierce and symbolic of strength and courage. A good first step is to attend a live raptor program or festival (see page 106) so that your youngsters can see these birds up close. You could also lend older children your camera, equipped with a good telephoto lens, and go on a photography expedition (not a bird walk—wink-wink) together. While raptors and songbirds are not always easy to spot and photograph in the wild, it's quite easy to take pictures of great egrets, cormorants, ducks, and other birds that stand still for long periods of time or ones that move slowly.

With more than 350 resident and migratory bird species in New York City, you won't be at a loss for subjects. And don't worry if you're not an ornithologist. It's okay to wing it while learning with your kids. Before I wrote this book, I didn't know a tufted titmouse from a towhee. As Laura Erickson explains in her excellent book, *Sharing the Wonder of Birds with Kids*, "Even a complete novice can help kids recognize and enjoy the birds around them, and learning bird identification together makes the experience for kids richer in many ways than when an expert adult simply dispenses the information."

Birds are a constant part of our lives and have long been part of popular culture, although we don't readily make the connections. Ask your kids why they think Toucan Sam is the Fruit Loops cereal spokesman (He's colorful like the cereal), or why so many sports teams are named for raptors, like the Atlanta Falcons and Philadelphia Eagles (raptors are large, powerful, and cunning). Birds also inspired the Wright brothers to flight and continue to represent freedom because they can fly away. Canaries were used for a long time to test air quality in mines; and, during wartime, pigeons carried messages that saved many human lives.

When it comes to watching birds with children, keep it simple until they're ready for more.

Remember, it's not about life lists, those personal tallies kept by serious birders who want to chronicle each and every species they've ever seen. It's about stuff kids can relate to—like the candy-apple red of a cardinal, the bullying of starlings, the enormity of a red-tailed hawk, the spring song of a robin, and the sheer magic of flight. Point out the differences in birds' beaks and feet, sizes and colors, and how these things allow specific birds to survive in their habitats. Most of all, make it fun: "That sparrow looks like he slept in his clothes!" or "That crow cackles just like Grandma when she hears a good joke." And remember: you're never too old to make believe; so go on, hop like a sparrow and waddle like a duck alongside your children.

Looking for one of the 325 species of birds recorded at the Jamaica Bay Wildlife Refuge

Don Riepe

Bigger Is Better

The bigger the birds (either in actual size or because they're close by), the easier it is for young children to appreciate them with unaided eyes. The big stuff includes ducks and other water birds, such as egrets, herons, and other waders, and some shore birds, including gulls. Backyard birds and pigeons are easy to watch, too.

Despite the bevy of kids' binoculars on the market, children are not ready for them until around age 7. A good one to choose is a midrange, lightweight, 7x35 model that is quick to focus. The first number means the image will appear seven times larger; the second number refers to the binoculars' aperture or opening—the larger the number the more light that comes through, brightening the image.

Children can practice using binoculars by moving and focusing on ten, fixed bird silhouettes placed in different spots in your yard or park. Make it fun by timing each "sighting" with a stopwatch. For preschoolers, pretend binoculars are just fine. Tape two toilet-paper rolls together side by side, punch two holes in the top of each tube, and thread a string or shoelace through so that your child can wear the "binoculars" around his or her neck. Obviously, this ersatz instrument won't enlarge anything, but it will help kids isolate a bird from its surroundings; and eventually children will feel comfortable using binoculars.

Ducks and Other Waterfowl

When it comes to bird watching with youngsters, a swimming duck is as good as . . . well, a sitting duck. Ducks are slow moving, colorful, and easy to spot on a lake or pond, even without binoculars. Whether it's a male bufflehead skidding into the water like a love-crazed surf-boarder or a canvasback preening its feathers, they're also very entertaining.

Since these birds take like ducks to water (to coin a phrase), look for them in oceans, marshes, ponds, rivers, lakes, and even really big puddles. All ducks have bills lined with fine hairs or teeth to strain or grip food, webbed feet for swimming, and waterproof feathers. When you see a duck nibbling near its tail, it's actually retrieving oil from a special gland; and then it then spreads that oil onto its feathers so that water will roll off, keeping the duck warm and dry. (To see how this works, dip your child's fingers in vegetable oil, then, pull a dry feather between her or his oily digits. Next spray the feather with water and watch the water roll right off.) When it's time to sleep, ducks often tuck their heads into their wings, even while bobbing on the water. Scientists have found, however, that ducks are only half sleeping; they close down one hemisphere of the brain, while keeping the other awake and attuned to danger.

Many characteristics and field marks set one duck species apart from another. The best time to experience a diversity of ducks is from late fall through late winter, although some species—like the familiar mallard—are year-round residents. During the winter, northern ponds and lakes freeze over, sending aquatic birds south in search of food. The colder it is up north, the better the duck watching is down here. But if a cold snap turns our lakes and ponds to ice, the ducks may temporarily travel even farther south in search of warmer temperatures and food.

During winter, most male ducks, or drakes, "color up" (songbirds color up in spring), achieving a brilliant plumage, like a fancy new outfit, to attract mates. Females, or hens, for the most part remain rather drab, wearing an unremarkable brownish coat that camouflages them from predators so they can safely look after their young. Many ducks will eventually return north to nest, while some, like the wood duck and the mallard, raise their families here.

Hundreds of ducks may spend the day floating around together, a kind of duck parade that provides ample opportunity for your kids to watch a single species and become familiar with field markings and other characteristics. It's best to view ducks when the temperatures are above freezing, not because your kids will complain less and your bones won't creak as much, but because ducks will vacate frozen water in search of thawed.

New York winters, however, provide plenty of 50-degree days on which to encounter rafts of ducks, which is what "flocks" of ducks are called. Look for northern shovelers, with their long, spoon-shaped bills that are unique in the duck world. Even the common male mallard boasts something no other duck has—a cute, tightly curled tail. Tell the kids that back in the old days (the 1950s), mallards inspired a trendy haircut called the "ducktail," or "D.A.," a hairstyle sported by nearly every high-school boy in the country and achieved by sweeping the sides of the hair back to a feathery point at the nape of the neck. (You may prefer going with ducktail so that you don't have to explain that D.A. is short for "duck's ass".)

Another fun thing to do is play "Dabbler or Diver" to distinguish between diving ducks and dabbling ducks. Dabblers, like mallards and gadwalls, sit high in the water and, when hungry, dip their heads into the water and strain out tiny insects and plants. Divers like buffleheads sit low on the water so that they can plunge down quickly and snag crustaceans and other animals. All ducks have lamellae—comblike structures on the edge of their bills, with the dabblers' being finer than those of the divers. Mergansers have long, slender bills with hooked ends and the sharpest lamella of all, which they use to catch and hold onto slippery fish.

The legs of dabblers and divers are also positioned differently. Dabblers' legs are set toward the middle of their bodies, allowing them to walk easily on land. Divers' legs are set further back so that they can paddle while diving; but this makes them awkward on land. Divers also prefer deep water—the middle of a lake or along coastal bays—while dabblers, or puddle ducks, enjoy shallow water. And when a duck is in flight, you can tell a dabbler by the colorful speculum (a bright patch of color) on its wings, like the brilliant blue patch of the Mallard.

When it comes to ducky courtship, young kids may not quite understand the intricacies; but they will enjoy the kooky antics of males trying to impress the opposite sex. The male common goldeneye swims around the female, thrusting his head back almost to his tail before rising in a spray of water. If there's a lot of head nodding and bobbing, it's duck love. Just tell the youngsters that this bizarre behavior is not unlike daddy doing cartwheels in his boxer shorts (or whatever is done in your family) to make mommy smile and, if he's lucky, get a hug. Return to your favorite lake or pond in summer to see resident ducks leading their progeny around the neighborhood just as in the children's classic, *Make Way for Ducklings.*

Resist the urge to feed ducks, geese, and swans. Lots of bread is not very nutritious for waterfowl. The birds aren't on the Atkins or South Beach diets; but feeding them all that bread is like feeding your kids cotton candy all day. Ducks need a balanced diet, and if they fill up on bread, they won't eat their dinner . . . the protein-rich plants and animals they need to stay healthy. They'll also rely too much on people for survival, eventually losing the ability to forage on their own. Uneaten bread left in the water also leads to harmful algae blooms and disease.

Ducks and Other Waterfowl You're Likely to See

When watching ducks with children, it's best to stick to lakes and ponds, where you'll see both dabblers and divers. For the most part, male ducks are the draw, because they're more colorful and easier to identify than the females.

Once youngsters are comfortable with binoculars and have mastered some patience, you may want to explore coastal bays like Jamaica Bay, Great Kills Harbor, Raritan Bay, and Pelham Bay for loons, scaups, and mergansers. A spotting scope is helpful on these trips. Dress warmly and don't forget your field guide—it not only helps you identify birds but shows the kids that what's in the book exists in real world.

Dabblers, or Surface Feeders

These waterfowl prefer shallow water where they can skim the surface and edges for food. Look for them on lakes and ponds.

American black duck—Drakes look a lot like hens, and both are often confused for female mallards, although American black ducks are darker in color and shier in disposition. They are also less common than mallards and usually only winter in New York City.

American coot—Although ducklike at first glance, this migratory bird is more chickenlike on closer inspection. Coots have big, goofy feet with lobed toes and sharp claws and bob their heads while swimming. Some people call them "mud hens," but they're neither duck nor

Bird-watching Field Kit

- Dress in layers and wear comfortable shoes.
- Earthy colors will help you blend in.
- Sun hat
- A field guide to birds of eastern North America
- Binoculars
- Journal or sketch pad
- Sun screen
- Insect repellent (in summer when the mosquitoes are biting)
- Camera
- Snacks and water

With ducks, as with other animal species, the male wears the colors.

chicken; they're part of the rail family, which includes clappers and Virginia rails. Coots are stubby, with short wings, tail, and bill; and they're mostly black, except for white foreheads, white bills, and dark-red eyes.

American widgeon—These dabblers hang around diving ducks, stealing their food as soon as the divers emerge from the deep. On the other hand, widgeons are keen to danger, flapping their wings and calling a loud "whee-whee-whew," warning nearby divers to flee to safety. Males have a bluish bill with black tip, grayish head with a green patch and white crown, and a cinnamon body with black-and-white tail feathers.

Brant goose—These little migrants travel thousands of miles from Baffin Island—an Arctic wilderness in northeast Canada—to winter here. They often feed among much larger Canada geese on mudflats and grassy areas. By April, they mosey over to the city's coastal bays to eat spartina and sea lettuce before heading home to breed. Noticeably smaller than Canadas, they have black heads but lack the white cheeks, and have a white zigzag on their necks.

Canada goose—These large black, white, and brown geese are North America's most com-

mon geese, often seen grazing in city parks. Watch them from a distance, especially during spring nesting season, when they will aggressively hiss and wiggle their necks until you go away. Geese mate for life and have strong family bonds. The city's geese are both resident and migratory, so if you hear a loud honk in autumn, look up for the familiar "V" formation as the lead goose blocks the wind for his trailing companions—all headed south for the winter. In April, look for fuzzy goslings.

Mallard—Males (see photo at left) have iridescent green heads, yellow bills, white neckbands, and chestnut breasts. Females (see photo below) are mostly brown but, like males have a bright blue stripe or speculum on their wings. Mallards nest in the city (typically in grasses and shrubs), so from May to July look for fuzzy, brown ducklings. If mom is leading her charges, she feels safe; but if she's guiding her babies from behind, she is worried about their safety.

Northern shoveler—If you see a duck with a bill that looks like it could flip pancakes, it's a northern shoveler, a wintering duck whose large, spoon-shaped bill is twice as wide at the tip than it is at the base. The brownish females have orange bills, while the green-headed males with yellow eyes have black bills. They also have white chests and rusty sides.

Mute swan—Although undeniably elegant, don't let these beauties fool you. Like Canada

geese, mute swans mate for life and will fiercely protect their young when threatened. Otherwise, they are quiet (unlike their trumpeting brethren), hence their name. The large white cob (male) and pen (female) are white plumed, with orange beaks with black bases, and long necks that often curve in an "S"-shape. In summer, look for cygnets (babies) riding atop their parents for warmth and protection.

Snow goose—These pure-white geese with contrasting black wing tips travel in flocks and are wonderful to see in flight, with wing spans of as much as 65 inches. One of the nosiest geese, they are also a thrill to hear when the reach for the sky. These strong flyers begin arriving en masse in early September, and then in early spring fly 3,000 miles back home to nest during the brief Arctic summer. They are one of the few species that can withstand the Arctic's harsh environment.

Wood duck—With their combed-back crown feathers, distinctive red eyes, and iridescent green heads with purple markings and white lines, male wood ducks are a sight to behold. But they're reclusive; so don't count on seeing them often—although they sometimes hang out in a raft of mallards. They are one of the few ducks that roost and nest in tree cavities (often returning to the same site year after year), some doing so right here in the city. After hatching, the down-covered babies can safely jump from their nests, even from heights of 50 feet, and will swim to find their own food.

Divers

These waterfowl obtain their food by diving under the water and, therefore, prefer it deep. Look for them in the middle of large lakes, reservoirs, and—sometimes—ponds and along coastal bays.

Bufflehead—These ducks are great to watch because they're constantly diving under water, staying submerged for seemingly minutes at a time. (For fun, have your child count how long they stay down.) Then they pop

Geese, gulls, ducks, and others—they're all here.

back up, like corks breaking the surface, before diving again. Males have a large, white patch extending from their eyes to the backs of their heads. They also have a white breast, stomach and sides, black back and wing tops, and gray bill. Unlike most ducks, buffleheads (North America's smallest diving ducks) form long-term monogamous relationships.

Canvasback—These large ducks have a distinctive sloping forehead that merges smoothly with their bills. Males have cinnamon-colored heads, black breasts and rumps, gray-white backs, grayish-black bills, and red eyes. Canvasbacks—so named, some say, because of the texture of their plumage—stay in large groups and fly off quickly when disturbed, hitting speeds of up to 70 miles per hour.

Common goldeneye—With transfixed yellow eyes, this wintering bird looks hypnotized. Males have blackish-green heads and are easily identified by the white patches between their eyes and black bills. They also have white chests and black backs and tails. Listen for the whistling sound their fast-moving wings make in flight.

Double-crested cormorant—This ducklike bird doesn't have an oil gland to keep its feathers waterproof. Rather, it hangs its wings out like the wash, allowing the breeze to dry its feathers. Great divers and underwater swimmers, these goose-sized birds have greenish black feathers and feed mainly on fish close to the bottom.

Hooded merganser—Both males and females have head crests that can be raised, usually during courtship or when they are perturbed, and lowered when they're at rest. Males are mostly black and white (a white patch extends from the top of the head to the eye), while females are reddish. These compact ducks are sometimes called "saw bills" because of their long, slender, serrated bills. Their streamlined bodies and stiff, rudderlike tails make them agile speedsters under water.

Pie-billed grebe—This secretive, ducklike bird has a skinny neck and big head and hides from enemies by quickly sinking into the water, leaving only the tip of its stubby bill and nostrils above the surface. In winter, the ivory-colored bill of this brownish bird lacks its signature black ring and throat. But you're more likely to see this grebe in early fall, when it first arrives. A threatened species in New York State because of declining freshwater marshes, it also frequents lakes and ponds, and even brackish waters.

Ruddy duck—Unlike most other ducks, male ruddies are kind of dull in winter, mostly grayish with black bills and white cheeks. (Females have a little white in the face with a black line through it.) But in spring, males develop bright-chestnut backs, and their bills turn turquoise—a bit bizarre, yet a striking contrast to their black-and-white heads. It's possible to see some blue bills in late spring before the ruddies fly north, but you'll more likely encounter rafts of these small, stubby, cocked-tail ducks in winter.

Places to See Ducks and Other Waterfowl

Pelham Bay Park (Bronx)—Search the Lagoon (behind the Orchard Beach parking lot) for wintering ducks, including American black ducks and buffleheads. Then walk northeast to Twin Island (near the Orchard Beach Nature Center) on Long Island Sound, where loons, scaups, and other water birds congregate. In January, harbor and harp seals are often seen out on Middle Reef, north of Hart Island.

Nesting swans may be seen throughout the five boroughs.

Van Cortlandt Park (Bronx)—Scores of ducks and some swans may be seen at Van Cortlandt Lake. Look for nesting wood ducks and their young from May 15 to June 15.

Brooklyn Bridge Park (Brooklyn)—Look for Brant geese, cormorants, and other water birds in the cove between the Manhattan and Brooklyn Bridges. A free field guide to the cove is available by calling 718-802-0603.

Gerritsen Creek (Brooklyn)—Located next to the Salt Marsh Nature Center, the creek hosts a variety of wintering ducks. Brant geese are often seen across the street, on the lawn next to the Marine Park parking lot.

Prospect Park (Brooklyn)—Prospect Lake is a great place to see wintering ducks, including coots, shovelers, and even gorgeous wood ducks. There are also year-round populations of easy-to-observe Canada geese, mute swans, and mallards.

Central Park (Manhattan)—Check the bird log, which has been kept since 1975, at the Loeb Boathouse on the eastern shore of The Lake. Otherwise, look for wintering ducks, including mergansers, coots, canvasbacks, shovelers, ruddies, and others at the Jacqueline Kennedy Onassis Reservoir (mid-park, between 85th and 94th Streets). Smaller numbers of ducks frequent the Harlem Meer (enter at 100th Street and Lenox Avenue).

Jamaica Bay Wildlife Refuge (Queens)—Look for wintering ducks, including mergansers and ruddies. Huge flocks of snow and Brant geese are common in late fall and early winter at the West Pond.

Clove Lakes Park (Staten Island)—Clove Lake and adjoining Martling Lake and Brooks Pond mostly harbor ring-billed gulls, Canada geese, mallards, and mallard hybrids, and sometimes boast a wood duck. Sit on the rocks along Martling Lake for a cozy, tree-shaded view of ducks and geese year round.

Places Best Explored with a Spotting Scope or Binoculars

Breezy Point (Brooklyn)—In winter, visit the fishing jetty that juts out into the Atlantic Ocean at the tip of Breezy Point and scan for loons, as well as mergansers and other sea ducks.

Floyd Bennett Field (Brooklyn)—Raptor Point and the Boat Ramp on the eastern side of the park are good places to see wintering sea ducks, including mergansers. Also look for loons, grebes, and American widgeons. You won't need a scope to see numerous Brant geese in the grasslands along the old runway, east of the Ryan Visitor Center.

Little Neck Bay (Queens)—Look for wintering waterfowl, including Canada and Brant geese, canvasbacks, northern pintails, greater scaups, common goldeneyes, buffleheads, and others.

Conference House Park (Staten Island)—From the beach, search the Arthur Kill and Raritan Bay (that's New Jersey across the way) for Brant geese, buffleheads, common goldeneyes, and others.

Great Kills Park (Staten Island)—Head out to Crooke's Point and scan the Atlantic Ocean for wintering sea ducks or walk over to Great Kills Harbor and watch for long-tailed ducks.

Long-legged Waders

When the weather turns warm, it's time to introduce your kids to long-legged waders. Children will find these large birds easy to see, and the waders' search for food is quite dramatic. Egrets and herons, especially, are stealthy hunters that wade silently and deliberately through shallow water in pursuit of food. Their aim is amazingly exact, put into play by extending their necks forward and pointing

There's surf, sand, and sun—but this ain't no day at the beach. Birds rule—whether endangered least terns are swooping down Alfred Hitchcock-style to protect their territory or equally endangered piping plovers nesting on their own parcel of federally protected turf. A trip to Breezy Point offers a vivid lesson in compromise, a way to show your kids that there is a place for both wildlife and humans. We must learn to share the earth.

Every year, stocky, little piping plovers fly up from Florida and sometimes farther south to raise their young in the city, in places like Breezy Point and—to a lesser extent—in Arverne and Jacob Riis Park on the Rockaway Peninsula. The birds don't build nests in trees; they lay their eggs in little dugouts right on the beach. Over the decades, piping plovers have lost much of their nesting habitat to development and recreational use, leaving only 2,500 pairs worldwide, with 1,400 of them concentrated along the Atlantic Coast, many of those right here in New York.

These tiny shore birds, 6 inches tall, are like cotton balls on toothpicks, fast-moving toothpicks, that is—because plovers run in sudden stops and starts like windup toys. They are the color of sand, and camouflage well, and have a black band across the forehead from eye to eye and a black ring around the base of the neck. Plover chicks are extremely independent, leaving the nest to feed themselves within hours of hatching.

While plovers quietly stand sentry at their nests, fast-flying least terns, sometimes called "sea swallows" because of their forked tails, take to the air to scare you away from their colonies, which are a little farther back in the dunes. At about 9 inches, they may be North America's smallest terns, with yellow beaks tipped with black, yellow legs, gray-and-white bodies, and black caps, but they are fierce. If you and your children enter tern territory, they'll scream "kip-kip-kip-kiddeek" as they dive bomb to frighten you away. And while it is intimidating having terns swoop at you, it's sweetly domestic to see them fly back and forth with fish in their mouths for their young.

To safeguard plover and tern nesting sites, volunteers and city and national Rangers erect corrals around their fragile neighborhoods. These keep beachgoers from stepping on nests and convey the message to stay away. People, however, do sit on the beach a stone's throw from the barricades, making for an interesting juxtaposition. If adults are frightened from their nests, eggs and young become vulnerable to such predators as gulls, crows, and stray cats and dogs.

To limit the birds' exposure to humans, Rangers and volunteers lead a limited number of free summer tours to the nesting sites. (In fact, it's the best way to get onto Breezy Point, since parking at the beach is restricted from April 15 to September 15. The rest of Breezy Point is a private community and closed to the public.) Visitors stand outside the nesting area and look through binoculars, making this a trip suitable for kids comfortable with binoculars. It's also a bit of a haul up a sandy path. Younger children might find it more fun hunting for shells along the wrack line. For dates, call 718-318-4300.

There's also a smaller site between Beach 45th Street and Beach 56th Street along Rockaway Beach. The site is closed to the public while the birds are nesting between mid-March and late August. The birds discovered this site in 1996, after the beach was closed because of a lifeguard shortage. The site harbors interesting beach plants, including endangered sea-beach amaranth. For information, call 311 and ask for the Urban Park Rangers.

their needle-sharp bills downward, before . . . Whamo! . . . they flawlessly spear a fish.

There is an elegant side to these birds, too, especially in spring, when breeding causes the males to breathtakingly fan open the wispy feathers on their heads, breasts, and tails and morph into giant snowflakes in order to appeal to the opposite sex. You might tell your children that during the late 19th century, these birds were hunted for their feathers, which decorated women's hats, and that they nearly became extinct. Today, federal law protects them, allowing us to see the magic of their flight—wings outstretched, necks neatly tucked in, and long legs streaming behind them like wind-blown kite tails.

Long-legged waders are fairly easy to find in summer, hanging out in fresh- and saltwater marshes, along lakes and ponds, and on tidal flats. During winter, they migrate south, many of them to the Florida Everglades. In addition to herons and egrets, there are also ibises— large birds with long necks, skinny legs and long toes (to help them stand in mud and sand), and slender bills designed to impale their catch. Glossy Ibises probe for their food rather than spear fish, so their bills slope downward like sickles. Herons and egrets keep their necks in an "S" shape when at rest and feed singly, but often nest in colonies. They build huge stick nests perilously high up in trees despite their large size. Many heron, egret, and ibis rookeries are on the city's harbor islands, where there is privacy and relative freedom from predators.

Look for the following long-legged waders at the water's edge:

Black-crowned night heron—This stocky bird is relatively small for a heron (23–28 inches tall) and would surely appear taller if it were not hunched over much of the time. It doesn't have a super-long neck like other herons and likes to forage for food at night. It is gray and white, with red eyes and a black bill and head, from which hang a few long, white feathers.

During summer, great egrets are common throughout the city and can be seen stalking food at the water's edge.

Glossy ibis—Look closely at this seemingly black bird and you'll notice a greenish-purplish iridescence, which gives this ibis its name. About 20–24 inches tall, it has a bill that curves downward, allowing it to investigate the mud for such prey as fiddler crabs and crawfish.

Great blue heron—The largest shore birds on the Atlantic coast, great blue herons stand up to 4 feet tall, with 6-foot wingspans and beaks about 5 inches long. Mostly gray-blue, they have white heads with a black line above and behind the eyes, yellow beaks, and golden eyes; and they can swallow fish much larger than their skinny necks could seemingly accommodate.

Great egret—These birds don't display their breeding plumage from head to tail. Rather, a cape of feathers cascades down their backs. A bit smaller (3 feet tall, with 55-inch wingspans) than great blues, adult great egrets are white, with yellow bills, and black legs and feet. While flying, they hold their necks in a more open "S" than other herons and egrets.

Green heron—This small heron (16–22 inches tall) has a green sheen to its dark feathers, a rust-colored neck and chest, black bill, and yellow legs. If it senses that it is being watched, it jerks its tail and raises and lowers its crest to appear big and bad and frighten intruders away.

Snowy egret—This bird is distinguished from the great egret by its smaller size, black bill, and yellow legs and feet. It likes to shuffle around the water, kicking up goodies to eat.

Places to See Long-legged Waders

Floyd Bennett Field (Brooklyn)—At the northern end of the park is the North Forty trail. Walk west to the bird blind at the Return-A-Gift-Pond, which is especially rewarding after spring rains.

Gerritsen Creek (Brooklyn)—Just behind the Salt Marsh Nature Center and along its trail are many long-legged waders hugging the water's edge.

Central Park (Manhattan)—The Lake, particularly from Bow Bridge, is a good vantage point, although you can scan more of the lake's nooks and crannies by going out on a rented rowboat (see chapter 5, Paddling with Kids).

Alley Pond Park (Queens)—Take the Cattail Pond trail from the Alley Pond Environmental Center parking lot to an observation deck overlooking Alley Creek, then follow the trail around the Alley Pond Park wetlands.

Jamaica Bay Wildlife Refuge (Queens)—The West Pond Trail offers many opportunities to see egrets, herons, and ibises.

Mariner's Marsh Park (Staten Island)—Ten ponds dot this 107-acre area, with birds flying in from nearby rookeries to forage for food.

Shore Birds and Sea Birds

Shore birds share a rhythm with the waves, running to dry sand as the waves roll in and then, as the waves recede, rushing in for a brief moment to forage, before the waves again drive them away. It's a carefully choreographed dance (and method of survival), with the surf playing the music and the birds providing the show.

Every spring, shore birds and sea birds leave their wintering grounds down south and stop in New York City on their way north. Some stay to nest—the piping plover and American oyster catcher, for example—but most are just pausing here to rest and refuel. Still others, such as sanderlings, are mostly winter residents, arriving when their Arctic homes freeze.

Shore birds are well adapted to the coast and have perfect beach bodies—not all bronze and

The Lake in Central Park is a great vantage point for seeing all sorts of birds.

muscular, but rather often buff-colored like the sand, or brown, gray, tan, and sometimes speckled. This helps them blend into the background, camouflaging them from predators. Their legs are long for their small bodies; and needle-thin bills allow them to probe the sand for tiny crustaceans and mollusks. Some feast on delectable horseshoe crab eggs laid on the shore in May and June. While this may seem to your kids like stealing, explain to them that this is simply the cycle of nature. To keep warm, some shore birds stand on one leg, with their faces tucked into their bodies. And since there are no trees on windy shorelines behind which to seek shelter, shore birds often use one another as windbreaks, each taking its turn at being the buffer.

As cute as they are, shore birds may be difficult for beginners to identify because many of them have similar colors. There are, however, distinctive facial markings and breeding plumages that usually set one species apart from another. Rather than worry about identifying each species, watch shore birds with your child and talk about how their bodies are adapted for life on shore. Long legs help them wade easily through water; long, thin bills are perfect for probing the sand and mud for buried critters; and dull colors help conceal them from predators. Long, pointed wings help them fly fast and far.

Some shore birds you may encounter are:

American oystercatcher—This large bird has a striking orange-red bill that works like an oyster shucker's knife. Flat and twice as long as the bird's head, it is perfect for prying open bivalves. American oystercatchers have white bellies, dark backs, and yellow eyes ringed with orange that stand out from their black heads. They arrive in large flocks in late March and early April.

Black skimmer—These birds are a bit goofy looking. They have long black bodies (about 18 inches) on short orange legs, white faces and necks, and orange-and-black bills—and they use the longer bottom part of their bills (the

American oystercatchers arrive in large flocks in late March and early April.

mandible) to skim just beneath the water's surface for fish and crustaceans. The best time to see these summer residents is at dusk.

Common tern—These black-capped, white-and-gray birds have deeply forked tails, red legs, and red bills tipped in black. They dive into the water for prey, mostly small fish, and nest in colonies on the sand. Smaller than least terns, at 8–10 inches, they aggressively defend their nests against intruders, including humans.

Greater yellowleg—These migrants—mostly brown-black with white dots in summer—have very long, bright yellow legs that allow them to feed in greater depths than other shore birds. They also have a slightly upturned bill, which they swing from side to side as they feed.

Sanderlings—These gray-backed, white-bellied, black-legged shore birds seem to play "catch me if you can" with the surf, but are really just waiting for the waves to retreat, so they can dig for tasty mollusks and crustaceans. Look for large flocks along the beach in winter, doing their "two step forward, one step back" dance.

Sandpiper—There are several types of sandpipers, including semipalmated, least, and spotted. Most have tan, gray, or brown backs, white bellies, and dark spots on their chests. They're generally as small as sparrows, but have long legs that move them in fits and starts along the water's edge. Some nest here, while others pass through during migration or are only winter residents.

Places to See Shore Birds

The best times to see a variety of shore birds is during the spring and fall migrations, and typically on unpopulated shorelines.

Fort Tilden and neighboring **Jacob Riis Park** (Brooklyn)—Look for plovers, terns, and other shore birds along the beaches.

Salt Marsh Nature Center (Brooklyn)—The trail behind the nature center offers great opportunities to see skimmers at dusk; while the mud flats behind the center attract many shore-bird species.

Jamaica Bay Wildlife Refuge (Queens)—The East Pond is the premier place to see shore birds, from late July through the end of August. The manmade pond is drained in mid-June specifically to create a 24-hour mud flat and provide foraging habitat for migrating shore birds. Look for a variety of sandpipers and plovers, as well as greater and lesser yellowlegs.

Goethals Pond (Staten Island)—Look for sandpipers, yellowlegs, and other shore birds during August and September. There is a viewing trail behind the Sunset Gardens mobile home community, located near the Goethals Bridge toll plaza.

Great Kills Park (Staten Island)—The park's salt marsh is a good place to see shore birds at low tide. Follow the short path that leads from the northeastern end of Parking Lot A.

Greater yellowlegs have very long legs that allow them to feed in greater depths than other shore birds.

Sky Dancers

In early spring, at dusk, male woodcocks perform a crazy love ritual to get the females' attention, propelling themselves hundreds of feet into the air, twirling and whistling before cascading down and landing like a boomerang in their original spots. They'll do this about 20 times an hour, before tuckering themselves out and turning in for the night. AZ bird's gotta do what a bird's gotta do, especially when his plumage isn't exactly spectacular (brown and gray) and he's less than handsome—kind of plump with a big nose emphasized by large, set-back eyes.

This spectator sport is good for older kids with patience, because you will stand around for a while waiting for the high-flying antics. The show begins when a male woodcock introduces himself with a nasal, sawlike sound that sort of mimics a wet, squeaky shoe. Then without warning, he'll zip up, a pigeon-sized bird with frantically flapping wings silhouetted against the darkened sky. Within seconds, he has gone so high that he disappears completely. Then a sweet kind of cheeping begins—a sound created by his wings. This means he'll soon be coming in for a landing, spiraling faster and faster until he's back down on earth.

You can witness this spectacle on free annual trips organized usually in March and April by both the Urban Park Rangers (dial 311) and the American Littoral Society (718-318-9344). New York City Audubon (212-691-7438) also sponsors guided bird-watching events in addition to their annual Birdathon each May. If you wish to go alone, one good spot is a grassy area at the Jamaica Bay Wildlife Refuge. While most shore birds stick to the coast, the quirky woodcocks like moist, open spaces close to trees. Take the trail left of the visitor center and walk about a block or so in. When you see a fire hydrant on your right, stop. The open woodcock-dancing area is across from the hydrant, on the left side of the path.

Backyard Favorites

Watching backyard birds is a nature lesson disguised as fun. As birds fly into and out of your yard, alighting on tree branches or calling to mates, observing them is not only entertaining, it hones important skills of observation and differentiation. Watch them for as long as you like, depending on your child's patience and interest.

You and your kids may wish to record the birds visiting your feeders and help the Cornell Lab of Ornithology with research on winter migration and bird populations in your neighborhood. As citizen scientists, the data you compile from November through April will be used to draw conclusions about, and detect changes in, backyard bird populations in communities all around the country. This information will be used for education and conservation. Participation in Project Feederwatch (1-800-843-BIRD; www.birds.cornell.edu//pfw/) is $15 annually, and includes a research kit with bird-feeding information, a bird-identification poster, a wall calendar, data forms, and a quarterly newsletter.

Bird watching is best in the morning and early evening, when birds are fueling up for the day or snacking before nightfall. The variety of birds will provide plenty of easy teaching opportunities. If a hummingbird shows up, tell your children how its long, thin beak allows it to poke deep into long-throated flowers to retrieve nectar. Point out how a cardinal's short, chunky bill is a nifty seed cracker. Once you recognize how differently each bird's beak is designed, it become easier to figure out what they eat.

Watching bird behavior is especially entertaining when the birds act like . . . well, like kids—swiping seeds from other birds or hogging the bird feeder. Kids can relate to these acts of aggression as well as the more gentle side of birds—for example, when a male cardinal gently places a seed into the beak of his loved one.

You can help attract birds to your yard, balcony, or fire escape by setting up bird feeders. Encourage youngsters to get involved by having them make feeders like the easy pinecone feeder—simply smear a pinecone with peanut butter, roll it in bird seed, and hang it outside. Or cut a rectangular hole in an empty, washed-out milk carton, decorate the carton with twigs, leaves, and other natural materials (a glue gun works great), thread a string through the top, fill with seed, and hang in a tree. Children also love to hide inside big boxes; so next time you have an old appliance carton, make a bird blind out of it. Cut a viewing hole into the box, place it outside, and have your kids climb in and, safely hidden, wait for the birds to arrive.

Bird feeders are particularly important in winter when natural food, mostly insects and seeds, is scarce. But don't just throw any seed into a feeder. Just like your own family, in which one child loves peanut butter and jelly and the other prefers macaroni and cheese, birds have their favorite foods. Stay clear of birdseed mixes; many of them have a lot of filler, which is just junk food for birds. The best food to start with is black-oil sunflower seeds; they are high in fat and have thin shells that lots of birds can easily crack. (The striped variety has a thicker shell.) But you might experiment with other seeds, like millet, cracked corn, and niger (a goldfinch favorite).

Bird-feeder designs and where you place them also play roles in attracting birds. It's best to keep feeders near natural areas—like trees or shrubs—for the widest variety, but some birds will visit feeders even on fire escapes. Tray or platform feeders attract ground feeders, like blue jays and dark-eyed juncos, while house finches and chickadees like house or hopper feeders. Tube feeders are also good for small birds, including sparrows.

Bird feeders also attract squirrels, and they'll perform amazing feats to get at the food. These agile creatures think nothing of dangling upside down from a tree limb and dipping into a feeder. Some people put baffles on their bird feeders, concave accessories that are like slippery hills to squirrels. Sometimes they work, sometimes they don't. Other people smear fat on the feeder and the area around it so squirrels will slide off the surface. Still others stick to safflower seeds, which squirrels are said to dislike.

You might also put suet (high-protein beef fat) in an onion bag or wire-mesh cage available at hardware stores and botanical gardens, and hang it from a tree branch. Or simply smear the suet on the tree to attract woodpeckers and nuthatches; but feisty starlings and squirrels like suet too. Some plants, including sunflowers, black-eyed Susans, berry bushes, and goldenrod also offer some tasty treats. Set out some water for birds (especially if there's a summer drought), and watch them bathe and drink.

In summer, fill hummingbird feeders with homemade nectar (four parts boiling water mixed with one part sugar, and then cooled) to attract the only hummer found in the New York City area, the ruby-throated hummingbird. These tiny creatures (about 3 inches long) with needle-thin bills, are metallic green, iridescent red, and white (the males), but often appear as a blur because of their constantly propelling wings (53 beats per second in flight). They also eat insects (hang an orange nearby to attract yummy fruit flies) and savor nectar from red, tubular flowers (a perfect fit for their beaks), so consider growing some in your garden.

It may take time for birds to discover your feeders, especially window feeders. If nobody stops by, sprinkle some seeds on the ground or sill, or consider moving the feeder. And keep your feeders clean by washing them with soapy water, and rinsing and drying thoroughly, about once every two weeks, twice a week for hummingbird feeders; and rake the ground below your feeders so old food and bird waste don't pile up.

When spring arrives, the kids might roll up some dryer lint into a ball, wrap it loosely with string, and hang it from a fence or low bush. They could even incorporate some shredded material from their old clothes. This will provide birds with ready supplies for making nests. It is magical watching birds pull the wad apart, picking and choosing their building materials—a piece of your son's once favorite T-shirt or your daughter's fancy tights. Encourage youngsters to draw pictures of what they imagine the birds' nests will look like on the basis of what was taken from the ball.

Backyard Birds of Winter

Feeding birds is generally a winter activity, helping them get through the cold, food-scarce season. When the weather warms up, they will forage on their own, although it's nice to leave some sugar water out for summer hummingbirds. Some common backyard birds are:

Black-capped chickadee—These tiny, mostly black-and-white birds are so friendly that kids will have them eating from their hands. Or watch one of these chipper visitors grab a seed from a feeder, then retreat to a nearby perch where it holds the seed with its feet while pecking it open. These inquisitive residents are great hoppers and clingers, and a joy to watch.

Blue jay—These big, crested, blue birds—10 to 11 inches long—like whole raw peanuts, among other seeds and nuts. When one of these native jays shows up at your feeders, the other birds will scatter, fearful of this boisterous bully. Blue jays are complex migrants, and you should look for them year round—some stay while others head south for the winter.

Dark-eyed (or **slate-colored**) **junco**—These soft-looking, tiny gray birds with white bellies and pink beaks are frequent winter visitors, usually foraging on the ground beneath feeders. Pay attention to which one in the flock eats first and which one last. Older males are usually at top of the pecking order, with the youngest females (more brown than gray) at the bottom—but because they all travel together, everybody gets to eat.

Downy woodpecker—These small (6 inches) black-and-white woodpeckers walk along trees looking and listening for insects to eat. Males, with a red spot at the back of their heads, tend to stay high up, chiseling deep into tree trunks and branches. The females have shorter bills, which they use to pry under bark.

European starling—These messy, noisy birds travel in large flocks and weren't New Yorkers until 1890, when a birding organization thought it would be great to import to America ever bird mentioned in Shakespeare's works. Among them were starlings, which get a quick mention in *Henry IV*, and today number 200 million in the United States. Watch these dark, spotted, iridescent birds use their yellow, pointed beaks to steal food from other birds and one another.

House finch—Native to the American West, these rosy-headed and -throated sparrow-sized birds were sold in New York City pet stores in the 1930s as "California linnets." When Audubon Society employee Richard Plough (later, a founding member of The Nature Conservancy) recognized them as federally protected house finches, he notified authorities. To avoid fines, dealers released their birds, paving the way for their proliferation on the East Coast.

Mourning dove—These sleek, softly beige-gray native birds with little heads and long tapered tails feed on the ground and call "oooah-ooh-ooh-ooah"—the low, sad-sounding song that gives them their name. Mourning doves swallow seeds whole, using their muscular gizzard to grind up both shells and seeds. Originally a farm bird, this symbol of peace has adapted well to the city but is hunted as game in 39 states.

Northern cardinal—The male's bright red coat is spectacular, like fire in the snow. Even the female—more olive than red, but also with distinguished crest and candy apple beak—is attractive. Cardinals mate for life and often visit feeders as couples, with males sometimes feeding their mates tasty little bon-bons. Both males and females sing, often performing loud and clear "cheer, cheer, cheer" duets.

Northern mockingbird—This bird's Latin name, *Mimus polyglottos*, means "many-tongued mimic," and that's exactly what mockingbirds do—imitate other birds, repeating each call several times before moving on to the next. During spring, unmated males sing all night long until they find a mate, and they'll keep you awake if you sleep near an open window. Mockingbirds are medium-sized, mostly gray birds that are beautiful in flight, when their white outer tail feathers and wing bars flash.

Ruby-throated hummingbird—This summer visitor, which lives as far south as the Gulf of Mexico, is the only hummingbird species east of the Great Plains. Like a helicopter, it can fly backwards, but is usually seen jetting from spot to spot, hovering at each juice bar to sip.

Sparrows—Most of the so-called sparrows frequenting feeders are house or English sparrows, which are really a type of finch. They were introduced into the U.S. from Europe about 150 years ago, by a man who thought they would control worms devastating city trees. These brown birds with their black bibs (or throats) are now ubiquitous in all 50 states. Unfortunately, they keep many native, true sparrows away; but if you're lucky, the song sparrow, a shy, yet melodious vocalist, may visit your feeder, but in smaller numbers. Song sparrows like to pump their long tails, and they have lateral crown stripes and a dot in the center of their chests. Some migrate, some don't. Another native sparrow and winter visitor is the white-throated sparrow, a beautiful singer with white head stripes and yellow spots in front of their eyes.

Tufted titmouse—Adorable, small, gray birds with perky crests, rust-colored flanks, white bellies and faces, dark eyes, and short, pointed bills, these little acrobats turn themselves upside down to retrieve seeds from feeders or insects from under tree bark. These outgoing, endearing year-rounders, which are related to the chickadee, are great fun to watch.

White-breasted nuthatch—These 6-inch birds with black foreheads and caps, blue-gray backs, and white undersides may be found year round in the woods and at backyard feeders. They use their long, straight bills and ability to creep upside down on tree trunks to probe for insects and other food.

Public Bird-Feeding Stations

If you don't have a place to hang a bird feeder, or are plagued by squirrels and feral cats, there are plenty of places around the city where bird feeders are set up for your enjoyment. Some are just outside huge, picture windows, allowing for inside viewing, while others are located near park benches, so you can sit and watch the constant flying in and flying out of a variety of feathered friends—some of which you may not see at your own feeders, including hairy woodpeckers and red-breasted nuthatches. Don't forget your field guide!

Most public bird-feeding stations operate during the colder months when food is scarce, so check before going at other times. Good spots for feeder watching include:

Prospect Park (Brooklyn)—A tube feeder and suet cage hang inconspicuously on Breeze Hill, just southeast of the Prospect Park Audubon Center. Proceed down the Lullwater Trail from the Audubon Center. After the rustic arbor, walk about a half block more, then scramble up the slope and look for feeders between two large pines. If walking east across the Terrace Bridge, turn into the trees at the second fire hydrant on Hill Drive. There is also a feeder on the second level of the Audubon Center.

Central Park (Manhattan)—The premier bird-feeding station, complete with benches for long-term sitting, is at Evodia Field in the Ramble, not far from Bow Bridge. There are about 12 feeders, each filled with a different type of seed, offering a smorgasbord that attracts a great variety of birds

Shorakkopoch Rock, Inwood Hill Park (Manhattan)—While you won't find any bird feeders here, simply standing at the rock in the morning with some black-oil sunflower seeds in hand will attract hungry woodpeckers, nuthatches, tufted titmice, and chickadees within feet of you, with chickadees sometimes perching on your hands.

Sara Delano Roosevelt Park (Manhattan; between Broome and Delancy Streets)—Every morning, but particularly on summer Sundays, Chinese men meet here with delicate birds perched in bamboo cages, sharing an ancient tradition and filling the park with bird song. Anyone can watch from a park bench as the men coax their *hua mei* birds (a type of thrush once favored by Chinese emperors) to belt out a tune or harmonize together. The concert begins at 9 AM and lasts through 11 AM, sometimes later.

Jamaica Bay Wildlife Refuge (Queens)—Feeders and benches are just outside the back door of the visitor center.

Blue Heron Nature Center (Staten Island)—Feeders are behind the nature center and may also be viewed from inside the center. There are bird-banding demonstrations at the feeders on Saturdays, from 1 to 4 PM, from October through April. Small, numbered metal rings with serial numbers (corresponding to the bird's vital statistics) are attached to each bird's legs. This helps researchers study bird movement, longevity, behavior, and other traits and habits.

Since 1996, Cornell University and Wild Birds Unlimited have maintained a series of bird feeders that may be viewed by anyone around the world via the Internet. A live Web cam delivers images of woodpeckers, goldfinches, cardinals, and others every day from dawn to dusk. To watch these birds in real time, go to: www.wbu.com/feedercam_home.htm.

Watching a Single Species

When you really want to get to know someone, there's nothing like a one-to-one relationship. The same holds true when it comes to birds, and there are plenty of people-friendly pigeons, gulls, sparrows, and starlings waiting for an audience. They don't mind if your kids watch them behave badly as they swipe food from one another or do the funky chicken to catch another bird's attention. Just sit on a park bench and study their nuances—the way they walk (some birds hop, pigeons walk or run and bob their heads), the patterns and colors of their feathers, and the differences in their beaks. Have your kids watch and take notes—this could be fodder for a science-fair project or research that may greatly help scientists.

Pigeons

Pigeons are perhaps the easiest and most amusing species to observe. And while you're at it, why not participate in a scientific activity as a family. Through a program called Project PigeonWatch (1-800-843-BIRD; www.birds.cornell.edu/ppw), scientists at the Cornell Lab of Ornithology are relying on regular people to record the number of pigeons, various colors of pigeons, and courtship behavior seen within flocks in their neighborhoods. Consider it your child's first job as a field scientist. The cost of participation is $15 a year and covers tally and data sheets, a color poster of pigeon color morphs, research and guide materials, and the *PigeonScope News* newsletter, to which you may send submissions.

Locate a flock in your local park or any place where pigeons congregate and pull up a seat. Paying special attention to these birds helps kids see them as individuals, not merely members of a flock. There may be eight boys in your son's class, but two have blond hair, four have brown hair, and two have black hair. There's also a lot of color variation among urban pigeons, both male and female, especially around their necks. This is unique in the bird world as male birds are usually one color and females another. Scientists call these color types in pigeons "morphs," and they study how color may or may not determine mate choice or dominance within a flock. How many color variations can you and your children spot?

When the weather warms up, pigeons also begin acting . . . well, cuckoo. The males get loud, puff up their iridescent neck feathers, and strut around in circles, perfectly normal behavior for a male flirting with a female. If impressed by a male's little performance, the female pigeon will decide to become his life's love. She may even nuzzle her beak into the male's beak. The male celebrates by beating his wings together in a kind of applause. Every year the two will replay this dance in a kind of renewal of vows.

Urban pigeons are descendents of wild pigeons, or European rock doves, brought here in the 1600s and domesticated by humans. Eventually, many escaped and quickly adjusted to city life, scavenging and nesting on building ledges that resemble cliffs—the rock dove's natural habitat.

Once your youngsters get to know pigeons, they'll want to stick up for them and help others see their goodness, just like Bert from Sesame Street, who is perhaps the world's most famous pigeon aficionado. Pigeons are busy street cleaners, consuming leftovers that would otherwise pile up on our streets. During wartime, their swiftness and homing instinct allowed them to carry messages that saved lives. To this day, many urbanites have a special relationship with pigeons, flying them from their rooftops as pets. But most of all, pigeons are doves of the street and an overlooked symbol of peace.

Gulls

If you've ever seen a gull try to devour a sea star or steal someone else's food, you know that these noisy scavengers can be endlessly entertaining. Resourceful and territorial, these sea birds really know how to eke out a living on shore, aggressively screeching and winging their way to food, eating everything from fish to garbage. But first and foremost, they are graceful flyers that seem at one with the sky.

Gulls have webbed feet, long, narrow, slender wings, and strong beaks, and they are usually gray, white, and black. Most people refer to all gulls simply as "sea gulls," but there are actually many gull varieties. Four are seen regularly in New York—herring gulls, ring-billed gulls, great black-backed gulls, and laughing gulls. Adult herring gulls are about 2 feet long and have gray backs, or "mantles," gray wings with black tips, white breasts, and yellow bills. They are seen year round. Ring-billed gulls look a lot like herring gulls, but are smaller, with a black ring around the ends of their bills. When it's time to breed, red rings develop around their yellow eyes. They are generally around most of the year, except for early summer. Greater black-backed gulls are large birds (as long as 31 inches) with black backs and

The ring-billed gull is one of four species of gulls regularly seen in the city.

wings and grayish eyes, and can be seen throughout the year. Laughing gulls migrate here in late spring to nest and are known for their loud "ha-ha-ha-ha-ha-haah-haah-haah" call. They have telltale black heads, white crescents above and below their eyes, white chests, and dark gray mantles.

So sit back with your kids and watch a flock of gulls, usually a generational gathering of toddler, teenaged, and adult birds. Despite being of the same species, each age group has its own look. That's how it is with gulls; it takes two to four years for them to achieve full adult plumage. Young gulls of all species are dirty looking, usually a mottled gray or brown, depending on their age. Usually the youngest are mostly brown and adolescents are gray mixed with brown. A good way to distinguish between ages is through the "Gulls Galore" program of the Cornell Lab of Ornithology. Citizen scientists like you and your children choose a site where gulls congregate and then record such information as types of gull, ages, number of gulls in the group, and behaviors. For information, go to www.birds.cornell.edu/programs /urbanbirds/ubs_GUPMainEN.html.

Taking Flight with Older Kids

When Peter Dorosh was 14, a brilliant scarlet tanager flew into his backyard in the shadow of the Brooklyn–Queens Expressway, inspiring both awe and a lifelong interest in birds. Today, he is president of the Brooklyn Bird Club. If your own fledgling takes an interest in birds, get some binoculars and a field guide and see what you can inspire for his or her future.

Before heading out, choose a habitat you'd like to investigate together—woodland, shoreline, lake, meadow, or marsh. By visiting different habitats, kids learn and see how birds are specifically adapted to survive in each habitat. For example, shore birds have long, thin bills to probe the mud and pull out food, while raptors often perch high above it all to get a bird's-eye view of their next meal.

Then consult your field guide for pictures and descriptions of birds that frequent the specific habitat you are visiting. Make a mental note of any obvious field marks that will help you identify birds in the field. You may also want to check out two websites that provide some information on recently seen species and their locales. They are www.nycbirdreport .com and www.virtualbirder.com/vbirder/real birds/rbas/NY.html, which also has a hotline at 212-979-3070.

Once in place, slowly scan the landscape. Stand still or sit down every so often to wait for birds to sweep by. Simply staying in one spot—becoming just another part of the landscape—is often the best way to see birds. When you see a bird, notice its size and shape. Is it smaller than a sparrow or larger than a pigeon? Is its head crested or smooth? Does it have a long neck or short neck? Focus on field marks, those colors or patterns that identify a bird as belonging to a specific group or single species. Beaks and bills also provide clues to a bird's type, as well as to its eating habits. Birds that spear fish have long, pointed beaks, while predators (like hawks) have hooked, sharp beaks. Feet help distinguish a bird's kind, too—ducks have webbed feet, while passerines (perching birds) have three toes in front and one longish toe in back that help them cling to branches. Notice, also, how a bird flies—in short spurts close to the ground or soaring high in the sky? Birdsongs are also great indicators, but they are more difficult to discern.

Keep trips short enough so your children don't get bored; encourage questions; rave like crazy when they spot something (you can literally put feathers in their caps); and pack enough snacks and drinks to keep them satiated, hydrated, and happy. Don't overload them with too much information. Simply initiate discovery and take it from there. They'll return home with a few bits of information each time you go out; and each subsequent trip will add to their store of knowledge. And when your child asks questions, don't worry if you don't have the answers—figure it out together. Most of all, make it fun.

Also consider going out with experienced birders to be assured of seeing something. There's no surer way to put a damper on further outings than to go birding with youngsters and come up dry. While most birding clubs discourage kids on their trips, some groups welcome older kids, so long as they are accompanied by an adult and can maintain quiet. Other organizations specialize in family trips and welcome the younger set.

But remember, it's the rare bird who takes to birding immediately; so if your child gets bored, don't push him or her. Try exploring nature in other ways—beachcombing, hiking, or fishing—throwing a few bird sightings in here and there. "A child has to react positively to birds and show an interest without pressuring them," says Dorosh. A chance meeting with a great horned owl, a red-tailed hawk, or even a scarlet tanager may be all it takes to initiate a lifelong curiosity and interest in birds.

Songbirds

When spring arrives, it's the early birder who catches the worm. Migrating birds flap their wings all night to get from there to here, and morning is when they've settled down for a good meal. Think of it as breakfast with the birds! Even if you can't rustle your child—or yourself—from sleep at sunrise, you can try later; but by lunchtime, activity dwindles as many birds take to their siestas. The same is true during fall migration, although birds are easier to find in spring because there's still little leaf cover, the birds are more vividly plumed, and they can be heard singing their hearts out in search of mates.

Once you're out there, teach your kids to "pisch." Have them put their lips together and take a deep breath. As they let their breath out through slightly opened lips, they should make a "p-sh-sh-sh" sound. They should repeat this exercise several times and then wait. If nothing happens, they should try several times more, and then move on to new spot. All the while, listen for bird song. When you hear one that you recognize—a blue jay, for example—show your child a picture of it in your field guide to make it real, just in case you don't get a glimpse. Most of all, be quiet and move slowly, because most birds let you come only within 30–40 feet of them.

Millions of songbirds migrate through New York City, with some species staying for summer to breed. Within the mix are more than 200 species of songbirds, with warblers and flycatchers alone accounting for dozens and dozens of varieties—enough to make even a seasoned birder's head spin. Many of these birds are small—about 4–5 inches long—and are difficult for kids to see and identify. If you have a real birder in your midst and want to do some "warbling," consult a field guide to identify the many species you may encounter. In the meantime, stick with more obvious birds, including these favorite species (in addition to those identified above, under "Backyard Birds of Winter").

American crow—There's no mistaking these big black birds with their loud "caw-caw-caw" calls. In size, they are second only to the raven, the country's largest songbird and one that figures prominently in Native American culture as "the great trickster." Intelligent and sociable, crows were once numerous in New York City, but have decreased significantly because of the West Nile virus.

American goldfinch—These small, bright yellow birds with black caps and wings have a playful way of flying in waves. Sociable birds, they travel in flocks and are sometimes referred to as wild canaries because of their singing. Look for them during the day in weedy fields, forest edges, gardens, and any place where thistle grows—their favorite seed.

American robin—Robins are often celebrated as harbingers of spring, yet you might spot these orange-breasted birds in the dead of winter. These "winter robins" are actually northerners in search of warmer weather. Our robins have migrated south. When spring arrives and we hear lots of robin song, these are our robins, having returned home to breed.

Baltimore oriole—These pretty orange and black birds make the coolest nests, pouches that hang from tree limbs. After they leave Mexico in spring, they sometimes hang out in our open woods, singing their flutelike song all summer long. A bit smaller than robins, their name refers to the male's colors, which resemble those in the coat of arms of Lord Baltimore, who headed Maryland when it was a colony.

Cedar waxwing—These elegant berry eaters sometimes line up in a row and pass a morsel from bird to bird, down the line, until one of them eats it. A soft, beautiful brown with yellow on their bellies and with gray backs, males and females look alike, and have neat crests, long wings, and black face masks.

Eastern bluebird—New York's state bird, the bluebird is a cutie with blue wings, back, head, and tail, brown chest, and white belly. But it's pretty rare in the city, preferring quiet, leafy, rural areas; although bluebirds have been spotted in a meadow behind the historic mansion in Van Cortlandt Park. Even statewide, it is listed as a species of special concern, its numbers dwindling because of decreased farmland, loss of nesting sites, and competition from aggressive house sparrows and starlings.

Eastern towhee—You'll often see this bird—with its reddish eyes, black head, neck, and shoulders, white chest, and rusty wings and sides—at the top of a tree. Its song is distinctive.

It sounds like it's saying "Drink your tea," dipping down for a low note on "your" then soaring for a high note on "tea." If you get your kids reciting this silly singsong phrase first, they'll find it easy to recognize in the woods. Towhees like to scratch around in the brush, like chickens, for seeds and insects. Be especially quiet, because they're easily spooked.

Gray catbird—If you hear something like meowing in the woods, it's probably not a stray cat, but a catbird making its signature sound. Slate gray with black caps and long tails that they like to flick, catbirds like messy places—tangled shrubs and thickets, where they forage for a variety of food ranging from berries to insects. These 8-inch migrants seek high perches—hence the saying, "Sitting in the catbird's seat"—meaning to have the advantage in a situation.

Monk parakeet—From the campus of Brooklyn College, to the Green-Wood Cemetery, to Marine Park, tropical parrots are squawking their hearts out throughout Brooklyn. Monk parakeets were first spotted in the late 1960s—some say a combination of released pets and imports that escaped from broken crates at Kennedy Airport. Although natives of South American mountains, they don't try to migrate in winter, but live here year round by building huge, nicely insulated stick compounds. (They're the only parrots that don't nest in cavities.) Mostly chartreuse, they have gray necks and faces that resemble religious attire, hence their name. A huge nest sits atop the entrance gate to the Green-Wood Cemetery at 5th Avenue and 25th Street in Brooklyn. A few have also been spotted in Pelham Bay Park and on City Island in the Bronx.

Purple martin—After leaving Brazil in spring, these shiny, eggplant-colored swallows are totally dependent on humans for nesting sites, usually little wooden houses with small openings. That's because way back when, some say, Native Americans attracted them with hollowed-out gourds, which the birds liked. Colonists adopted this tradition, so that today, Purple martins will nest only in gourds and martin houses, and actually like the company of humans. The best place to see them—just before dusk in late June and July, when the babies poke their heads out of the holes—is at Lemon Creek Park on Staten Island, where a colony has existed since 1953.

Red-winged blackbird—Beginning in late February, these marsh lovers leave their winter homes in places as far south as Costa Rica and return here. When they spread their black wings, a brilliant red patch edged with yellow is revealed. Look for them perched on cattails or other tall plants, the males puffing up their impressive shoulders to attract mates.

Rose-breasted grosbeak—These handsome birds have chunky, pinkish bills and black-and-white bodies with rose-colored, triangular breast patches. They fly here from Mexico and South America in April and May. The male helps incubate the eggs, all the while sweetly singing a song, a somewhat hazardous endeavor when predators are near.

Scarlet tanager—Aptly called "flame of spring," the scarlet tanager arrives from South America dressed in crimson with contrasting black wings. Look for him in the tree-top canopy (especially oaks) in spring. Once fall arrives and he's done impressing females, Mr. Fancy Pants molts his royal robe, taking on the dull olive green frock of the female.

Tree swallow—Flocks of these adorable flyers with teeny-weeny beaks, glossy green-blue coats, and white bellies fly into town beginning in March. A great place for your children to see them up close (they don't mind people watching them) is the Jamaica Bay Wildlife Refuge, which has lots of tree swallow nest boxes for their convenience. Watch them veer this way and that way through the air, gobbling flying insects on the wing.

Almost everyone has a childhood memory of keeping a baby bird in a shoebox, feeding it mushy cereal (the worse possible food for fledglings) and trying to nurse it back to health. But how many of these little creatures actually survive to fly the coop? Not many; and that's because birds are, after all, wild animals that have a better chance at survival if left alone in the outdoors. And those that need a little extra care are best left in the hands of people trained in the art of bird rearing. If you do find a bird in need, however, there are some things you can do to help it along.

If the bird doesn't have feathers, it's a hatchling that should be returned promptly to its nest. If you can't find the nest, make one. Use anything that has drainage—a plastic berry box or any plastic container with holes punched into the bottom—and cushion the bottom with nonabsorbent material like straw, grass, and dry leaves. Secure the nest (try nails or duct tape) as high as you can on the shady side of a tree, and gently place the bird inside. The worried parents will be grateful. Just like people, birds have a strong urge to nurture their young and will likely be listening for the chirp of their lost babe. If the parents don't return within an hour (and they won't if you stick around), call a licensed wildlife rehabilitator.

If the bird is feathered, can hop, and is obviously not injured or in danger, leave it alone and wait for the parents to return. You may want to place the bird in a shrub or tree to keep it safe from stray cats. Just because a bird is on the ground, doesn't mean it needs to be saved. It's a fledgling, and has been given the go ahead to leave the nest—and it may simply have landed on the ground while practicing to fly. If its parents do not return after two hours (leave the area so they'll feel safe to return), call a licensed wildlife rehabilitator. Sometimes it's even safe to leave the fledgling alone for a day or two; birds have territories and parents will often continue searching for a couple of days.

If the bird is injured, immediately call a licensed wildlife rehabilitator. These are trained individuals legally permitted to care for wild birds. You'll be asked to refrain from feeding the bird, put it in a warm, comfortable box (you may want to try a heating pad on a low setting) and place the box in a quiet area. Stress and handling limit the bird's chances for survival, so avoid peeking. And remember, adult birds will not abandon offspring that have been touched by human hands. That's just an old wives' tale, something probably made up by parents to keep their kids from bringing home every injured bird. Most birds have a poor sense of smell and won't know you've intervened at all.

To obtain help for an injured bird—or other animal, call the Staten Island–based United for Wildlife Rehabilitation and Education Center, at 718-979-5704. The Special Licenses Unit of the New York State Department of Conservation's Division of Fish, Wildlife and Marine Resources also maintains an updated list of wildlife rehabilitators in the five boroughs, as well as information on becoming a wildlife rehabilitator. For information, call 718-482-4900. You may also view a list of licensed wildlife rehabilitators on the Web site of the New York State Wildlife Rehabilitation Council, at www.nyswrc.org/rehabbers.html. You can also find information on locating a rehabilitator at www.nwrawildlife.org/page.asp?id=111.

If you find an injured bird in any New York City park, call the Urban Park Rangers at 311.

Places to See Migrating Songbirds

It's a good idea to pick up a map, usually available at a park's nature center or visitor center, to help orient you. Some maps are available online at the city Parks Department website, www.nycgovparks.org, and that of Partnerships for Parks, www.itsmypark.org. Also, if a ranger is on duty, ask where the best places to see birds are.

Van Cortlandt Park and **Pelham Bay Park** (Bronx)—Walk virtually any trail for sightings of spring and fall migrants.

The Green-Wood Cemetery (Brooklyn)—If your kids aren't creeped out by roaming through a cemetery, they can enjoy some great birding (and history) here, from 8 AM to 4 PM. A member of the Audubon Cooperative Sanctuary System, Green-Wood wants you to visit; and the guard at the gate (25th Street at 5th Avenue) will even give you a free map and point out the dozens of monk parakeets flying into and out of the huge nest atop the main gate. Check the ponds for kingfishers and waterfowl.

Prospect Park (Brooklyn)—During the first two weeks of May, birding is superb in Prospect Park. Some good spots include the Ravine, Midwood, Breeze Hill and North Lullwater, Lookout Hill (the highest spot in the park), and Rick's Place. Pick up a map of bird-watching sites at the Prospect Park Audubon Center, or online at www.prospectparkaudubon.org/map.html.

Central Park (Manhattan)—Three good spots for birding are the Ramble in midpark, the Ravine, above 96th Street, and the North Woods in the upper park. You might also look for red-winged blackbirds around Turtle Pond, next to Belvedere Castle.

Inwood Hill Park (Manhattan)—Walk west from the nature center to the hilly woods and look around for birds. The area known as the Clove is especially good.

Clove Lakes Park (Staten Island)—Enter at Clove Road and Cheshire Place, cross the stone bridge from the parking lot, climb the hill, and meander around the wooded hillsides to see a variety of songbirds.

Forest Park (Queens)—The Yellow Trail, accessible from Park Lane South and Grosvenor Road, wraps around a pond and is a good place to see birds, particularly in spring, before what's called the Watering Hole dries up.

Fort Tilden (Queens)—Walk along the Back Fort Trail, which begins west of the visitor center, just past the Rockaway Artist Alliance building. There's a tick notification sign there. Check trees and brush for songbirds, including eastern towhees, Carolina wrens, warblers, cowbirds, thrushes, and others.

Jamaica Bay Wildlife Refuge (Queens)—This is a superb place to see birds year round. Scout through the North and South Gardens for olive-sided flycatchers, blue grosbeaks, and prothonotary, hooded, Kentucky, worm-eating, and mourning warblers—among many others.

Raptors

With their lethal beaks, dangerously sharp talons, and strong bodies, raptors readily capture the imagination. These are fearsome predators, as they ambush a mouse or bird, and majestic in their command of the skies. Unlike delicately built smaller birds that nosh on seeds, berries, and insects, owls, hawks, falcons, eagles, ospreys, harriers, and vultures are all meat eaters. (Vultures, however, don't hunt; they nibble on the dead.) And they don't shop at the butcher—they hunt, some by night, others by day, seizing unsuspecting mice, birds, reptiles, fish, and other animals for breakfast, lunch, and dinner. Such is the chain of life.

While few kids will witness a raptor actually tearing into its lunch (although it does happen), there are many places in New York City where families can see birds of prey—at organized events and in the wild. From the annual hawk migration in the fall—when hawks may be seen flying south for the winter—to raptor programs and live demonstrations offered by the Urban Park Rangers and other groups, families can learn what it means to be a raptor and why these federally protected birds are critical to our environment. (For one thing, they keep rodent populations in check, while vultures—the world's cleanup crew—eat carcasses before they rot and cause disease.) Even raptors like peregrine falcons and American bald eagles, whose survival was threatened not too long ago, are making a comeback—with peregrines nesting on bridges and building ledges, and eagles visiting the New York City area by hitching rides on ice floes floating down the Hudson River each winter.

Because they eat meat, raptors are built differently from songbirds, shore birds, and ducks. They have muscular legs and feet, with sharp, hooked claws (talons) to catch, grasp, and carry their prey. Their curved beaks are great for tearing flesh; and their long, broad wings let them soar effortlessly on air currents while hunting, helping them conserve energy that would otherwise be wasted flapping their wings. They focus their large eyes quickly and are said to see eight times better than humans, able to spy a juicy grasshopper from many dozens of feet away; owls have even better eyesight than diurnal (or day hunting) raptors, which allows them to hunt deftly in the dark.

Owls

If you've ever walked on a park path or city hiking trail, you may have brushed by an owl. By day, they roost in trees that are surprisingly close to passing people. At night, these nocturnal raptors soar into the darkness, using their amazing senses to hunt for delectable rodents and, sometimes, other birds.

Owls have sharp, hooked bills and talons, excellent night vision, and soundless flight thanks to fringes on the edges of their feathers, which allow air to pass through, eliminating any flapping sound. And they have shorter wings than most raptors, because they don't hunt from great heights. Their eyes are fixed in their sockets, but specialized neck muscles allow them to turn their heads so that they can see through a 270-degree panorama. They also have asymmetrical ears—slits on the sides of their heads, one lower than the other—which allow them to pinpoint sounds. Owls also have flat faces and facial disks that help funnel sounds to their ears, which can detect the sound of a mouse stepping on a twig up to 75 feet away. And those cute, feathery things on top of the heads of some species of owls are not ears, but "ear tufts," used to attract mates or sometimes just to look fierce.

Spotting owls takes a little knowledge, some detective work, and a lot of patience. It's mostly a winter activity (some owls are only winter residents), so the amount of time you and your children want to spend scouting trees may be limited. The best way to get started is by going out with a naturalist or ranger who knows where owls hang out. Each winter, the Urban Park Rangers offer free owl walks and even host night walks in the southern part of Central Park to see, or at least hear, screech owls—whose call is incredibly enthralling when heard in the dark. The rangers also offer owl workshops, during which kids can learn about the variety of city owls and dissect owl pellets.

Owls cough up pellets, which are something like the hairballs that cats spit up. If you pick through a pellet, you'll find fur or feathers and bones from the rodents and birds that owls eat whole. Owls can digest the flesh, which is discharged as excrement, or "whitewash." The remainder of the prey is regurgitated in a neat little package. By probing a pellet, kids can find out just what an owl has eaten for dinner. You can also try this at home by ordering sterilized owls pellets from Carolina Biological Supply Company, at www.carolina.org, or by calling 1-800- 334-5551.

If you want to look for your very own pellets, hit the woods and look under evergreen trees. The tree's bark is sometimes marked by whitewash that has dripped down from the branches above. Don't be fooled by tree sap, which is also whitish. Owl whitewash is very white, like plaster. If you find it, have your children look up into the tree, sorting through the branches with their eyes. Owls are very still and may be very high up or just a few feet from you. If you see an owl and it's just before dusk, wait for the "fly out," just as the little girl does in the children's classic, *Owl Moon*. That's the time when owls leave their roosts to hunt for food. And if you see anyone else walking around with binoculars, ask if they've seen any owls.

Owls You May See in New York City

Barn owl—These 15–20 inch owls are unique among their kind, with sweet, white, heart-shaped faces outlined in brown, dark eyes, white breasts with buff, yellow, and tawny shadings, and no ear tufts. I like to call them "moon-faces." They don't hoot or whinny, but hiss and shriek like fighting cats. Historically, they've nested in barns and silos; but in New York City they often raise their young in nesting boxes set up by park rangers.

Eastern screech owl—You have a better chance of hearing these small owls at night than seeing them during the day, when they stay inside tree holes or blend in with tree bark. Unlike the great horned owl's familiar "whoo-whoo," the screech owl's cry is a couple of descending whinnies, followed by a low trill—something like this: "wheeeee, wheeeee, quo-hohoho." In 2001, the Parks Department released 18 eastern screech owls into Central Park (the last had been previously recorded in 1955), as part of Project X, a program to restore native species to city parks.

Great horned owl—This is the big daddy of owls, an impressively large (18–24 inches

Great horned owls are known for their lage size and prominent ear tufts, and boast a wingspan of more than 4 feet.

tall), fierce hunter with a wingspan of 4.5 feet. It will grab an animal 2–3 times larger than itself and even eats smaller owls. Brownish-gray and with large yellow eyes, intense looking creature had long been the official rep for deliciously greasy Wise potato chips. (Now they use just the eye.) When kids say "who-who-whooo," they are imitating the great horned owl, which nests in the city between February and April.

Long-eared owl—These winter residents drew quite a crowd in the winter of 2003–2004, when five were discovered roosting in a conifer a stone's throw from Central Park's Bow Bridge. These secretive birds are similar to great horned owls, but are smaller (13–15 inches) and more slender, with ear tufts that are closer together.

Northern saw-whet owl—These tiny winter residents (7 inches) are the smallest owl in the East and are fairly approachable, as they roost low in evergreens. They do not have ear tufts, are reddish-brown with white vertical streaks on their foreheads, and appear roundish as they hunker down on their branches. They toot rather than hoot.

Some Good Places to Look for Owls

Kazimiroff Nature Trail, Pelham Bay Park (Bronx)—Northern saw-whet owls sometimes winter in the trail's young pine forest, while great horned owls frequent more mature pines or perch atop tall snags, watching for prey. The cavity of an old northern red oak, halfway along the trail, has served as a great horned owl's nest.

Central Park (Manhattan)—Wintering long-eared owls have roosted near Bow Bridge, while screech owls are sometimes heard in the park at dusk. A barn owl recently roosted near the Ross Pinetum.

Inwood Hill Nature Trail, Inwood Hill Park (Manhattan)—Follow the trail up into the higher elevations and look for small stands of

The Jamaica Bay Wildlife Refuge has one of the densest populations of nestng barn owls in the state.

Don Riepe

white pines that have been host to screech and long-eared owls.

Owls have also been seen in Van Cortlandt Park (Bronx), Blue Heron Park (Staten Island), Jamaica Bay Wildlife Refuge (Queens), Alley Pond Park (Queens), Prospect Park (Brooklyn), and even the Brooklyn Botanic Garden. When in the woods, check pines, cedars, and other evergreens.

Diurnal Raptors: Hawks, Falcons, and Eagles

Unlike most owls, hawks, falcons, and eagles are diurnal raptors, meaning that they hunt during the day. As with owls, the males tend to be smaller than the females. Some say it's because the females need to be big and bad to ward off intruders to their nests. Each of these raptors is outfitted differently. Some soar high and are easy to spot, while others hover low. Some eat fish, others prefer rodents and birds. With slender bodies and long, narrow, pointed wings designed for speed, falcons are the fastest of all raptors, clocking speeds of more than 100 miles per hour. Peregrines can cruise at 55 miles an hour and dive bomb their prey at up to 200 miles an hour. In most cases, diurnal raptors have a bony ridge over their eyes to shield them from the sun while hunting.

In the fall, raptors migrate as far away as South America, making the long-distance trip by riding on thermals (updrafts of warm air) to cut down on physical effort. (On a hot summer day, show your kids the wiggly air that emanates from a car's hood or a hot open parking lot. That's a thermal.) Unlike songbirds, raptors migrate during the day—lucky for us! So, if you're in the right place at the right time, your children may see dozens, even hundreds, of hawks, eagles, ospreys, and falcons heading to warmer climates. Other raptors are year-round New York City residents, particularly the red-tailed hawk, which nests in several of our parks and even on a building in Manhattan.

Hawks and Other Diurnal Raptors You're Likely to See

American bald eagle—When chosen as our national bird in 1782, there were plenty of bald eagles around New York. By the 1960s only one active nest remained in the entire state. Since then, DDT has been outlawed, the Hudson River has been cleaned up, and forested areas along the river are being restored with the hope that someday they will once again support eagle populations. These huge, glorious white-headed raptors (up to 3 feet long, with a 6–7.5 foot wing span) have been seen flying over Central Park and hitching rides on ice floes headed down the Hudson, hunting for fish over the sides. The Parks Department began hand rearing and releasing eaglets (who don't get white heads until they're 4 years old) in Inwood Hill Park in 2002. Some of the fledglings have been seen north of the city; but the goal is for them to return to Inwood to nest and breed, as they did in the old days.

American kestrel—The American Kestrel (8–12 inches long) is a pretty, petite falcon with large, dark eyes, a small beak, and black smudges running down its white face, which act like a football player's cheek black—cutting down the sun's glare so it can hunt more productively. It is super fast in flight, zeroing in on big insects, small mammals, and is quick enough to nab even small birds. Females lack the male's blue-stone-colored wings, but both have rusty tails and backs and sound a shrill "killy-killy-killy." Look for them throughout the year.

Broad-winged hawk—These long-distance migrants can be seen during their fall migration soaring on warm air currents as they fly as far south as South America. Look for a black-and-white-banded tail on an otherwise brownish bird that is about 16 inches long with a 3-foot wing span.

Cooper's hawk—This woodland hawk's rounded tail is long in proportion to its wings and helps it steer through the trees for prey. At 14–20 inches, it is larger than the square-tailed, similarly colored sharp-shinned hawk and sports a rusty, streaked breast and a grayish-blue back. Juveniles have yellow eyes; adults, red.

Merlin—Merlins look like mini-Peregrine Falcons, but with strongly barred tails. These dark-colored, 12-inch-long raptors don't hover for food, but simply pluck insects, bats, and birds from the air with their talons.

Northern harrier—These long, slender raptors—also called marsh hawks—hunt more by sound than do other raptors and, like owls, have a facial disk that directs sounds to their ears. Unlike most raptors, they fly close to the ground (except during migration), usually over fields and marshes, looking for birds, rodents, and amphibians. The males are pale gray; the females, brown—and both have the signature white rump patch. They nest in the city but are a threatened species in New York State.

Fledglings of our national bird have been released in Inwood Hill Park. They don't achieve their white heads until they reach 4 or 5 years of age.

The Inwood Hill Park Overlook, just above the Hudson, offers great opportunities for seeing migrating hawks in fall.

Osprey—These eaglelike fish hawks (2 feet long, with a 5-6 foot wing span) like to be near water because they just love fish. When it spots a fish, an osprey dives from as high as 100 feet, plunging into the water and then carrying away its catch (head facing forward to reduce wind resistance) grasped in its talons. These raptors are white and dark brown, with white heads smudged with horizontal, dark-brown cheek stripes.

Peregrine falcon—This falcon looks like it's wearing a black helmet. One of the fastest birds in the world, it dives as fast as 200 miles an hour, whacking its prey senseless with razor-sharp talons. By the 1960s, there were no breeding pairs of peregrine falcons left in the United States. But thanks to DDT prohibition, stricter laws, and reintroduction (by the Peregrine Fund at Cornell University), these 17–20-inch slate-colored raptors with black sideburns have made a comeback, particularly in New York City, which hosts the world's largest population of nesting Peregrines—about 16 breeding pairs. Peregrines mate for life and have adapted to the city by building nests on bridges and high-rise ledges and feasting on the city's pigeons.

Red-shouldered hawk—These hawks do indeed have red shoulders that are difficult to see in flight. Look instead for red, white, and brown-barred underparts, a banded tail, and a translucent area near the wingtips. These big hawks are more colorful than red-tails and tend to frequent woodlands near swampy areas, feeding on rodents, reptiles, and amphibians. They build their nests only halfway up a tree, while red-tails prefer to be higher up.

Red-tailed hawk—This biggie is the one you'll most likely see perched in treetops or circling overhead, emitting a loud, hoarse scream. Beginning in March, red-tails—believed to mate for life—nest in many of our parks, including Central and Prospect Parks (about 35 feet up in the fork of a tree). There's even a pair on one Fifth Avenue balcony—Pale Male and his mate. The two sexes look alike, with red tails, plumb brown-and-white bodies, and dark bands of spots on their bellies.

Places to Watch the Hawk Migration

Thomas Pell Wildlife Sanctuary, Pelham Bay Park (Bronx)—Ospreys are common in the sanctuary's wetlands. Look for these birds of prey dive-bombing into the water.

Nethermead and the **Audubon Center, Prospect Park** (Brooklyn)—The open area of the Nethermead, near Terrace Bridge, is a good place to scan the skies for red-tailed hawks, which also like to perch in the trees across from the Audubon Center.

Belvedere Castle, Central Park (Manhattan)—From mid-September through early November, the Urban Park Rangers host an annual watch at the castle (midpark at 79th Street, and the second highest point in the park), inviting families to scan the skies for passing hawks. On a clear day with northwest winds, viewers may even see hundreds of broad-winged hawks.

The Overlook, Inwood Hill Park (Manhattan)—Follow the park trail to the Overlook, just above the Hudson River, which offers great opportunities for seeing migrating hawks in fall. There are no buildings in sight, just the majestic river, big skies, the lovely Palisades across the way, and plenty of soaring hawks.

Battery Harris East, Fort Tilden (Queens)—Between mid-September and late October, this former military base is one of the best places to watch hawks flying south along the Atlantic Coast. Spectators gather atop this old World War I armament located along the Back Fort Trail, which has been refashioned into an observation platform (with lots of stairs to climb). The New York City Audubon Society recommends visiting on a clear to partly cloudy day with northwest winds between 10 and 20 miles per hour. The field behind the visitor center is also a good place from which to scan the sky for hawks.

Moses Mountain, High Rock Park (Staten Island)—Take the Greenbelt's Yellow Trail to the top of the mountain for spectacular views and hawk watching. Or join Protectors of Pine Oak Woods, Staten Island's oldest environmental group, for a family-friendly guided hike to the top from mid-September to late October.

Raptor Viewing Events

Prospect Park Audubon Center (Brooklyn) (near the Lincoln Road entrance to the park)—In September, the center hosts a Hawk Family Weekend, a two-day event with live raptor demonstrations, an early-morning hawk watch from the center's observation deck, hawk crafts, stories, and a hawk-calling contest.

East Meadow, Central Park (Manhattan) (at 97th Street and Fifth Avenue)—Every October, the Urban Park Rangers host a free Falconry Extravaganza, an afternoon-long event featuring live raptors, including hawks, owls, and eagles, and flight demonstrations showcasing the birds' skills and speed. There's also information on the history, ecology, and conservation of raptors as well as on the Rangers' own wildlife-management projects in the city's parks.

Inwood Hill Park (Manhattan)—Most people never get within 50 feet of a baby bald eagle, but from June through September you may visit City Parks Department Falconer Tom Cullen and his eaglets at a hack site (an artificial nest and release tower) in the park. If the eaglets have fledged (all part of the department's species reintroduction program), Cullen may be out tracking them. If you plan to visit, call Inwood Hill Park at 212-304-2365 to see if Cullen is around—or just take your chances.

Model Boat Pond, Central Park (Manhattan) (on the East Side, between 72nd and 75th Streets)—On the west side of the pond is a telescope fixed on a pair of red-tailed hawks that nest between February and June above the 12th-floor window of a Fifth Avenue apartment building overlooking the park. The scope belongs to photographer and hawk watcher Lincoln Karim, who welcomes passers-by to take a peek. (Or bring your own binoculars.) The male hawk—named Pale Male by the park's hawk watchers—arrived in 1991 and quickly seduced a mate, First Love, with a dead pigeon. Together they built the first hawk's next constructed on a manmade structure in New York City. The pair successfully fledged young in 1995. First Love died from eating a poisoned pigeon, but Pale Male returns to the same place every year to raise a family with his current partner, Lola. In December 2004 the building's co-op board had the nest, and the spikes holding it in place, removed. Protestors and plenty media pressured the board to reinstall the spikes so the hawks may continue nesting there.

Karim's website, www.palemale.com, is filled with photos and is a great way to introduce your kids to New York's hawks. The website's up-to-date information on the red-tailed couple's domestic life will capture your children's imaginations and allow them to develop a relationship with these birds.

Floyd Bennett Field (Brooklyn)—Scan the skies above the park for wintering hawks such as red-tailed hawks, Cooper's hawks, sharp-shinned hawks, American kestrels, merlins, and northern harriers. Peregrine falcons nest on one of the towers of the nearby Marine Parkway Bridge and occasionally make hunting forays into the park.

Organizations That Welcome Young Birders

The Urban Park Rangers offer free family-friendly bird walks throughout the year. To get a copy of their seasonal calendar, call 311 and ask for the Rangers, or fill out the form at www.nycgovparks.org/email_forms/Rangers/mail_form.html.

During migrations, the Bronx Zoo opens its gates at 7:30 AM for free bird walks along the Bronx River, near the Zoo's Bronx Parkway entrance. Kids are welcome, if they can get going that early! To register, call 718-220-5095. For additional information, you may also call 718-220-5131.

Each year, the New York Botanical Garden (Bronx) offers 90-minute bird walks on specific Saturdays—except during January, February, and August. While anyone may participate, older children who can be quiet and patient are preferred. A grounds fee is required. For more information, call 718-817-8700 or go to www.nybg.org.

New York City Audubon (212-691-7483) welcomes families on their bird walks to places like Central Park and Jamaica Bay Wildlife Refuge, among others. Some are free; others cost a nominal fee. Families can also learn all about long-legged waders during NYC Audubon's journey to Heron Island on "A Boat Cruise Along the East River," with stops to view rookeries on some of the city's island. NYC Audubon also publishes *Look Around New York City*, a publication for kids interested in birds. It is available in printed form or may be downloaded from their website at www.nycaudubon.org/kids/lanyc.

On weekends, families may enjoy free afternoon bird walks provided by the Prospect Park Audubon Center (Brooklyn). Field guides and binoculars are available. Call 718-287-3400 or go to www.prospectpark.org.

During the spring migration, the Battery Park City Parks Conservancy (Manhattan) offers free birding for all ages at Robert F. Wagner Jr. Park along the Hudson River. Binoculars and field guides are available for borrowing. Call 212-267-9700 or go to

What Makes a Bird a Bird?

Birds have one thing that no other animals have—feathers! Feathers help them stay warm and are used to attract mates. Birds molt their feathers annually, replacing them with brand new ones, just as you and your children go shopping for fresh sets of duds at the beginning of the school year.

Feathers also help most birds to fly, although some—like ostriches and penguins, have big or bulbous bodies that make it difficult for them to get off the ground. Most birds, however, are built for flight, and wings are only part of it. These warm-blooded creatures have streamlined bodies and their hollow bones make them as light as can be.

And all birds lay hard-shelled eggs. Unlike humans, who bear live young, birds incubate their eggs by sitting on them, keeping them warm until the chicks are ready to crack open the shells and come into the world. While growing inside their eggs, the little birds are able to breathe because the shells have microscopic pores that allow oxygen in and pass carbon dioxide out.

www.bpcparks.org.

During migrations, the Linnaean Society of New York (a natural history organization established in 1878) offers walks through Central Park (Manhattan) "For Birders of All Ages," but they start early—at 7:30 AM. For information, call 212-935-0273 or go to www.linnaeansociety.org.

Bette Midler's New York Restoration Project periodically offers free family-friendly bird walks in upper Manhattan parks like the new Swindler Cove Park on the Harlem River and Highbridge Park. Call 212-333-2552 or go to www.nyrp.org.

Most of the bird walks offered by National Park Service rangers and volunteers within the Gateway National Recreation Area (Queens, Brooklyn, and Staten Island) are geared toward adults, but kids can attend if they're able to withstand the concentration and patience needed to walk around with a bunch of adults. For a calendar of events, call 718-354-4606 or go to www.nps.gov/gate/pphtml/ events.html.

Find out where the birds are on one of the city's free bird walks.

When birds build nests they recycle materials like twigs, dried grass, string, lint, and even human hair.

The Alley Pond Environmental Center (Queens) offers bird walks for families. For information, call 718-229-4000, or go to www.alley pond.com.

The Queens County Bird Club welcomes nonmember families on their half-day trips at local places like Oakland Lake and Alley Pond Park. For information, go to www.qcbc.all.at or send an email to avian@nyc.rr.com.

The High Rock Environmental Center (Staten Island) offers free bird walks for kids 8 and older. For information, call 718-351-3450 or go to www.sigreenbelt.org.

The northeast chapter of the American Littoral Society offers free family-friendly shorebird and waterfowl walks, as well as a hawk watch, year-round. For a calendar of events, go to www.alsnyc.org or call 718-318-9344.

Migration is like that old vaudeville joke that kids just love: "I just flew in from South America, and boy, are my arms tired." Well, that's what birds do twice a year—make the trip away from and back to their homes or nesting grounds. It's an instinctual behavior that goes back millions of years, a timeless journey shared by mother birds, grandfather birds, great grandmother birds, and so on and so on.

Birds don't migrate because it's too cold for them; they migrate because they have to follow the food supply—otherwise they'll starve. Some species, like hummingbirds, dine on flower nectar, so they must go where flowers are in bloom—in winter that means tropical places like Central America. Other birds eat insects, so they travel where these creatures are active, usually where winters are mild. Although birds are well outfitted for the trip, it's a tiring and often dangerous one. There are storms and winds to endure, predators to dodge, and—for newbies—unfamiliar terrain to navigate.

Timing is everything. Explain to your child that just as we avoid traveling during a raging thunderstorm, birds will also sit out bad weather and cover greater distances during good weather and when there are favorable winds to help them along. Birds need hospitable places to rest and refuel; but many of these oases are, unfortunately, being developed for golf courses, vacation homes, and condominiums—resulting in fewer migrants surviving the flight.

Kids who are good with binoculars might see oodles of neotropical migrants (birds that winter way south and nest in temperate zones) stopping by or passing through their neighborhoods and parks. That's because we live within what is called the Atlantic Flyway (one of four major migratory routes in North America) and along the coast, which tends to have higher concentrations of migrants. Tell your youngsters that the flyway is simply a highway for birds. We can't see it, but birds can—navigating by the stars and geological features, and by using their inner compasses.

The spring migration generally begins in late February (with the increase in daylight hours) and continues through mid-June, with songbird migration hottest in May. The fall migration runs from September to October. For some species, New York is the final stop; for others it's a layover before they head farther south or north, depending on the season. Since there isn't a lot of green space for migrants to fan out throughout the city, birds tend to congregate in city parks and along shorelines, brightening the season, and our days, with their presence.

Ducks and geese also migrate, but in reverse—many Arctic species come here in winter (it's like South America to them) and return north in the spring to breed. Shore birds migrate pretty much when songbirds do, arriving at or passing through in early spring and leaving or passing through in early fall.

Not all birds migrate, however; and within certain species, some migrate and others do not. In fact, about 20 percent of the 650 bird species that nest in the United States and Canada don't migrate. Woodpeckers, for example, can pick hibernating insects out from under tree bark during winter; while other insect-eating birds switch to whatever food is available, including the dried tops of shrubs and flowers and the contents of backyard bird feeders.

A wonderful and evocative documentary to watch with your children is *Winged Migration*, available on DVD, which captures the journey of migrating birds in a way never before done, with astonishingly up-close shots of actual flights that will amaze kids.

NIGHTS ON THE TOWN

Camping Out

The tent is up and you and the kids are singing around a campfire, toasting marshmallows a perfect golden color outside, creamy inside. Darkness has crept in, but that doesn't stop you and the children from entering the nocturnal forest with only flashlights lighting the way. The youngsters are frightened by dead trees silhouetted against the midnight blue sky, but not scared enough to turn back and retreat into their sleeping bags.

It's a beautiful night—memorable and made all the lovelier because you are camping in what for many urbanites is their own backyard, a New York City park. The campsite is private and spacious (the public has left for the day), far from playgrounds and baseball fields, in a place where woods, wildflowers, and ponds rule. You're the first on your block to give urban camping a try and it opens your eyes to just how much nature thrives so close to your home.

If the woods give you the willies, maybe you and your kids are better suited to a snooze at the zoo or aquarium, where the environment is controlled. You're still sleeping among the animals, but now you have a backstage pass to their private world.

Camping with the Urban Park Rangers

A nearly full moon casts some light on the night as families follow an Urban Park Ranger into the woods in search of screech owls. It may come as a surprise, but these hard-to-spot nocturnal creatures haunt the fragment of Manhattan forest in Inwood Hill Park. After the ranger plays several minutes of a recorded owl call—ascending whinnies followed by a tremolo that sound more turkey than owl— something in the distance answers. Everyone walks silently toward the sound and the

recording is repeated. But this time the wait is short, as the unmistakable call of an actual screech owl cuts through the night. Moments later, two owls fly out of the woods and land on a nearby branch. Disbelief and then wonder permeate the air, and the experience is almost religious. These owls are not characters in some Discovery Channel program; they live among us in skyscraper-stacked Manhattan and seeing them in their natural habitat is nothing short of glorious.

While the Urban Park Rangers can't guarantee an experience like this, you certainly will see New York City in a new light if you join them on one of their family camping programs. Activities may include stargazing, orienteering, fishing, campfires, bird watching, nocturnal walks, storytelling, and nature crafts—with the highlight, of course, sleeping safely inside your sleeping bag and zipped up in your tent under the watchful eyes of the rangers.

Each program and site is unique to the park hosting it, with no two experiences ever the same. One trip included a history buff and his daughter—both seemingly pulled from the pages of a textbook—dressed in period clothes and spending the night in a replica Revolutionary War–era tent. During another program, kids watched in amazement as a Ranger hand fed two abandoned baby sparrows. Nothing is canned or rehearsed; everything is spontaneous, as nature intended.

Individual camping in New York City parks is prohibited, so the Urban Park Rangers began leading supervised family camping trips in 2001 as part of their Explorer Programs. The trips are held in each borough and have included the Salt Marsh Nature Center in Brooklyn, Central Park in Manhattan, Van Cortlandt Park in the Bronx, Blue Heron Nature Center on Staten Island, and Alley Pond Park in Queens. Some sites are wooded, while others are grassy or on the grounds of historic houses. It may not be the Adirondacks; but for children this is simply camping, and it is great fun.

The one-night sleepover begins around dinnertime and concludes the following morning—and usually attracts families with kids between 6 and 11, although younger kids and teens join, too. Ranger activities bring everyone together beautifully, with kids from different city neighborhoods and backgrounds meeting on common turf.

If bringing young children, keep in mind that the evening is jam packed with activities, including night walks, and bedtime is around 11 PM, although you may bow out at any time. It's difficult to get to sleep early, however, because there are usually goings-on around the campsite. At bedtime, kids sometimes have difficulty winding down from the day and giggle late into the night. So don't plan on getting a great night's sleep—

This is the Bronx . . . not exactly wilderness, but the site is warm and inviting—and there are free marshmallows!

especially considering that campers are awakened early, usually between 6 and 7 AM, so that the site can be broken down. Campers are then free to go home or spend the day at the park on their own; although sometimes there is a planned activity, such as a bird walk.

Rangers provide the tents for free, but campers must bring their own food, flashlights, and other gear, including sleeping bags. These are great trips for beginners because campsites are usually near bathrooms. Rangers help with tent setup and occasionally do a snack-and-beverage run (civilization is usually just blocks away). If the campsite is a fair distance from the meeting place, the rangers generously truck all your gear to the site—as you would expect in New York City . . . right? There are no personal taxis, however, and campers must hoof it to the site; but it's not a long trek and the rangers often make a scavenger hunt out of it.

The program is very popular and space is limited. Reservations are required and must be made

only on a date and time specified by the rangers. Camping dates and reservation call-in times are listed in the rangers' free calendar of programs, which may be requested by dialing 311 and asking for the Urban Park Rangers, or going online at www.nycgovparks.org/sub_about/parks_divisions/urban_park_rangers/pd_ur.html. Here's a sampling of what you can expect:

Camping in Van Cortlandt Park, the Bronx

Using only a compass and mysterious clues, campers steer their way through the woods along the 1.4-mile Cass Gallagher Trail, named for a local environmentalist who helped save Van Cortlandt Park from destruction. This one-hour lesson in wilderness navigation without handy trail markers is called orienteering, a popular outdoor recreational and competitive sport since the 19th century that is as exciting and suspenseful as a treasure hunt.

Orienteering requires concentration, and some of the older kids eagerly try to guide themselves along the way, while smaller children are happy simply to hold the compass and pretend to go north or south. Everyone learns a bit about nature in the process, including how Native Americans carved the trunks of tulip trees to make canoes. Luckily, the Urban Park Rangers are leading the pack and nobody gets lost.

Tents are pitched near the park's historic Van Cortlandt House, the oldest house in the Bronx, built in 1748 and now a museum. Views from the tents include the gorgeous, old, fieldstone manor, but also bustling Broadway with its bright Burger King sign, a safe distance away. At night, floodlights outside the mansion stay on for security. Not exactly wilderness, but this is the Bronx, and the site is surprisingly quiet and comfortable.

At night there's a campfire and a night walk, with some stargazing with an amateur astronomer, who points out several constellations as well as the seven stars of the Big Dipper. During the 19th century, slaves called this asterism (which is part of a constellation) the Drinking Gourd and used it to guide them to freedom in the north.

Camping at the Salt Marsh Nature Center, Brooklyn

The nature center may be on busy Avenue U, but the campsite is out back, in a quiet horseshoe-shaped space with beautiful views of Gerritsen Creek, the surrounding salt marsh brilliant with seaside goldenrod, and the big sky.

After pitching tents, the rangers lead a 1-mile sunset walk through the marsh in search of shore birds and bats. They point out two grasses important to the marsh—salt-marsh cordgrass and salt-meadow cordgrass—and explain how they support a vast network of animal life. The salt-marsh cordgrass, with its lime-yellow tinge, is particularly pretty in the late sun. The rangers also point out tall, thick reeds known as phragmites, an invader that interferes with the growth of the much-needed salt-marsh grasses.

Black skimmers, funny-looking shore birds with very long, bright orange beaks, skim the water for food, using their long lower mandibles as scoops. Meadow crickets chirp, black-crowned night herons fly through the darkening air, and then dozens of bats appear overhead, snapping up insects. Sky is everywhere, interrupted only briefly by a few apartment buildings and allowing everyone to appreciate the rare beauty of the sun slipping beneath the city horizon.

Afterwards, kids make Popsicle stick photo frames for pictures of birds or animals cut from nature magazines, then move outside for stories and games. Everyone is asked to create a nature name, using the first letter of her or his first name as a starting point—names like Caleb-Caterpillar, Lucas-Lion, and Sharon-Shooting Star. There's a 5:45 AM wakeup to go on a sunrise bird walk, although some people stick to camp and watch bleary-eyed as the sun slowly rises from behind the marsh and the cormorants and herons begin foraging for their meals.

Camping on Central Park's Great Hill, Manhattan

Central Park is the one place you thought you would never be after dark; but there you are, without a lock and bolt on your tent, sleeping comfortably with your kids out in the open and after hours. With the Urban Park Rangers as sentries, it's a privilege to camp where no one you know has camped before; and the experience gives your children bragging rights when they get home. They can tell their friends that they spent the night in one of the world's most famous—and infamous—parks.

Central Park's Great Hill, the third highest point in the park, is a lovely place to pitch a tent, surrounded by tall trees and songbirds. The meeting site, the Dana Discovery Center, is a short walk from Fifth Avenue and 110th Street. At the Center, you and the kids pick up bamboo fishing poles and corn bait and fish in the 11-acre Harlem Meer, a catch-and-release site where more than 50,000 fish are stocked—bluegills, largemouth bass, chain pickerel, and catfish. Locals suggest crushing the corn before hooking, making it easier for the fish to grab onto.

After fishing comes an orienteering walk, following the rangers past noisy Lasker pool (an ice-skating rink in winter) and into the quiet woods. Compasses and clues help everyone get around among the trees, and ultimately to the campsite on the Great Hill. Along the way, rangers point out several wonders, beauties, and enjoyments of nature. You will also pass park landmarks, such as Huddlestone Arch, covered with yellow forsythia in spring. The bridge is supported by its own weight, constructed of stones ranging in weight from one to 20 tons. Next is the Loch, a meandering stream that feeds the Meer and leads into the Ravine, a stream valley with five manmade waterfalls created by various dams along the Loch. This is the park's rugged backcountry, the 90-acre North Woods, a deciduous forest of oak, hickory, maple, and ash trees that screens out the city's skyscrapers.

The trail gets a little steep, with some rocks to climb, and can be challenging for very young children. Rangers point out chunks of Manhattan schist (which comprises 90 percent of Manhattan's bedrock), the prickly fruit of a sweet gum tree, screech owl nesting boxes (the owls were reintroduced to the park in 1998), and a 19th-century fortress. Built in 1814, the Block House is the park's oldest structure, a vestige of the past, before Central Park was even created, when the high ground provided an important military vantage point.

The campsite on the Great Hill is spacious and grassy, and ringed by lush American and English elms. After dinner, volunteers from the Amateur Astronomers Association set up powerful telescopes, inviting campers to peer at the planet Venus and moon craters and explaining that the sky is pink because city lights are reflected by the clouds. Then there's story time and a ranger-led nocturnal walk along the park's dark pathways, a thrilling opportunity to spend some time with the night, before going to sleep in the great urban outdoors.

Camping in Inwood Hill Park, Manhattan

Inwood Hill Park may be in Manhattan, but there is little of the city about it once you get away from the playgrounds and head into the

The moon shines bright over Inwood Hill Park camping sites.

deep woods. This is real, dense forest with hills and rocks, Native American shelters, and glacial potholes, tall tulip trees and brilliant wildflowers—all of which make the walk to the campsite a wondrous event. There's even a gigantic erratic rock, said to be where Europeans and Native Americans finalized the sale of Manhattan to the white man.

The campsite itself is spectacular, more remote than some of the other Urban Park Ranger sites, a meadow filled with songbirds near an overlook with views of the Hudson River and New Jersey Palisades. There are no bathrooms here, but the Rangers make periodic shuttle trips via park van to the nature center down the hill.

The program begins with a great scavenger hunt that keeps kids busy during their trek up the hill, with rangers pointing out Manhattan's last remaining bit of natural salt marsh, interesting trees, and such avian marvels as a large red-tailed hawk nest. The trail leads to an area of huge rocks left behind by the Wisconsin ice sheet during the last Ice Age and later used as shelters by Native Americans. These inviting rocks are accessible, and kids love to climb them and explore.

The trail gradually ascends and eventually comes to an open area at the edge of the woods. This is one of the highest points in Manhattan, at about 260 feet. Tents are pitched in the wildflower-covered meadow, but it's the view that keeps everyone enraptured—especially at sunset, when the golden orb slips behind the trees of the New Jersey Palisades. In the fall, this is a great place to watch migrating hawks. Summer brings lots of butterflies.

After a picnic dinner, the rangers test all the moms, dads, and older kids on their knowledge of the night sky. Then it's off for a ranger-led nocturnal walk through the dark woods to listen for screech owls. Flashlights are turned off, an owl-call recording is played, and a response is heard in the distance. The soundtrack is played again, and two owls swoop

Sleeping with this icon just outside your tent is the ultimate childhood fantasy.

down onto a nearby branch. A flashlight is turned on, putting them in the spotlight for only a brief minute. But how wonderful a sight!

Camping with the Little Red Lighthouse, Manhattan

This outing is more than a camping trip. It's a chance to step into the pages of a classic children's book. If you don't remember *The Little Red Lighthouse and the Great Gray Bridge* from your own childhood, you've probably enjoyed reading it to your children. This 1942 tale features a seemingly outdated, proud little lighthouse that frets about being replaced by the new George Washington Bridge, but then proves itself indispensable. Sleeping with this icon just outside your tent is less a lesson in nature than other overnights, but it is the ultimate childhood fantasy.

Everyone meets at West 181st Street and Plaza Lafayette and then takes a longish walk downhill to Fort Washington Park and the site of the lighthouse on the shores of the Hudson River. There's a din from traffic on the nearby bridge, but it's tempered by the serenity of the river itself. Families sit on waterfront rocks and watch tugboats chug by on the river Native Americans called Mahicanituck. Kids watch the wakes left by passing boats and count the minutes lapsed between them.

When evening falls, campers roast marshmallows, make s'mores, and listen to a fireside reading of *The Little Red Lighthouse and the Great Gray Bridge*. Then there's a flashlight tour of the lighthouse, built in 1880 and originally sited at Sandy Hook, New Jersey. It was moved here in 1921 to help boats navigate along this part of the Hudson. The lighthouse interior is dark and flashlights are necessary for making your way up the tight spiral staircase to a short ladder climb, and then through a hatchway to the top. From the beacon, you can see the lights of midtown Manhattan and the Empire State Building to the south.

But there's nothing like sleeping alongside a river and waking up to the visual magnitude of the George Washington Bridge's huge shadow cast on the trees of the New Jersey Palisades across the way. The tents come down early, but there's always time to linger along the shore.

Note: If you don't want to camp out, but wish to tour the lighthouse, call the Urban Park rangers at 311 for a list of seasonal tour times. The Rangers also host a Little Red Lighthouse Festival in September, attended by thousands.

Camping in Alley Pond Park, Queens

Tents are pitched in a wooded area near the nature center, and despite the nearby playground and athletic fields, the backdrop is a forest brimming with wildlife. Birds cruise back and forth at dusk, joined by the buzzing song of leaflike katydids (in mid- to late summer) and the flight of little brown bats above a clearing.

Unlike the rangers' other camping programs, which are held periodically at different sites all over the city, camping at Alley Pond Park is a regular program during the summer on Friday and Saturday nights. It includes a barbequed dinner of hot dogs, hamburgers, and garden burgers, with s'mores for dessert, all provided by the rangers. Dinner is followed by a ranger-led night hike that often reveals a host of creatures big and small.

A ranger's sharp eyes spot a Fowler's toad crossing the path and everyone gets to touch its bumpy, cold skin. The walk continues in complete darkness, with flashlights turned on only occasionally to see what else might be near. There's some movement in a tree; two adorable young raccoons are nestled in its branches and peer back at their visitors. To hold the interest of children, the rangers constantly look under rocks and logs and rustle through leaves for anything that moves. In addition to a millipede and slug, three spotted salamanders, black with bright yellow spots, are discovered hiding under a rock.

After the walk, everyone hangs out for a while enjoying a seldom-experienced side of a city park, the darkness—when all is quiet except for the sounds of insects, and empty except for the urban campers. There's time to consider the night sky, play in the nearby playground, or hunker down in your tent until morning, when the wilderness becomes a city park again.

Camping in Blue Heron Park, Staten Island

Block after block of suburban subdivisions fade into memory upon entering the grounds of the Blue Heron Nature Center, fringed with brilliant wildflowers and tall trees. After camp is set up in a grassy area behind the center, there's an easy evening walk along the park's Meadow Loop. The rangers provide plenty of information that young minds can grasp, explaining how trail markers are read, pointing out the star-shaped leaves of sweet gum trees, and turning over logs to look for salamanders and other moisture-loving creatures.

During a stop at Blue Heron Pond, the rangers explain that this is a vernal pond, a depression in the ground left by glaciers and which is filled only when conditions are wet enough—usually in spring. Unlike ponds with underwater springs that provide a constant source of water, a vernal pond is fed by rain and snowmelt. It's a great place for breeding insects and amphibians, and indeed the banjo-string call of the green frog fills the air. At times along the trail, the bright windows of suburbia intrude on the woodsy landscape, but quickly disappear at the next bend thick with trees and white blooming wild roses.

Afterward, families make dream catchers, circular, weblike objects derived from Native American beliefs and said to ward off bad dreams. Dream catchers require some adult supervision and are a bit complicated for little hands. In the process, kids and parents learn about Staten Island's indigenous Lenni Lenapes, one of the first Native American people to come into contact with European settlers.

After scary stories in the outdoor gazebo, everyone calls it a night. In the morning, there's a short bird walk along Spring Pond Trail, with the rangers providing binoculars. Even without birds, the pond is a nice wake-up tonic, with water lily flowers, gorgeous blue lupines, and wild phlox in bloom.

Camping in High Rock Park, Staten Island

High Rock Park is very woodsy, with hills and ponds that make you feel as if you've driven many miles to camp for the night. The rangers guarantee this sense of seclusion by setting the tents in a small clearing a comfortable distance

Wake up to this friendly totem tree during the High Rock Park Campout.

from the nature center and bathrooms, with only a tree carved with a totem face as company.

At dusk, everyone takes a short walk through the woods to Loosestrife Swamp, named for the native swamp loosestrife (also called water willow) that grows within the wetlands and blooms pinkish-purple in summer. Nighttime sounds include the tapping of a red-bellied woodpecker and the quacks of mallards flying to a nearby kettle pond, which was created by blocks of ice left behind by retreating glaciers. Rangers engage kids with questions like, "Are salamanders reptiles or amphibians?" and provide tips on reading trail markers, recognizing poison ivy, and listening for screech owls.

Later, there's an astronomy lesson in the park parking lot, with the rangers putting the sky into context for the kids. Among other things, they explain that we see only one side of the moon, because the so-called "dark side" always faces away from Earth. And the amount of moon that we see on any given night depends on the position of the orbiting moon relative to Earth and the sun. The youngsters (and the grown-ups, too) learn that, in fact, the moon doesn't glow at all, but is illuminated by the sun.

Before bed, there is a campfire and s'mores and a group reading of a book about owls, with each camper reading a page out loud. On the walk back to camp, a salamander crawls across the path on his way to somewhere, too.

Camping at Willowbrook Park, Staten Island

This advanced campout is not about the rusticity of the site, but the journey getting there—a 2.5-mile nature walk starting in High Rock Park and ending in the picnic area of Willowbrook Park. The trek is best suited to kids aged eight years and older, but the rangers allow even young children to attempt the hike, arranging for a park van pick-up at midpoint for those who simply can't walk any farther. And you don't have to backpack your gear in, because you drop it off at the site before starting out on the trail.

Campers begin at the Yellow Trail in High Rock Park and soon connect with the White Trail, exploring a portion of Staten Island's 2,800-acre Greenbelt, an area four times as large as Central Park and featuring mostly natural areas, with some traditional parks. The walk initially crosses some streets, but then becomes relatively remote, with chance encounters with other people slim to none. The trail also becomes muddy and a bit overgrown at points, giving it a true wilderness feel. The moist woodlands are dotted with skunk cabbage and vernal ponds and filled with tall trees and wildflowers such as jewelweed (used by Native Americans to relieve poison ivy itch) and mugwort (used by Native Americans to ward off mosquitoes). Kids get to cross plenty

of wooden bridges over streams and there's even a ruin in the woods—a big, old chimney remaining from a family farm now nearly all reclaimed by nature.

It feels strange popping out of the woods into Willowbrook Park, with its mowed lawns, tidy pond with catch-and-release fishing, barbeques, and gorgeous carousel decorated with a variety of animals and Staten Island historic sites. But after exercising your child's inner Huck Finn through the woods, it's a relief to sit down at a picnic table, grill some dinner, and simply relax. The tents are pitched near the merry-go-round and comfort station, within sight of a residential street but fringed by woodlands with plenty of morning birdsong.

Roughing it at Floyd Bennett Field, Brooklyn

Now that you've set up your own tent and braved a night on the town in your sleeping bag, try something a little more primitive. At the southern end of Brooklyn, between Flatbush Avenue and Jamaica Bay, is an unlikely, yet singular sensation, a pristine overnight retreat that rivals anything outside the city.

Forget about being sandwiched between RVs and other campers. The two gorgeous sites at Floyd Bennett Field—Camp Goldenrod and Camp Tamarack—are private, spacious, clean, grassy expanses surrounded by trees, trees, and more trees. Here's a slice of Eden in the city, big-sky country where you can watch the sun set and the moon rise. And it's the only place in New York where you may legally sleep with your kids under the stars, totally on your own, with no rangers and no planned activities, other than those you come up with yourself.

The campsites are open year round (for the truly hardy!) and are managed by the Gateway National Recreation Area. A permit costs $50 for up to three nights of camping, by reservation only. The sites are located next to one another, with ample trees separating them; but it's rare that both sites are used at the same time. Camp Goldenrod accommodates up to 50 people, Camp Tamarack, 100; but most campers are single families and small groups. The site is all yours for the duration of your permit, whether you are one person or 100.

After picking up your permit when you arrive, you're on your own. That means no ranger chaperone or all-night watchman, no organized programs, and no expert naturalists to point out the poison ivy and migrating warblers. The rangers will provide a park map and suggest activities within Floyd Bennett Field and its environs, but a good time is totally up to you.

But don't worry, there's plenty to do. While you can't swim in Jamaica Bay, you may fish (see chapter 9, Goin' Fishing) and there's a

Floyd Bennett Field is the only place in the city where you can camp out on your own.

great place just across from the Camp Tamarack entrance—an old seaplane ramp and a beach from which you can do a little seining with your kids (see chapter 6, Exploring the Shore). At the other end of the park is an easy nature trail (see chapter 2, Nature Walks) with a bird blind for spying on birds and other critters lazing around the pond. There is also a large community garden open to the public, a great place to watch butterflies and bees. There's even a children's garden and periodic programs for kids.

In autumn, look to the sky for migrating hawks and monarch butterflies or snip a piece of oriental bittersweet (with red berries that pop through yellow shells) to decorate the camp picnic table. Owls can sometimes be seen in winter, while spring brings migrating songbirds and new plant growth. Summer can be hot and buggy (so don't forget mosquito repellent), but it's also a good time to walk (suitable for older kids) over the Gil Hodges/Marine Parkway Bridge and spend the day at sandy Jacob Riis Beach. Be mindful of ticks, too.

At night, the only sounds are made by crickets (truly!) and perhaps a passing plane en route to John F. Kennedy Airport across the bay. Kids love running around the campsite at night with flashlights, like giant fireflies, before gorging themselves on gooey, oh-so-bad-for-you-but-oh-so-good s'mores melted over a campfire. In addition to the on-site fire pit and grill, each campsite also features a shelter (in case of rain) and nearby bathrooms that are clean.

If the kids want a little break from nature, Hanger B to the right of the seaplane ramp has dozens of antique aircraft on view, many of them being lovingly restored by the Historic Aircraft Restoration Project. Members of this small group of volunteers are happy to greet impromptu visitors and give free tours during the day on Tuesdays, Thursdays, and Saturdays. National Park Service Rangers also give free tours of the old airport's control tower, New York City's first. Then there's

Brooklyn N-Trak, a local group of train hobbyists, who periodically set up their entire railroad world (usually on Sundays) in the Ryan Visitor Center, while a group of model airplane enthusiasts are out every day flying miniature planes and helicopters from one of Floyd Bennett Field's old runways.

But the real thrill is camping out on your own; and if you forget a few things, don't worry. It may feel like the great outdoors, but Kings Plaza mall is five minutes down the road. That's one of the strange perks of camping in the city. You can rough it or not, depending on your comfort level. And while safety has not been a problem at the Floyd Bennett sites, it's wise to carry a cell phone just in case you need to contact the park police, who are stationed nearby.

For a permit application, call Floyd Bennett Field at 718-338-3799 or stop by the Visitor Contact Station, the first building on your right after entering the park.

Sleeping with the Animals

It's one thing for your children to cuddle up for the night with stuffed kangaroos and sock monkeys and such, but how about giving them the chance to listen to the loud ranting of courting peacocks at night and hungry, barking sea lions in the morning. The Wildlife Conservation Society welcomes families to novel slumber parties at the Bronx Zoo, Central Park Zoo, and New York Aquarium—where you and your kids will have free rein while the doors are closed to the public, going

Getting close to the animals during the Bronx Zoo Overnight Safari

behind the scenes with zookeepers and educators to hold, help feed, and learn tons about the resident animals. Each program is packed with activities and games and hosted by knowledgeable educators, who disguise learning as fun, wowing kids with plenty of animal petting, artifact handling, and nifty crafts to take home.

Family Overnight Safari at the Bronx Zoo

**2300 Southern Boulevard
Bronx, New York
718-367-6898**
www.wcs.org

Offered three times annually. Ages 6 and older, with one adult—$250 ($125 per additional person); members $220 and $110, respectively

It's not cheap and it's not wilderness, but it is sleeping outside in a tent at the Bronx Zoo.

And this thrice-annual event (once monthly in May, June, and September) is so popular there's practically a stampede to get in. Some families consider sleeping at the zoo an important ritual and attend year after year. So if your kids want to sleep with the animals, watch for the zoo's February program guide and immediately book a spot, because by April all 600 slots (about 200 per program) are usually filled. The zoo provides all beverages, ice cream, lots of snacks, and breakfast in the morning. Participants bring their own a tents, sleeping bags, and a picnic dinner.

The program begins after the zoo has closed to the public, about 5:30 PM. There are between 25 and 30 staffers and volunteers who make sure everyone has a good time; they are a well-oiled machine, cheerful, professional, and on the ball. Check-in is easy, with each family greeted by a zoo employee or volunteer, who helps get your belongings to one of four campsites, which have been near the World of Darkness (nocturnal animals), the World of Reptiles, the Crane Walk, and the African Savannah. Everyone also receives a personal itinerary, which details where you'll go after pitching your tent and eating dinner with the other campers. Each camper gets a colorful pin that identifies the group he or she will travel with through the zoo—for example, the Boas, Armadillos, Leopards, or Frogs. These groups are usually based on age, so young campers travel with young campers, teens with teens, and so on.

Before exploring the zoo, a high-energy pep rally gets everyone psyched for the evening. The crowd cheers for returning campers, recognized for their years of attendance, with hoots, hollers, and applause. Then all join their animal groups and each group follows its leader to one of four activity stations, set up exclusively for the night. Traveling around in small groups assures that no station is ever crowded, because there's only one group at a station at a time.

Activities (which can change yearly) have included, for example, Predators on the Prowl, an indoor *Jeopardy!* game, during which everyone learns something new, such as how frogs eat. Well, since you ask . . . their tongues, unlike ours, are attached to the front of their mouths, which is great for capturing insects on the tongues' sticky surfaces, but useless for pushing food down their throats. That's where frogs' bulging eyes come into play. When frogs want to swallow their food, they blink their eyes, pushing their eyeballs down into their heads, applying pressure on the food in their mouths, and sending it down! Everyone meets animals in person, too, like the tiny, big-eared fennec fox, the smallest wild dog in world.

Educators at another station demonstrate how scientists work in the field, using radio collars and transponders placed on animals to keep track of and study their behavior. There are plenty of artifacts on hand, also, to illustrate how field biologists use them to make assumptions about an animal they haven't seen. For example, if scientists find a set of buffalo horns, they measure them from tip to tip to determine the animal's size. Other programs include detective work in the mouse house, using clues to identify individual species, and such animal demonstrations as close encounters with a two-toed sloth, a legless lizard, and other unique creatures.

Like most of the city's campouts and sleepovers, this is a late one, with folks turning in around 11 PM, with wake-up at 6:45 AM, the day starting with a zoo-provided breakfast and followed by a morning chock full of activities. Unlike the previous night, families are free to pick and choose what they'd like to do (or do nothing)—going on a nature walk along the Bronx River, which runs through the zoo, for example, or visiting the Reptile House or the Children's Zoo—before handing their own personal zoo back to the public at 10 AM.

Snooze at the Central Park Zoo

**830 Fifth Avenue
New York, New York
212-861-6030**
www.wcs.org

Offered in fall and winter. Ages 7-10, with an adult—$180 ($30 per additional person). Members $160 and $30, respectively. No more than two children per adult.

Spend the night at the Central Park Zoo's overnight program and you may have a macaw land on your head. Offered three times a year, from October to February, this rain-forest–themed sleepover accommodates about 10 families, who spend the night in sleeping bags on the floor of one of the zoo's education buildings. But the best part is having the zoo's fantastic rain forest, inhabited by rare tropical creatures, all to yourself.

The program begins around 7 PM, with kids making craft items such as rainforest tote bags, followed by games that help break the ice. Each child and parent gets a picture of a rainforest animal taped to her or his back; and then all walk around engaging in questions and answers designed to reveal their animal selves. They also learn a little about the rainforest.

Then families take a nocturnal walk through the zoo to visit the rainforest animals, including cotton-topped tamarins, Rodriguez fruit bats, leaf-cutter ants, scarlet ibises, and bright blue *Dendrobates azurius* frogs. While the insects, reptiles, amphibians, and some mammals are behind glass (or in the case of the red-bellied piranhas, in a tank), most of the exhibit is open, with birds and bats flying freely among lush plants.

After this first visit, there are more games, including a rainforest–themed obstacle course and a skit—performed by two educators playing the parts of customs officer and self-absorbed passenger—designed to teach children the value of protecting endangered species. Campers and the educator-passenger line up to declare whether or not they are bringing any fruit, animals, or veggies home from the rain forest, with the guilty passenger unapologetic about her ocelot fur and caiman pocketbook (two endangered species). Campers also meet a snake and a Madagascar hissing cockroach, play Rain Forest Jeopardy!, and make believe they are box turtles to learn about the impact of lost habitat. Campers stand inside a hoop that represents their home. A greedy developer comes along to build, forcing the box turtles to squeeze into neighboring hoops. As hoops (habitats) are lost, fewer turtles survive, going from threatened to endangered; and finally, when no hoops remain, they are brought to extinction.

Before turning in for the night, everyone revisits the rainforest and helps put the animals to sleep by covering the glass partitions with

Educators introduce kids to rainforest animals during Central Park's Snooze at the Zoo.

tarps. The zoo provides some tropical bedtime snacks, including fresh mango and papaya, and also serves breakfast in the morning. Then campers go behind the scenes to watch zoo keepers prepare the animals' morning meals— fresh fruit, for the most part, diced and sliced to perfection—and afterwards join the keepers in the rainforest to watch the animals eat. Food dispels any animal apprehension and lots of them come out of the trees and plants, with birds sometimes flying onto campers' heads.

Sleep in the Deep and Bedtime with Belugas at the New York Aquarium

Surf Avenue and West 8th Street
Brooklyn, New York
718-265-FISH
www.wcs.org

Ages 5-12, with an adult—$145.00 nonmembers; $130.00 members;

A low barrier keeps aquarium visitors from getting too close to the beluga whales and reflected sunlight on the glass tank can make it hard to get a good view of the creatures that inspired Raffi's biggest hit. But when you sleep at the aquarium, you step over the barrier, put your face right up to the glass, and watch these beautiful Arctic creatures dance playfully in the water or pose with their flippers out to one side just for you. You may even see two whales hug.

The New York Aquarium's Bedtime with Belugas and Sleep in the Deep programs (age-appropriate versions of the same program) are open to about 15 families per session, with campers sleeping in the Explore the Shore building, surrounded by huge aquariums filled with exotic fish, their slow, watery movements mesmerizing. Sleeping quarters are pretty snug, with sleeping bags lined up on the floor, cheek and jowl with one another, a pajama party with a bunch of strangers.

Campers make lots of personal visits to the aquarium's animals, including Danny, Spanky, and Willie, three otters who failed "wilderness school" and so came to live at the aquarium. But most of all, everyone learns about whales, how some have teeth while others have baleen, which strains plankton (tiny and microscopic sea creatures and plants) from ocean water. Kids get to hold baleen (which feels a lot like thick, wiry hair) and whale skeleton jaws, then make whale bookmarks and giant whale puppets that they later parade in front of a projector light in a nautical pageant. After some snacks provided by the zoo, everyone gets to hear a reading of *Ibis: A True Whale Story*, by John Himmelman, a wonderful tale about a humpback whale that gets caught in a fishing net. By 10 PM all participants are in their sleeping bags, with most kids opting to watch a video called *Andre*, about a bottlenose dolphin.

In the morning campers help themselves to a zoo-provided continental breakfast, then feed chunks of fish to sea stars and go behind the scenes to the tops of aquariums where they drop handfuls of fish and tiny shrimp to the creatures below, and then rush down to the exhibit to watch the fish feast. There are visits to the penguins at Sea Cliffs and aquariums filled with huge bass, sea turtles, stingrays, and brilliant coral-reef fish. Then it's off to the Aquatheater to meet a bottlenose dolphin. Instead of sitting in the audience bleachers, everyone stands on stage with the trainers and the dolphin to learn how these very smart, social mammals are trained to perform for the public through a reward system with helpful props decreased as the animal learns its tricks. One kid is picked from among the campers to assist the trainers, but it's fun for all as they stand just feet from a real, 400-pound bottlenose dolphin.

Note: As of publication, the Prospect Park Zoo and Queens Zoo are not offering sleep-overs because of funding cuts. The programs will be reinstated if and when additional financial support becomes available.

Nighttime Is the Right Time

As night falls on the city, we retreat to our homes and apartments and turn on the lights, dispelling the darkness. Black is the night and that's probably why many of us tend not to venture into it with our children. It is unfamiliar, suggests danger, and inspires fear. While I'm not advocating that anyone stroll after hours in deserted parts of the city, I do suggest that families explore the night safely with a group, opening up a wonderful world with which we have sadly lost connection.

The night may seem still and empty, but it has a rhythm and a life of its own. It's an active time when birds migrate, plants grow, slugs and snails feed, crickets sing, and stars shine. It is a magical realm, virtually unexplored by we lovers of light.

Moonlight's the right light for city camping.

If we embrace the darkness, especially with our children, we can recapture some of the balance lost in our lives. As Michael J. Caduto and Joseph Bruchac write in their book, *Keepers of the Night*, native cultures do not see night "as a time that disturbs the order of things in our lives . . . it is considered a crucial part of the balance established by the Creator."

So embrace the nocturnal world by bringing it into the lives of your children and yourself. Experience its rhythms, be fascinated by its verve, seek solace from its soul; but most importantly, as Caduto and Bruchac advise, "be part of it, not apart from it."

Night Walks (Ages 4 and Older)

Walking in complete darkness is instinctually uncomfortable for human beings. That's because we depend very much on our sight—and let's face it, you can't see well in pitch black. And what we can't see, we often fear. That's why it's great to go out with guides who will lead the way. They also often know where nocturnal animals are likely to hang out—raccoons,

woodcocks, owls, bats, and spring peepers—and they'll lead you in the right direction.

If your children are leery about going on a night walk, try holding their hands and letting them choose a nocturnal animal to protect them during the walk, an animal they can think about whenever a little fear strikes.

Secondly, give them their own flashlights so that they have some control in illuminating the area around them. Remind them that vampires and ghosts are storybook characters and the sounds they are hearing are made by harmless animals living their lives. In fact, most animals are more afraid of the kids then they should be of the animals.

Help your kids blend into nature by symbolically rubbing a safe, scented plant on them to seal the bond. Keep your first walk short, with a quick return route should your youngsters want out.

One of the benefits of walking along a beach, through a forest, or around a pond at night is seeing and hearing nocturnal animals you wouldn't otherwise encounter. Nighttime walks also provide a fresh perspective on nature, allowing you and your kids to experience it in a new and interesting way. For one thing, scents are more pronounced at night. If your children are comfortable in the dark, you may want to abandon the flashlights altogether, because the light scares many animals off—except for moths and other insects. So leave the flashlights on, if these creatures interest you. After your eyes adjust to the darkness (about 30 minutes), you'll achieve night vision and be able to see fairly well, especially if there's a full moon. You might also cover your flashlight lenses with transparent red cellophane, which will provide some light but which many animals cannot see, even when it's shining directly at them.

Organizations That Offer Night Walks

Urban Park Rangers

Dial 311
www.nycgovparks.org/sub_about/parks_divisions/urban_park_rangers/pd_ur.html

The Urban Park Rangers offer free, guided, nocturnal hikes in every season and in every borough. In the past, walks have occurred in Alley Pond Park, High Rock Park, Inwood Hill Park, Blue Heron Park, Van Cortlandt Park, Forest Park, Marine Park, and Central Park. And they sometimes focus on specific topics, such as bats or insects.

Gateway National Recreation Area

718-318-4340 (Jamaica Bay Unit, Brooklyn and Queens)
718-987-6790 (Great Kills Unit, Staten Island)
www.nps.gov/gate

Free, guided, nocturnal walks are offered throughout the year at the Gateway National Recreation Area, particularly at the Jamaica Bay Wildlife Refuge in Queens and Great Kills Park on Staten Island. The outings range from the harvest moon and dunes at sunset to horseshoe crab and woodcock mating walks.

Protectors of Pine Oak Woods

718-761-7496
www.siprotectors.org

This Staten Island environmental organization hosts sunset/moonrise walks to Moses Mountain in High Rock Park throughout the year and especially encourages families to participate in the short hike to the top. They also host owl prowls in various Staten Island parks.

Bicycling by Moonlight (Ages 10 and Older)

Now that you've walked the night, imagine bicycling with your children in a pitch-black city park, with nothing to ponder but strange nocturnal sounds and trees silhouetted against the night sky. At first this may seem like a creepy proposition; but heading out with a group of night riders who have been doing this for 10 years really takes the edge off.

Time's Up is a not-for-profit environmental group that promotes a more sustainable, less toxic city. The group began the rides as a way of promoting car-free parks. Today they offer rides year round (even in winter!), three times a month: one in Central Park, one in Prospect Park, and a Central Park–Riverside Park combo. The rides proceed at a leisurely pace and are completely safe, with guides at both the front and rear of the group. Stops are made to enjoy scenery or some other facet of nature.

Children are welcomed on the rides, but they must be comfortable cycling in a group, know how to use the gears on their bikes, and not be afraid of the dark. They must also be able to bike about 10 miles (although the Prospect Park ride is shorter) and stay up late. The rides start at either 9 PM or 10 PM and may last up to two hours. Lights are recommended, especially for the Prospect Park ride, which is the darkest.

Youngsters who can handle all this will be rewarded with an after-hours experience filled with funhouse-like treats, the glow of the moon up above, perhaps a screech owl call from the left, rustling of leaves from the right, even a rat scurrying across the lane, and best of all, no cars! In other words, it doesn't feel like the city.

For information on joining one of these rides, visit the Time's Up website at www.times-up.org, or call the ride hotline at 212-802-8222.

Stargazing (All ages)

In a 24-hour city like New York, where all the lights bleach out celestial details, it's tough to get kids wowed by the night sky. But if you look hard at the sky and appreciate what can be seen, you and your children will soon realize that even the bright lights of the big city can't block everything out.

Take the moon, for example. It's always there and can be seen from wherever you live (except on nights of the new moon). Even toddlers can enjoy the moon, especially when parents express wonder at its changing shape from full moon to half moon to sliver moon. Reading folktales like "Why the Moon Gets Smaller," as retold by Bill Gordh in his book and audio cassette, *15 Easy Folktale Fingerplays*, helps feed this fascination with the moon.

Older kids can begin to understand the phases of the moon and that the moon's shape doesn't change at all. In fact, the moon doesn't even glow, but reflects the light of the sun. Explain to your children that the moon has a near side (which we see) and a far side (which we never see). When we look at the moon we are seeing that portion of the near side being illuminated by the sun. This is caused by the moon's ever-changing relationship to the sun and Earth, a cycle that repeats itself about every 28 days. When the moon is full, for example, the sun, Earth, and moon are in a nearly straight line, with Earth in the middle. This line up allows the entire near side to be lit by the sun. (Earth is also half illuminated by the sun as it rotates, which causes night and day.)

If your children are old enough to use binoculars or a telescope, they can investigate some of the moon's details, including craters, ridges, mountains, and valleys. Craters are deep pits on the surface of the moon, with more than 30,000 visible from Earth. They were created when space rocks, or meteorites, hit the moon. The dark parts are *maria*, the smoothest parts of the moon, created by lava that flowed over and covered old craters.

It is even possible to see planets in the city sky, including Venus and Jupiter, and the rings of Saturn, as well as meteor showers and stars—although we only see a fraction of the nearly 3,000 stars visible to folks out in the country. And the sky isn't the same from night to night. As Earth orbits the sun we are given a window onto different parts of the universe. This process is completed over the four seasons, so that the summer sky is different from the winter sky; but every winter sky is the same from year to year. Older youngsters can get acquainted with the night sky by studying sky maps that provide glow-in-the-dark seasonal layouts. Younger children simply enjoy seeing the shimmering lights and reciting with their parents that old, familiar "Twinkle, twinkle little star. How I wonder what you are."

If your children are serious about exploring the night sky, it's best to check out some astronomy programs before investing in what can be a very expensive hobby. Stargazings are held throughout the city, primarily in areas least affected by light pollution, such as Floyd Bennett Field in Brooklyn and Great Kills Park on Staten Island. Most are free or low cost, and include experts eager to share their equipment and knowledge with inquisitive kids.

Programs and Festivals

Amateur Astronomers Association of New York (Ages 7 and Older)

Gracie Station
P.O. Box 383
New York, New York
212-535-2922
www.aaa.org

Founded in 1927, this organization hosts free monthly stargazings at Carl Schurz Park in Manhattan, Cadman Plaza and Floyd Bennett Field in Brooklyn, and Great Kills Park on Staten Island. Outings are cancelled when temperatures fall below zero or when it rains. From October to May, the club also hosts free lectures at the American Museum of Natural History, although the topics may be over the heads of most youngsters.

The club's Web site features a "clear sky clock," so you can check sky conditions before heading out, and highlights the monthly points of interest in the night sky.

Alley Pond Environmental Center (Ages 7-12)

228-06 Northern Boulevard
Douglaston, New York
718-229-4000
www.alleypond.com

This nature center features astronomy programs led by astronomer and teacher Mark Freilich. Past topics have included the moon's features, the Milky Way, the summer triangle, the Pleiades star cluster, and the Orion nebula. Each program includes an indoor lecture followed by outside viewing with a telescope. There is a fee.

Urban Starfest (Ages 9 and Older)

Central Park's Sheep Meadow (mid-park between 66th and 69th streets)
Annual event in October
www.nycgovparks.org

Each October, the Urban Park Rangers together with the Amateur Astronomers Association of New York celebrate the universe in a free evening event, with telescopes for viewing the sky as well as talks and exhibits on constellations, phases of the moon, seasonal skies, and other things celestial.

Urban Park Rangers

Dial 311
www.nycgovparks.org/sub_about/parks_
divisions/urban_park_rangers

The Rangers offer free tours and discussion of the night sky in parks throughout the five boroughs.

Campfires

Campfires and camping go hand in hand; so if your children want to enjoy an evening filled with the scent of wood smoke, the sweetness of roasted marshmallows, and the mesmerizing flicker of orange and yellow flames, take them camping (see Camping Out, earlier in this chapter) and build a fire.

But if you'd rather sit by a fire without committing to sleeping under the stars, consider one of the Gateway National Recreation Area's campfire programs held at Floyd Bennett Field in Brooklyn and Miller Field and Great Kills Park on Staten Island. Never build a campfire in any city park, because you may find yourself on the wrong side of the law. The Gateway programs offer a safe place to enjoy the night with your children and some park rangers. In addition to the fire itself, you may hear or see nocturnal creatures, enjoy some campfire songs and storytelling, and keep warm on a chilly night.

For information, call 718-987-6790 (Great Kills), 718-351-6970 (Miller Field), and 718-338-3799 (Floyd Bennett Field), or visit www.nps.gov/gate and go to the Gateway National Recreation Area's "Special Events" listings. Clay Pit Ponds State Park Preserve (718-967-1976) on Staten Island also hosts periodic campfires.

Kids can participate by collecting tinder materials from the ground: dried twigs, branches, shredded bark, and leaves. Never break or rip anything from live trees or shrubs. When your campfire is going, gather in a circle around the fire—perhaps sitting on mats to avoid damp bottoms—and warm up with a campfire song. Have your children choose special campfire names, something they feel close to in nature—like a plant, animal, or constellation. Then go around the circle until everyone has shared a story, a joke, or a special thought. Afterward, everyone might hold hands, close eyes, and listened to the sounds of the night for a few minutes. End the evening by singing another campfire song.

If you have a yard with an area free of trees and a clear sky overhead, you might start your own small campfire. But keep it small. Build a fire ring by scraping out a shallow depression, lining the bottom with small pebbles, and surrounding the circle with larger stones to contain the fire and ashes. Place a small pile of tinder in the center of the ring. Next, build a tepee of small sticks around the dry leaves and twigs, and then stack larger sticks around, and up to the height of the tepee. Continue adding larger branches to build up the wall, careful not to cover the top. Light the leaves and twigs with a match (never use flammables like lighter fluid or gas) and wait for the fire to burn. As the fire grows, you might put some larger branches on top, being careful not to collapse what you've already built. When you're done with your fire, pour some water on it and stir the ashes with a stick until you're certain that the fire is completely out. Then cover the ashes with dirt.

Bats

When daylight turns to dusk, it's time to call it a day and head for home, leaving parks and open spaces to the creatures of the night. But if you hang around for just a while, you may be able to treat your children to one of nature's most spectacular displays—bats in flight.

Bats live all around the city—mostly little brown bats and big brown bats, and some red bats—spending their days hanging upside down in secluded spots, safe from predators and the public. But at night, they zoom into the skies, devouring insects on the wing, eating half their body weight every night, and never getting fat. That's because they have high metabolisms and expend plenty of energy flying around all night. So next time you are *not* bitten by a mosquito, thank the bat that may have swallowed 600 of the pests in one hour.

Bats have an unusual way of getting around in the dark and no, they are not blind. They simply rely on their hearing and a process called echolocation. By bouncing high-frequency sound waves off just about everything in their path, bats use the returning sound, or echo, to pinpoint both obstacles and food, detecting size, texture, shape, direction, and distance. These clicking sounds are beyond the range of human hearing, but a bat detector makes these sounds audible so you can track bats during their nocturnal flight. If your children are very interested in bats, you may want to invest in a pocket-size bat detector, which costs about $80 and is available at www.acorn-naturalists.com. It's thrilling to stand in the dark and hear a bat approaching from the left or the right and then watch as it swoops and dips for its meal while silhouetted against the night sky.

Bats fly but are not related to birds. Like us, they are warm-blooded mammals (the only ones that fly) that have hair, bear live young, and feed their babies milk. Unlike us, however, they hibernate during winter, have backward-facing knees and weak legs that make it difficult for them to stand, but strong tendons that allow them to comfortably hang upside down and sleep without expending any energy. They also wrap their ample wings around themselves like blankets, forming a tight package that enables them to squeeze into crevices and other hiding places where predators cannot find them.

Summertime at dusk is the best time to see bats, and humid nights are particularly good.

Bring your kids to open areas where night-flying insects abound, near ponds or lakes and even under streetlights, where moths serve up a delightful meal. Arrive about 30 minutes before dusk and wait. Insect-eating birds called nighthawks are often the first fliers to appear, but they are bigger than bats and have white stripes on their wings. When the bats arrive, you'll know it because they fly erratically, in a frenzy to eat bugs. Your children may have dozens of bats flying above their heads; but don't worry, they won't get tangled in their hair. That's a myth, just like the one that all bats carry rabies. Only about one-half of 1 percent contracts the disease. And bats don't suck blood. Only vampire bats in Mexico and Central and South America even like blood and they don't suck; they lick blood from cuts in animals' skins.

Some Places to Watch Bats

Bronx Zoo's World of Darkness and Jungle World exhibits, Bronx

The Gerritsen Creek Trail, Salt Marsh Nature Center, Brooklyn

Prospect Park, near Dog Beach and the entrance to the Ravine Trail, Brooklyn

During the summer, Paul Keim of the Brooklyn Bird Club hosts bat watching in Prospect Park using a bat detector to locate and identify them. For information, call Keim at 718-875-1151.

Central Park's Great Hill, Manhattan

Jamaica Bay Wildlife Refuge, Queens

Spring Pond, Blue Heron Park, Staten Island

In the summer, naturalist Cliff Hagen presents a bat program here. For information, call 718-967-3542.

Lightning Bugs

Most children are familiar with the glow of lightning bugs, their tiny lanterns appearing at dusk and flashing throughout a summer's evening. It's practically a rite of passage to gather these bits of magic in a jar, hoping to accumulate enough to make a living lantern. But they're best watched flying in complete freedom, their lights illuminating our own memories of playing with fireflies and reminding us to share the wonder with our children.

The city is full of lightning bugs, which inhabit backyards and parks from June through August. They like moist lawns, fields, and woodland edges. By day, they hide out in plants and trees. But come dusk, they are truly spectacular, commanding the night with their tiny searchlights.

Any child can catch a lightning bug to view up close. These beetles fly slowly and produce a greenish glow, easily revealing their location in the dark. And they don't mind being touched, as long as your children are tender with them. They won't bite or pinch and are not poisonous. They fly as high as 5 feet from the ground, and frequently much lower—so even the smallest child can take one from the air and examine it.

The reason male lightning bugs fly so low flashing their lights is to get noticed by females on the ground. Only the males fly; females are flightless. If a female is attracted to a male's signal and also recognizes him as one of her own species, she flashes back. There are about 200 species of lightning bugs in the United States and each has its own flash code—for example, quick single flashes, long flashes, continuous glows. After exchanging flashes back and forth, the male flies to the female to mate.

This attractive light is not battery-powered; rather it's the result of a chemical reaction that takes place in the tail end of the insect's abdomen. Have your children touch the light: it's cold, not hot. This is called bioluminescence and it intrigues scientists who are exploring its use in cancer treatment. On a more frivolous level, chemists have learned to synthesize the insect's light-producing chemicals to make the glow sticks and light necklaces that kids love wearing on Halloween.

Sadly, my own childhood memories of lightning bugs include kids who smeared the insect's abdomen on their arms to watch the smudge glow for ten minutes, killing the firefly. A more humane way to enjoy lightning bugs is by catching one in a jar and observing its flashing for about five minutes. (Make sure you punch holes in the jar and provide some moisture, like a damp paper towel or an apple slice.) Have your kids write down the number of flashes it makes, how long they last, and the time between flashes. Then set the beetle free in the area where it was found. Return to the same spot an hour later and repeat the experiment. If your children notice a different flashing sequence from the new firefly, it's probably a different species. Again, release the insect and, this time, make believe it is flying into the night sky to join the stars.

Nature Funnies

It's only natural for kids to . . . well, kid around. Here are some silly nature jokes that will crack you and them up.

● ●

Why did the maple tree cry?

It was a real sap.

What kind of shoes do snakes wear at the beach?

Water Moccasins.

Why did the dinosaur cross the road?

There weren't any chickens back then.

What do rain clouds wear under their silver linings?

Thunder pants.

Why did the spider buy a car?

So she could take it out for a spin.

Why do hummingbirds hum?

Because they don't know the words.

What birds drink a lot?

Swallows.

Where does an evergreen tree keep ice cream?

In its pine cone.

What tree barks?

A dogwood.

What did the little bird say to the big bird?

Peck on someone your own size.

Why do birds fly south for the winter?

Because it's too far to walk.

Where does a tree pack its belongings?

In its trunk.

What did the branch say to the twig?

Stick with me, kid.

How do you catch a school of fish?

With a book worm.

What did the judge say to the unruly skunk?

Odor in the court.

Why is the sky so high?

So birds won't bump their heads.

 # 5 PADDLING WITH KIDS

If you've ever thought about paddling with your children, New York City is probably not your first choice for a maiden voyage. But it should be. The city is surrounded by water, with 578 miles of coastline. There are bays, rivers, and tidal estuaries, not to mention inland lakes and ponds and tributaries. And it's all close to home.

Until recently, people have been cut off from much of the waterfront by highways, trade, and industry, which in turn often polluted the city's waters. In recent years, however, the city's waterfronts and waterways have experienced a renaissance. First of all, they're cleaner than they were a century ago, thanks to good laws, remediation, and environmental stewardship; and many now support a diversity of marine life. This improved quality has prompted communities to reclaim their waterfronts by pressuring government to restore native habitats, create waterfront parks, and—best of all—provide easy public access. Ferries and water taxis now crisscross from shore to shore, providing commuters with a new way of seeing their city. And more and more people, including families, are plying the city's waters for fun in kayaks and canoes.

Now, you don't need to own a boat, canoe, or kayak to push off. Plenty of organizations give families a crack at paddling, and even the smallest children will enjoy cruising around a pond or lake. But be warned: once you and your kids weigh anchor, you'll want to return to the water again and again and may even be inspired to join a paddling club or own your own boat one day.

Before you go that far, though, test the waters with your youngsters. The first thing you'll notice is just how wonderful it is to be on the outside of the city looking in, really a unique perspective that you can't get any other way. The water is uncluttered, a wide-open world providing some much needed physical and mental space between you and the crowded, high-energy metropolis. Paddling is slow, so there's no rushing around; and this gives kids the chance to explore their surroundings, from shorelines harboring turtles and frogs, to sweeping skies of birds and clouds, to gorgeous views of the city. Then there's the sheer joy of dipping toes into the water. Lastly, paddling in a small boat is intimate, inviting leisurely conversation with your kids or simply appreciating the experience of being on the water together.

Plying the City's Lakes

The easiest way to enjoy time on the water with young kids is by renting a rowboat or pedal boat in one of the city's parks. The water is calm, the boats are all the same size, and you can paddle or pedal around or explore the shore as much or as little as you like. All rentals come with personal floatation devices, which children are required to wear.

The best time to head out is on an overcast day, because the boats do not have canopies to shield you and your children from the sun. If you go out when it's hot and sunny, be sure to bring sunscreen and a sun hat. Try not to go out during the heat of the day, since heat and physical exertion combined—you and the kids will either be rowing with your arms or pedaling with your feet—can lead to a meltdown. If traveling with small children, you may also find yourself getting all the exercise.

Another pleasant time to go out is late in the day, when the city is quieting down, the light is perfect, the sky is changing, and wildlife can be seen foraging for their last bite of the evening. And there you are with your kids, soaking it all up before heading home for the night.

Prospect Park Lake, Brooklyn

(Ages 2 and Older)

Kate Wollman Rink and Prospect Park Audubon Center
718-282-7789 or 718-287-3400
www.prospectpark.org

At Kate Wollman Rink—Pedal boats: each seats 4. Mid-May through mid-October: Thursday–Sunday and holidays, noon–5 PM (until 6 PM, July 1–September 6). $15 an hour, plus $10 refundale deposit. Restrooms in Wollman Rink. At Prospect Park Audubon Center— Electric boat rides: seats 14. 25-minute narrated tour. Mid-May through September: Thursday–Sunday and holidays noon–4:30 PM (until 5:30 PM, July 1–September 6); departs every half hour. $5, 13 and older; $3, 3–13; children 2 and under free. Restrooms in the Audubon Center.

Fishermen reel in bluegills, perch, and large-mouth bass, dragonflies skirt the surface for insects, and yellow water lilies bloom. At 60 acres, Prospect Park Lake is Brooklyn's largest freshwater lake; but it's also a fake, created by park designers Frederick Law Olmsted and Calvert Vaux and fed by a tap like the one in your bathtub, only much, much larger.

The lake is wide open, with a few islands and nooks and crannies to explore, and mostly quiet, except sometimes on summer weekdays when day campers show up en masse. Then, there can be a wait for a boat. It's best going out later in the day or on the weekend for a bit more solitude. Look for frogs, turtles, swans, all four species of gulls, including laughing gulls, and 10 species of duck. Trees along the shoreline provide beautiful texture and reflections in the water.

If boating means letting someone else do the work, take your kids on a 25-minute guided tour aboard an electric boat. The trip begins at the Audubon Center on the Lullwater, a quiet channel frequented by egrets and herons. Some of them may even be nesting in trees overhead.

While paddling around the city's lakes, look for yellow blooming water lilies.

After cruising under the Lullwater and Terrace Bridges, the boat reaches Prospect Park Lake and then heads back to its starting point. All along the ride, passengers learn something about the making of Prospect Park and its ecology. In addition to these more general trips, the *Independence* hosts periodic twilight rides for adults ($25), complete with wine and cheese and followed by a nature walk—as well as family-friendly aquatic and bird-watching trips ($10 adults, $6 kids). Reservations are required.

Central Park Lake, Manhattan

(Ages 2 and Older)

Loeb Boathouse, off East Drive at 74th Street
212-517-2233, ext. 3
www.centralparknyc.org/virtualpark/ thegreatlawn/loebboathouse

Rowboats; each seats 4. March through October, 10 AM–5 PM, weather permitting. $10 per hour, plus $30 refundable deposit. Guided gondola ride; seats 6. Summer: Monday–Friday, 5–9 PM and Saturday–Sunday, 2–9 PM. $30 per half hour. Restrooms in Loeb Boathouse.

Of all the lake boating in the city, this is my favorite. It's not only beautiful—with views of Loeb Boathouse, Bethesda Terrace, and Bow Bridge and the city peeking out from behind the trees—the journey includes twists and turns that give the impression that you've paddled really far. The 22-acre lake was created from a swamp by the park's designer, Frederick Law Olmsted. There are four wooden boat landings along the lake—one at Wagner's Cove, two along the western shoreline, and one along the Ramble shoreline by Bow Bridge—at which you may dock, if you wish. Look for turtles on exposed branches, birds in the trees, ducks in the water, and long-legged waders along the shore.

If you get to the park too late to rent a rowboat or don't want to do all the rowing yourself, you can set sail in an authentic 37-foot Venetian gondola during the summer. The kids will get a kick out of the singing gondolier dressed in straw hat, striped shirt, and black pants sculling you all around the lake using a single oar.

Afterward, you may want to explore the Ramble, behind the boathouse (where young-sters enjoy climbing huge boulders) or visit the nearby Conservatory Water, where you may rent a model sailboat to navigate along the water.

Paddling with your kids is the perfect way to slow down and enjoy the view.

Flushing Meadows-Corona Park, Queens

(Ages 2 and Older)

Boathouse, east side of Meadow Lake 917-805-3946

Pedal boats and rowboats: each seats 4. June through October, weather permitting, 10 AM to 8 PM. $15 per hour. Portable restrooms.

Meadow Lake is New York City's largest lake at 84 acres and was created for the 1939–40 New York World's Fair. During the 1964–65 World's Fair folks were able to cruise the lake aboard an amphibious vehicle called the Amphicar, which was showcased at the fair. Today, in addition to fishing and boating on the lake, basic sailing lessons are available from the American Small Craft Association (fee; 718-699-1951).

While it's not the city's most scenic lake, with few lush stands of trees and marred by highways along the perimeter, turtles and long-legged waders forage along the shores, and gulls and terns ply the air. You can also see remnants of both World's Fairs, including the famous Unisphere and the towering New York State Pavilion. And because the lake is so large, there's plenty of water on which to practice your rowing.

Afterwards, visit some of the park's cultural institutions, including the New York Hall of Science (718-699-0005) and the Queens Museum of Art (718-592-9700), the latter featuring the famous panorama of New York City, a

9,335-square-foot cityscape representing 320 square miles of the city and featuring 895,000 building models (3:30 PM, weekend tours).

Clove Lakes Park, Staten Island

(Ages 2 and Older)

**1150 Clove Road, across from the Lake Club restaurant
718-442-3600**

Rowboats: each seats 6. Pedal boats: each seats 4. Daily June–October, 9 AM–dusk, weather permitting; weekends in May. $10 per hour. Restrooms in the fieldstone park building called Stonehenge.

The park has three lakes, all connected by a stream, but you may boat only on Clove Lake. The 5-acre lake was created in the 19th century by damming a brook that ran to the Kill van Kull. There's a stone footbridge to row under and a small island in the southeast portion of the lake that you may circumnavigate; but be careful of going aground, because the water is shallow here. If you stop your boat for too long, gaggles of Canada geese will surround you, looking for handouts. This close encounter gives kids an opportunity to see these geese close up—large, long-necked geese with black bills, black heads and necks, and white cheek patches. The lake also has mallards and domestic ducks during summer. Less common are great egrets and other herons that stand on the shoreline looking for fish. If you see one, stop the boat, and keep some distance or the bird will fly off. Watch how these elegant birds use a bit of birdie yoga as they methodically get into posture to spear a fish unannounced.

Afterward, you may want to visit the park's two other lakes, Martling and Brooks, by foot via a paved, circular path. In the park's northwest section is a huge, 300-year-old tulip tree, the oldest living thing on Staten Island. The Staten Island Zoo is nearby, just north on Clove Road.

Canoeing

Once your kids are beyond the toddler stage (although some folks start their children canoeing as young as two), it's time to give them a taste of canoeing, which dates back thousands of years to when Native Americans used canoes to hunt, fish, and travel.`

Today, most people canoe for fun, and it is a perfect family activity. In most cases, a family of four fits into one canoe. Larger families can split up into two canoes. Kids under 8 don't provide all that much power, but they like running the paddle through the water and feeling like they're moving the canoe. Depending on individual skill and willingness, youngsters older than 8 are able to contribute more to the cause.

There are plenty of free programs around the city that help uninitiated families test the waters. These are short and sweet outings, the perfect recipe for giving your children a taste of paddling without boring or scaring them to death. All the rides are on calm water and led by experienced rangers or canoeists.

While personal floatation devices are provided, it's a good idea to bring your own if you have a child under 50 pounds, as most places don't carry that size. Also pack an inflatable cushion, old pillow, or even a Back Jack portable chair in case your child is asked to sit on the floor in the middle of the canoe. (This is the case with young children or when there are two adults and one child). If you are one adult and one child, chances are the adult will sit in the stern to steer, while the child sits in the bow to help paddle or just go along for the ride. When working together as a team, both paddlers' strokes must be coordinated.

While you and your children will get some instruction before shoving off, there are a few things to keep in mind. Experts suggest that you stay low when boarding the canoe (keeping your center of gravity low so as not to rock

Everyone pitches in during Urban Park Ranger canoe outings.

the canoe) and use your oar to stabilize yourself. Once inside the craft, some canoeists prefer kneeling with their rear-ends resting against the seat, again to keep their center of gravity low.

Most of these introductory rides are brief; but stay out only as long as your child enjoys it. For little kids, you may want to bring some waterproof toys, perhaps a plastic fishing pole with fake fish on it or something else they can drag along through the water, so they don't get bored simply sitting in the canoe doing nothing. Inexpensive binoculars and a disposable camera (in case they get wet) will help occupy older children who may want to explore and record their surroundings.

The Urban Park Rangers Canoe Program

(Ages 8 and Older)

**Various locations citywide
Dial 311**
www.nycgovparks.org/sub_about/parks_
divisions/urban_park_rangers/pd_ur.html
Weekends, April through October. Free; but preregistration required.

The city's park Rangers offer beginners' programs on lakes, creeks, and other calm waterways in parks throughout the city, with dates posted in the Rangers' quarterly calendar of events. The programs begin with a quick lesson on canoe strokes and safety, and each individual is required to wear a PFD (personal flotation device, or life vest). Most programs require that a ranger accompany you and your child in the canoe, in which case one person will sit in the middle on the canoe floor and not paddle; but you can always switch places. Some programs let you go out on your own, while rangers paddle nearby in their own canoes. Most programs are about one hour in duration; and in some locations—a creek or lagoon, for example—participants are required to stay within certain boundaries. Lakes are pretty much explored in their entirety.

While you can't wander off and canoe to your heart's content, the rangers' programs are a good way to find out if a child likes canoeing. Besides the canoeing experience itself, the programs also provide a great way to look around for birds and other wildlife. The easiest trips are on local ponds and lakes, including Wolfe's Pond on Staten Island, Inwood Hill Lake in Manhattan, Crotona Lake in the Bronx, and Oakland Lake in Queens. Gerritsen Creek in Brooklyn is a favorite, with the beach crawling with fiddler crabs and the shoreline dotted with herons and migrating shore birds.

Bronx River Alliance

(Ages 8 and Older)

One Bronx River Parkway
Bronx
718-430-1846
www.bronxriver.org

Weekends, May through October. Free; but preregistration is required, and donations are appreciated.

There's only one true river in the city and it's the Bronx River, which flows 23 miles—13 through southern Westchester and 10 through the Bronx—before emptying into the East River. The East, Harlem, and Hudson Rivers (at New York City) are actually estuaries subject to the ebbs and flows of nearby salt-water bodies. By comparison, a true river runs downstream in one direction before flowing into another body of water. It carries fresh water and is fed along its course by streams and other tributaries.

The Bronx River served Native Americans well, as it was flush with fish and other wildlife. Colonization changed the river, which figured prominently in the War for Independence and later accommodated industry along its banks. By the turn of the 19th century, it had become horribly polluted, then neglected and almost forgotten. In recent decades, however, hundreds of volunteers have been committed to improving the river, so that today parts of it are clean enough to once again support wildlife—wood ducks, egrets, songbirds, and other creatures—and inspire people to canoe its currents.

One group committed to the river's future is the Bronx River Alliance, which invites families to paddle the Bronx portion of the river in a series of public programs designed to foster stewardship of the river. The free trips are offered first to Bronx residents, although people from other boroughs are welcomed to participate when space is available. Kids 8 through 18 must be accompanied by an adult. Participants are expected to portage (carry) their own boats at points where the river is interrupted by a dam or waterfall; and each canoe is limited to three people.

The Alliance, in partnership with the New York City Department of Parks & Recreation, offers several types of public outings. Participants may choose to explore the lower river, where it empties into the East River and has a particularly urban feel, or the upper river, the "green" section that runs through the New York Botanical Gardens and Bronx Zoo and includes waterfalls and pristine corridors. To get a more accurate experience of the river, it is best to do the full river tour—six miles from 219th Street in Bronx Park to Concrete Plant Park at the mouth of the East River—to experience both the upper, natural parts of the river as well as the lower, more industrial stretches. This trip, and the upper-river trip by itself, includes three portage sites.

Perhaps the most exciting day in the life of the Bronx River is the annual Bronx River Flotilla in April, the official start of the paddling season. Hundreds of folks turn out for this event, which covers six miles of the river, beginning at 219th Street and culminating with music and other family activities in Concrete Plant Park, the abandoned site of the Transit Mix Company, now being transformed into a public park. Canoeing is open to experienced paddlers, but the festival at the park is open to all and includes free canoe rides in the area alongside the park.

Gateway National Recreation Area Introduction to Canoeing

(Ages 4 and Older)

Dead Horse Bay, Flatbush Avenue, Brooklyn
718-338-3799
www.nps.gov/gate/pphtml/events.html
Weekends, twice monthly, June through September. Free; but preregistration required.

This one-hour cruise around Dead Horse Bay is a bit more challenging than some of the Urban Park Ranger trips, because you are not canoeing a river or lake, but rather a bay, an enclosed area that is part of the ocean and therefore affected by tides and weather—conditions that make each outing unique.

The rangers maintain a policy of one adult per one child, which means that if you have two children, you must participate with another adult. This comes in handy, also, if one of your children decides at the last minute that he or she doesn't want to set out. Most children are asked to sit on cushions in the bottom of the canoe, where they like to play with the boat's baler while their parents paddle. Kids around 8 or 9 can try their hand at paddling.

The program begins with a reasonably thorough briefing on how to get into and out of a canoe safely. Rangers also go over paddling technique, including forward and backward strokes, as well as draw and pry strokes that move a canoe sideways. Then the rangers push off from the beach launch and conduct an in-water demonstration for landlubbers. Afterwards, all board their Old Town canoes with mesh seating and follow the lead ranger for an excursion around Dead Horse Bay. One ranger even goes out in an outboard in case someone needs to quickly get back to base.

Tell your kids that Dead Horse Bay is named for horse-rendering plants that operated here in the mid-19th and early 20th centuries, processing horse remains into glue and fertilizer. The rangers say old horse bones sometimes still wash up on the beach.

After launching, the flotilla heads north and paddles under some piers belonging to the Gateway Marina. Then it's off to a small beach, where the overall skill of the group and the weather conditions are assessed. Kids get to do a little beachcombing during this nature stop, scavenging for shells, feathers, and seaweed; they'll see such shore birds as skimmers and sanderlings, and waders such as great and snowy egrets feasting on aquatic critters.

If everyone is doing fine, the group continues around Dead Horse Bay, before returning to the launch area. If not, canoeists practice in a still area before retracing their route back to the launch. Depending on the weather, the bay's western side might be choppy or exhibit a bit of swell, causing enough excitement so that canoeists get a feel for the bay. And then there's the wake of the occasional passing boat, providing paddlers with a momentary thrill.

Basic Canoe and Kayak Terms and Strokes

- **PFD:** Personal Flotation Device (life jacket)
- **Bow:** Front of boat
- **Stern:** Back of boat
- **Port:** Left side of boat when facing bow
- **Starboard:** Right side of boat when facing bow
- **Cockpit:** Opening in the deck of a kayak where paddler sits
- **Portaging:** Carrying your boat out of the water and around a rapid, waterfall, or other break in the course
- **Put-In:** The place from which boats are launched into the water
- **Blade:** The widened end of the paddle that does the work in the water
- **Grip hand:** The hand on top of the paddle
- **Shaft hand:** The hand on the shaft or length of the paddle
- **Forward stroke:** Used to propel the boat. Performed by paddling close to the boat from bow to stern
- **Back paddle:** Used to slow the boat or move it backwards. Performed by paddling close to the boat from stern to bow
- **Draw Stroke:** Used to move the boat sideways. Performed by placing the blade well out from the canoe and pulling it directly toward the side of the canoe
- **Forward Sweep Stroke:** Used to turn the boat. Performed like the forward stroke, except that the stroke is swept out in a wide arc
- **Reverse Sweep Stroke:** Used to turn the boat. Performed like the back paddle, except that the stroke is swept out in a wide arc
- **J Stroke:** A steering stroke that helps keep the boat straight without changing sides. Performed by starting with a forward stroke, then slowly angling the stroke until the blade rudders the canoe
- **Grab Loop:** A loop of rope on the bow or stern, which is useful for grabbing onto in an emergency situation.

The Gowanus Dredgers Canoe Club

(Ages 4 and Older)

**126 Fourth Place, #2
Brooklyn
718-243-0849**
www.gowanuscanal.org

Weekends, March through November. Free.

This volunteer organization, based on the Gowanus Canal in Brooklyn, invites families to paddle the 2-mile canal during its walk-up canoe program. For dates, it's best to consult the club's Web site calendar. If you have your own life vests, especially if your child is under 50 pounds, bring them along, as the club doesn't always have life vests for children.

This is a wonderful place to witness first hand how nature is reclaiming the urban landscape. The canal was built in 1855—literally cut into the landscape via what was Gowanus Creek—as a direct way of bringing goods to Brooklyn, which was then the third largest city in the country and growing rapidly. Heavy industry lined the canal, running from the mouth of New York Harbor and terminating at what is today Douglass Street. When highway transportation became more popular after World War II, the canal's decline began. Industry slowly left, although today there is a rock-crushing business and some big box stores along the canal. The once-bustling waterway became a dumping ground where nothing at all could live.

So where does nature come into it? In the late 1980s, long-time residents and newcomers banded together to pressure the government to clean up the canal. It wasn't until the late 1990s that 2,000 contaminated tons of mud were dredged from the bottom of the canal; and then, in 1999, a long-broken pump that brought fresh water to the stagnant waters was finally repaired. Curious people started canoeing and kayaking the canal, reclaiming it as a recreational resource. They noticed crabs and fish returning to the water and cormorants feeding along the shores. The once-dead canal, named long ago for Chief Gowanus of the local Canarsie Indians, was slowly being resurrected.

While the water is still pretty disgusting, the ecosystem is slowly improving. Plying the waters with your child, you'll often find yourselves paddling alone through what at first seems a desolate industrial graveyard riddled with trash, dumpsters, and heavy machinery. Treated sewage exits from holes on the sides of the canal walls; but after a heavy rain these outflows become so overwhelmed that untreated sewage flows into the canal.

On closer inspection, however, you'll notice wildflowers growing out of cracks in the canal, and shrubs and small trees pushing their way through abandoned truck tires. Morning glories wrap themselves around poles and concrete slabs, masking the old ways. There is bird song, and a great egret may fly overhead while a catbird calls from the shore. Nature resounds—and rebounds—with hope and power, and this is the place to see it at work.

The club keeps four canoes at the end of 2nd Street, just beyond Bond Street, as well as life vests and paddles. You will be asked to sign a waiver, provided by the American Canoe Association, which provides the club with insurance. On walk-up canoe days, a pretty low-key event, a club member drops a canoe into the water (which can be a bit difficult at low tide), helps you and your children board, and provides some tips on paddling safely in the canal. It's an easy flat-water trip along calm waters where there's little if any other boat activity. At trip's end, you will be asked for a small donation, which among other uses goes toward improving the pretty primitive canoe launch.

If you decide to join the club ($25 annual fee; plus $75 to use the equipment), you'll be given a key to the canoe locks and storage bins, allowing you and your children to launch a canoe in the canal whenever you like. If you own a kayak or canoe, you may use the launch at any time, free to explore side channels. If you venture out of the canal and into Gowanus Bay and New York Harbor, paddling will be a little trickier because of tides, currents, and boat traffic.

Note: The Gowanus Dredgers are assisting a local initiative, the Long Island City Community Boathouse, in establishing a similar program on the East River and nearby basins and coves in Long Island City. For information on the group's progress, go to www.LICBoathouse.org.

Sebago Canoe Club

(Ages 4 and Older)

**1440 Paerdegat Avenue North
Brooklyn, New York**
718-241-3683
www.sebagocanoeclub.org

Twice annual weekend open house during summer, 10 AM–5 PM. Call for dates. Free.

The Sebago Canoe Club sits on land where Canarsie Indians once encamped, a small site along Paerdegat Basin and a short paddle to nearby Jamaica Bay. The club occupies little more than a shacklike clubhouse, with kayaks and canoes stored in large metal containers and with a small, shaded picnic area that hugs the shore. But what the club lacks in appearance, it possesses in substance. Established in 1933, it's one of the oldest in the Northeast, a nonprofit, volunteer organization made up of folks who simply like getting out on the water and who, in recent years, have made an effort to interest the public, including families, in canoeing, kayaking, and sailing right in their own backyards.

Twice during the summer, the club hosts a day-long open house to attract both experienced and inexperienced paddlers. To ensure that you have a great day with your kids, arrive as early as possible, before sea breezes kick up later in the day, making it a little more difficult to paddle. You'll find a small, laid-back world unto itself, so make sure you find someone to take you out onto the water. It may take a little walking around, interrupting people while they're chewing on hamburgers, but it's worth the initiative.

While kids cannot go out in kayaks (an increasing presence at the club) unless they are 16 or older, younger children can canoe with their parents, who will have to sign a waiver. If you have your own personal floatation devices, bring them, as the club has a limited supply. An experienced canoeist—most likely canoe chairman Andy Novick, with one of his young children—will accompany you, providing tips on paddling. You will stay mostly in protected Paerdegat Basin, a 1.25-mile-long channel that empties into Jamaica Bay. If you look south, you'll see the Belt Parkway crossing over the water. Just beyond that is Jamaica Bay.

There's plenty of nature for kids to explore in and around the area—wetlands, beaches, and islands and lots of waders, such as egrets and great blue herons, patrolling the shore, as well as gulls, oystercatchers, and skimmers flying overhead. A marina next door to the canoe club provides ample opportunity for kids to study boats coming in and out of dock. There's a breeze in the air as you slowly cruise the waters and it feels like a vacation.

After your outing, you'll be expected to help carry the canoe to the rinse station to wash off deteriorating salt water and then to put the canoe away. Youngsters may run around the 1-acre grassy grounds and will probably find other kids to play with. There's also food at the open house, so they may just want to munch on hot dogs or some chips.

If you like what you see at Sebago, you may consider joining the club; a family membership is $250 a year and, among other benefits, allows you to use the club's equipment, so you won't have to buy a canoe in space-starved

Sebago Canoe Club, one of the oldest clubs in the northeast, welcomes families to paddle around Jamaica Bay.

New York. As a beginner, you'll have to stick to the basin; but eventually you'll be allowed to venture farther out into Jamaica Bay—once the canoe chairman judges your canoeing skills to be sufficient. Once okayed, you're free to take your kids out to explore distant marshes scattered around Jamaica Bay's 16,000 acres, part of the Gateway National Recreation Area. You may circumnavigate Canarsie Pol to the north, an uninhabited island of about 225 acres, or paddle over to nearby Fresh Creek to see nesting snowy and cattle egrets and great black-backed gulls. But keep your distance and be careful not to disturb the birds. At dusk, skimmers use their bright orange bills, whose lower mandibles are bigger than the tops, to scoop food from along the water's surface. Sunset is particularly beautiful, a golden time when most of the leisure boats have docked for the day and the only things breaking the surface are you and the occasional fish.

More than providing equipment, membership unites you with a group of expert paddlers, from whom you will learn. (In addition to kayakers and canoeists, the club has sailors, rowers, and flatwater racers.) The club also offers advanced instruction for a nominal fee. To ensure that you and your family become active club members, you'll also be required to give 10 hours of your time to the club—tending the garden, helping out during open house, or doing a little administrative work, among other tasks. And you'll have access to the club's rustic cabin at Lake Sebago (where the club was founded) in Harriman State Park, just an hour's drive from the city. If you become really proficient and buy your own canoe, storage space is available.

Kayaking

Kayaking has become extremely popular in the waters around the city, but it's nothing new. The kayak is a highly maneuverable vessel originally made from animal hides stretched over an animal-bone frame and used primarily by Inuits to quickly skirt chunks of ice in Arctic waters.

Today, kayaking is a recreational pastime. Perhaps you've seen urbanites out on the wide and mighty Hudson, paddling their small boats among huge Circle Line and other sightseeing boats, tiny minnows in a sea of sharks and whales. Those who prefer kayaking to canoeing swear by it, citing—among other things—the kayak's better aerodynamics and relative stability. These days, kayaks are often hipper than traditional canoes.

But an entire family cannot sit together in a kayak, since most kayaks are designed for one person, some for two. Moreover, most kayaking programs in the city are not open to young kids, since most don't have tandem kayaks and will not let a child go solo. One exception is the Downtown Boathouse, which does have

tandems and allows kids as young as 4 to go out with an adult for a 20-minute paddle in a stretch of the Hudson River. (Youngsters 16–18 may go it alone as long as a parent or other adult is present.) Other organizations require participants be at least 10 years old.

Downtown Boathouse, Manhattan

(Ages 4 and Older)

241 West Broadway
Manhattan
(646) 613-0375 or (646) 613-0740
www.downtownboathouse.org

May 15 through October 15, at three locations on the Hudson River—Pier 26, between Canal and Chambers Streets, weekends and holidays, 9 AM–6 PM; Pier 66a at West 26th Street, weekends and holidays, 10 AM–5 PM; and the 72nd Street Dock, weekends and holidays, 10 AM–5 PM. Pier 26 also features weekday evening kayaking, usually on Fridays, from June 15 to August 31, from 5 PM–7 PM. Free.

You have to love people who volunteer their time to give landlubbers a free taste of riding the waters. And that's exactly what the folks at the Downtown Boathouse do; they suit you and your children up for a safe trip on the sea, give you a little instruction (about "two seconds worth," quipped one volunteer), and send you out onto the Hudson.

Actually, you must stay within the protected embayment area near the pier, which offers plenty of opportunity to tool around and practice your strokes. And it may be hard work; unlike a pond or bay, the Hudson River is subject to strong currents and winds that will test your strength.

Pier 26 is the only one of the three locations equipped with child-sized paddles; elsewhere, young ones can simply enjoy the ride—without paddles—in the bow or middle of the kayak, depending on how many adults are in the boat. Only one child is permitted in a kayak at a time. So if you have two children, you'll need two adults, although the boathouse staff is happy to watch one of your kids while you paddle with the other.

While on board, make sure your child doesn't wiggle around or stand up, because—although the kayaks are unsinkable—you may capsize. These are tandem sit-on-top kayaks, not the cockpit type, and are self-bailing, which means water that splashes into the boat drains out through holes in the bottom. It also means that you will get wet, something kids just love. The Pier 26 site also has a changing room, while the other sites do not.

This is a first-come, first-served program, and participants must abide by the organization's rules, which mean wearing a personal floatation device at all times, signing a liability waiver for yourself and your children, and knowing how to swim—although they don't give you a test; and, besides, how many urban four-year-olds know how to swim? It's best to try kayaking in the morning, when fewer people are out and the river is calmer. Peak times are from noon to 4 PM on sunny weekends. On sunny days, of course, make sure that your kids are slathered with sunscreen and wearing hats.

Even the youngest children can enjoy kayaking along a stretch of the Hudson River.

Inwood Canoe Club, Manhattan

(Ages 10 and Over)

**Dyckman Street Boat Basin and Marina
212-463-7740**

Sunday, 10 AM–12:30 PM, Memorial Day through the end of September.

Despite its name, this long-standing club is more about kayaks than canoes, although they do occasionally launch dugouts. This is a club for families with older kids who think they may want to get serious about paddling. The best way to get involved with the club is by consistently attending the club's open houses, so the club can get to know you and assess your skills with each outing on the water.

Every participant must be able to swim; and are also required to wear a personal floatation device and sign a waiver before going out on the water. "It's not a treacherous river, but it is open water with tides, currents, winds, waves, and traffic," says Commodore Antonio Burr. "If anything goes wrong, we want you to be able to self-rescue."

The kayaks are unsinkable, sit-on-top types, and there are tandem kayaks available so you and your child can paddle together. You will get some instruction, with paddling at first restricted to the cove near the boathouse. As you and your child hone your skills, you will be invited to venture gradually farther out on the river. "The more we get to know you, the more adventuresome the trips become," says Burr. In general, the club paddles on the Hudson River from the George Washington Bridge to 215 Street, and also east to the Harlem River.

The club wants to build a relationship with guests before offering them membership, which requires that members help out around the boathouse, cut weeds along the shore, and perform other housekeeping chores. The club has been around since 1902 and was once a competitive club that turned out Olympians. While more recreational these days, it is again building a club racing team to enter regional competitions.

Manhattan Kayak Company, Manhattan

(generally, Ages 10 and Older)

**Pier 63, at the Hudson River
and West 23rd Street
212-924-1788**
www.manhattankayak.com

Four-hour class. $160 per person.

Most of the students in the class will probably be adults, but if your child is at least 5 feet tall, he or she may take Basic Paddling I with you and learn how to paddle a kayak on the Hudson River. Half the course is on dry land, where you'll learn all about equipment, how to enter and exit a kayak, basic paddling techniques and strokes, and how the currents of the Hudson River work. Later, out on the river, you'll apply what you've learned indoors, with you and your child working together in a tandem kayak.

The company also sells boating equipment, offers kayak storage ($500 annually), and con-

ducts a wide variety of trips and tours for experienced kayakers. There's also a kids' kayaking camp in the summer, through Chelsea Piers (212-336-6846).

For the Experienced Kayaker and Canoeist

If your family has experience kayaking or canoeing, there are places around the city from which to launch your own canoe or kayak. (There are no canoe or kayak rentals in the city.) Most of the launches are overseen by the New York City Department of Parks & Recreation and require a permit. Others are free launches managed by a club or nonsanctioned spots that paddlers have adopted as their own.

Before setting out on the water, it is wise to leave a "trip plan" with a family member or friend in the event of an emergency. Everyone is also expected to wear a personal floatation device (life jacket). The city recommends that each vessel have the following on board: a bailer, lines for bow and stern, extra line, a distress flag, sound-producing device such as a horn or a whistle, flares or a flashlight, a first-aid kit,

National Estuaries Day

New York City is surrounded by water. Much of that water converges in an area known as the New York/New Jersey Harbor, an estuary where salt water from the ocean mixes with fresh water from rivers and tributaries. These coastal habitats are important spawning grounds and nurseries for many fish and other sea creatures and also provide people with places to swim, paddle, and bird watch.

While the continued health and protection of estuaries is a year-round effort, they are publicly celebrated on the last Saturday of September, known as National Estuaries Day. Leading up to this event are tons of free, family-friendly programs ranging from boat tours and fishing to nature walks and beach cleanups hosted by government agencies and local nonprofits, and held from mid-September through early October. For a calendar of events, call 212-637-3787 or visit the New York–New Jersey Estuary Program at www.harborestuary.org.

sunscreen, drinking water, a compass, charts, tide tables, duct tape, and waterproof containers for some of these items.

City Parks Department Launches

You must have a permit to launch a canoe or kayak from any Parks Department launch. Permits are $15 per season. Call 212-360-8133 or download an application at www.nycgov parks.org.

Bronx

Pugsley Creek Park

Foot of Soundview Avenue at Clason Point
Explore: East River
Parking available.

Orchard Beach Lagoon, Pelham Bay Park

Explore: Lagoon and Long Island Sound
Parking and restrooms available.

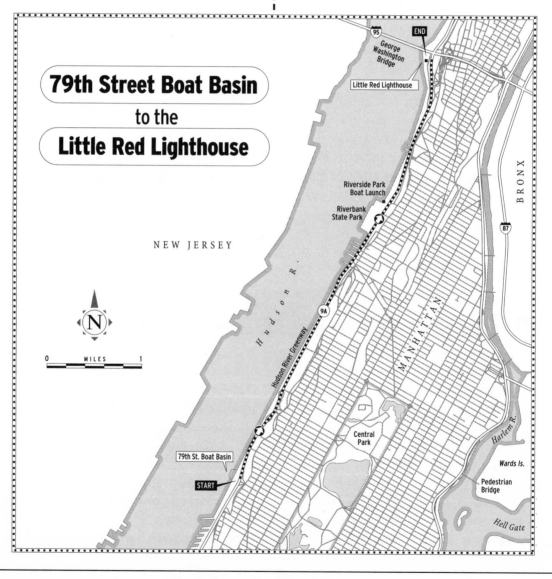

79th Street Boat Basin to the Little Red Lighthouse

Brooklyn

Louis J. Valentino Park, Foot of Coffey Street, Red Hook

Explore: Buttermilk Channel and East River
Parking on Van Dike Street.

Manhattan

West 79th Street Boat Basin

Explore: Hudson River
Street parking.
Storage available; $250 per season (May–October / November–April), $500 per year.

Riverside Park, foot of 140th Street

Explore: Hudson River
Parking.

Inwood Hill Park, foot of Dyckman Street

Explore: Hudson River
Street parking.

Queens

Bayside Marina, off the Cross Island Parkway, at the foot of 28th Avenue

Explore: Little Neck Bay
Parking

World's Fair Marina, 122-01 Northern Boulevard, off Grand Central Parkway

Explore: Flushing Bay
Parking.

Other Launches

Brooklyn

Floyd Bennett Field, Gateway National Recreation Area

718-338-3799

At old seaplane ramp
Explore: Jamaica Bay
Parking available; Gateway car-top boat permit required.

Staten Island

Lemon Creek Park, Johnston Terrace and Bayview Avenue

Operated by Lemon Creek Mariners 718-356-7235

Explore: Raritan Bay
Free parking

Great Kills Park, Gateway National Recreation Area

Boat launch at mid-park, east side
Explore: Great Kills Harbor
Parking available; Gateway car-top boat permit needed for boat ramp lot, although free parking is nearby in Lot E.

Old Place Creek Gulf Avenue at the start of Western Avenue

Unofficial launch
Explore: Lower Arthur Kill
Street Parking.

6 EXPLORING THE SHORE

The shore is more than a retreat for sunbathers and sandcastle builders. It's a rough neighborhood; a place pounded by waves, soaked, and then depleted of water; a place where winds blow ruthlessly and the sun blazes unhindered by the shelter of trees. For millions of years, the place where land meets sea has been the site of life on the edge, and only the toughest plants and creatures survive.

Seventy-one percent of our planet is water; and New York City is right in the thick of it, with hundreds of miles of shoreline, from the relentless Atlantic Ocean to quiet bays and marshes and river and creek banks. And while many of our shores are developed into public beaches, residential communities, and industrial sites, there's still plenty of wildness peppered with shells, seaweed, sponges, crabs, fish, and other creatures. There are even sand dunes in the city, fragile, shifting hills just barely held in place by grasses and plants with long roots and thick, salt-tolerant leaves.

With just a little effort, a day at the beach can become a day of discovery. There are shells to inspect, tidal pools to explore, and shallow water to sift through. Our shores support a wide variety of creatures integral to the food web, which includes humans. You might teach your children that it really is not a dog-eat-dog world out there. No creatures pick on someone their own size if they can help it. Most creatures look for something smaller to swallow. Microscopic plankton are eaten by shrimp and clams, which are eaten by tiny fish, which are eaten by larger fish, which are eaten by still larger animals . . . and by us. So the health of the seashore is important to the survival of us all.

The seashore is affected by tides that rise and fall around every 12 hours, providing every day with two high tides and two low tides. Perhaps most astonishing for children is learning about the powerful connection between these waters so close to home and that glowing orb in the night sky, the moon. Teaching them the basics of tides is another opportunity to illustrate the interconnectedness of everything.

Tides are caused mostly by the moon's gravitational pull. As Earth rotates, the oceans nearest the moon swell. On the earth's opposite side, another bulge forms to balance out the planet. In between the high tides come low tides. The sun plays a role as well, although a lesser one. When the sun and moon are aligned with Earth (about every two weeks), their combined pulls create the highest tides of all—spring tides. On alternating weeks, when the sun and moon are at right angles to one another, their gravitational pulls oppose one another and cause lower-than-average tides—neap tides. What a great time to explore the seashore with your children, when much of it is exposed.

Tides affect what is called the littoral zone, the shore area between the highest and lowest tides. This area is divided into four sections: the low-tide zone, which is almost always wet; the middle-tide zone, which may be alternately wet or dry; the high-tide zone, which is wet only at high tide; and the spray zone, which is usually dry but receives an occasional mist of salt water. Each zone is unique and home to specific animals and plants, from crabs and herring gulls to burrowing mollusks and sand fleas.

When you investigate the shoreline, outfit your kids in rain boots or old canvas sneakers (and make sure they take care when walking on slippery, algae-covered rocks). Wear hats, sunglasses, and sunscreen. Take along a pencil and notebook for record taking, a magnifying glass for seeing things up close (or minimicroscope, if you have one), a pail and shovel for digging, a magnet, and a field guide to the North Atlantic seashore. Don't walk anywhere where you may become stranded when high tide rolls in.

Rather than bagging a bunch of shells to take home, have fun with your children on the beach. Everything need not be a consumer experience and shells, seaweed, and other shore stuff are better off where they are, serving as food and shelter for living animals. This is also a good way to teach your kids that nature wastes nothing. Even the salt in the water is derived from nature, a combination of different rock minerals and decomposing plants and animals.

So take photos of your children's treasures or sketch them in a notebook. A quirkier activity involves searching for pebbles, shells, feathers, and other seaworthy debris and then using them to fill in and decorate an outline of your child made in the sand. Try creating shell ears, pebble smiles, and feathery hair for a completely silly day at the beach.

Beachcombing

Your child picks up a shell from the beach, admires its shape or color, and perhaps listens for the sounds of the ocean. When this happens, it's a good time to point out that every shell once had an animal living inside it. When they were alive, these invertebrates (having no backbones) looked like blobs, but they were more than just Silly Putty or slime. Inside each of them were internal organs that allowed them to eat, live, and make babies, just like humans and other animals. The shells are simply what's left behind when the animal dies, much like our bones.

Kids of all ages love sifting through sand, perhaps turning up a corkscrew-shaped whelk-egg case or a delicate moon snail with a spiral design. Sea glass, pebbles, and driftwood that have been knocked around by turbulent water for years are smooth and satiny. Even the sand itself is worth exploring, a colorful mix of pulverized rocks and shells.

The best time to explore the beach for shells and animals is at low tide, when the greatest swath of sand is exposed. This is also when you'll find the wrack or strand line, a messy streak of old wood, sea sponges, crabs, shells, barnacles, and garbage that have been washed up on shore and left behind when the tide moved out. The bounty is particularly rich after a storm or when there is a full moon, when tides are strongest.

Beach strolling is especially fun once the summer crowds have gone. Off season, you may find yourself alone at the shore with your kids, a wonderfully private experience in an otherwise crowded city. Of course, in nature, you are never alone. Ducks bob on the water, while shore birds hunt for aquatic life teeming below the surface—that cool and shady area to which marine life retreats to escape predators and the hot sun. Nature is also never quiet. The air is punctuated by crashing waves and by squawking gulls and terns flying overhead.

Seining

Exploring the shore is more than a stroll on the sand. On a warm day, kids love getting wet; and if you plunge in with them, seine in hand, you'll find an exhilarating hands-on way to teach them about coastal ecology. All you need is a seining net (a 10–12-foot-long net works best with kids), water shoes, two pairs of waders to keep warm and dry (you can leave them home during summer), and a goldfish bowl or jar. Seines are generally 4 feet deep and have weights along one side and floats along the other. Poles attached to the ends are used to drag the seine through the water, trapping fish and other aquatic creatures. Nets and waders are available at most bait and tackle shops.

Seining goes back thousands of years. Weary of catching slippery fish with their hands, ancient humans figured out how to capture seafood with nets. Today, on a much larger scale, commercial fishermen still seine to haul in tons of fish at a time. On a smaller scale, families might seine from a beach for fun and get a closer look at what lives under the sea.

It takes two to work a seining net. Each person grabs an end, keeping the weighted side on bottom and the buoyant side on the top. Walk into the water with your backs to the shore, keeping the net in a half-moon configuration, curved between you and your child. Slowly drag the net out from the shore, keeping the poles touching the bottom so that the sea creatures don't escape. Don't tow so hard that you pull the weighted edge off the bottom or pull the floats under the water. Go out about waist deep for the littlest person and then walk the net around so that it is perpendicular and then again parallel to the shore. Continue dragging

Seining is an exhilarating hands-on way to teach kids about coastal ecology.

the net; and when you pull the seine onto the beach, keep the weighted edge on the bottom or you'll lose everything inside.

You're likely to have hauled in some mud snails, clams, pretty, brightly-speckled reddish calico crabs, small fish, and even some northern pipefish (a slender, long-nosed relative of the seahorse), as well as sea lettuce (a seaweed) and sea walnuts (a nonstinging type of jellyfish that kids can safely touch). If the Gulf Stream (an extremely fast-moving and warm ocean current that originates in the Gulf of Mexico) has segued into your part of the ocean that particular day, you may even net a tropical fish.

Gently put a few specimens into your jar or goldfish bowl filled with ocean water, quickly easing the rest of the catch back into the ocean so they can return to their lives at sea. After viewing the sea creatures (leaving them in the jar no longer than 15–20 minutes), gently return these beings to the sea as well. After you're done with your net for the day, rinse it with fresh water and let it air-dry.

Gateway National Recreation Area, in conjunction with the American Littoral Society, offers periodic seining programs at Floyd Bennett Field in Brooklyn, usually led by local marine biologist Mickey Cohen. An affable, knowledgeable educator, he's fantastic with kids, even providing a kiddy-sized seining net so the little ones may try their hands at this ancient art. Kids also get a hand lens for closer inspection of their catch. For information on Gate-way's next seining program, call 718-338-3799, or log on to www.nps.gov/gate or www.alsnyc.org.

Investigating Tidal Pools

For children, a seemingly endless beach or the vast ocean might be overwhelming. Kids often relate best to life on a smaller scale. (Think about how many protagonists in children's literature are creatures like mice or bunnies.) So the rich and complex, but miniature world of tidal pools is ideal for small children. These watery enclosures are ripe for exploration because the animals are confined within a space that can be easily studied. Creatures that live in tidal pools—puddles formed by the advance and retreat of the tides—are always waiting for high tide to wash over them, replenishing their miniature worlds with oxygen, food, and water. Without high tides, these confined spaces would become increasingly difficult to live in, as the water slowly evaporated and became saltier, hotter, and depleted of oxygen. Creatures in these impoundments also have few escape routes and are easy prey for birds.

So show your kids how each creature, as it waits for high tide to restock its home or set it free altogether, finds ways to survive—some mollusks and snails hold water in their shells to stay wet, while others burrow into any available wet sand or mud. Fish and other creatures hide under seaweed or rocks. Everyone just hangs on. It's a life of extremes and of quick adjustments, suitable for plants and animals that can adapt under the baking sun and withstand the violence of powerful waves.

The best place to find tidal pools is along a rocky coast, like that of Twin Island at Pelham Bay Park; but pools can also be found in marsh mud and even in depressions on sandy beaches. Visit at low tide (check the newspaper for tide times in your area) and gently turn over rocks and swish the seaweed around to see if anything is hiding underneath. Look for barnacles and other creatures attached to rocks, but don't remove them. If the tidal pool is deep, use your sea scope (see page 154) to get a closer look.

Some Good Spots for Beachcombing, Seining, and Exploring Tidal Pools

Twin Island, Pelham Bay Park (Bronx)—The rocky coastline along Long Island Sound is the southernmost part of the same coast you'll find in Maine. It's a great place to find slipper shells and tidal pools. On the sandy areas near Two Trees Island look for fiddler crabs in summer.

Gerritsen Creek at the Salt Marsh Nature Center (Brooklyn)—The shoreline at the corner of Burnett Street and Avenue U is a great place to see fiddler crabs in summer.

Fort Tilden Coastline (Queens)—The area between Beach 175th Street and Beach 193rd Street has lots of huge surf clams, among other creatures.

Great Kills Park (Staten Island)—You'll see lots of periwinkles, ribbed mussels, fiddler crabs —and maybe some hermit crabs, too—at the park's salt marsh. Visit at low tide and watch the shore birds as they eat. Crooke's Point, at the park's southwestern tip, is a great place to find jingle shells.

Ward's Point, Conference House Park (Staten Island)—This sandy shoreline faces Raritan Bay and New Jersey and is covered with shells, including moon snails and slipper shells.

Floyd Bennett Field Seaplane Ramp (Brooklyn)—This is a great place to go seining for pipefish, sea walnuts, silversides, and other marine animals. Also try Deadhorse Bay, on the west side of Flatbush Avenue. Follow a short trail to the beach (sometimes called the

Millstone Trail, because there's an old Millstone on the path)—and wear old sneakers or water shoes at all times. The area is a former landfill that has been breached by storms, so you can expect glass and trash.

Seashells and Their Inhabitants

When your kids start picking up shells on the beach, call them bone collectors and watch a chill run up their spines. Shells are the external skeletons (exoskeletons) of soft-bodied animals called mollusks, which include creatures such as snails, clams, oysters, and mussels. Mollusks make their shells by extracting calcium from the water they swim in and the food they eat. Their mantle, or skin, then secretes this calcium into a hard shell, which gives the animal shape and helps protect its fleshy body from predators.

When an animal is alive, the shell is usually brownish. It doesn't reveal its beach look until the animal dies and the shell's protective

Clams, oysters, mussels, snails, and other mollusks make shells from calcium.

coating, called the periostracum, is lost. Sometimes you can tell a mollusk's age by counting the growth lines, or ridges, on its shell, something that's done easily with clams. Some mollusks, such as squids, have no shells; but most are either bivalves (two valves or shells) or univalves (single shelled) and have a single foot that helps them get around.

Sand

Children can do a little treasure hunting and learn the source of sand by examining its minute particles up close, using either a hand lens or a portable microscope.

Sand is made up of tiny grains worn off of large chunks of rock either during glacial movement or by the constant pounding of winds and waves over time. These minuscule jewels come in a variety of colors and shapes. For example, colorless glasslike fragments are quartz (or silica), pink or red pieces may be garnet, while yellow or tan crystals with flat sides are feldspar. Magnetic minerals like iron (or magnetite) are also found in the sand, so have your kids run a magnet through the sand to see these tiny particles cling to the magnet's surface. It's also fun to gather sands from a few different places to see the differences in their compositions—the result of local rock sources and conditions.

To get an idea of how sand compositions differ around the world, go to www.chariho .k12.ri.us/curriculum/MISmart/ocean/sand intr.html. This Web site was developed by a Rhode Island teacher who also invites kids from around the world to trade samples of sand from their hometown beaches.

Clams

If you've seen a minigeyser in the sand, it was probably made by a clam. These bivalves dig deep with their single foot, send up a siphon to draw water in, filter out food, and spit the water back out. The bump where their two shells are joined is called an umbo. If there's a hole there, the clam was likely sucked out by another creature. Notice how the shell's smooth interior is perfect for sheltering the clam's soft body.

Atlantic jackknife clam—This long, slender bivalve looks like an old-fashioned straight-edged razor and is sometimes called the razor clam. Speedy diggers, jackknife clams can burrow down about 24 inches in one minute.

Atlantic surf clam—These big, thick-shelled guys are shaped like rounded triangles and can grow to 7 inches. They're the largest clams on the East Coast.

Hard-shell clam, or **northern quahog**—These 2.5- to 4-inch long clams hang out about 3 inches below the surface, so try digging for them. Native Americans made beads from the purple interiors of these shells, using the beads for jewelry and wampum.

Making a Seascope

If your kids want to get a good look at what's under the water, they don't have to submerge their heads and look around underwater. Instead, help them make a homemade seascope so they can spy on marine life and keep dry.

Just cut the top and bottom off a half-gallon milk or orange-juice carton. Then cover one opening with a large piece of plastic wrap, holding it in place with rubber bands and taping the ends of the wrap to the sides of the container until it's water-tight. Your child can then stick the plastic-wrapped end into the water and peer into the open end!

Soft-shell clam—This clam is too big for its 3-inch shell, so its siphon sticks out the side. These chalky-looking bivalves have thinner shells than their hard-shell brethren and are called steamers on restaurant menus.

Other Bivalves

Atlantic bay scallop—Beautifully shaped and textured like a fan, these exquisite shells come in white, yellow, gray, and orange. Bay scallops are unique in the bivalve world because they can fly through the sea like underwater birds, opening and closing their symmetrical shells like wings. In mythology, it is said that Aphrodite/Venus, the goddess of love, rose from the sea on a scallop shell. (For the artistically inclined child, you may want to trot out a photo of Botticelli's *Birth of Venus*, sometimes called "Venus on the Halfshell.")

Jingle shell—This thin, pearly shell looks like mother-of-pearl and gets its name from the sound made when many of them are strung together and rattled. They're also called mermaids' toenails, because of their translucent, pale yellow, silver, and orange colors.

Mussel—Found along coastlines and bays, mussels tend to hang out together, clinging to rocks or each other by tiny threads called byssi. At high tide, they open up and use hairlike cilia to strain out tiny plants and creatures to eat. People enjoy eating blue mussels. Ribbed mussels, usually found in salt marshes, are edible, but bitter.

Eastern oyster—Often jammed together in crowded beds, the thick, bumpy shells of these oysters make up collections of one-of-a-kind specimens, shaped by the environment in which they grow and live. They're best known for the pearls they make when a bit of sand becomes lodged between shell and mantle. Eastern oyster pearls, however, are worthless, because they lack brilliance.

Univalves (Gastropods)

Gastropod means "belly-footed animal," and that's because these animals have a single shell and one flat foot that helps them get around. But they don't hop; the foot's muscles contract and expand, enabling the animal to slowly creep along, often leaving a trail of slime. Many gastropods have pointy, spiral-shaped shells like snails, but some have flat shells. When the animal retreats into its shell, a plate called the operculum seals the opening, keeping the creature moist and insulated and safe from predators. If you find one, put it in a jar of seawater with a piece of seaweed or a rock and watch the creature emerge, sending out its foot for moving and its sand-papery radula, or tongue, to eat. Some gastropods eat meat, drilling holes into bivalves and sucking out their squishy bodies.

Atlantic slipper shell—These 1- to 2-inch shells make excellent shoes for dolls; each is shaped with a lip attached to a sole. Slipper shells are sedentary creatures and are often found in stacks, with males on top and females on the bottom. The ones in the middle are in the processing of changing from male to female, in order to maintain an even number of sexes within the stack for reproduction purposes.

Eastern mud snail—Usually brownish and covered in algae, these 1-inch snails are very common in the summer, when hundreds of them can be seen on mud flats along the coast.

Limpet—Shaped like a little bowl, some with a hole at the top, limpets hang out in shallow places they've created in rocks with their hard shells. They may leave to graze on seaweed but always return to the same spot. Many have tortoiseshell markings and are between 1 and 2 inches long.

Moon snail—This animal has a taste for and spends a lot of time beneath the sand hunting for them. It uses acid on its radula to soften the clam's shell before drilling and digging the animal out to eat. Moon snails are beautifully round, about the size of a golf ball, with a spiral design, and come in creamy white, gray, tan, silver, and pink. Sometimes their egg collars are found on the beach—wide, pliable rings of tiny eggs held together with mucus and sand.

Periwinkle, or **marsh snail**—Periwinkles come in many varieties, but are usually brownish and seen stuck to seaweed and marsh grasses or rocks, vacuuming up algae with their very long tongues. Their shell is about 1 inch long and conical.

Whelk—With wide shells that taper almost to a point, local whelks include the knobbed whelk (tannish on the outside, with a bit of orange inside, and with bumps on the fat part of its shell) and the channeled whelk (with a smoother shell that is tan or gray and a pink inside). These large snails grow to 7 inches and use the narrow part of their shells like a knife, shucking clams to get inside to the flesh. A great find is a whelk egg case, a long necklace of yellowish disks, each of which once held a baby whelk, complete with shell. The small holes in the disks what they used as their escape hatches.

Crustaceans

Crustaceans also wander or live along the shore and in the water, and include crabs, shrimps, beach fleas, and barnacles. They usually have hard shells, or carapaces and three jointed body parts—head, thorax, and abdomen. They're marine animals that breathe through gills, like fish. Members of the arthropod family, they're related to spiders.

Robins sing and crocuses emerge from the ground, but a sign of spring that often goes unnoticed is the onshore spawning of hundreds, sometimes thousands, of horseshoe crabs in late May and early June. Since most kids love dinosaurs and other prehistoric creatures, they'll be intrigued to learn that these ancient beings with helmetlike bodies and long spiky tails are the closest living relative to one of earth's first life forms. Horseshoe crabs hark back to trilobites, sea-faring arthropods related to spiders—and not crabs—that existed 300 million years ago, even before dinosaurs roamed the earth. Incredibly, they have survived. And they've somehow picked up the misnomer, "crab."

There are four species of horseshoe crabs worldwide, with three of them far off in the East Indies and East Asia, where the Japanese have long celebrated them in poetry and painting and honor them as reincarnations of Samurai warriors. In Japan, there's even a horseshoe crab museum. The fourth species is right here on the East Coast, offering us the rare treat of witnessing this spectacle of life up close.

Most of the time, horseshoe crabs lie half concealed in ocean sediment about 70 feet offshore. But as soon as the longer days of spring arrive, light sensors on their bodies tell them to come ashore and start new families. Kids will enjoy seeing dozens of these bizarre creatures all hooked together doing their thing.

The females are larger than the males and have scissorlike claws, while the smaller males have hooklike claws that allow them to latch onto their lady friends. Dragging the males along, females burrow 6 to 8 inches into the sand at the high-tide line and deposit tiny bluish-green eggs. This spawning coincides with the northern migration of shore birds leaving Central and South America on their way to nesting grounds in the Arctic.

The horseshoe crabs' eggs provide critical nourishment for the birds, without which they would never be able to complete their flight of thousands of miles. Thirty-five species of birds eat the eggs—from migrating red knots, ruddy turnstones, and sanderlings to such year-rounders as glossy ibises and laughing gulls. The eggs also feed fish that other birds live on.

Point out to your kids how other sea creatures rely on horseshoe crabs. Barnacles, slipper shells, blue mussels, and others attach themselves to these little Sherman tanks. Some stay married to the crabs forever, while others simply hitch a ride.

Instill in your children the truth about horseshoe crab tails. They are not dangerous. They help the crabs stay on course as they navigate the sand and mud, and help them right themselves when they've flipped upside down. However, they often lie stranded on the beach when the tide goes out. A fun and rewarding late-spring activity is to take your kids on a walk and do some horseshoe crab rescue. When you see one on its back, kicking its legs frantically, do it a favor and turn it over. Unassisted, the crab may die.

Today, the horseshoe crab's 300-million-year undisturbed lifespan is threatened by modern life, particularly habitat destruction due to pollution and development and overharvesting for use as bait and nitrogen-rich fertilizer.

The medical industry even takes its toll, bleeding the animals for a special clotting agent used to test injectable drugs and medical devices for harmful endotoxins that may cause life-threatening diseases in humans. The animals are returned to the water, but there is a 10 percent mortality rate.

A good way to see tons of horseshoes up close is by joining a free, guided walk at the Jamaica Bay Wildlife Refuge in Queens, led by the American Littoral Society (718-318-9344). The walks are usually offered three times a season, usually on nights of full or new moons, when the tides are high.

The National Park Service also offers programs at Great Kills Park on Staten Island, where hundreds of horseshoe crabs can be seen on the harbor side of Crooke's Point. These curious creatures may also be seen at Dead Horse Bay at Floyd Bennett Field in Brooklyn.

Other hot spots include: the North Channel Bridge in Queens (park in the west parking lot and walk 20 feet); Raritan Bay at Conference House Park on Staten Island; Plum Beach in Brooklyn, between Exits 9 and 11 on the Belt Parkway; and Pelham Bay Park in the Bronx.

The Urban Park Rangers sometimes lead tours at Pelham Bay Park in the Bronx, while the Alley Pond Environmental Center occasionally hosts walks to Little Neck Bay in Queens.

Barnacles

They may look like mollusks, but these hard-shelled creatures are actually crustaceans. In their larval stage, they look like tiny shrimps and hang out with zooplankton. But once they become adults, they settle down by gluing themselves upside down to rocks, shells, and other hard surfaces, usually in colonies, reaching out of their mini-volcano-shaped shells only to eat. At high tide, each animal feeds by stretching its threadlike legs (cirri) from the shell's opening and filtering food from the water. At low tide, the legs are pulled inside and the door is closed tight until the tide rolls in again.

Crabs

If it walks sideways, has a round body, a carapace (shell), and ten legs, one pair equipped with pincers, it's a crab. And those pincers hurt, so pick up a crab only from the back for closer inspection. If a crab loses a leg, it grows a new one. If your child spots shells scattered along the shore, explain that they may not be the remains of dead crabs, but rather shells that have been molted. Look for a split at the back of the molted shell, through which the crab crawled out. Crabs with new shells are called "soft shelled" and some are delicacies in restaurants. Once the shell matures, it's a hard-shelled crab. You can tell a crab's sex by the tail, or flap, that's tucked under its body. If it's wide, you're looking at a female; if narrow, a male. Crabs have long, stalklike eyes for seeing in all directions and feelers to feel and smell their way around.

Atlantic mole crab—These funny-looking crustaceans don't look like typical crabs and don't move sideways. They look like tiny, walking helmets that move backwards. You can find these egg-shaped creatures where the waves

Kids' favorites, male fiddler crabs sport one pincer larger than the other.

break on the shore; once exposed, they quickly bury themselves in the sand to hide from the shore birds that love to eat them. Mole crabs don't have pincers so they can't hurt you.

Blue-claw crab—These crustaceans are excellent swimmers, with paddles for back legs. They're also known for their sweet, white meat—they're scientific name, *Callinectes sapidus* means "beautiful swimmer that is savory." Males are distinguished from females by their abdomens, or "aprons," on their undersides. Males have inverted T-shaped aprons, while mature females have inverted U-shaped aprons. Juvenile females have inverted V-shaped aprons. Females also have red tips on their blue claws.

Fiddler crab—This small, odd-looking crab has one pincer larger than the other (on the male) which is often held across the body as if playing a fiddle. But these guys aren't into bluegrass music; they're just trying to attract females with their pumped up arms. Kids love sneaking up on these crabs, which are usually found in crowds during low tide in summer, trying to catch them before they dart into their sandy burrows to hide. But stick around quietly and they'll emerge once again.

Ghost crab—The best time to find these big-eyed crabs is at night in the upper beach zone where they feed. But even then, these nocturnal animals are hard to see, because they are quick to burrow into the sand; and when they are above ground, their grayish-white carapace blends well with the sand. If you sit quietly for a while, though, you may see them walking toward the moon when it's full.

Hermit crab—These crabs don't have shells, so they're always looking for a home. They scour the land for secondhand quarters to move into, usually the cast-off shells of dead snails. And as they grow, hermit crabs are forced to abandon their homes and seek out larger, more spacious quarters.

Lady, or calico, crab—These crabs are also great swimmers, with paddle legs, but they're only about 2 inches long and are not good for eating. They are pretty to look at, though, with red and purple speckled shells. Their molts are often found on the beach.

Spider crab—These round-bodied crustaceans have very long legs and are usually covered with algae, a plus in helping them to camouflage themselves.

Other Sea Creatures

Atlantic menhaden, or **bunker**—Most people wouldn't want to eat these small fish with the big heads, because they are very oily and bony; but the oil pressed from them is rich in omega-3 fatty acids and is used to enrich everything from pasta to sports drinks. Native Americans used these herring-like fish as fertilizer. They are silver with a distinct black spot behind their gills.

Atlantic silversides—These light-colored, translucent, slender fish are easy to spot because they swim close to shore, often in schools. They have a silver stripe outlined by a narrow black stripe along their sides and are integral to the ecosystem because bigger fish, like striped bass, and birds, like terns and cormorants, eat them. Fisherman also use these 5-inchers as bait.

Jellyfish—Be careful of jellyfish, because many of them sting (that's how they catch food), including the moon jellyfish, the clear beauty with the flower pattern in the center. They are mesmerizing to watch as they open and close their bodies and swim through the water. Comb jellies, on the other hand, don't have stingers (pneumatocysts), but collect food using sticky cells called colloblasts. These jellies include sea walnuts, oval-shaped, transparent animals with faint vertical stripes on their bodies. They're bioluminescent, meaning they glow green at night when disturbed.

Northern pipefish and **seahorses**—Both of these long, slender animals, whose bodies are encased in bony rings, swim with their heads up and their tails down, with males carrying and giving birth to live babies. They are also sometimes called tube-mouths because of their elongated snouts. Seahorses have horselike heads and monkeylike tails that they hook to plants and other objects to stay anchored. Pipefish are a little more eel-like, with a small fin at the ends of their tails.

Plankton—If you have a microscope, bring it along to study these tiny creatures, without which marine life would not be possible. Zooplankton are animals and phytoplankton are plants. Dip a jar in seawater, then use a dropper to put just a bit of water under the microscope. You'll see all sorts of strange-shaped, wriggling creatures. Plankton comes in many varieties.

Sea stars—Most sea stars have five radiating legs with light-sensitive eyespots at the tips. The dot (usually orange) in the middle of a sea star's spiny body isn't an eye, but a madreporite, a pore that takes in water to help move the flexible tube feet on the animal's underside. To eat, sea stars wrap themselves around bivalves, pull the shells open, and push their own inverted stomachs through their tiny mouths (in the center of their undersides), eating and digesting the bivalves right in their own shells. Like crabs, sea stars can grow a new arm if one is lost.

Skate egg cases—If you find a small, black rectangle with tendrils at the ends, it's the egg case of a skate, a flat, bottom-dwelling ray fish that lays eggs rather than bear live young. The capsules (sometimes called mermaid purses) are buried in the sand, so they look like submerged kelp and are safe from predators.

Sponges—Real sponges look nothing like the lemon-colored darling of the younger set, SpongeBob, who looks more like a scouring sponge. Sponges are irregularly shaped, primitive animals with no internal organs and no real skeletal structure. They are simply a bunch of cells that breathe, feed, reproduce, and eject waste through their fibrous nook-and-cranny bodies. They come in a variety of shapes and colors, but most of those found in our area are brown.

Seaweeds

Seaweeds are marine algae that come in reds, browns, and greens, depending upon the depth of water in which they live. Red seaweeds grow in the deepest waters, brown in the midrange, and green closer to shore. Although plant-like, seaweeds do not have roots, stems, and leaves like traditional plants, but do photosynthesize. Instead of roots, they have holdfasts that attach them to the sea floor.

In addition to providing shelter for tiny invertebrates and many other sea creatures, seaweeds are a food source not only for shore dwellers, but for people, who consider them quite healthful. While your kids may squeal in disgust at the idea of eating seaweed, you might tell them they gobble it up all the time, because seaweed derivatives are used in ice cream, puddings, and chocolate milk, among other foods.

Bladder wrack—This olive-brown, branching alga is covered with air pockets that kids just love to pop. These bubbles allow the seaweed to float to the top of the ocean and get the sunlight needed to survive and grow. Often found washed up on the beach and attached to rocks, bladder wrack is the original source of iodine.

Chenille weed—A beautiful red seaweed with many branches, chenille weed is covered with soft leaves that look like hair.

Dulles—This brown or dark-red seaweed feels leathery and often grows on or near kelp.

Irish moss—This branching alga is usually purplish-red with brushy, curly tops. Edible, it is said to have helped many Irish people survive the Great Famine of the 1840s. It contains carrageenan, a starch-like, no-calorie substance that is today used to thicken ice cream, salad dressings, and other foods.

Kelp—Look for kelp—long, flat blades with tails—in mussel beds and under docks.

Sea lettuce—This familiar, grass-green algae comes in crinkly, thin sheets that are often seen lying around on sand and rocks at low tide. It is a favorite food of periwinkles (a type of snail), and some people enjoy it in their salads. For a humorous look at sea lettuce, read the children's story, *Harry by the Sea*, by Gene Zion.

Coastal Plants

Show your kids that in many ways the beach is like a desert, but without the cacti. It's a harsh environment, where plants cling to the sand and bake in the sun. Plants that thrive in this environment have deep root systems that hold them in place and help them find scarce fresh water underground. Their small, tough, and sometimes hairy leaves help them retain moisture. These plants do not grow very tall and are flexible enough to withstand heavy winds, pounding waves, and saltwater spray. Some of them hold the dunes in place and are the foundation on which larger plants later grow. Most of these plants are found on shorelines closed to swimming, because they would never survive foot traffic, volleyball games, and beach blankets.

American beach grass—This plant is the glue that holds sand dunes together. Its deep root systems grow out parallel to the surface, every foot or so sending up tillers, or new shoots, which then form clumps of grass that act like wind barriers.

Beach heather—This short, bushy plant has green, fuzzy leaves, and in late spring, it has golden blooms that flower only for a short time.

Beach pea—This pretty native vine has purple flowers in summer and can be found crawling along dunes, its tendrils keeping the plant in place. Its seed pods look like garden pea pods and are edible.

Beach plum—Native to the Atlantic coast, this plant produces dark-purple, cherry-sized fruits in August that, although too tart and bitter to eat out of hand, make a tasty jam. New stems are reddish brown and the shrub sprouts pinkish-white flowers in spring, even before the leaves show up.

Examining bladder-wrack, a seaweed with air pockets that help it float.

Salt-spray rose—One of the most recognizable beach shrubs, these roses are pink or white with yellow centers, and are later replaced by cherry tomato-like rose hips that make a soothing tea and tasty jelly high in Vitamin C. As its name implies, this Asian import tolerates the salty sea spray that would do in the delicate roses of Valentine's Day bouquets.

Sea beach amaranth—This endangered plant has spinach-like leaves that are rounded and have a notch at the ends, and reddish, fleshy stems. It is not tolerant of foot traffic and therefore forms its wide, low-growing mats on beaches usually closed to the public and occupied by endangered shore birds.

Sea rocket—This native, prostrate succulent grows along the high-tide line and has tough, rubbery, wavy-toothed leaves that lock in moisture. It's named for its two-jointed seed-pods, designed to allow one half to break off and be carried away by the ocean to disperse its seeds elsewhere, while the other half stays attached to the plant to reproduce at the same location. Look for whitish to pale lavender flowers with four petals in June and July.

Seaside goldenrod—This plant grows up to 8 feet tall and sports many long clusters of bright golden flowers in late summer, providing food for butterflies and insects. Its leaves are long, fleshy, and pointed.

Coastal Upland Plants

Exploring coastal uplands with your kids is a good way to show them that nothing lives in isolation, that everything is interconnected. Once shore plants have stabilized beaches and enriched the soil, larger plants may take root farther back from the ocean and bays, eventually forming uplands. There you'll find taller shrubs and trees that are less tolerate of salt and strong winds and often depend on the dunes and barrier beaches to protect them. Show your children how these trees and shrubs are often stunted from salt spray and growing in saline soils and twisted from blowing in the wind.

Autumn olive—Introduced from Asia in the 19th century, this invasive plant features leaves that are green above and silver below. It grows as a shrub or small tree. In spring, it has small, light yellow, trumpet-shaped flowers and in fall produces red berries, which songbirds like to eat.

Bayberry—A large shrub or small tree with dark green leaves, bayberry is highly scented and in the fall produces grayish-white berries that are covered with wax and grow in clusters close to the branches. Colonists boiled the berries and collected the floating wax to make bayberry candles.

Black cherry—This native flowering tree is gorgeous in spring, when long pendulous clusters of fragrant white flowers are in bloom, usually the same time that tent caterpillars build their silky nests in the forks of the tree's branches. The glossy green leaves turn yellow and rose in the fall.

Dwarf, or **winged**, **sumac**—This small native tree appears to have green wings growing on its branches. Its leaves are compound, made up of many oval leaflets that grow opposite one another. Sumac really stands out in the fall, when it is covered with large plumes of dark red fruit that grow in tall clusters. These slightly hairy berries hang on through the winter, providing food for wildlife.

Eastern red cedar—This aromatic native evergreen doesn't have needles, but rather flat, scaly leaves. In June, juicy blue berries covered with a white powder appear, favorites of cedar waxwings but toxic to humans. Many Native American tribes consider this the tree of life and burn its wood as incense in sweat lodges and purification rites. Wood shavings from this tree are used to line gerbil cages.

Japanese black pine—This import from Japan is an interesting looking, irregularly shaped evergreen, which often has lots of twisted branches. Its needles are about 5 to 7 inches long and are grouped in pairs. Japanese black pines are known for their white "candles," the new sprigs that grow at the branch tips.

Shadbush—This native shrub or small tree has pretty, star-like flowers with five thin petals in April and May and is so named because that's the time when shad fish leave the Atlantic Ocean to swim upriver to spawn. The blueberry-like berries produced in June are important to wildlife and were eaten by Native Americans,

Annual Beach Cleanup

A family can explore the shore and at the same time do something good for the environment. Every year, on the third weekend of September, volunteers all over the world head to local beaches and help clean them up. Some join already organized groups, others assemble friends and neighbors in the cause, while still others head out as a families, adopting their own beaches.

Working side-by-side with your children in an enjoyable yet meaningful way opens up discussion about the world we live in and the role we can play to improve it for everyone. Kids learn how trash gets on the beach in the first place—from careless people simply littering to eroding landfills unleashing trash directly into the water. And when garbage is tossed into the street, storm water often carries it right into our street sewers, whose outflow ends up in the ocean, which in turn washes that garbage onto the beaches.

You can make picking up trash fun by playing a game to see who can find the weirdest piece of garbage or the most bottle caps. Everything picked up is documented and used to create educational materials and to lobby legislators for cleaner beaches and coastlines. Organized in New York City by the American Littoral Society, more than 10,150 volunteers cleaned and documented more 334,421 pounds of debris at 351 beaches across the city in 2003.

If you want to join a group or organize one of your own, contact Barbara Cohen, New York State Beach Cleanup Coordinator, at 718-471-2166 or at alsbeach@aol.com. She will conduct a phone workshop with you so that you can explain the whole program to your volunteers. Or visit www.alsnyc.org.

who dried them for use during the winter. They also mixed the berries with dried meat and animal fat, creating "pemmican," a portable meal that they took on hunting trips. It is said the berries helped to delay meat spoilage. Colonists used the berries in jams and pies.

Virginia creeper—One of the first plants to change color in fall, turning from green to red, Virginia creeper is a native vine whose "leaf" is actually a compound leaf consisting of five leaflets spread out like a fan. It often climbs trees and crawls on the ground, which makes it easy for chipmunks to reach the blue berries it produces in the fall. The berries are, however, poisonous to people, who sometimes confuse this vine with poison ivy, which has three leaves.

 **7** # GARDENS GROW CHILDREN

With children spending increasing amounts of time indoors behind computers, in front of televisions, and in indoor play spaces, it's more important than ever to get them outside. And there's no better place to do that than in a garden, be it a public or community garden or a plot of your own.

Gardens not only soften the edges of urban life; they are beautiful, calm oases where families can spend time exploring together, free from unwelcome, sometimes overwhelming city stimuli. Gardens put children in touch with the vital cycles of nature, of which they are a part. Kids quickly learn that plants are living things, too—they are born, grow, breathe, eat, and reproduce. As they connect with gardens more and more, youngsters discover the interdependence of all living things—for gardens are not simply soil and plants, but worlds filled with inter-relationships among plants, insects, birds, worms, mammals, other creatures . . . and people.

Children are naturally inquisitive and will discover that there's always something new in the garden, from a seedling pushing through the soil and a praying mantis egg case attached to a branch to a swallowtail butterfly collecting nectar and raspberries ripe enough to pick. Over time, kids will learn to love, respect, and understand the garden and its inhabitants—from the creepiest spider to the thorniest bush—and eventually mature into environmentally conscious adults with lots of happy childhood memories in the garden.

Visiting Public Gardens with Children

You don't need a home garden to engage your children in the wonder of plants and their wildlife communities. Public gardens around the city have sensational hands-on gardening programs that allow kids to experience first-hand the journey from seed to plant. Many of these places also include children's gardens, where kids can climb on tree stumps and boulders,

The city's public gardens offer an array of family programs in which kids can make nature journals, plant seeds, and more.

walk along mulched trails, and touch and smell everything growing in a plot of land created just for them. These public gardens also offer a bouquet of seasonal events with music, crafts, games, and plant appreciation for all ages.

While the children's gardens are wonderful, that doesn't mean youngsters will be bored in the rest of the garden. Small children may be disinterested in botanical names and formal garden design, to be sure; but there are plenty of creative ways to explore public gardens with your kids. Unfortunately, some parents think botanical gardens are only for adults—like a friend of mine who, when invited to bring her son to join me and my boys at a local garden, remarked, "But what is there for them to do?"

Where do I start? Little children love making tree rubbings or scouting around for unusual or particularly vivid flowers. Older children can go beyond the aesthetics of a plant to understand why different species thrive in specific environments. Infants are happy just crawling in the grass or rummaging through autumn leaves for the sheer tactile pleasure of it all.

Once you've decided to visit a garden with your kids, it's good to start with a ground plan—something to guide you along, but with freedom to deviate if your children seem intrigued by one specific aspect of the garden. Your child should always carry a hand lens, so as to look more closely at plants and the insects that crawl on them. Binoculars are also a good idea, because gardens are filled with birds.

Begin exploring a garden with toddlers by looking for colors. Have them find individual flowers that are red, yellow, pink, orange, white, and so on. You might also look for plants with silly-sounding common names—like old-man cactus, lady's slipper, and red-hot poker—and on the basis of observation, guess why they are named that way. There's even a book by Diana Harding, entitled *Some Plants Have Funny Names*.

Let your noses lead the way to an herb garden, where scents are as varied as tangy lemon verbena, onion-like chives, perfumey lavender, and aromatic basil. Ask your children to sniff around for something familiar and tell you what it reminds them of—oregano and pizza or fennel and licorice, for example.

Since gardens are more than the plants that grow there, look around for animals that live in the garden, from spiders and praying mantises to ladybugs and honeybees.

Collect acorns and pinecones and do something fun with them at home, like rolling pinecones in peanut butter and birdseed for a quick feeder, or combining acorns and pinecones into an "all-natural" turkey. Glue the acorn onto one end of the pinecone for a head, adding googly eyes and a piece of red felt for a wattle. Then glue long pieces of construction paper to the opposite end for tail feathers. Put a small bit of clay on the bottom to keep the turkey from rolling.

Once youngsters are in grade school, they have the ability to dig deeper into the plant world and may be eager to explore plant structure and how insects work with plants to secure both their futures. Explain to them that plants need to be pollinated to produce seeds. That means moving bits of pollen from the male part of the plant to the female. Most flowers can't do this on their own. Corn is pollinated by the wind, but insects, particularly bees, are the chief pollinators of plants. In their travels from flower to flower, collecting nectar to feed their queen and community, bees brush up against pollen. As they flit about, landing here and there, some of the pollen gets dusted onto the female parts of flowers, thereby fertilizing them so they can produce seeds.

Gardens are also great places for scavenger hunts because there are so many different varieties of plants and trees. Come up with an age-appropriate list of 12 items, with younger children seeking out such things as a red flower, a leaf with pointed lobes, a singing bird, a honeybee, and so on. Older kids can look for things like leaf galls, a plant with thorns, signs of a spider, two different kinds of seeds, a flower with five petals, and so on. Don't let your kids collect these specimens; just have them check them off on their list.

Try focusing one of your visits on trees alone, using the self-guided walks in *New York City Trees*, by Edward Sibley Barnard, as your guide. Or simply watch butterflies, often colorful and always delicate, like tiny faeries in a perfect world. Some gardens have special butterfly gardens, planted with flowers that attract these winged gems; but keep an eye out for butterflies throughout the garden.

Lastly, visit the garden in spring, summer, autumn, and even in winter to see how Mother Nature changes her wardrobe every few months, just like us. After a while, your children will be able to tell the time of year by what's in bloom rather than by the calendar. A good guide to the city's gardens is *Garden Guide: New York City*, by Nancy Berner and Susan Lowry.

While it's fine to just stop and smell the roses, there is something more to be gained by noticing the trees for the forest and learning the who's who in this vast plant community. For every season, there's a reason and an order.

New York Botanical Garden

**Bronx River Parkway
and Fordham Road
Bronx
718-817-8700**
www.nybg.org

Seasonal events; family programs; farmers' market; bird walks; gift and plant shop; tram that makes stops throughout the garden; free daily tours; café; family picnic area; restrooms.

Of all the city's public gardens, this botanical paradise offers many reasons to visit with young children, from hiking the garden's 50-acre forest to exploring the Everett Children's Adventure Garden. Dig for worms at the

The spring-blooming pink lady's slipper is one of our rare plants.

Howell Family Garden or squeeze through the crack of a huge rock left behind by a glacier. Linger and get intimate with the garden, soaking up all that a wetland or butterfly garden has to offer. Listen for the "jug-o-rum, jug-o-rum" of male bullfrogs (hint: they're near water), inspect the inside of a flower, and have fun building a human-sized bird's nest.

The garden is immense—250 acres—so don't expect to see it all in one day. You can always return, perhaps during another season when the garden will look and feel like an entirely new place.

Open—April-October: Tuesday through Sunday and Monday holidays, 10 AM-6 PM; November-March: 10 AM-5 PM. Closed nonholiday Mondays, Thanksgiving, and Christmas. Grounds admission fee, with separate fees to the adventure garden, rock garden, conservatory, and tram. Combination tickets are available. Kids under 2 free. Grounds admission is free on Wednesdays and Saturdays, 10 AM-noon. On-site parking (fee).

Enid A. Haupt Conservatory

It is forever summer in the Enid A. Haupt Conservatory, the world's largest Victorian glasshouse, which highlights ecosystems found around the globe, from rainforests to arid lands. The 90-foot-tall greenhouse is so big it supports tremendous specimens, including a giant saguaro cactus, fruiting banana trees, and an African kapok tree that has grown here for more than 100 years. Tell your children that in the wild, kapok trees flower at night and are pollinated by bats!

At the door, youngsters can pick up a colorful cartoon guide sheet ($1.00) that will help them search for plants that dinosaurs ate and plants used to make medicines, chocolate, and coffee. There's also a kids' audio tour of the conservatory, narrated by children and free with conservatory admission.

Everett Children's

The New York Botanical Garden is 250 acres of nature's beauties and pleasures.

Adventure Garden

The 12-acre Everett Children's Adventure Garden is playfully designed for kids under 12, complete with flower-covered caterpillar topiaries whose coats change with the seasons and kid-sized lily pads that spout water when pounced on. A special favorite is the Boulder Maze. Many parents take it easy here, sitting on a bottom rock while their kids scale their mini-Mount Everest, pleased with themselves as they ascend higher and higher to a lookout. There's not much shade here, so it can get pretty hot in the summer.

Across the way is Beth's Maze, a labyrinth of child-high hedges for kids to navigate. There's also an area where kids can build human-sized bird's nests by weaving thick reams of rope and twine through metal forms. This is a wonderful opportunity to become a bird with your child, chirping together while building the nest. When it's done, dispose of any inhibitions and sit inside with your fledglings and offer them some imaginary worms. Later, as you walk around the garden, help your children find real bird's nests in the trees.

If it's raining on the day you visit, don't fret and run home. While the plants get their thirsts quenched, wait out the storm in the well-staffed and well-stocked Discovery Center, with demonstrations ranging from ice-cream making, using ingredients found in nature, to programs on various creatures—bees, ants, flies, and hummers, for example—that pollinate plants and help produce fruit and seeds. Exhibits and programs change about every six weeks. There's also a great collection of nature books, puppets, puzzles, and games to share with your child.

This is a "Touch, Please!" kind of place where kids can handle giant pinecones, bark chunks, various types of acorns, and other bits of nature, or

Kids love climbing on the the giant boulder maze in the Everett Children's Adventure Garden.

become young scientists investigating pollen and leaves under a microscope. Older youngsters can even get a grip on the scientific method of "classification" used to group specimens by similarities and differences in order to identify them. Sometimes, staffers pull out live millipedes, tarantulas, and tadpoles for kids to meet. There are also hands-on nature crafts, like making field guides and scented tissue-paper flowers.

Back outside is a pond with tadpoles, duckweed, and water hyacinths that bloom lavender in mid-summer and a kidney-shaped touch tank with aquatic plants that kids can lift up to inspect the roots. Helpful field guides on birds and pond life are available in the gazebo on the bridge.

On the other side of the pond is the Mitsubishi Wild Wetland Trail, a short, dry pathway that goes through a swampy habitat that is of vital importance to the food web and our own survival. Along the trail, listen for the "check" or "oh-ka-lee" call of red-winged blackbirds.

Children and adults both will enjoy the naturalistic plantings and beauty of the Everett Children's Garden. One bed is planted specifically for hummingbirds, with lots of tubular, red flowers that attract hummers, with their color and slender "throats" perfectly suited for the tiny birds' thin, nectar-collecting beaks. Butterflies, including huge tiger swallowtails and monarchs, have a field day on the numerous butterfly bushes with purple, white, and pink flowers shaped a lot like lilacs.

During warmer months, the garden is so lush that kids really have fun navigating the various leafy paths that lead to nooks and unexpected educational displays tucked here and there. To get the most out of your outing, make sure you play along, investigating and interpreting signs for them. When you're done, enjoy a picnic lunch at the nearby Family Picnic Area.

Ruth Rea Howell Family Garden

Located on the far east side of the botanical garden and often overshadowed by the Adventure Garden, the Family Garden is often overlooked by visitors. And that's too bad, because this is where kids get to touch the earth and its bounty.

How a Plant Works

When a plant is born, everything it needs for its first few days of life is stored in the seed. After that, it's on its own. Plants are the only living things that must make their own food. This complex food-producing process is called photosynthesis, which plants achieve by absorbing sunlight through their green leaves, water through their roots, and carbon dioxide from the air—and mixing it all together to make carbohydrates (for themselves) and oxygen, which is released back into the air and is critical to our own survival. Roots do not feed plants, but anchor them to the ground and draw in needed moisture and minerals. Most plants have both male and female parts. When the pistil (female part) is dusted with pollen (male reproductive cells), seed production begins. In most cases, pollen reaches the pistil through pollination, often effected by bees, other insects, and birds—and, sometimes, even bats. While flowers are beautiful to look at, they're really designed to attract pollinators. As the pollinators flit from flower to flower, they are picking up pollen and brushing some of it off onto the pistils of other flowers. The pollen then lengthens and makes its way down into the plant's ovary, where seeds are produced for the following year.

While many botanical gardens restrict their children's gardens to kids registered in their programs, this garden invites families to drop in and help plant seeds, harvest crops, and weed—whatever the staff happens to be doing when you visit. There are whimsical gardens here—like the Kitchen Garden, where plants are nestled in stoves and sinks; and the Carnival Garden, complete with a planted mini–merry-go-round. Themes change yearly.

Pitchforks stuck into compost piles invite kids to poke around heaps of organic material in various stages of decomposition, and occupied by millipedes, worms, sow bugs, and other insects hard at work turning it all into nutrient-rich humus. There are also two worm-digging stations with trowels and knee-pads, so that family members can kneel side-by-side and prospect for worms. A tiny pond supports tadpoles and other aquatic life.

There are also four heritage gardens tilled by volunteer families who grow produce important to specific cultures, such as Native American, Chinese, Korean, and Caribbean. This is a great opportunity for children to discover "new" veggies, herbs, and plants that may

Flower-covered caterpillar topiaries sport "coats" that change with the seasons.

not be sold in their local supermarkets, as well as learn how these plants are eaten or used in natural medicines and decorations.

All the walk-in programs, including crafts under the gazebo, are free. The garden is open to families from 1 PM through 5:30 PM, Tuesday through Sunday, April through October. It is closed to the public in the mornings (when children's gardening programs take place there). For your convenience, the garden tram stops right at the gate.

Exploring the Native Forest

It may come as a surprise, but sheltered within the perfect trim of the New York Botanical Garden are woodlands that have never seen an ax—a bit of urban nature left untouched. This rare, primeval forest with its 200- to 300-year-old trees is one of the last such places in New York City and comprises 20 percent of the garden's total acreage. Despite its sanctity, families are invited to wander its quiet paths, passing adorable chipmunks, florescent mushrooms, and medleys of wildflowers.

Walking these woods is a wonderful way for children to see the difference between cultivated gardens and nature left on its own. This is a healthy forest comprised of layers: the forest floor (mainly leaf litter and decaying branches, logs, and fruit); the herbaceous layer (wildflowers, ferns, and other small plants); the shrub layer (tree seedlings and woody plants); the understory (tall shrubs and short trees); and the canopy (the leafy roof of the tallest trees).

The entrance to the Forest Trail is opposite the Wild Wetland Trail and Everett Children's Adventure Garden. It's best to pick up a map at the garden entrance. Most people walk straight on the main trail, which eventually crosses the Bronx River; but if you explore the side trails, you'll encounter fewer people and feel like you've driven upstate for a day's outing.

Soon after starting this 1-mile walk, you'll see a native tree on your right that is, well, exfoliating. It's called a shagbark hickory, and

Kids spin the carrot at the New York Botanical Garden to learn all about plants.

its gray bark peels off in long, wide, curled strips. Give it a touch. In autumn, the tree produces a thick-husked fruit that squirrels and chipmunks hammer away at to get to the sweet kernel inside, sort of like biting a lollipop to get to the Tootsie Roll center.

Look for false Solomon's seal, a wildflower with long leaves that produces a creamy white plume in spring and a cluster of reddish-pink berries in late summer. Orange, trumpet-shaped flowers hang like gems from the jewelweed plant in late summer, attracting hummingbirds. Rubbing some stem juice on you is said to relieve poison ivy itch and other skin rashes.

Take the second left. There's a tiny vernal pond on your right, where mallards sometimes swim. Odd Jack-in-the-pulpits also bloom along this trail in spring; but they're hard to see because they're green, only about 12 inches high, grow in the shade, and usually hide beneath three big leaflets. They are so named because the club-like stem on which the tiny flowers grow looks like a person preaching within an old-fashioned pulpit—which in this case is actually a spathe, a leaf-like funnel with a wavy, pointed hood that prevents water from accumulating inside the spathe and washing away the pollen.

Continue for a short while until you reach a "7" marker next to a large red oak tree (the number corresponds to a long-defunct, self-guided trail brochure). To your right is the 23-mile-long Bronx River, the city's only freshwater river, which originates in Westchester County and runs through the Bronx, eventually emptying into Long Island Sound. Wood ducks like to hang out here. Once polluted by industry, the river is enjoying a renaissance as community and environmental groups help restore it and welcome people to its shores via new waterside parks, bicycle paths, and canoe trips. (See chapter 5, Paddling with Kids.)

Something wonderful was discovered along this trail in 1987—a Native American petroglyph, or rock picture, depicting a turtle and probably carved between 1000 and 1600 C.E. Turtles figured prominently in the creation myth told by the local Lenni Lenapes. If your children want to see the petroglyph, it's on display in the Enid A. Haupt Conservatory, right before the desert area.

Turn around and return to the main path. Turn left. You will come to the remains of a 300-year-old oak felled in a storm. Garden personnel have sawed the tree into large chunks, providing kids with a great opportunity to study its rings. Tree detectives are called dendrolochronologists, and they can determine the age of a tree and the conditions under which it grew from year to year by interpreting these rings.

Explain to your children that every year trees grow a new layer of wood around their trunks and branches—a ring. Each ring has two parts: a wide light-colored band (springwood, because it grows the most in spring) and a thin-

ner dark-colored band (summerwood, when growth slows down). Help your children count the rings from inside out, beginning at the dark core or heartwood. Then count backwards from the outside in to determine how old the tree was when your children were born and when you were born.

What else do these rings tell us about this tree? Was this a good place to grow? Were there any traumatic events in this tree's life? Look closely at the "cookie" (what a cross-section of trunk is called). A wide ring indicates a good year with plenty of sunshine, water, and nutrients. Narrow or misshapen rings reveal drought, cold, disease, competition from other trees, and other stresses.

If the season is right, you may notice plenty of blackberry bushes along the trail. Also, keep watch for a small, spiny, tropical-looking tree called Hercules' club (its branches widen at the joint, giving them a club-like appearance) and sometimes the devil's walking stick (because of its thorns). It produces blackish berries in fall, favorites of cardinals, thrashers, and other birds.

Despite its wildness, the forest has been affected by humans, as evidenced by the many nonnative plants growing here, like Japanese honeysuckle, garlic mustard, and Norway maples. Explain to your children that way back when, these plants were imported from other countries because they looked nice in gardens or because their fruits tasted good. Their seeds then dispersed. They found footholds and began crowding out native plants. Since they're not from these parts, they have few natural enemies, like insects and diseases, to keep them in check. That's why they're called "invasives," because they have invaded the local ecosystem.

You'll soon come to a bridge that crosses the Bronx River. Interestingly, this bridge is featured in the opening sequence of *Sesame Street*, with Big Bird dancing across it. Stand on the bridge for a while and let your children watch the water rush by. Rather than crossing the bridge, turn right and you'll soon see a stream flowing beneath lots of jewelweed, a summer-blooming, orange flower that attracts hummingbirds. In spring, look for dragonfly nymphs resting on the bottom of the stream.

Turn right onto Azalea Way, which leads out of the woods. In spring, this area bursts with color. The path also has lots of tall, straight tulip trees, once used by Native Americans to make canoes. When you come to the interpretive Forest Edge Trail on your right, pause for a quick lesson on the importance of forests and the differing attitudes of Native Americans and early colonists toward the forest. In spring, a sea of gorgeous blue Virginia bluebells blooms. In early spring, look for the yellow, nodding heads of tiny trout lilies. This ends your walk.

Split Rock and the Rock Garden

Near the entrance to the Rock Garden is a huge boulder with a dramatic split right down the middle. Kids never tire of walking through the crack in the rock, a glacial erratic pushed here thousands of ago and still in the same spot.

While here, stop by the Rock Garden to see the minigardens in stone containers on the left as you enter. Worlds unto their own, they may inspire a similar project at home, especial-

Kids love to squeeze through the crack in this glacial rock at the New York Botanical Garden

ly if you don't have a yard. Using tiny plants and flowers, pebbles, and driftwood, you and your child can design, cultivate, and tend a tiny plant universe so compact, yet so full of variety. The garden's Shop in the Garden has a wonderful selection of teeny-weeny rock-garden plants that will help get you started.

Farmers' Market

From June through October, kids can meet New York State farmers and sample what they reap from the earth, including delicious raspberries in June, peaches and tomatoes in summer, melons in September, and apples and gourds in October. Free demonstrations—which have included rainwater harvesting, attracting butterflies to the garden, composting, and soap making—are held from noon to 2 PM on the second and last Wednesday of each month. The market is in Tulip Tree Allee and is open on Wednesdays from 10 AM–3 PM.

Holiday Train Show

The annual Holiday Train Show, on display in the glass-domed Enid A. Haupt Conservatory from November through January) is a family favorite. What kid doesn't like choo-choos chugging along lengths of track, passing into and out of tunnels, crossing bridges, and wending around tight curves. While the show has plenty of local significance—the miniature buildings and structures are replicas of historic places in and around New York City—the exhibit is also about nature.

Designer Paul G. Busse uses gourds, berries, pinecones, twigs, and other natural ingredients to handcraft everything from the Statue of Liberty to the Brooklyn Bridge. The Guggenheim Museum is stacked with layers of mushrooms. The clock tower atop City Hall is constructed of honeysuckles, acorns, cinnamon sticks, dusty miller, and bittersweet. Rockefeller Center is complete with angels made from okra pods, grapevines, hickory nuts, sea grass, and raffia. The stained-glass windows of Street

Patrick's Cathedral include Siberian iris seed ponds, poppy seeds, eucalyptus pods, pinecone scales, and grapevines.

After visiting, why not create some botanical architecture of your own at home with your children using found twigs, leaves, and bark as well as beans and seeds bought at a supermarket or garden shop. Glue guns, available at craft stores, provide sure-fire mortar. If your house or apartment building were made of plant materials, what would it look like? How about your school or favorite restaurant? The possibilities are as varied as nature itself.

Wave Hill offers one of the best nature-themed family art programs in the city.

Wave Hill

**675 West 252nd Street
Bronx
718-549-3200**
www.wavehill.org

Family art projects and programs; seasonal events; garden tours; wildlife walks; urban nature writing program for teens; girls' science camp; gift shop; café; restrooms.

Wave Hill doesn't have a children's garden, but it does have some of the best family art programs in the city, held from 1 to 4 PM every weekend throughout the year in the Kerlin Learning Center. The center has an inviting art-studio feel with spirited children's artwork, and there's no shortage of materials or educator enthusiasm. Projects are linked to the seasons and often include music and some outside time,

like sketching in the forest or moving through the air like a butterfly.

The garden also has a 10-acre woodland with a mulched path suitable for any age. The trail begins just inside the garden entrance, to the left, and meanders through a grove of rhododendrons (beautiful in late spring), a white pine grove, and a larger deciduous forest. You'll also stumble on a lovely resting place—a little nook with a tree-trunk table and log seating—where you can sit and listen to the sounds of the forest.

Among the garden's festivals is the annual Buzz-a-Rama in September, when kids can watch bees make honey, try on beekeeper's gear, meet the garden's volunteer beekeepers, and make their own artistic beehives. Another program invites the public to watch tree climbers and pruners at work.

In addition to the garden's flower, herb, aquatic, wild, and other components is one of the most spectacular views of the Hudson River and New Jersey Palisades, a star attraction during fall foliage. In the visitor center, you may pick up a free self-guided tour featuring 12 of the garden's most impressive trees. Of special interest to children is the big-leaf magnolia with enormous leaves up to 30-inches long.

Open—April 15-October 14: Tuesday-Sunday, 9 AM-5: 30 PM; until 9 PM on Wednesdays in June and July; closed Monday, except Memorial Day, Labor Day, and Columbus Day. October 15-April 14: 9 AM-4:30 PM, closed Monday. Fee for those 6 and older. Free all day Tuesday, 9 AM-noon on Saturday, and throughout December, January, and February.

If you've ever wondered how a container of decaying organic matter can be at all interesting to kids, you haven't dug through it with a stick, looking for millipedes, sow bugs, earthworms, and other critters busily eating away and turning the mess into nutrient-rich soil. Insects are endlessly fascinating to many kids, although they do make others squeamish. Once you explain to your children that insects are the earth's recyclers, chances are they'll have a new-found respect for the little creatures.

Composting also teaches kids to differentiate between good garbage and bad garbage. To quote a really terrific song by Tom Chapin:

Good garbage breaks down as it goes;
That's why it smells bad to your nose.
Bad Garbage grows and grows and grows.
Garbage is supposed to be composed.

Send home the message by burying a nylon stocking filled with vegetable and fruit peels and plastic material, like cutlery or your kid's favorite toy car. When you dig it up in three months, the plastic will be unchanged, while the organic materials will have been transformed into soil.

Once kids learn that banana peels, watermelon rinds, and autumn leaves don't have to be thrown in the trash, but can be magically transformed into something soil-like, they'll be hankering for a compost pile of their own. All you need is a compost bin (available at gardening stores, botanical gardens, and Web-based sources) with a screened bottom, which allows insects and microscopic critters in, but keeps squirrels, mice, and rats out. For this reason, I don't recommend an unprotected compost pile. If you don't have a yard, your kids can easily and safely compost small amounts of organic material in countertop worm bins.

Simply chuck in all your organic waste—veggie and fruit remains, coffee grounds, egg boxes, old flowers and weeds (if they haven't gone to seed), and other organic matter. It's best to maintain a good mix of green and brown items, like kitchen scraps and dried leaves, so the compost doesn't become too mushy or too dry. It's also a good idea to aerate the heap; using a pitchfork or composting tool, about once a week to keep it light and fluffy so it doesn't become too compressed.

Once your compost heats up, show your kids how the temperature inside the bin differs from the temperature outside the bin. This is best done during cooler temperatures, for the starkest contrast. As thousands of insects, microscopic bacteria, fungi, and worms busily nibble and digest the garbage, they release heat. The real workhouse is the lowly earthworm that constantly tunnels through and loosens the compost, allowing water and air to circulate. Their castings (poop) are high in minerals and organic matter.

When your compost looks like really black dirt (called humus), it's ready to mix into the garden or indoor plant pots, enriching the soil without commercial fertilizers. What you and your children have done is simply replicate what nature does naturally. Plants die and leaves fall to the ground, and then they decay with the help of the same critters attracted to your compost bin. That hearty smell in the forest comes from humus. If compost didn't happen, the forest would be buried under mounds of dead leaves, logs, and other organic waste.

Explain to your kids that by composting they are recycling, helping to reduce the volume of garbage in landfills and creating a valuable product—all for free. It's their way of keeping their earth from becoming one big mountain of garbage.

Brooklyn Botanic Garden

**1000 Washington Avenue
Brooklyn
718-623-7200**
www.bbg.org

Family programs and seasonal events; free weekend guided tours; summer self-guided garden walks based on annual theme; café; garden shop; resource library; restrooms. No picnicking.

The Brooklyn Botanic Garden hosts wonderful seasonal events at which families may dance to hoe-down music, make nature crafts, plant seeds, or pretend to be pollinators. Its Children's Garden is the nation's longest operating gardening program for children, opened in 1914. The garden's 52 acres also provide a place to explore nature, from playing in the Discovery Garden to going on a scavenger hunt in search of caterpillars, butterflies, seeds, and other offspring of the earth.

The Fragrance Garden is one of the few places where kids may pick leaves and flowers and crush them to release their varying scents. Be sure to take a whiff of pineapple sage, which really smells like pineapples, and the licorice plant, which smells good enough to chew.

The lily ponds are gorgeous in midsummer with candy-colored flowers floating on the water and visits by mallards and the occasional heron. But perhaps most interesting to youngsters are lotus-seed heads (late summer) that resemble the tops of watering cans. Explain to your children that the seed head will eventually drop face down into the water, releasing its seeds, which will then float down, take hold in the mud, and send up new plants.

When temperatures turn cold, you and your children might embark on a botanical safari in the garden's Steinhardt Conservatory, a series of glass houses featuring different habitats. Enter the Desert Pavilion and pretend you're in Arizona. In the Tropical Pavilion, make believe you're visiting a rainforest. And in the Warm Temperate Pavilion imagine being in the Mediterranean or South Africa. Kids also get a kick out of the pint-size trees in the Bonsai Museum.

Open—April-September: Tuesday-Friday, 8 AM-6 PM; weekends and holidays, 10 AM-6 PM. October-March: Tuesday-Friday, 8 AM-4:30 PM; weekends and holidays, 10 AM-4:30 pm. Closed Mondays (except holidays, excluding Labor Day), Thanksgiving, Christmas, and New Year's Day. Fee, but free for children under 16. Free for everyone all day Tuesday, and 10 AM-noon Saturday. Mid-November-February, free all weekend. Always free for seniors on Fridays.

Discovery Garden

This small, intimate garden for kids is divided into two parts: the Children's Discovery Zone, with nooks and crannies best explored by preschoolers; and the Family Nature Trail, a short, mulched path that meanders past ferns, bamboo, trees, flowers, and water.

Kid favorites in the Discovery Zone include a weeping mulberry tree whose branches sweep the ground and must be pulled back like a curtain by kids wishing to sit on one of four stumps nestled under this umbrella of a tree. The private space is like a secret clubhouse for kids. At a long water table filled with aquatic plants, including floating water moss, feathered water fern, and water hyacinth, kids experience how some plants grow in water without soil. Children are encouraged to pick up the plants and examine their roots.

Look for butterflies on the garden's white and purple butterfly bushes, joe-pye weed, black-eyed Susans, and bee balm—all planted to attract them. Solar-powered panels generate the sounds of grasshoppers, crickets, and bees. There's also a tepee to sit in near the aquatic plants and a box full of pinecones in which little ones can play—a kind of nature's ball pit.

To enter the Family Nature Trail, kids and their parents walk through an arch covered with a hummingbird favorite: trumpet vine. Many kids then immediately dash off to the water pump to push the handle up and down as in the old days, letting water flow down a series of descending bamboo canals and into a slate-edged stream. Scales set up in shady nooks invite youngsters to pile on the pinecones, mulch, and branches to see which harvest is the heaviest. And there are, of course, flowers everywhere, some with fuzzy leaves that beg to be touched, others with delightful scents that seduce you to smell.

One special tree along the trail is the dawn redwood. Tell your children that this is an ancient tree thought to be extinct until it was rediscovered in China in the late 1940s. Seeds were later distributed to arboretums and gardens around the world, introducing the exotic tree to a larger audience

Children's Garden

While the garden is open only to children registered in the Botanic Garden's programs, the miniature farm with statuesque sunflowers, squat squashes, stands of corn, and bean tepees is easily enjoyed from the garden path or cozy roofed sitting nooks bordering the garden. Here is a chance for children to try and identify the foods that they eat, as they grow and not as they're displayed in a supermarket. Planting boxes along the perimeter of the 2-acre garden are flush with interesting plants and labeled to explain the plants' uses. The Johnny Appleseed apple tree, growing in a large container along the path, provides the perfect opportunity to recount the true story of the 18th-century nurseryman who spent 49 years of his life walking the American wilderness and planting apple trees. Many books tell his fascinating story.

Native Flora Garden

Upon entering this native-plant garden, you and your children will immediately notice the absence of symmetry and orderliness seen in most other areas of the Brooklyn Botanic Garden. This is a wild place, where kids may explore different habitats (and the plant life peculiar to those habitats) that exist within 100 miles of the city and conveniently pulled together in this 2-acre site. From bogs and pine barrens to a deciduous forest and a kettle pond, this is nature close to home, a collection of trees, shrubs, and wildflowers that preceded any introductions from Asia and Europe. Native Americans knew the value of these plants and used many of them in their day-to-day lives; these plants are firmly American.

As you and your kids follow the maze of dirt paths, see how many plants you can recognize from previous outings in the woods or other natural places. Trees include sugar maples, from which maple syrup is made, and American beech, trees often inscribed with sentiments of love. Explain to your kids that just as a cut in our skin invites infection, these carvings leave the trees vulnerable to disease.

If visiting in spring, look for the tightly curled fronds of emerging ferns. Once they straighten out later in the season, you'll be able to tell them apart—from the frilly delicateness of the lady fern to the softly-toothed sensitive fern. Point out the interrupted fern, so named because the line of sterile green leaflets on the stem is "interrupted" half way along by some brown fertile leaflets, which ripen and drop in early summer, leaving a gap on the frond. If your youngsters are familiar with cinnamon sticks, they'll get a kick out of the cinnamon fern, which produces long, cinnamon-colored rods in early summer.

When you pass the evergreens in the border mound, show your kids that next to nothing grows under an evergreen. That's because the needles are very acidic, creating an environment that few other plants can tolerate.

Native wildflowers abound, from spring bloomers like bloodroot and marsh marigold to late summer bloomers like goldenrod, iron-weed, and joe-pye weed, the latter named for a Native American who used the plant to cure sickness in colonial times. Ask your children if they would like to be named for a plant and what that name would be.

Some amusing plants include wetlands-loving buttonbush (aptly named for its white, ball-like flowers and whose round fruits persist through winter, providing food for birds and other wildlife) and prickly pear cactus, a native cactus whose pads are covered with spectacular yellow flowers in early summer. Pink turtleheads are late season, snapdragon-like bloomers with flowers that, in profile, resemble turtles' heads. Bright red cardinal flowers bloom during the late summer migration of hummingbirds, which pollinate the red flowers.

Above: Cinnamon fern produces long, cinnamon-colored rods in early summer.

Left: Native prickly pear cacti are covered with spectacular yellow flowers in early summer.

Below: Sensitive fern's soft fronds die back at the first frost.

The garden is filled with bird song and it's common to see cardinals darting back and forth. A pleasant place to linger for a while is the kettle pond, brilliant with blue flag iris in spring and visited by plenty of dragonflies and birds looking for insects to eat. Show your kids the tall brown cattails in the water, cigars on a stick. The brown parts on top are actually lots of tightly-packed flowers.

As you and your children walk along the garden's paths in summer, you may notice a sweet scent emanating from the sweet pepper bush's long, white blooms. Another lovely smell is emitted by crushing the leaf of the spicebush plant, a shrub with yellow flowers in spring and beautiful red berries in early autumn.

The Native Flora Garden is closed November through March.

Japanese Hill-and-Pond Garden

Youngsters love hanging out at this garden's viewing pavilion, feeding bread to dozens of huge, hungry koi fish and slow-moving turtles (which the garden doesn't seem to mind). The koi are particularly mesmerizing, crowded together at the water's surface in a flurry of orange, white, black, and red, mouths wide open, and furiously vying for every tiny morsel. A black-crowned night heron often stands across from the pavilion watching all the excitement in what is meant to be a spiritual place.

You may want to point out to older children some of the beautiful symbolism built into the garden, from the evergreens denoting eternal life to the waterfall signifying life's constant change. Japanese gardens are designed to balance humankind and nature, and this one includes a 1.5-acre pond and an island shaped like a turtle, a traditional symbol of longevity. The red *torii* (gateway) in the middle of the pond indicates the presence of a shrine dedicated to a harvest god, which is tucked in between some white pines on the far side of the pond. To see the shrine, or just to take a nature walk, follow the path that circles the pond.

Gardener's Resource Center

A little-visited gem is the Gardener's Resource Center on the second floor of the administration building, just above the Visitor Center. In addition to attending weekend story hours for kids 5 and older, parents may visit with their children and peruse shelves of gardening and nature books. Drop in and do some quick research on lasagna gardening while your kids read the latest edition of *Ranger Rick* or one of the many books in the children's section. Wrap up your visit with a little storytelling of your own. The center is open from 1:30 PM to 4:30 PM, Tuesday–Saturday, April–October and Tuesday–Friday, November–March.

Weekend and Weekday Discovery Programs and Family Programs

Held year-round from 1 to 3 PM in the Discovery Garden (in the Steinhardt Conservancy during winter and early spring) are 20-minute walk-in workshops for kids 3–10 years old accompanied by an adult. The programs are in sync with the seasons and may include planting bulbs in autumn, gardening in spring, and seasonal scavenger hunts.

On selected weekdays, parents with youngsters 3 through 6 can drop by the Discovery Garden between 1 and 3 PM for 15-minute workshops, which include digging for worms, pressing flowers, planting seeds, and making a botanical craft to take home.

The garden also offers other periodic walk-in programs for kids, as well as family programs, which in the past have included outdoor landscape painting for parents and children 8 and older. Parents may also participate with their 3- and 4-year-olds in a basic gardening program offered during the week. There is also a drop-off children's gardening program for kids 5 through 13. The best way to find out about the garden's programs is by picking up a *Get Green!* program guide at the garden or by logging onto zwww.bbg.org.

Self-Guided Summer Garden Trails

Each year, the garden publishes a different self-guided summer trail map focusing on a specific theme in the garden. The free guide helps visitors and children see the garden with fresh eyes. One year the garden produced a butterfly and hummingbird trail. Another year, it focused on plants used in different cultures. Garden programming often complements the theme. Trail maps are available at the Visitor Center.

Parts of a Flower

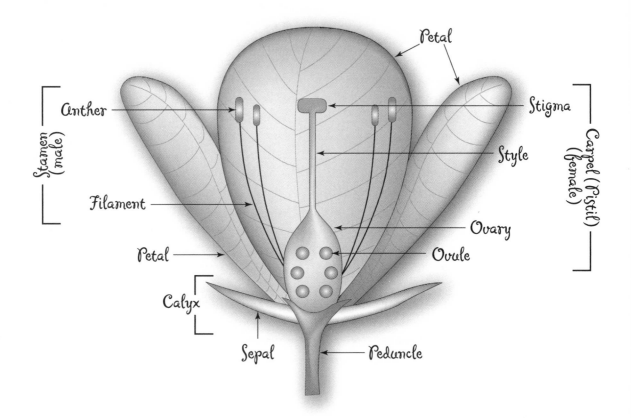

Flowers may be pretty, but their main purpose is to seduce pollinators inside to help plants produce seeds for the next generation. They lure pollinators, like bees and other creatures, with their colorful petals and intricate interiors, which include both male and female parts. When a bee lands inside a flower, pollen (a yellow dust) from the flower's anther (male part) sticks to the bee's body. When the bee visits another flower of the same kind, some of the pollen brushes off onto the flower's sticky stigma (female part). Once this happens, each tiny grain of pollen grows into a long tube that will meet down in the flower's overy (female part). Genes from the pollen (male) mix with genes in the ovule (egg in the female) and produce seeds.

Queens Botanical Garden

**43-50 Main Street
Flushing
718-886-3800, ext. 229**
www.queensbotanical.org

Family programs and events; garden maps; family garden tours; exhibits; plant shop; restrooms.

One of the garden's biggest family events is its annual Gardening Day, held in late April. Every year has a different theme, a recent one being "Getting Back to Our Roots"—which engaged children in tasting a variety of edible roots and making a "root view" by planting seeds in clear jars so that they could watch their plants grow at both top and bottom and learn about plant structure. The 5-hour event also includes plenty of adult and family programs, music, art, and demonstrations.

Weekends are pretty special, also, with "Just for Kids!" (fee), an afternoon family program in which everyone participates in gardening workshops, nature crafts, seed saving, cultural uses of herbs, and other activities.

While the children's garden is reserved for those registered in programs, there are plenty of other gardens kids will love visiting, including the bee garden. You can't walk into the garden buzzing with bees, but it's easy to watch from the sidelines as they fly into and out of their hives. There's also an observation hive near the garden's front gate that provides a cutaway through which kids can view the amazing work of bees.

Your youngsters will probably ask you what the frenzied comings and goings are all about and it may be a good time to talk about the importance of bees. As bees go from flower to flower, they brush up against pollen (the tiny powder-like male reproductive cells of seed plants), which are then brushed off into another flower, reaching the female part of the plant. Once this is done, the plant produces seeds, which grow into next year's plants. Explain to your children that without bees and other pollinators there would be no flowers, no crops, and no food.

The shady, woodland garden, with its wood-chip paths and its stream, is also a nice place to wander with kids. In autumn, explore the nearby 21-acre arboretum for fall foliage, and show your children how different tree species turn different colors. For example, a gingko always turns yellow, never red, in the fall. Every tree species contains its own assortment of pigments, colors masked in summer by a super-productive green coloring and food producer called chlorophyll, which all trees have. Younger kids may enjoy making leaf rubbings, while older youngsters might collect different kinds of leaves, flatten them in a flower press (or put them between two sheets of waxed paper and then into the middle of a big book) to create a leaf album that includes species names as well as locations and dates found.

The garden is constructing a new "green system" administration building and visitor center, which will highlight how nature can be harnessed to manufacture energy and recycle resources. One roof will convert sunlight into electricity, while another will be inverted to collect rainwater, which will then be mixed with gray water (used sink water), cleaned, and used in the garden. A third roof will be a "green roof" covered in plants, which will naturally cool the building, absorb rainfall, and provide a habitat for wildlife. On-site exhibits will explain the technology to visitors.

Open—April-October: Tuesday-Friday, 8 AM-6 PM; Saturday-Sunday, 8 AM-7 PM. November-March: Tuesday-Sunday, 8 AM-4:30 PM. Closed Monday, except legal holidays. Free. Plant shop is open April-September, 11 AM-5 PM, and on weekends through mid-October.

Staten Island Botanical Garden

**1000 Richmond Terrace
Staten Island
718-273-8200**
www.sibg.org

Various gardens, including a children's secret garden and maze; children's summer workshops; special events; garden tours; restaurant; restrooms.

The Staten Island Botanical Garden is one of the organizations found in what is collectively called the Snug Harbor Cultural Center. The center's 83-acre site, with wonderful Greek Revival buildings and other noteworthy architecture, was built in the 19th century as a home and hospital for retired seamen. Today, it is a national historic site and the fastest growing cultural institution in the city, with the Staten Island Botanical Garden occupying a large chunk of its northwestern section.

Small children thoroughly enjoy Connie Gretz's Secret Garden, a whimsical delight featuring a 38-foot-tall medieval castle, a hedgerow maze, and a walled secret garden based on Frances Hodgson Burnett's classic children's book. After navigating the maze, kids climb to the top of the castle for an aerial view of the intricate pathways and surrounding kingdom.

Nearby is the New York Chinese Scholar's Garden, a one-of-a-kind re-creation based on scholars' gardens in 14th-century China and described as an architectural interpretation of nature. Indeed, the building is mostly open to the elements, its details a celebration of nature—from banana-leaf–shaped doorways to tall rockeries representing the mountains of China. The floors are studded with black and white river rocks, while many of the plants have symbolic meaning in everyday Chinese life. Spring is a good time to visit, when many of these plants are blooming.

Children of all ages enjoy exploring the garden's various rooms and courtyards, looking

Kids can climb to the top of this Medieval castle in the Secret Garden at the Staten Island Botanical Garden.

for koi in the reflecting ponds and listening to the waterfall. Older kids may go on a scavenger hunt of sorts as they walk through the garden, unearthing the many ways in which the building and its garden relate to nature. To help in this investigation are four different guides—large, color-coded, take-along cards available for borrowing (no cost) at the garden entrance. Each guide explores something different, including the meanings of plants and architectural elements that pay homage to nature—rivers and mountains, moon-shaped doorways, and bat-shaped door pulls. Even the building's flying eaves look like the wings of a bird.

Grasshoppers, butterflies, and other insects hang around the more than 200 plant species in the Perennial Garden, where something is always in bloom from April through October. While most of the plants are not labeled, you can still challenge your children's senses by asking them to find one thing in the garden that represents taste, smell, sight, hearing, and touch. If visiting in late summer, for example, consider this: for taste—the huge mounds of nasturtiums in the *potager* garden behind the greenhouse (the leaves and flowers are edible); for smell—fragrant gardenias in the greenhouse; for sight—odd-looking artichokes growing in the potage garden or the supreme beauty of the pond lilies; for hearing—the sound of the pond fountain or buzzing of a bee; and for touch—dry seed heads or the fuzzy leaves of lamb's ear.

And what kid doesn't like walking through tunnels? So, before leaving, be sure to amble through the Allee, a long, pathway shaded by 120 European hornbeam trees that arch to create an overhead canopy. The Allee is located to the west of the *potager* garden. Another enjoyable walk is along a short, circular path hugging the 20-acre Wetlands, an uncultivated area of

Staten Island's Chinese Scholar's Garden is a one-of-a-kind re-creation of 14th-century China's architectural interpretations of nature.

the garden, dotted with cattails, jewelweed, and other water-loving plants. It is north of the Secret Garden, just down the hill.

Open—Most of the gardens are open every day from dawn to dusk and are free to explore. There is a fee to enter the New York Chinese Scholar's Garden, which also includes entrance to the Secret Garden. Both gardens are open April 1-October 31, Tuesday-Sunday, 10 AM-5 PM; and November 1-March 31, Tuesday-Sunday, 10 AM-4 PM.

Gardening at Home with Children

If your children want to do some gardening at home, fertilize their enthusiasm by giving them space in the yard or buying them their very own containers. Better still, team up and work in the garden together. Choose plants that excite the senses—from fuzzy lamb's ear and fragrant peppermint to touch-sensitive mimosa and wooly bunny tails. Kids also love extreme plants, which range from giant sunflowers, to miniature Jack-be-little pumpkins, to strange-looking vegetables like gourds, Easter-egg radishes, yellow tomatoes, blue potatoes, white pumpkins, and purple peppers. They also like growing things they can easily eat, including carrots, cherry tomatoes, berries, and even edible flowers.

While infants obviously cannot garden, they can enjoy hanging out with mom or dad in the garden, noticing butterflies and birds as they fly by. A good way to keep little ones close to the grass but safely corralled is by placing them inside an enclosed, free-standing playden.

Once they become toddlers, they'll want to help around the garden, planting seeds and bulbs and watering plants. Help them by digging the holes, but let them drop in the seeds, and don't worry about symmetry. Let them have fun. Seeds with short germination times work best—radishes, salad greens, zinnias, marigolds, and beans, for example. They can sprout in just a few days. Buy a children's watering can with tiny holes so the plants aren't drowned by enthusiasm. Young children also love mulching plant beds, because they get to move messy stuff from one place to another. You may, however, want to mulch around tender seedlings yourself, so that they're not suffocated. And if your toddler just wants to dig, let him till the soil in new beds before planting or in an area set aside for him. Getting dirty is part of the fun.

When it comes to older kids who can take on responsibility and think creatively, working their own plant beds or containers based on specific themes works wonderfully. Include them on your trips to the nursery or pour over seed catalogs together in winter, letting them pick out what they want to grow. If they choose something unsuitable for your soil or conditions, explain why it won't work. If they insist, let them plant it anyway, turning the experience into a scientific experiment, so that they might see for themselves how a plant thrives or does not thrive in a given environment.

Some themes that work well include an "eating garden" filled with edible flowers like Johnny-jump-ups, nasturtiums, violets, daylilies, calendula, garden sorrel, squash blossoms, and yucca petals; or a "pizza garden" with basil, tomatoes, garlic, oregano, and different colored peppers. When everything is ready to harvest, make a pizza using these homegrown ingredients.

Another great project is a bean tepee, which allows kids to grow plants vertically while providing a shady hideout. All you need is a 6-foot circle of space, 6 to 8 wooden poles 6–8 feet long, heavy twine or wire, and scarlet runner bean seeds. To build the tepee framework, set the poles around the edge of the circle, spaced evenly. Gather the upper ends of the poles together and tie with twine or wire.

The bean tepee is a great home-gardening project.

Push the bottoms of the poles deep into the ground. Then thread twine within the tepee framework like a spider's web, so plants can grip as they climb. Don't thread any twine in the space between the two poles designated as "the doorway". Plant the bean seeds around the base of each pole, water them, and wait for them to grow. You may want to put some hay or mulch inside the tepee to cushion the clubhouse. The tepee will eventually be covered with green leaves, brilliant red flowers, and, later, long pods filled with edible beans.

Even before the weather warms up, youngsters can experience the miracle of growth by starting seeds indoors under long florescent grow lights available at garden shops. It's like having a laboratory in the house. First, have your children fill individual cells of a seed starter tray with moist starter mix—a lightweight soil that makes it easy for seedlings to burst onto the scene. Before planting, read the seed package carefully, because some types of seeds do better when soaked overnight. Make sure that the kids label the cells so that they'll know what they've planted. After they have planted the seeds, a few to every cell, the most important thing is to keep the soil moist. Covering the trays, or flats, with plastic wrap until the seeds emerge works well. Also, most seeds need some warmth to germinate. Garden shops sell propagation mats that slide easily under flats and help to mimic spring temperatures.

Once seeds sprout, the grow lights should be left on between 14 and 16 hours a day and kept about 6–12 inches above the flats. The first leaves to appear are called cotyledons and have everything the plants needs to get started. Once the plant has two sets of true leaves, the seedlings should be transplanted to larger containers and fertilized half strength. Before transplanting outside, your children should slowly acclimate the seedlings to the outdoors by bringing them out during the day for a few hours, gradually lengthening the time and going from a shady, protected place to sun. In a few days, the young plants will be ready to go in the garden.

If your children become disappointed that some seeds didn't sprout, explain that Mother Nature never intended that all seeds germinate. That's why flowers produce so many seeds—to ensure that some will sprout and continue the species.

Planting a Garden

Before getting started it's a good idea to check your soil's pH—that is, how acidic or alkaline it is. While each plant has an ideal pH range in which it likes to grow, many plants, generally speaking, can grow in a range of 5.0 to 6.5. Also aerate the soil by turning it over with a pitchfork or claw to loosen it up, and then add compost or organic fertilizer.

Most plants are either annuals—plants that have one growing season, or perennials—plants that return year after year. When gardening with children, stick with annuals because they can be started from seed and will flower all summer long. Perennials have a defined and shorter bloom period and, when started from seed, may take a couple of years to flower.

Easy sun-loving plants that can be started from seed or purchased as seedlings include nasturtiums, zinnias, marigolds, cleome, sunflowers, petunias, celosias, and all vegetables. One perennial that blooms throughout the season and is worth having in the garden is butterfly bush, whose long, lilaclike blooms attract butterflies.

Shade gardens seem less exciting because they tend to showcase texture and shape rather than flowers. But if that's all you have, try planting impatiens, begonias, or fuschias. A shade-loving perennial that kids adore is bleeding heart, with its dangling heart-shaped blooms that appear in early spring.

To keep your garden blooming, deadhead (pick off) spent flowers to encourage the plant to produce more flowers.

Gardening Without a Backyard

Just because you don't have a yard doesn't mean your children are destined to be wallflowers. The sun rises and shines each day, air always surrounds us, and water is always on hand. All the kids need from you is a flowerpot or container—large or small—potting soil, seeds or seedlings, and—voila!—they have their very own minigarden plot. Pour the soil into the container, place the seeds or sprouts in the soil, water the soil, and have your children place their new botanical world outside in the sun and air—on a fire escape, front steps, even the sidewalk in front of your home or apartment, making a proud statement that they are committed to beautifying their block.

Kids can also spruce up neighborhood tree pits, which are often in need of a little makeover. If the pit is not in front of your own house, your children might ask the neighbors whether they would mind a little redecorating. Chances are they'll welcome it!

Tree-pit soil is often compacted (impeding the flow of air and water to the tree's roots), so you'll have to help your children improve the soil by aerating it, adding a little fresh topsoil, if necessary, and topping it with mulch. Such flowers as impatiens, begonias, ferns, coleus, and hostas—which can tolerate the shade of a tree in full summer plumage—work well. To protect the flowers and the tree, you may want to consider installing a tree-pit guard. Also have your children paint a little sign that pulls at the heartstrings of passers-by, imploring them to be kind to the flowers.

Gardening doesn't have to be outdoors and relegated to the warmer months. A fun and easy indoor gardening activity for youngsters is growing sprouts that the whole family can eat in sandwiches or salads. Sprouts are nutrition-packed baby plants. Many kinds of seeds, beans, and nuts can be used to grow sprouts, from black beans and chickpeas to sunflowers and lentils. And you don't need soil.

Have your children soak a small handful of untreated seeds (available at whole-food stores) overnight in a clean, glass jar covered with cheesecloth secured by a rubber band. In the morning, they should strain the water from

Starting seeds with children can be a rewarding experience.

the jar through the cheesecloth. Then rinse the seeds with fresh water and strain again. Set the jar aside. Once each subsequent day, rinse and strain the seeds until the sprouts grow and are ready to eat. All this usually takes between two and five days, depending on the seed.

Another great indoor activity is forcing spring bulbs to bloom out of season. In the real world, bulbs need to experience a period of cold before they can bloom; so in this little experiment, children will simply have to make it seem like winter. Put a hyacinth bulb in a small brown paper bag and date the bag. Place the bag in the refrigerator for 12–14 weeks. After this cold period, remove the bag and put the bulb in a special bulb-forcing vase found in

Planting a Street Tree

Imagine a world without trees. It would be bleak and soulless. Trees have long been revered for what they readily provide—beauty and shade, furniture, pencils, paper, fruits, and nuts—and as powerful spiritual presences. They are, after all, the longest-living organisms on earth.

So why not mark a special time in your family's life by planting a street tree? Everyone can sit down together and leaf through photos of city-friendly species before deciding on a tree, then plant it together and take turns watering it and learning how to prune it. Your children might take responsibility for the tree pit itself and plant some flowers; and over time, as the tree grows, you can all record its progress from year to year.

You can request a free tree from the city, but may have to wait up to two years to get it. Or you might foot the bill and plant the tree immediately, either by yourself or by hiring a landscaper. Depending on how you do it, the cost can be between $500 and $800.

For more information, call 212-227-1887 or visit www.treesny.com.

most plant and garden shops) with the bulb's pointed side up. Fill the glass with water until it touches the bottom of the bulb. Anchor the bulb in place with some pebbles. Your children will soon see the roots grow, and in a few days the bulb will also sprout. Make sure that the water always reaches the base of the bulb.

Easier still is forcing paper-whites and amaryllis, which appear in garden shops in autumn, because they don't need a chilling period. Paper-whites bloom in 3–5 weeks, amaryllis in 6–8 weeks. Paper-whites look best planted in groups, while any amaryllis is impressive all by itself. Plant paper-white bulbs about a half inch apart in a dish two-thirds filled with pebbles, maintaining the water level at the base of the bulbs. Place in a cool, dark place for two weeks. When shoots appear, move to a cool, sunny spot. Amaryllis can be planted in soil, keeping the bulb one-third to one-half exposed above the soil. It does best with at least four hours of sun a day and watering once a week.

Community Gardens

If gardening with other families interests you, join a community garden and learn from the best of them. Many community gardeners have been tilling the urban soil for years, accumulating knowledge and experience that they're eager to share with the next generation of gardeners. Most gardens are always looking for volunteers to help around the garden or plant an entire plot by themselves, as long as they keep up with the weeds and keep it looking marvelous. And what better way to tap into our agrarian roots then by gardening side-by-side with other families—people of different ages and cultures as diverse as the garden itself just digging in, so to speak.

Community gardening is about more than getting your hands dirty and reconnecting with the earth; it's about connecting with one another for the benefit of the entire community.

Some gardens are beautiful oases, like the Liz Christy Garden on the Lower East Side (www.lizchristygarden.org), with a pond, beehive, grape arbor, fruit trees, berries and a wildflower habitat. The Clinton Community Garden in Hell's Kitchen (www.clintoncommunity garden.org) has an annual summer solstice celebration and an Oktoberfest, where they sell honey made by their own bees. The Floyd Bennett Field Garden in Brooklyn (www.fbga .net) has nearly 600 plots and offers free children's programs and how-to gardening workshops for adults. The Community Farm in Prospect Heights hosts an annual Pumpkin Smash, during which post-Halloween jack-o'-lanterns are smashed to bits by kids just for the fun of it and then deposited into the garden's compost heap. This garden, at 252-256 St. Mark's Avenue in Brooklyn, also operates a rainwater collection system.

If you don't have the time to get involved in a community garden, you can visit any community garden with your family. Each garden is required to post public hours and all Green Thumb gardens are required to be open a minimum of 10 hours a week, usually on one weekend and one weekday evening. Many gardens also host festivals and offer public programs.

For information on community gardens, call 212-788-8070 or visit www.greenthumbnyc .org. To find a garden near you, go to www.oasis nyc.net/gardens/cenycmapsearch.asp.

Community Garden Organizations

Green Thumb

**49 Chambers Street, Room 1020
New York, New York
212-788-8070**
www.greenthumbnyc.org

Established in 1978; provides technical assistance and materials to community gardeners.

Seasonal festivals abound in the city, including this spring puppet parade in Prospect Park.

Green Guerrillas

**214 West 29th Street, 5th floor
New York, New York
212-402-1121**
www.greenguerillas.org

Established in 1973; helps grassroots groups strengthen community gardens through volunteerism, advocacy, youth programs, and financial assistance.

Neighborhood Open Space Coalition

**232 East 11th Street
New York, New York
212-228-3126**
www.treebranch.com

A public space and community garden advocacy organization.

A Brief History of Community Gardens in NYC

New York City has the largest concentration of community gardens in the country—numbering more than 600 throughout the five boroughs. Most of these green places were once depressing, city-owned, empty lots filled with weeds and junk. The city didn't do anything about them because, back in the 1970s, it was knee-deep in a financial crisis. At the same time, the environmental movement had gained momentum, inspiring urban gardeners to cultivate these abandoned lots. Volunteers hauled out old cars and washing machines, raked up glass and nails, and turned what had been eyesores into Edens. The city supported these efforts by providing temporary leases and, in 1978, created Operation GreenThumb, which to this day provides gardeners with materials, grants, and technical assistance, including educational workshops.

Over the decades, many of these gardens have grown to be beautiful—with ponds, tall trees, and community centers—and it seemed that they would flourish forever. Indeed, the city seemed disinterested in these plots until the mid-1990s when Mayor Rudolph Guiliani announced that all vacant land—including community gardens—would be auctioned off to the highest bidder for residential housing development. This sent shock waves through the gardening community. But the gardeners quickly organized and, dressed as cucumbers and daisies, even protested at City Hall. Many people and other organizations came to their aid, specifically the Trust for Public Land and the New York Restoration Project, which at the eleventh hour in 1999 agreed to purchased 114 of the gardens from the city and preserve them forever. There are still many more community gardens in need of protection, and some have already been bulldozed to make way for buildings.

New York Restoration Project

31 West 56th Street
New York, New York
212-333-2552
www.nyrp.org

Restores gardens and public spaces in underserved city neighborhoods; and established a trust to maintain, preserve, and develop 60 gardens in perpetuity.

Earth Celebrations

638 East 6th Street
New York, New York
212-777-7969
www.earthcelebrations.com

A nonprofit organization dedicated to preserving community gardens and fostering environmental awareness through theatrical pageants, exhibitions, art & ecology workshops, and advocacy projects.

8 BICYCLING

To the casual observer, cycling in New York City is no ride in the woods. City cyclists are often seen dodging taxis, buses, and hurried pedestrians as they navigate the streets—not something you'd want to do with young kids.

But there are safe, car-free places in all five boroughs where families can pedal along tree-lined corridors, many with waterfront views. Indeed, no other means of city travel, except boating, makes you appreciate that New York City is an island community and how lucky we are to be surrounded by soothing waters.

Most of these car-free cycling trails are part of the city's growing Greenway System, a network of shared-use pathways designed to connect parks and communities. So far, 150 miles have been completed, with about 200 miles more to go. In the end, some greenway lanes will have to exist on city streets (the only means of connection in some areas), but 80 percent of greenways will be traffic free, scenic routes separated from roadways.

If you want to explore the city's waterfront and natural areas by bicycle, a good way to choose a route is by calling 311 and requesting a free City Cycling Map. As you and your children cruise along on your bikes, stay together and be watchful and considerate of joggers, walkers, and roller skaters who may be sharing the path. Carry plenty of water, an air pump, and a spare inner tube in case of a flat. And forget about flared pants, which might easily get caught in a bicycle chain. There are also some great citywide bicycling events that encourage family participation (see page 210).

Kids 14 and younger are required by law to wear helmets, and that also goes for tiny tots hitching a ride in tagalongs or seats on the back of mom's or dad's bike. Older siblings and adults should wear them as well—for safety reasons and by way of presenting positive role models. It's illegal to put a child under 1 year of age on any bicycle; and every child over 4 must ride his or her own bike, or one specifically designed to carry more than one person.

If you own a mountain bike, don't be tempted to ride it on any of the park's unpaved nature trails. That's illegal. Among other considerations, mountain-bike wheels tear up the ground, destroying vegetation and habitat, especially in ecologically sensitive areas, and promote erosion.

Bronx

Pelham Bay Park and Orchard Beach

Moderate 6.25-mile round trip.

Pelham Bay Park is the city's largest park, a 2,700-acre mix of woodlands, sandy beaches, bays, rocky shoreline, saltwater marshes, and meadows—and much of it is accessible or viewable by bicycle. This ride is particularly beautiful in autumn, when the trees are at their most colorful and the throngs of people have deserted Orchard Beach for the summer.

Start at the west end of the City Island Bridge and admire the views of Eastchester Bay to the south, Long Island Sound to the north, and anglers camped out under the bridge for a day's fishing. Then follow the bicycle path and keeping the woods on your left. When the path forks, stay left. You'll soon come to an open marshy area on your left, a pleasant place to stop, pull out the binoculars, and help the kids look for ducks, cormorants, egrets, and gulls.

The path then enters some woods flecked with wildflowers. Startled birds fly into the trees as you pedal by. When you reach a narrow, concrete walkway over the water (the Pelham Bridge), walk your bicycles across, periodically taking the time to inspect the marsh for long-legged waders and ducks.

Sometimes cormorants stand like statues on the rocks to dry their outstretched wings. The large, unnatural hump in the landscape is part of the now-defunct Pelham Bay Landfill.

After crossing the bridge, you'll come to a "Pelham Bay Park" sign. Bear left on the tree-lined path and into the park. Turn left at the first fork and right at the second fork, continuing to veer right in a circle until you reach the hard-to-miss Bronx Victory Memorial, complete with a 120-foot limestone pedestal and column crowned with a bronzed and winged angel of victory, a tribute to the 947 Bronx soldiers who died in World War I. In autumn, the linden and Norway maple trees surrounding the monument turn a golden yellow.

After viewing the monument, continue on the path, retracing your steps back across the Pelham Bridge. At the intersection with City Island Road, carefully cross the street (there is no light) and continue on the bicycle lane opposite the side you biked earlier. You'll soon be pedaling through a wooded area. Then you'll pass the Turtle Cove Golf Driving Range and arrive at a marshy area called Turtle Cove. This is another binocular stop; there are plenty of herons and egrets to see here.

The bicycle lane then crosses Park Drive and eventually leads to Orchard Beach. Here, you have plenty of options to explore. You can investigate the salt-marsh lagoon, which abuts the back of the Orchard Beach parking lot, or you can bike straight ahead to the beach, which can be loud and crowded during summer. Since cycling on the beach walk is prohibited, lock up your bicycles and explore on foot. Alternately, you may turn left at the beach and visit Hunter and Twin Island and the Orchard Beach Nature Center (see chapter 1, Nature and Environmental Centers), or turn right on the path that parallels the beach and head for the quiet south end of the beach, home to a beautiful meadow that attracts butterflies in summer. Large erratic boulders protrude from the grass and even from the sand, which at this

end is empty in summer because there are no lifeguards.

After exploring, return to your bicycles and cycle back along the path that brought you here. If you soon pass the trail marker for the Siwanoy Trail on your left, you're headed in the right direction. At the traffic circle, turn left and return to City Island Bridge.

Brooklyn

Owls Head Park to the Verrazano-Narrows Bridge

(Ages 6 and Older) Easy 4.5-mile round trip.

The ride along Brooklyn's western coast, where Upper New York Bay and Lower New York Bay meet in the Narrows, offers spectacular ocean views and cool breezes, making it a particularly pleasant outing on days when there seems to be no relief from the heat. Look for gulls bobbing on the water, and—in late summer—baby bluefish jumping out of the water. Lots of boats, from tiny sailboats to giant tankers, also ply the waters. You'll also see the Statue of Liberty and the Manhattan skyline. Pack a kite and fly it for a while when you reach an area just before the Verrazano-Narrows Bridge, one of the city's best kite-flying venues.

Begin your ride at Colonial Road and Wakeman Place in Bay Ridge and take the path that veers to the left. You're in 27.1-acre Owls Head Park, which sits high on a terminal moraine (where the Wisconsin glacier left boulders and rocks 10,000 years ago) overlooking New York Harbor. It was here that a former Brooklyn mayor built his mansion in the 19th century, later selling it to a wealthy man in the pressed-tin business, who in turn willed the property to the city as parkland.

As you ride along, notice the high area to your left, a slope recently replanted with native plants. The Belt Parkway and Upper New York Bay are to your right. At the next fork, bear right, passing a dog run on the right before reaching the intersection of Shore Road and 68th Street. Turn right onto the bike lane.

At 69th Street, turn right onto the 69th Street Pier, where a ferry from Brooklyn to Staten Island operated before the Verrazano-Narrows Bridge replaced it in 1964. The kids will love riding around the modernized pier, a popular recreational and fishing spot. After checking out the catches of the day, turn right onto the Shore Road Bike Path, pointing out to your kids how sunlight reflects like diamonds on the ripples of the water. In the near distance is the Verrazano-Narrows Bridge, named for Giovanni da Verrazano, who, in 1524, became the first European explorer to sail into New York Harbor.

When you reach the bridge (you'll actually be under the span), you and your children can marvel at the 693-foot towers, each weighing 27,000 tons and held together with three million rivets and one million bolts. The bridge is more than 2 miles long; and when it opened, it was the longest suspension bridge in the world. Across the way, on Staten Island, you can see Fort Wadsworth (built after the War of 1812) and Battery Weed (built just prior to the Civil War). There was once a light on top of Battery Weed to help guide ships, but the bridge also rendered it obsolete.

Lots of people gather near the bridge to fish, relax, and fly kites. Sometimes a group of fliers is there to help novices. For a quick primer on flying before you head out, check out www.gombergkites.com/how.html.

Turn around. On the return trip the Narrows gives way to the wider Upper New York Bay, with the Statue of Liberty and Manhattan skyline in the background. At the pier, turn right and then make another right into the 4.5-acre Narrows Botanical Garden (www.narrowsbg.org, or 718-836-1754), a volunteer-run oasis between 69th and 72nd

Streets. This use to be a dump before the locals took over. Now there's plenty of beauty to explore, including a native-plant garden, a butterfly garden, a dawn redwood grove, and a spacious lawn for lounging, all on the water. Among the garden's most popular annual events is its autumn Harvest Fair, featuring a canine-costume contest that will make kids roar with laughter. In fact, this is a very dog-friendly place, with plastic-bag dispensers located throughout the park for dog walkers' convenience.

After exiting the garden, turn left onto Shore Road. Return to the bike path and Owls Head Park, which itself has a wonderful collection of great trees.

Manhattan

79th Street to the Little Red Lighthouse

(Ages 9 and Older) Moderate 10-mile round trip.

Don't forget to pack a lunch, because once you get to the end of the line, you'll want to picnic next to the city's famed Little Red Lighthouse, right on the scenic shores of the Hudson River. When you're packing, include a copy of *The Little Red Lighthouse and the Great Gray Bridge*, by Hildegarde Swift.

The journey is as beautiful as the destination. For much of the way, the bike lane parallels the Hudson River, where gulls and cormorants ply the water for fishy tidbits. Heading north, you'll have an almost continuous view of the George Washington Bridge stretching from New Jersey to New York. Hefty rocks line the shore, inviting cyclists to sit down for a moment and watch the parade of boats sailing by.

This route—from the 79th Street Boat Basin to the Little Red Lighthouse—is the northernmost portion of the city's 13-mile Hudson River

Greenway, a multi-use trail that runs from Battery Park to Fort Washington Park and that will eventually connect with the Hudson River Trail system to Albany and Canada.

Start your ride at the 79th Street Boat Basin, getting to the bike lane by walking your bikes down some steps in Riverside Park. Mixed in with the sailboats and recreational boats at the basin are some houseboats where people live year round. In recent years, however, the city has stopped issuing year-round leases in favor of seasonal dockage, so the number of residents in this floating community is dwindling.

You will soon be diverted into bucolic Riverside Park—passing colorful gardens and folks passing the time quietly on benches—before heading down a slope and back along

The famous Little Red Lighthouse sits under the George Washington Bridge.

the Hudson River shore. You'll soon be riding on a stretch known as Cherry Walk (between 100th and 125th streets), so named because it is planted with—what else—cherry trees, the pink flowers of which blanket the path in early spring. The path here is really close to the river, so stop, take a break on the rocks, and dip your feet in the water.

When you reach one of the city's most popular supermarkets, Fairway, on your right, you'll be diverted from the waterside and detoured onto the street along 12th Avenue, which is not exactly scenic but is well marked with Greenway signs. (There are plans and funding to construct a waterside lane, with native plantings and a recreational pier on the site of Fairway's parking lot, which now interrupts the flow of the Greenway.)

The waterfront detour continues between 135th and 145th Streets, taking riders along a no-man's-land route behind Riverbank State

Park, which sits high atop a wastewater treatment plant that cuts people off from the water. There are also plans to build a welcoming inland route with plantings—but until then, this is probably the bleakest part of the trip.

You will soon be directed back into Riverside Park and to its waterfront view. In the distance is the George Washington Bridge, drawing nearer as you pedal north, a mammoth steel structure spanning the grand Hudson River. The route soon leads into Fort Washington Park, a narrow swath of waterfront parkland wedged between Riverside Drive and the river and named for an 18th-century fortification ordered built by General George Washington to protect New York from the British during the War for Independence. The fort stood on Manhattan's highest point, what is today the southern end of Bennett Park, just north of the George Washington Bridge. It was captured by the British in November 1776, in a devastating defeat for the Continental Army.

After you pass some tennis courts, the beloved Little Red Lighthouse will come into view, standing meekly at the foot of the bridge's massive Manhattan tower. This is the perfect place to stop for lunch, and there are picnic tables for your convenience. After eating, entertain your kids with a reading of *The Little Red Lighthouse and the Great Gray Bridge*, which recounts the building of the bridge from the wee lighthouse's point of view. When the lighthouse was deactivated in 1947, the book and the children who loved it played an important part in the beacon's preservation. The Urban Park Rangers give periodic tours of the lighthouse.

This is also a wonderful time to simply sit with your children on shoreline rocks and quietly watch boats sail up and down the river, creating wakes that slowly ripple their way to the water's edge before disappearing completely. Birds and gulls fly overhead, and the bridge seems like a giant eagle with its wings spread from shore to shore. To distract from the din of cars speeding back and forth across the expanse, try tossing—with your kids, of course—pebbles into the river. Then return to your bicycles and head south, back from whence you came.

Swindler Cove Park and the Harlem River

(Ages 8 and Older) Easy 7-mile round trip.

This is a great "let's pack a lunch and do a little biking kind of outing," with Swindler Cove Park as your base. Once full of junk and derelict boats half sunk in the Harlem River, Swindler Cove has been transformed into a gorgeous garden and park by Bette Midler's New York Restoration Project (NYRP), which has beautified other parks in Upper Manhattan and preserved community gardens around the city.

Swindler Cove Park opened in 2003 near the busy intersection of Harlem River Drive, 10th Avenue, and Dyckman Street; but you'd never know it, because it's tucked behind Public School No. 5, between the school and the Harlem River. This 5-acre park is often empty and quiet, a beautiful retreat with welcoming gardens and tall trees, waterfront views, winding pathways, a pond and wetlands, a nearby bicycle path, clean bathrooms, and picnic tables. It is particularly appealing in late summer, when the gardens are in full bloom.

A great way to get acquainted with the park is by attending one of NYRP's family programs, which range from birding to seining and are held throughout the year. For information, go to www.nyrp.org. Swindler Cove Park is open seven days a week from 10 AM to 6 PM.

After exploring the park, walk your bicycles along the path just left of the gardens and out to the greenway, with Harlem River Drive on your right and the Harlem River on your left. As you bike along, turn your eyes from the towering apartment houses across the way and instead look at the river itself—an 8-mile waterway that runs between the Hudson and

East Rivers. In the early 1900s, boathouses lined the Harlem and people came out in droves to watch club races. In an effort to revive this tradition along the river, the NYRP recently moored a new floating boathouse called the Peter Jay Sharpe Boathouse, a green and yellow Victorian-style structure that stands out boldly on the shoreline.

You and your kids may also want to examine the exposed bedrock along the right side of Harlem River Drive. Atop this rock layer is 119-acre Highbridge Park, which overlooks the Harlem River. After cycling under the Washington Bridge (1888) and Alexander Hamilton Bridge (1963), you'll pass under the landmark High Bridge, for which the park is named. This is the city's oldest bridge (1848), and was built to carry water by aqueduct from Westchester's Croton River to the city. (Pedestrians were once allowed to walk across the bridge, but it has been closed since 1970.) In 1872, the Highbridge Water Tower, which still stands in nearby Highbridge Park, was built to increase water pressure so that people living in high-rises on high ground could get water.

On a clear day, seven Harlem River bridges can be seen from the terrace at the base of the granite tower. If you want to see for yourself, join one of the Urban Park Rangers' occasional tours to the top.

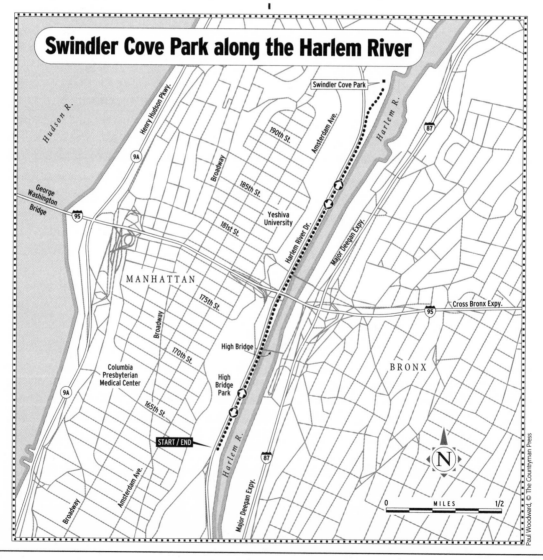

Swindler Cove Park along the Harlem River

When you come to a narrow overpass, at 166th Street, it's time to turn around and return to Swindler Cove Park.

Roosevelt Island

(Ages 7 and Older) Easy 4-mile loop.

Notorious during the 19th century for its crowded, poorly run institutions and hospitals, Roosevelt Island was revamped in 1975 as an island community in the middle of the East River. High-rises and plenty of parkland coexist with some of the island's surviving historic landmarks. Accessible by subway, tram, and bridge, the island is ringed by a 4-mile path used by walkers and cyclists. The best stops along the

path are at the wild south end, where the ruins of an old smallpox hospital mix with wildflowers and raw nature; the north end, where anglers fish beside a 19th-century lighthouse; and the west side, which provides unobstructed views of Manhattan and the East River.

If you cycle to the island via the Roosevelt Island Bridge (opened in 1955) connecting the island to Queens, begin at the corner of Vernon Boulevard and 36th Avenue in Queens. After crossing the bridge, you'll have to go down to the island itself via the elevator in the parking garage. Once at street level, proceed north on the path, keeping the river on your left.

If you and your children visit the island by subway or tram, you'll be let off on the west side

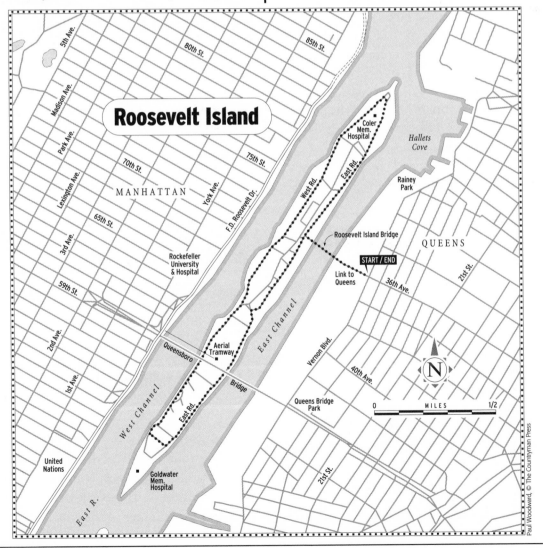

about mid-island. Just pedal onto the path and circle the island at your leisure.

Keep in mind that the southern end of the island, called Southpoint Park, is open during summer from 8 AM to 9:30 PM, during spring and autumn from 8 AM to 8:30 PM, and during winter from 8 AM to 6:30 PM. In addition to song sparrows, nesting Canada geese, gorgeous wildflowers, and other wildlife, this still-undeveloped 10-acre park is home to a 19th-century, Gothic-style smallpox hospital designed by noted architect James Renwick. Nature has reclaimed this shell of a building, with trees and shrubs sprouting from almost every window; and the views from here are spectacular. This is really a wonderful place for your children to commune with nature, a quiet spot often empty of people—a rarity in the city.

The northern end of the island is somewhat busier, a public park punctuated by a stone lighthouse also designed by Renwick. The rocks used in its construction are local, quarried on the island by prisoners housed in the island's prison (1828–1935). Fishermen often try their luck here. Just beyond the lighthouse there's a wonderful mulberry tree, which is loaded with delicious berries in June.

The Roosevelt Island lighthouse was constructed of local rocks quarried by prisoners.

Bicycle riding is popular on Roosevelt Island where nature mingles with 19th century architecture, like the famed Smallpox Hospital.

QUEENS

Alley Pond Park to Fort Totten and Little Bay Park

(Ages 8 and Older) Easy 6.5-mile round trip.

From wetlands and shoreline to a historic army base with stone forts, this ride along Little Neck Bay is scenic and spectacular, offering glimpses of wildlife and a circuit around Fort Totten, a military fortress built just before the Civil War, which—until recently—had been closed to the public.

The tour begins at Joe Michael's Mile in Alley Pond Park, a bicycle and pedestrian lane that runs along Little Neck Bay. It's named for the former drummer of the '60s rock group, Jay

Black and the Americans, who was also a founding member of the Alley Pond Striders, a local walking group.

The best way to access the path is by crossing busy Northern Boulevard at the traffic light just left of the Alley Pond Environmental Center. Do not cross the boulevard any other place, because it can be dangerous. Before crossing and starting your ride, take the kids to the Little Neck Bridge, just to the right of the environmental center on Northern Boulevard, where long-legged waders and shore birds are particularly plentiful, at low tide, in the salt marsh below.

When you start your ride, the Cross Island Parkway will be on your left and the bay on your right. Lots of wildflowers grow here—yarrow, goldenrod, jewelweed, evening primrose, common reed grass, and others. There are plenty of places to stop along the way and explore the shoreline with your kids. Your first opportunity is at a set of park benches on your right. From there, just scramble down some rocks and explore the beach at low tide, looking for tiny fish and ribbed mussels.

Returning to the path, you'll soon come to the Bayside Marina (718-229-0097), which you may want to visit on your way back. The marina rents boats as well as bait and tackle, so you and your kids—if you wish—can fish directly from the pier. The Bayside Anglers host an annual snapper derby here for kids (see chapter 9, Goin' Fishing). If you're hungry, try

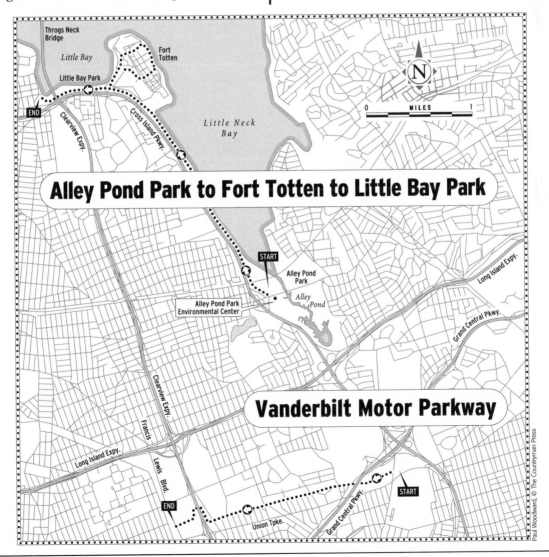

Alley Pond Park to Fort Totten to Little Bay Park

Vanderbilt Motor Parkway

Paul Woodward, © The Countryman Press

the snack bar—and sit outside at the picnic tables to watch the locals fishing.

Just before the Cross Island Expressway Exit 32/Bell Boulevard sign, you'll find, on your right, a sandy beach frequented by egrets and cormorants. Cormorants sit low in the water, only their heads and necks sticking up, like periscopes. When hungry, these dark-colored birds, sometimes called "crow ducks," submerge themselves, diving deep underwater and using their hook-tipped bills to nab fish. Egrets, on the other hand, are virtually motionless—they stand absolutely still on their long, lanky legs and hunt quietly with their eyes. Then, like a dart to its target, they stab their prey through the water and gulp it right down. Wintering ducks seen here include goldeneyes, pintails, and buffleheads.

Return to the path. The sound of the highway recedes, and you enter an area of tall trees and shade. When you come to a sign on your right that reads "Fort Totten Park," turn right and head into the new park, accessible only to cyclists and pedestrians. The path is in poor condition, but there are plans to resurface it and make it part of the Greenway system. Until recently, this military compound, built in 1857 to protect New York Harbor from invasion via Long Island Sound, was closed to the public. The federal government decommissioned it in 1995, giving 49.5 acres to the city for parkland. Another portion of the property is a fire-department training complex, with a small bit remaining an Army Reserve facility.

The park offers beautiful waterfront views, a historic parade ground, and a battery. The Bayside Historical Society is housed in the landmark officers' club, where it presents local exhibitions (718-352-1548). It is open Tuesday–Sunday, 11 AM–4 PM.

After cycling around Fort Totten—remember you'll have to pedal about 2.5 miles back—exit the complex the way you came in and turn right onto the bike path for a short pedal through Little Bay Park, which offers plenty of opportunities to investigate the shoreline. When the path ends, turn around and retrace your route, cycling under the approach to the Throgs Neck Bridge and remembering to stop at the Bayside Marina for refreshment before heading back to Alley Pond Park.

Vanderbilt Motor Parkway

(Ages 7 and Older) Mostly flat 5-mile round trip, with one big hill.

Here's an opportunity to cycle a portion of one of our nation's most historic byways, the former Long Island Motor Parkway, also known as the Vanderbilt Motor Parkway. In 1908, during the early automobile craze, William K. Vanderbilt Jr., a descendent of the New York Central Railroad Vanderbilts, built a racecourse for his Vanderbilt Cup Race. The venue was short-lived, closing in 1910 after some spectators were killed by a car. The Vanderbilts then expanded the course and turned it into a toll road used by thousands of motorists, who could travel 48 miles from Queens to Ronkonkoma, Long Island. In 1938, the more modern Northern State Parkway made this roadway obsolete; but lucky for us, the Queens section was preserved and re-opened that same year as the Queens Bicycle Path.

Almost 70 years later, this scenic 25-foot wide path still meanders through woodlands—now Alley Pond and Cunningham Parks. There are plenty of places to stop along the way to investigate woods and marshes, a pond, and playgrounds, or just to take a rest and eat lunch.

The ride begins at Winchester Boulevard, just north of Union Turnpike, with a severe hill that you may want to spare young children just starting out. Older kids, however, might welcome the early challenge.

To avoid the hill (and enjoy it on the downhill return trip), cycle into Alley Pond Park by turning left at Winchester Boulevard and riding under the Grand Central Parkway until you reach the park parking lot. With the lot behind you and soccer fields on your right, go straight to the Urban Park Rangers Adventure Center. Facing the nature center, take the path to your left, keeping the playground on your left. At the fork, bear left. Little Alley Pond is on your right. This is a great place to explore with kids, especially around May when thousands of tiny tadpoles are squirming around just off shore. By summer, some of these tadpoles will have become frogs. Ducks and long-legged waders also like to hang out here. The pond is especially beautiful in the fall, when surrounding trees are ablaze with autumn colors.

Return to the path, where you'll find several stairs. Walk your bicycle up the stairs and continue to some railings. Turn right. You are now on the Vanderbilt Motor Parkway and have successfully avoided the steep hill. The tree-lined path ahead is divided into lanes by painted dashes, so keep to your right so as to avoid cycling into oncoming pedestrians or other cyclists. On sunny days, the shade and coolness of the trees is very inviting. Listen for songbirds and look for squirrels and chipmunks darting across the path.

You will soon reach an underpass. The Clearview Expressway is above you. Cycle through and make a tight left into Cunningham Park. At the next fork, bear left. Continue through the woods, checking for blooming multiflora roses in late spring.

When you find yourself out of the woods, it's time to turn around. Either return to the Alley Pond Nature Center and adjoining playground, or continue to the very end of the Vanderbilt Motor Parkway, experiencing the tremendous downhill you may have avoided earlier when it was ascending. The nature center is also a good place to lock up your bicycles and go on a brief nature walk. The nearby Green Trail is rather short and takes about 30 minutes, passing through woodlands and past kettle ponds. Look up into the trees for rac-

coons. You may pick up maps inside the nature center, which is usually open on Saturdays from 10 AM to 4 PM.

Queens-Brooklyn Combination

Fort Tilden, Back Fort Trail

(Ages 6 and Older) Easy, flat 2.5-mile loop.

With its easy trail, wildflowers and wildlife, cool ocean breezes coming off the Atlantic, and fine views, Fort Tilden is a great place for family bicycling. The best time is early autumn, when you'll see dozens of migrating monarch butterflies fueling up on their journey south as well as migrating songbirds and hawks. Poison ivy is one of the first plants to turn red, making it easier to spot. Also look for black-and-orange milkweed beetles on the elongated seed pods of milkweed plants. As long as there's no snow on the path and you dress in layers, winter offers the chance to see all kinds of berries—frosty, spicy-scented bayberry; yellow-and-red oriental bittersweet; and the clustered, tan-colored berries of poison ivy. There are also wintering ducks, sanderlings on the shore and, sometimes, owls in the maritime forest.

But if summer is the only time you can get away, bring along water, insect repellent, and sunscreen and feast your eyes on plenty of wildflowers—snowflake-like Queen Anne's lace, purple milkweed, honeysuckle, daisy fleabane, mullein, yarrow, blue chicory, yellow coreopsis, and more. Some of them bloom into early autumn. Dragonflies dart in every direction.

The wide, pebbly path begins just west of the Rockaway Artists Alliance building, beyond a yellow swing gate (to keep cars out) and a sign reminding visitors to watch for ticks.

While cycling, notice gulls flying overhead and songbirds jetting from tree to tree.

After passing a large wooden cube on your right, one of several weather-worn sculptures placed along the trail some time ago by a New York–based artists group, you'll see a trail on your right that leads to a maritime forest sheltered by sand dunes and filled with wind-shaped trees and shrubs that can withstand the harsh coastal environment.

Stay on the path until you reach a giant, foliage-covered fortification on your right. This is Battery Harris East, one of twin armament batteries constructed during World War I to fend off possible enemy attacks. To view the annual fall hawk migration, birders climb to an observa-tion deck built by the National Park Service. Lock your bicycles to the chain-link fence paralleling the path and head up the 40 or so stairs to the top, where you will find great views of the Atlantic Ocean to the south and Rockaway Inlet to the north. Everything winged whizzes by up here—from butterflies, to birds, to airplanes—and it's a great place to observe the sunset.

Return down the stairs and walk across the path to the Pond Trail, a short .1-mile walk to a tiny freshwater pond where youngsters can sit on a log and watch dragonflies or throw bits of shell into the water just to hear them splash. There's also a bench to sit on, overlooking the dunes, the shoreline, and a few giant yuccas that bear long stalks of white bell-like flowers in July.

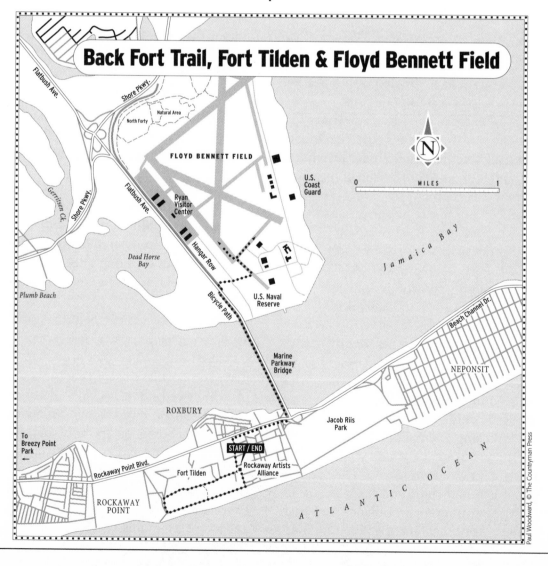

Back Fort Trail, Fort Tilden & Floyd Bennett Field

Paul Woodward, © The Countryman Press

Retrace your steps back to your bicycles, hop on, and continue along the path, turning left when you come to an intersection with a paved road, Beach 193rd Street. Notice the short, fuzzy rabbit-foot clover growing here. Ride past the fishermans' parking lot on your right. The path soon intersects with another paved road; Shore Road (or the Middle Road). Turn left here. Notice the vegetation on either side of the road; there are some pretty pines on the left and protected dunes on the right, blocking your view of the beach and shoreline. If you want to go to the beach, make sure you cross at designated areas, because the dunes are extremely fragile.

About a quarter mile farther on, you'll see a big, grass-covered hump on the left side of the road. This is an old munitions bunker, which is now covered with yarrow in summer.

You may also notice something called a "salt spray horizon." The tops of shrubs and trees are not straight, but rather grow at a 30-degree angle because of the effects of wind and salt. The trees and shrubs farther from the shoreline are less affected and therefore taller, while those growing closest to these harsh elements are more stunted.

When you get to the end of the road, blocked by a fence, turn left and cycle until you reach your starting point. Turn right, ending up back near the Rockaway Artists Alliance building.

Extended ride to Floyd Bennett Field

(Ages 9 and Older) Moderate .75 miles one way, with steady incline going out. Plus however long you ride in the park.

For a longer ride and some exploring around neighboring Floyd Bennett Field in Brooklyn, exit Fort Tilden at 169th Street and walk your bicycles across the Marine Parkway–Gil Hodges Memorial Bridge (1937), named for the former Brooklyn Dodgers first baseman and New York Mets manager. The bridge spans Jamaica Bay, an important habitat for migratory birds and other wildlife and part of the Gateway National Recreation Area. Resident peregrine falcons nest high up on the bridge, so watch overhead for these extremely fast predators.

Once you've crossed the bridge, you're in Brooklyn. At the end of the bridge is a traffic light. Cross to the east side of Flatbush Avenue and into Floyd Bennett Field, which opened in 1931 as the city's first municipal airport and later became an important naval station. It became a national park in 1974, when it became part of Gateway. Bicycling the park's wide, long, virtually car-free, old runways is a great way to explore the park, which also has a nature trail (see chapter 2, Nature Walks), a giant community garden, a hangar where historic aircraft are restored, and a model-airplane field, where enthusiasts fly tricycle-size helicopters and airplanes and welcome the public to watch from small bleachers.

When you finish exploring Floyd Bennett Field, return the same way you came via the Marine Parkway Bridge to Fort Tilden.

Staten Island

Great Kills Park to Crooke's Point

(Ages 6 and Older) Flat 2.75-mile round trip

The best way to explore Great Kills Park is by bicycle via the multi-use path that runs the length of the park to a peninsula that juts out into Lower New York Bay. Joggers, parents with strollers, and elderly folks also use the path, so keep an eye out while riding. Be careful not to go too fast; announce your approach with a bicycle bell, whistle, or a "passing on the right" or "passing on the left" call.

The first thing you and your kids will notice upon setting out on the path is that there is plenty of unobstructed sky, something rare in New York City. Lots of trees line the path, too, including sumac with its thick, red berry clumps in autumn, and ailanthus of *A Tree Grows in Brooklyn* fame. Wildflowers include Queen Anne's lace, goldenrod, and butter-and-eggs, the latter a yellow and orange snapdragon-like flower introduced in the 19th century by colonists who mixed its juice with milk to ward off flies.

After passing a sign for the model-airplane field and ranger station on your right (you can check them out later), you and your children will soon see the Lower New York Bay come into view on your left. Since it opens into the Atlantic Ocean, this has traditionally been the maritime entrance to Manhattan. The peninsula narrows here, with a public beach on the left and Great Kills Harbor on the right. Dotted with beautiful sailboats, the harbor appears much like one in New England.

After the beach, the path becomes gravel and practically empty, because most people don't venture beyond this point. Cars are prohibited from driving beyond the beach, unless they have a permit, most of which are reserved for fishermen. You can, however, purchase an annual naturalist's permit for $50, which allows you to park at the point and more easily explore the coastline and maritime forest with small children

This is the most peaceful part of the ride. Point out to your kids some of the plants growing along the sides of the trail: mullein, sumac, and seaside goldenrod, for example. In autumn,

The sand dunes on Staten Island's Crooke's Point are fragile ecosystems with a beauty all their own.

hundreds of migrating monarch butterflies fly here to "nectar-up" on their way south. Listen for birdsong year round, and look up to see passing egrets and flocks of terns. When you and your children arrive at the tip, look for salt-spray roses, bayberry, and sea rocket.

Walk your bicycles down to the beach, taking the sandy path to the right of the bathrooms, then lean them up against the trash can and explore Crooke's Point. This is the end of the peninsula, which is named for John Jeremy Crooke, a wealthy mining engineer, industrialist, and naturalist who lived here in a cabin in the 19th century and chronicled—through writing, photography, and specimen-collecting—the area's varied plants and animals.

Crooke's Point is still serene, with most activity produced by gulls and terns, the latter getting a little noisy if they think you are threatening their nesting sites. They are harmless, however, and fun to watch as they zip through the sky and scream at you and your kids. You may even see oystercatchers, black and white shore birds with long, oversized bills, who like to feed at the shoreline.

Explore—from a distance—the sand dunes; but don't walk on them. These fragile dunes are kept in place by American beach grass and other salt-tolerant plants. Look for sea rockets, with whitish-lavender blooms in late June and early July, followed by swollen, two-jointed seedpods that kids will find interesting—one segment breaks off and is washed away to begin a new plant elsewhere, while the other segment stays with the parent plant and seeds close to home.

Fishermen love it here; and most of them don't mind if you and your youngsters walk over to see what they've caught. One proud angler keeps a photo in his wallet of the 42-inch, 35-pound striped bass he hooked at Crooke's Point and is only too happy to show it. Most of the fishermen will also give you angling tips if you are interested in fishing there.

Since this is a wild beach, meaning that it is not opened to swimmers or sunbathers, there's plenty to see along the undisturbed wrack line. Walk along the shore with your children and search for shells and sea sponges, taking a peak in the water for jellyfish and sea lettuce. Or just sit a while and enjoy the sound of the water lapping the shore.

After you leave the beach, you and your kids may want to take a walk on the short, horseshoe-shaped White Trail. The trailhead is just across from the bathrooms. Or return to the bike path and explore other parts of Great Kills Park by bicycle, including a pond at the back of the education field station (on your left, with the turnoff right after the boat-launch sign) and a salt marsh (on your right, via a sandy path just after Parking Lot A).

Snug Harbor Cultural Center

(All ages) Various short paths

The Snug Harbor Cultural Center is a gorgeous 83-acre compound of botanical gardens and 19th-century buildings housing museums, all set within a pastoral landscape connected by paved paths along which families can bicycle together. There's a great children's museum and a maze-like garden (see chapter 7, Gardens Grow Children) designed just for kids, so it can be enjoyable to cycle around to various sites. One particularly wild path exists in the northeast corner and encircles a wetland, with an arch created by twisting branches and two bridges that kids will love pedaling through and across, respectively. Look for cattails, jewelweed, burdock, purple loosestrife, and Japanese knotweed, all in bloom in late summer.

Silver Lake Park

(Ages 6 and over) Easy 1.3-mile loop

Enter at Silver Lake Park Road and Forest Avenue. Go a short way on Park Drive, which has car-free hours on weekends and some weekdays. At the "V," take the path into the park, passing some benches on your left. You'll soon see some descending stairs on your right. Walk your bicycle down those stairs. (If you don't want to do this, you may take a shorter route by returning to Park Drive and cycling until you come to a path that cuts across the lake. At the end of this path, turn right onto the path that hugs the lake, following it around until it meets up with your starting point.) After descending the stairs, ride on the path that parallels the lake. On your right, you'll come to a .25-mile-long path that cuts across the lake. Cycle in and check out the view, looking for ducks, gulls, and cormorants. Water is all around you here, and only a few buildings protrude above the otherwise uninterrupted 360-degree view of tree canopies, which are particularly gorgeous in autumn.

Silver Lake was a natural lake fed by springs until it was drained in 1913 and converted into a reservoir, which opened in 1917, receiving water from the city's Catskill Mountain supply system. In 1971, the reservoir was replaced by two underground storage tanks, the world's largest.

This may be a good time to explain to your children that New York City gets its water from upstate sources, and that the water travels for miles and miles through massive tunnels, aqueducts, and pipes before it reaches our faucets.

Return to the path, careful to keep the lake on your right. A little more than halfway around the 101-acre park you'll see the Silver Lake Golf Course on your left. Not too long ago, bones were found beneath the 18th fairway, remnants of a 19th-century cemetery where thousands of immigrants with contagious diseases were buried.

The path soon meets up with Park Drive. Follow it back to your staring point.

If you're bicycling with children ages 10 and older, you can tour both Snug Harbor and Silver Lake Park in one outing. It's very easy to get from one park to the other, but the connecting route (less than a mile) is along the streets. If car traffic is a concern, you can

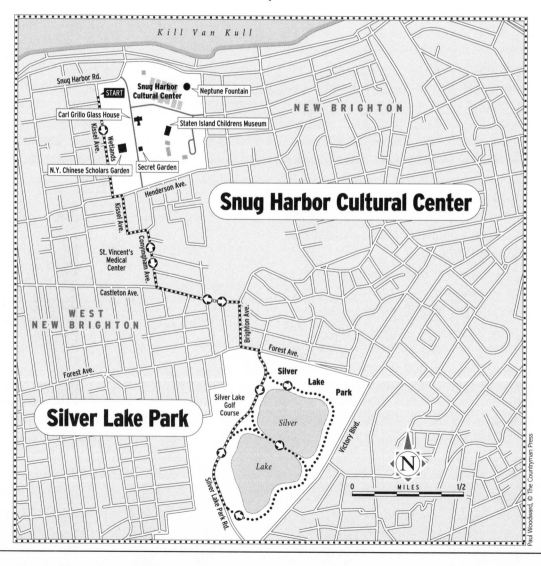

always ride on the sidewalks for safety. The ride from Snug Harbor to Silver Lake Park is pretty much uphill, so you'll be working hard; but on the way back, it's a breeze cruising along the sloping course.

Snug Harbor to Silver Lake Park, Connecting Route

(Ages 10 and Older) Hilly .75-mile route, followed by an easy .75-mile downhill return.

To get to Silver Lake Park, exit Snug Harbor from the Snug Harbor Road gate. At Kissel Avenue, turn left. When you reach Henderson Avenue, turn left again, then make a quick right back onto Kissel Avenue. Follow it around to the left, turning right onto Coyningham. At Castleton Avenue, turn left. Silver Lake Park will soon be on your right.

Bicycle Month

May is bicycle month in New York City, with plenty of bicycle advocacy groups and clubs offering family events throughout the five boroughs. For information, go to www.transalt.org, and click on Bike Month NYC; or call 212-629-8080.

The cycling path in Silver Lake Park takes you right across the lake.

The Park Drives

When some of the city's older parks were laid out in the late 19th century, park drives were created so that folks could escape the city by enjoying leisurely carriage and bicycle rides along green avenues. In fact, Frederick Law Olmsted and Calvert Vaux designed four dedicated transverse roads for Central Park to separate commercial traffic from pleasure riders.

The first car drove through Central Park in 1899, but it wasn't until the 1930s that automobiles really took over the park's drives. Although never built as commuter routes, the drives are now used by motorists as short cuts. For decades some have fought to ban cars from the parks, so that people could stroll, jog, cycle, and roller skate without fear of motor vehicles. The first car-free day in Central Park occurred in 1966. While cycling activists say there is still much to be done, the park drives do have car-free hours during which you and your children can pedal around the park, escaping the city hustle and bustle just beyond the trees.

Car-Free Hours
Central Park, Manhattan
Monday–Friday, 10 AM–3 PM and 7 PM–10 PM; weekends, 7 PM Friday to 6 AM Monday, except from the Monday before Thanksgiving through New Year's Day, when the drives are continuously open to cars, to alleviate holiday traffic.

Prospect Park, Brooklyn
Mid-January through week of Thanksgiving: weekdays, 9 AM–5 PM and 7 PM–7 AM; weekends, 7 PM Friday to 7 AM Monday. Monday before Thanksgiving through mid-January: weekends, 7 PM Friday to 7 AM Monday; holidays, 7 PM the day before the holiday to 7 AM the morning after.

Forest Park, Queens
Forest Park Drive, between Woodhaven Boulevard and Metropolitan Avenue, including Memorial Drive is open until 10 PM, when the park closes.

Silver Lake Park, Staten Island
Summer hours: weekdays 6 PM–9 PM; weekends, 6 PM Friday to 7 AM Monday; holidays, 7 AM–9 PM. At other times: weekend and holiday hours only.

Bicycle Rentals

If you don't own a bicycle, some shops will rent them to you. Transportation Alternatives, a cycling, walking, and public transportation advocacy group, maintains a list of Manhattan rental shops, as well as bike shops in other boroughs, at: www.transalt.org/calendar/century/rental.html.

You may also rent bicycles on site in three parks—Central Park, Flushing Meadows–Corona Park, and Hudson River Park—and quickly be on your merry way.

Loeb Boathouse–Central Park, Manhattan

at 74th Street
212-517-2233

Daily, March–October, 10 AM–6 PM, weather permitting. $6–$20 per hour (including helmet), depending on the bicycle. Must have identification and leave credit card, driver's license, or passport as deposit.

Cyclists may choose from among adult cruisers with foot brakes ($9), adult 21-speed bikes ($15), tandem bikes ($20), children's two-wheelers ($6), and toddler trailers ($6). Ask for a map to help guide you around the park. From the boathouse you can hop right onto the East Drive and begin exploring the park. Or head north, making a stop just east of the drive at the Conservatory Water, where kids can sail model sailboats. Continue north, taking in the nature around you, and eventually turn left (west) to Turtle Pond, just below Belvedere Castle—a great place to observe dragonflies, turtles, ducks, and other wildlife. Farther west, nestled on a hillside, is the 4-acre Shakespeare Garden, a good place to search for songbirds. If you visit this ever-changing landscape often enough, your kids will learn how to tell the time of year simply by recognizing what's in bloom—Virginia bluebells in March and black-eyed Susans in summer, for example. Ride south, following any path that follows the western edge of the Lake, passing Strawberry Fields and its "Imagine" mosaic dedicated to the memory of John Lennon. Turn left, now heading east, and pass Bethesda Terrace, after which you'll turn left (north) and cycle back to the Loeb Boathouse.

The boathouse serves food and has both indoor and outdoor seating. Afterward, you might meander into the Ramble for a while, entering right behind the rental kiosk, where you returned your bikes. Just a short walk in are some huge boulders that kids just love to climb.

Hudson River Park, Manhattan

Three locations: Pier 84 at West 44th Street; Pier 63 at West 23rd Street; and Pier 26 at North Moore Street.
212-967-5444 or 212-627-2020

April through October: Thursday and Friday, noon–8 PM; weekends, 10 AM–8 PM. $6-$9 per hour, depending on the bicycle. Identification and deposit required.

Renting a bicycle—adults' and children's, as well as toddler trailers—from any of these venues gives ready access to the city's beautiful, new Hudson River Park, a linear park that parallels the Hudson River for five miles, from just north of Battery Park City to 59th Street. A car-free bicycle lane known as the Hudson River Greenway borders the park's eastern side, so you don't have to worry about riding on the street.

Along the route are various places to stop, play, and learn, including the River Project ecology center at Pier 26 (see chapter 1, Nature and Environmental Centers), various free fishing (see chapter 9, Goin' Fishing), and kayaking clinics (see chapter 5, Paddling with Children), and many historic vessels—including, at Pier 63, the *John J. Harvey*, a retired fireboat built in 1931. There's also a trapeze school between Piers 26 and 34, where kids 6 and older can learn how to "fly through the air with the greatest of ease" while overlooking the mighty Hudson.

Flushing Meadows-Corona Park, Queens

Two locations: Meadow Lake Boathouse (northern shore of the lake); and near the Passerelle Building and Ramp (Park Center, near the #7 subway station).
917-578-5242 or 718-760-6565
www.flushingmeadowscoronapark.org

April through early September: daily, 11 AM–7 PM. $6–$20 per hour (including helmet), depending on the bicycle. Identification and deposit required.

There are single-seat bicycles for children and adults, as well as tandems, at both locations, but only Meadow Lake rents surreys, fun, four-wheeled, canopy carriages that accommodate four and are pedaled by the two people seated up front.

Most people renting bicycles at Meadow Lake cruise the perimeter of the 80-acre lake, which is about 2.5 to 3 miles around. The largest lake in the city, it and the park were created for the 1939-40 New York World's Fair. Today, parts of the path are in disrepair, but a proposal to bring the 2012 Olympics to New York City includes restoring the park and making Meadow Lake and its neighbor, Willow Lake, premiere rowing venues. Some areas around the lake are stark and treeless, while other spots host waders and shore birds, and the occasional angler, and are fringed by wildflowers and reed grasses.

Cyclists who rent near the Passerelle Building and Ramp, just east of the #7 subway stop, usually pedal quiet, tree-lined paths in the park's center. And there's lots to look at, too, including the 140-foot Unisphere, the giant, tilting steel globe, and the Rocket Thrower, depicting a muscular Greek god throwing a rocket into the stars, both remnants of the 1964–65 New York World's Fair. There are also several cultural institutions in the vicinity, including the Queens Museum of Art and the New York Hall of Science. You can even cycle over to the Queens Botanical Gardens (see chapter 7, Gardens Grow Children).

Bicycle Tours and Events for the Family

Urban Park Rangers

Dial 311
www.nycgovparks.org/sub_about/parks_divisions/urban_park_rangers/pd_ur.html

The rangers often lead bicycling tours of various areas, including the South Beach boardwalk and Silver Lake Park in Staten Island and the Salt Marsh Nature Center in Brooklyn, among others. Age appropriateness varies with each ride. For a schedule, pick up a copy of the rangers' calendar of events at any city park, dial 311, or go the Web site above.

Gateway National Recreation Area, Jamaica Bay Unit, Brooklyn–Queens

718-338-3583
www.nps.gov/gate/pphtml/events.html

One of Gateway's most popular trips is the 15.5-mile loop from Plum Beach, Brooklyn, to Breezy Point at the western tip of the Rockaway Peninsula, Queens. It is offered during spring, summer, and fall and includes five stops, with rangers telling the history of Plum Beach, Floyd Bennett Field, Jacob Riis Park, Fort Tilden, and Breezy Point. The tour starts and ends at the Plum Beach parking lot, located between eastbound Exits 9 and 11 of the Belt Parkway.

Central Park, Manhattan

212-541-8759
www.centralparkbiketour.com

Ages 7 and Older. Daily, 10 AM, 1 PM, and 4 PM, weather permitting. Closed January through March. Meet at 2 Columbus Circle (corner of 59th Street and Broadway). Adults, $35; children 15 and younger, $20–includes bicycle rental fee, helmet and escort.

Take the kids on a bike tour through Central Park and learn about both its nature and its historic sites like Belvedere Castle and Strawberry Fields, honoring John Lennon. Early autumn is a wonderful time to explore the park, with some wildflowers still in bloom and trees beginning to turn color.

The 2-hour tour is about 4.5 miles with nine stops, making it easy for grade-school kids to complete the entire course. Tandem bikes are available, but accommodate adults only. Children's two-wheeled bicycles are available. It's also best to arrive 15 minutes prior to the tour. Reservations may be made in advance, both online and by calling the above number.

Century Bike Tour, Central Park, Manhattan

(Toddlers and Older)

212-629-8080

www.transalt.org

Usually held in September. Meet at the Harlem Meer, in Central Park. Registration fee.

To encourage families to participate in the annual Century Bike Tour, bicycle advocacy group and sponsor Transportation Alternatives offers a 15-mile route that can be completed by many kids 9 and older. Even little kids can participate by riding along with their parents in a bicycle seat, trailer, or tagalong attached to an adult bike. While many of the event's 4,000 riders will cruise a full 100-mile course around four of the city's five boroughs, families ride 15 miles from Central Park's Harlem Meer to the carousel in Brooklyn's Prospect Park, an appropriate end.

All the pedaling is done on greenways, bike lanes, and low-traffic streets (marshals are posted for safety) and in parks, with participants even riding across the Brooklyn Bridge, along the scenic Brooklyn Heights Promenade, and past Empire Fulton–Ferry State Park on the East River. Free transportation is provided back to Central Park for those who need it.

9 GONE FISHIN'

There's something eternal about catching a fish when you're a child. The memory of waiting for a nibble and the adrenaline rush of reeling in your squirmy treasure never seems to fade. I don't fish much these days, but I warmly recall fishing with my dad. On my refrigerator, I keep a photo of myself, a jack-o'-lantern–toothed girl with her finger in the gill of a big fluke. It makes me feel connected, to the past and to nature and it's something I like to be reminded of.

I'm all grown up now and, while researching this book, began to relive the excitement of fishing as a child by fishing with my own children, watching other kids hook a fish or scramble to the "biting spots," eager to catch one of their own.

There is, indeed, great fishing in New York City, and you don't need to know an awful lot to fish with your children. Good places to start, especially with younger children, are local lakes and ponds where even the simplest rod will yield a bluegill or pumpkinseed. There are also programs that lend rods and reels and provide some instruction. And many experienced anglers wetting their own lines are often willing to provide tips and assistance, especially if you're fishing with children.

Once your kids get good at freshwater fishing using bait, its time to fish the same spot using lures—artificial bait made to look like fish prey—to attract usually bigger fish, like largemouth bass. Fishing with lures requires a bit more skill, with the angler casting out and reeling in over and over again to seduce the fish, rather then simply plunking a baited hook in the water and waiting for a bite.

Freshwater fishing in the city is catch-and-release only, and you must use hooks without barbs so as not to injure the fish. Kids under 16 don't need a license to fish but adults have to obtain state fishing licenses, available at tackle shops and some sporting-goods stores. The last weekend of June is always designated "Free Fishing Days" in New York State, to give folks a chance to test the waters without a license. For further information, call 718-482-4900, or go to www.Decemberstate.ny.us/website/dfwmr/fish/fishregs/fishlicense.html.

Once youngsters graduate from freshwater fishing, they may want to try some saltwater fishing from a pier. This type of fishing is more specialized, often requiring heavier tackle and, in some cases, a heftier pole (but not always). More nuanced saltwater fishing, like surf casting and fly fishing, is best left for a time when your children are older and stronger and have some fishing experience.

A license is not required for saltwater fishing, and you may keep your fish—although there are size and quantity limits, as well as health advisories pertaining to the consumption of certain species of fish. In general, children and women of childbearing age should not eat local fish. For more information, call 1-800-458-1158 or go to www.health.state.ny.us/nysdoh/fish/fish.htm.

While fishing is a seasonal activity, with specific species present or abundant at certain times of the year, fishing in New York City is generally best from April to June and then from September to late November. And you never know what you'll catch, what with 250 species swimming the various waters of Jamaica Bay, the Hudson River, and other waterways and lakes in all five boroughs. Most of the water is cleaner than it was at the turn of the last century, but there are still problems with PCBs and heavy metals dumped into the water decades ago.

The real fun of fishing, anyway, is catching fish, so it's best to exercise catch-and-release etiquette with all fish. While some people believe that even catch-and-release fishing is cruel (there are contrary views on whether or not fish feel pain as we do), I think that there's much to be gained by being out in nature fishing responsibly with your children.

For one thing, kids get to see first hand what makes a fish a fish and how their body design helps them survive in the water. Youngsters also learn how different fish have adapted differently to life underwater. For example, flounders are flat because they live at the bottom of the sea and have a brown "upper" side that helps them blend into the ocean floor and protect themselves from predators. Streamlined fish like striped bass are fast swimmers and often live in open water. Bring along a field guide to help you in your discussion with your children.

Catch-and-release is also a good way of instilling a conservationist ethic in your children. Fish stocked in lakes and ponds are often there specifically to help water bodies maintain an ecological balance. For example, some species consume algae blooms that in abundance can be toxic. Releasing saltwater fish lessens the human impact on local commercial fisheries, so there will be fish to reproduce the following year.

Once you've decided to go fishing, come

Remembering Your First Fish

The New York State Department of Environmental Conservation (DEC) wants kids to always remember the first fish they catch and will commemorate the big moment by sending youngsters a special award. All you have to do is provide the DEC with the following information: species of fish caught, size, where caught, date caught, and your child's name, address, and phone number. Send the information to: My First Fish, NY State Department of Environmental Conservation, Bureau of Fisheries, 625 Broadway, Albany, NY 12233

up with a definite plan so that your children's first experience with fishing is a positive one. If you have time, visit the site you intend to fish and see what successful anglers are doing and where. Ask them questions. Many anglers say that a sure-fire hit is taking your kids snapper fishing in late summer when these finfish are nearly flying out of the water.

When it comes to gear, the sizes and varieties of monofilament (fishing line) alone will make your head spin. But you can keep it simple. For fun, help your kids make their own rig. You'll need a 5- to 10-foot bamboo pole or branch (depending on your child's height), fishing line (6–8 pound works well) at least as long as the pole, a barbless hook, and a plastic bobber (or float). Kids love picking out their own bobber, because bobbers come in a variety of shapes and even feature cartoon characters. Tie one end of the line tightly to the pole's tip, perhaps cutting a notch to keep the line in place. Tie the hook to the other end of the line and then attach the bobber 2 or 3 feet up from the hook. If the hook touches bottom (it shouldn't), adjust the bobber accordingly. Drop the line in the water and when you get a bite, just pull up the fish. This is a great way to go fishing with little kids who would have trouble operating a mechanical reel.

If you're not that handy dandy, there are plenty of kids' rod-and-reel starter kits on the market. These will work for both freshwater and saltwater fishing, although they may need to be rigged differently. Don't let children use grownups' poles; they're simply too heavy and too long. If you want a little extra help buying a rod, visit a bait-and-tackle shop that sells them and you'll get individualized attention. They'll also gladly rig your child's pole. But pay attention, because kids invariably tangle their lines or get their lines snarled with somebody else's line—and they'll need you to come to the rescue.

Kids as young as 5 can learn how to cast, as long as you practice with them, using a casting plug instead of a hook at the end of the line for safety. The best place to do this is in a park or a large backyard. Experts recommend that beginners use comfortable pistol-grip rods fitted with spin-casting reels, which allow the easy release of fishing line with the touch of a thumb button.

When it comes to bait, some freshwater fishing programs use corn kernels, because they're cheap and easy, although sunfish can have a hard time biting through the shell. Squishing the kernels before hooking them helps. Sunfish will also go for hot-dog bits. While there's nothing like a good, old-fashioned worm, this may not instill a respect for all life. On the other hand, you might perhaps explain the web of life to your children and how one thing eats another to survive. It's your choice. If you do use a worm—one you've dug up from the garden, retrieved from your compost bin, or bought at a bait shop—push the hook through the worm's midpoint three times and let the ends dangle. Don't dig for worms in parks—it's illegal.

When you think you have a fish, slightly tug the line to set the hook in the fish's lip. Then haul the fish in, gently remove the hook (cut the line if the fish has swallowed the hook; and don't worry, it will eventually dissolve), and let your children get a good look at the fish and photograph it before sending it back on its merry way as quickly as possible. Don't take any caught fish home as pets; they won't survive. Wetting your hands before handling a fish helps protect the fish's protective coating, the slime that you feel.

Consider making fishing part of a larger outing that includes bicycling, going to the playground, flying a kite, or eating out at a favorite restaurant. If the day becomes a wash, regroup by skipping stones on the water, searching for turtles or crayfish, preserving leaves in a flower press, or simply pointing out the beauty of nature. Read *Not a Nibble*, by Elizabeth Honey.

Fishing with children isn't always easy, so don't make it more difficult by going out on a cold or a very hot day. Bring snacks and keep the outing short. As with birding, most young kids don't have the patience for lots of fishing; so when your child wants to call it a day, call it a day. And don't fish yourself—pay attention, rather, to your child's rod to better his or her chances of catching something. Lastly, make your outing a special event with mementos. Take lots of photos or even some video, and help your children create a record of the day by drawing and describing their fish in a "Book of Catches" before throwing them back.

Fishing teaches patience—an important skill in a world increasingly dependent on immediate gratification—and hones concentration skills as well as good hand-eye coordination. As their fishing skills develop, your kids will also gain confidence. And then there's the sheer adventure of suddenly seeing the unseen, that moment when a fish is pulled from its watery world and into ours for just a brief visit.

Best of all, maybe the next time your child sees someone toss a cigarette butt or candy wrapper into the water, he or she may speak for the fish, aware that life exists in this watery wilderness.

Fishing with Younger Kids (Toddlers and Older)

When going fishing for the first time, start with a pond or a lake in a city park, where you will find sunfish, perch, catfish, and bass from late spring through early fall. Sunfish are the most popular and include many varieties such as crappies, bluegills, pumpkinseeds, and large- and smallmouth bass. Their dorsal and anal fins have sharp, rigid rays that help keep them from being eaten by larger fish.

Freshwater Fish You May Find

Black crappie—These sunfish travel in schools and are usually between 8 and 12 inches long, with highly compressed bodies that are silvery green with black blotches. They also have a depression on their foreheads above the eyes and tend to feed during low-light hours.

Bluegill—The first thing you notice about bluegills is their beautiful blue cheeks and gills, which stand out from their brownish back and brown to orange sides. About the size of pump-kinseed sunfish, they'll bite just about any-thing, including corn. Males tend to the nests after females release their eggs and leave for deeper waters.

Chain pickerel—This long olive-green fish, with contrasting light green chain-link-fence–like patterns, is often used to control sun-fish populations. A predators, it will waylay anything it can swallow, even fish as big as itself (usually about 14–19 inches). Chain pickerels have sharp, needle-like teeth and long snouts, and they like to hide near or under plants.

Channel catfish—Catfish have whiskers or barbels around their mouths, which help them feel around for and taste food. Blue-gray and sil-very-gray to blue-black in color, and often with speckled sides when young, channel catfish

The annual fishing derby at Prospect Park always produces smiles.

have forked tails and sharply-spined dorsal and pectoral fins. They often feed at the bottom of rivers and ponds.

Common carp—This 12- to 25-inch fish is usually brownish, yellowish, and greenish, with two pairs of barbels (or whiskers) on its upper jaw. Its dorsal and anal fins are saw-toothed and sharp. Introduced to the United States from Asia in the 19th century, this fish sometimes considered a nuisance here; but in China it's a symbol of great wealth. An amusing children's book is Barbara Cohen's *The Carp in the Bathtub*, about a Jewish woman who plans to make gefilte fish and keeps her huge carp fresh by letting it swim in the bathtub. Grass carp, found in the Harlem Meer, resemble common carp, but are usually more silvery white and lack barbels.

Golden shiner—This usually small minnow (2.5–7 inches) is silvery, with golden-brown or reddish fins and an olive back. Shiners travel in schools and often stay near shore. They're used as bait and prey food for larger fish.

Largemouth and **smallmouth bass**—The largest members of the sunfish family, these guys are fun to catch because they put up a fight, particularly the smallmouth bass. Adult smallmouths are generally 14–17 inches long and do, indeed, have smaller mouths than do largemouths. They are usually greenish with vertical bands across their bodies. Adult largemouth bass have a long, dark, horizontal stripe along their sides.

Pumpkinseed—The most abundant sunfish in New York State, pumpkinseeds are as colorful as tropical fish, with orange-red bellies and golden-brown bodies mixed with bluish-green. They also have a bright red spot on the tips of their gill flaps. They are typically 5–6 inches long, hang out in large numbers in shallow water close to shore, and are usually willing to go for your bait.

Yellow perch—Along with sunfish, perch are pretty easy to catch and are most active in the morning and evening. They travel in schools, so it's a good idea to change location if none are biting in a particular spot. Be careful releasing perch from hooks because they have sharp spines and sharp gill plates. Generally between 6 and 12 inches long, they're yellow with black vertical bars on their sides.

Places for Freshwater Fishing

There are freshwater fishing opportunities in every borough. If you visit on a day when the fish just aren't biting, consider my "Plan B" activities, all of them close to the fishing holes.

Bronx

Indian Lake, Crotona Park

3 acres. Across from the nature center, at Claremont Parkway and Crotona Park East.
Plan B: Check out the Crotona Park Nature Center, Crotona Pool (free, in summer), or one of the park's four playgrounds.

Van Cortlandt Lake, Van Cortlandt Park

30 acres. Inside Van Cortlandt Park, at West 240th Street and Broadway.
Plan B: Visit the Van Cortlandt Park Nature Center, go for a short hike, or check out the historic Van Cortlandt House Museum inside the park, at West 246th Street (718-543-3344). A horseback riding facility is located in the park at West 254th Street (718-548-4848).

Brooklyn

Prospect Lake, Prospect Park

57 acres. Enter the park at Vanderbilt Street and Prospect Park Southwest to reach the south side of the lake, or at Parkside and Ocean Avenues to reach the east side of the lake. Prospect Lake has the largest concentration of largemouth bass in the entire state, according to the New York State Department of Environmental Conservation.

Plan B: Rent a pedal boat, visit the Prospect Park Audubon Center, or ride the nearby carousel.

Manhattan

Harlem Meer, Central Park

11 acres. Inside the park at West 110th Street, between Lenox and Fifth Avenues.

Free bamboo poles are available for borrowing at the Dana Discovery Center at the Meer from mid-April to mid-October, Tuesday–Saturday,

---

Tackle Box Starter Kit

- Fishing Pole (entire setup)
- Bait
- A few extra pre-tied hooks
- Extra bobbers and sinkers
- Net
- Fingernail clippers (for snipping lines)
- Bucket (for filling with water, if you want to look at fish for a few seconds)
- Needle-nose pliers (for removing stubborn hooks)
- Absorbent cloth (for cleaning hands between baiting and fish releases)
- Field guide on local fish (for identification)
- First-aid kit (in case you get bitten by a fish or stuck with a hook)
- Food and refreshments
- Camera
- Tracing paper and pencil

---

10 AM–4 PM and Sunday, 10 AM–2 PM. Picture ID required.

Plan B: Explore the Dana Discovery Center, go for a short hike in the North Woods, or enjoy the playground across from the Meer.

Queens

Baisley Pond, Baisley Pond Park

25 acres. At the intersection of Rockaway, Supthin, and Baisley Boulevards.

Plan B: Visit the playground, where a sculpture of a mastodon commemorates the discovery of mastodon molars and a bone fragment found during the dredging of Baisley Pond in the late 19th century.

Kissena Lake, Kissena Park

8 acres. Inside the park, near the intersection of Oak Avenue and 164th Street.

Plan B: Visit the nearby playground or the Historic Grove, which dates back to colonial times, when it was created by famed nursery-man Samuel Parsons. The grove includes 100 tree species from Europe and Asia.

Meadow Lake, Flushing Meadow-Corona Park

100 acres. In the park's southern end.

Plan B: Rent a bicycle or surrey and cycle the perimeter of the lake, or rent a boat and take to the water.

Oakland Lake, Alley Pond Park

15 acres. Near 223rd Street and 46th Avenue.

Plan B: Walk or bicycle around the perimeter of the lake or visit the nearby Alley Pond Environmental Center.

Staten Island

Clove Lake, Clove Lake Park

5 acres. Inside the park, near the Lakeside Café.
Plan B: Fish Clove Lake Park's two smaller ponds, Brooke's and Martling's; rent a boat; or enjoy the park's playground, where you'll find a whimsical sculpture called "A Bird Named Goldilocks."

Silver Lake, Silver Lake Park

51 Acres. Midpark, which is bounded by Forest and Victory Avenues and Clove Road.
Plan B: Bicycle around the reservoir or visit nearby Snug Harbor.

Willowbrook Lake, Willowbrook Park

5 acres. Inside the park, at Victory Boulevard and Eaton Place.
Plan B: Take a ride on the park's gorgeous carousel, which depicts Staten Island scenes, or take a walk in the nearby woods.

Wolfe's Pond, Wolfe's Pond Park

15 acres. Inside the park, just off Hylan Boulevard and Cornelia Avenue.
Plan B: Go for a nature walk or head to the park's beach.

Saltwater Action (Ages 5 and Older)

When it comes to saltwater angling, nothing beats fishing for snappers, or baby bluefish, with your kids. Once the snappers start biting, there's no stopping them. That's because they travel in schools to feed; and when they encounter a school of prey fish, they go into a feeding frenzy that makes the water look like it's boiling. Sometimes, the snappers even jump

The Urban Park Rangers sponsor fishing clinics around the city, including this one at Willowbrook Lake.

out of the water. When snappers are in the area, it's guaranteed that you and your children will spend more time catching fish than waiting for them. If this doesn't hook them on fishing, nothing will.

Snappers arrive in large numbers around piers and jetties in mid-August and stay through September. Now, that doesn't mean they're always hanging around a pier just waiting for you. You have to be there when the snappers are running with the smaller baitfish. Anglers recommend fishing close to high tide, usually an hour before the tide is full or within an hour after it has started to go out.

Snappers are the progeny of bluefish—ferocious predators with powerful jaws and sharp teeth that rip the heads off their prey, leaving scraps floating on the water for hungry flocks of gulls. Don't worry. Your child's light tackle cannot handle these big guys. Bluefish migrate along the Atlantic Coast during the various stages of their development. The largest bluefish, sometimes called gorillas or alligators, may be as big as your toddler and can top 30 pounds, while most bluefish are in the 4–10-pound range. Gorilla blues may weigh as much as 100 pounds! Medium sized blues are referred to as cocktails (4 pounds, and 10 inches long), while snappers are the tiniest at 4–10 inches.

Your kids can use the same spin-casting rod described on page 215 and light tackle with 4- to 6-pound monofilament line. Keep two feet of line between the bobber and the hook, preferably a snapper hook. Use small spearing for bait. If your children are older, they might try luring fish with a "snapper popper," a 3-inch piece of cone-shaped Styrofoam that floats on the water. When the line is tugged, the popper creates a commotion—bubbles and noise that mimic the look and sound of baitfish trying to escape a predator. Predatory fish in the area, in turn, think that there are tasty, juicy fish nearby.

Crabbing

Another straightforward and exciting saltwater activity for kids is crabbing for blue claws. It's not only fun telling the males from the females by looking at their undersides, but interesting to see how crabs are related to spiders. Both are arthropods, meaning that they're invertebrates with jointed legs and bodies and exoskeletons. Blue claws are also rather beautiful, with olive-green bodies and vivid azure pincers. These pretty pincers, however, will draw blood, so be sure to hold the crab firmly with your thumb and forefinger at the rear, where its claws cannot reach you.

Crabbing is best in summer, particularly July and August, and on a moving tide—meaning when the tide is moving in or out. (Note that crabbing is prohibited in city parks but permissible elsewhere.) The equipment is simple—a fishing line or string with a weight and a chicken neck (bait) tied to the bottom. Slowly drop the line into the water, letting it hit bottom, then tie the free end to the dock or some other stationary object. It may take crabs a little while

to smell your food. Every so often, slowly and carefully pull the line up until you see one or more crabs clinging to the chicken. Pull too fast and the crab may let go. When the crab has reached the point where you can easily get a net under it, do so, and shake the crab into the net. You can also bait a collapsible crab trap, but this method lacks the drama of the hand line.

Now the crab temporarily plays educator to your children. Notice how the width of the shell (which may be as much as 9 inches wide) is twice as long as the length. Turn the crab over, being careful not to get pinched, and show your kids its underside. Males, or "jimmies," have long, inverted "T" shapes on their undersides, while mature females, or "sooks," have an inverted "U" with a pointed top, like the shape of the Capitol building. They also have painted fingernails, or red claw tips. Immature females, or "she-crabs," display a pyramid, or inverted "V," shape. If a female is carrying eggs, she's called a "sponge," because that's what the orange mass of eggs (about two million of them) clinging to her abdomen looks like. Don't touch or upset this egg mass and immediately release these precious females back to the sea, so the babies have a chance at survival.

If you find a crab that feels kind of soft, you have a "peeler" that has just molted its shell. As crabs grow, their hard shells split open and they swim out the back. It takes several days for the new shells to harden; and until they do, the crabs are vulnerable to predators. Soft-shell season begins with the first full moon in May and continues through early fall. Male crabs often protect molting females by cradling them in their legs, but they have ulterior motives. Once females shed their old shells, they mate, with males later cradling their soft females until their new shells have hardened. Then the guys bolt to look for other willing females.

Snapper and Blue Claw Hangouts

Bronx

Under the City Island Bridge, City Island

Brooklyn

Canarsie Pier, Canarsie
69th Street Pier, Bay Ridge
Steeplechase Pier, Coney Island

Manhattan

Various locations along the Hudson River, including Wagner Park, Battery Park City Pier 25, Hudson River Park (at North Moore Street) Pier 45, Hudson River Park (at West 10th Street), West 79th Street to West 96th Street, under the George Washington Bridge, at West 179th Street.

Various locations along the East River (Manhattan side) include Stuyvesant Cove, East River Park under the Manhattan Bridge, Lighthouse Park (Roosevelt Island), East River Esplanade, at East 96th Street.

Queens

Joseph J. Addabbo Bridge, Howard Beach
Pier 4, Gantry Plaza State Park, Long Island City
Bayside Marina, Bayside

Staten Island

Lemon Creek Pier
Ocean Breeze Pier, Midland Beach

Advanced Saltwater Fishing

Most saltwater fishing, like surf casting and fly fishing, are best left to older kids and to children who have been fishing for a long time or have parents who are proficient anglers. It often requires more sophisticated gear and techniques that might easily frustrate new anglers.

You can try out a little saltwater fishing without investing in all the necessary equipment and know-how by participating in one of the city's

Fish Anatomy

Fish are cold-blooded animals that live in the water. They breathe by taking in water through their mouths and forcing it back to their gills (basically the fish's lungs). Here, oxygen in the water is absorbed into the blood stream, while carbon dioxide leaves the blood and is pumped back into the water. The water is then expelled through the gills.

Fish are designed to swim through the water using their various fins, especially their tail fins. Most fish have bones, but some, like sharks, have cartilage. Important fish parts include:

- Dorsal fin—the fin on the upper part of the body, toward the middle
- Caudal fin—the tail fin
- Anal fin—the fin on the underside of the body, near the tail
- Pelvic fin—each of the paired hind fins on the sides of the body, toward the tail
- Pectoral fin—each of the paired fins on either side of the body, near the head
- Gills—fleshy organs used for breathing and located on the sides of the head
- Lateral line—a series of sensory pores along the sides of the body that help fish sense vibrations in the water
- Scales—overlapping bony plates designed to protect a fish's body (Some fish, such as catfish, have skin instead of scales.)

many fishing clinics, where your children will receive some instruction and a free loaner rod and reel, and oftentimes can watch the catches of the day swimming in a pier-side aquarium.

Family Fishing Programs and Kids' Contests

Urban Park Rangers

(All ages, depending on the type of fishing)

Various sites, citywide
212-360-2774
www.nycgovparks,org/sub_about/parks_
divisions/urban_park_rangers/pd_ur.html

The rangers offer both freshwater and saltwater fishing in a wide variety of locations. Loaner rods and bait provided. Free.

I Fish NY

(All ages, but recommend for 8 and Older)

**New York State Department of
Environmental Conservation
Various Sites Citywide
718-482-4022**
www.dec.state.ny.us/website/dfwmr/
recfsh14.html

Weekends, mid-day during warmer months. Free.

A program of the New York State Department of Environment Conservation, the I Fish NY

It's great fun to stand in the water while fishing at Twin Island in the Bronx.

sport-fishing clinics are designed to get kids (and adults) interested in fishing and, hopefully, give birth to future environmental stewards. Youngsters receive everything they need to get started, from a fully-equipped 7-foot saltwater fishing pole to sand worms, bunker, and squid bait. The poles are relatively heavy, so small children will need help holding them up.

Before dropping hook, line, and sinker, kids visit four educational stations. The ecology stop features an aquarium with fish and other sea creatures from local waters, including blue-claw crabs, baby flounders, hermit crabs, and snapper blues. The fish-biology station focuses on fish anatomy. The casting station provides technical know-how. The rules and regulations station discusses, among other topics, the size and quantity of fish that may legally be taken from the waters. The program, itself, is catch and release.

Then you're pretty much on your own, with educators passing by every now and again to see how it's going and to answer any questions. Keep in mind that the fish aren't always biting, so your child may become disappointed if she or he doesn't catch anything. Some of the fish caught take center stage in an aquarium for all to see and are released later.

In the past, clinics have been held at Canarsie Pier in Brooklyn and the Ocean Breeze Fishing Pier on Staten Island, although the DEC hopes to broaden the program's scope. The best way to find a fishing clinic near you is by calling the DEC's New York Regional

Freshwater fishing is a favorite pastime in some city parks.

office at 718-482-4900, or by going to www.December state.ny.us/website/dfwmr /seasons /00ffdcln.html.

Brooklyn

Macy's Annual Fishing Contest

(Ages 15 and Younger)

**Prospect Lake
Prospect Park
718-965-8951 or
718-965-8999**
www.prospectpark.org

One entire week in July, usually 10 AM–2 PM. Free.

Since 1947, Macy's department store has sponsored an annual fishing contest open to anyone 15 and younger and held for one week at Brooklyn's Prospect Park. If you've never fished before, this is a good place to start. The free program includes all fishing equipment and bait, which is not simply handed over to kids, but earned after they walk through three stations to get the lowdown on fish and fishing. They learn what a fish is, how aquatic ecosystems work, and how to fish safely.

Then it's off to Prospect Lake for a chance to hook a winner. Prizes (usually a rod and a tackle box) are awarded to the child who catches the first fish—and then daily for the largest fish caught and the most fish caught.

Manhattan

Annual Fishing Jamboree

(Ages 5-12)

**Harlem Meer, Central Park
Inside the park, at 110th Street
between Fifth and Lenox Avenues
212-860-1370**
www.centralparknyc.org

Annually, in September; call for date and time. Free.

Kids compete for prizes, get their faces painted, listen to stories, and participate in other family activities in this annual fishing event open to about 150 youngsters. A contestant entry form must be filled out in advance to register. The forms are available at the Dana Discovery Center or on the Central Park Conservancy Web site, above.

Go Fish (Hudson River)

(All ages, but recommended for 5 and Older)

**Robert F. Wagner Jr. Park,
Battery Park City
212-267-9700**
www.bpcparks.org

Designated days in spring and fall, 10 AM–2 PM. Free.

Run by dynamic and knowledgeable marine educators and volunteers, this catch-and-release program gives families a chance to fish and learn about the Hudson River ecosystem at the same time. Kids beam from ear to ear after reeling in a striped bass or even a seahorse, and then stand mesmerized in front of a 25-gallon aquarium, watching their fish swim. And the venue is gorgeous—with views of the Statue of Liberty, Ellis Island, and the Upper Bay. Sailboats and motorboats pass by. Gulls soar overhead.

"The aim of this program is to get kids thinking about the river, how it used to be when you couldn't find a fish in it because of pollution, and how it is now, and how we can all keep it clean," says Bill Fink, the Marine Education Coordinator for the Battery Park City Parks Conservancy, which runs the program.

In the 1960s, the Hudson River was declared dead, a casualty of industrial wastes and chemicals discharged into the river. Today, more than 40 species of fish live in the Hudson—from anchovies and eels to sea robins and white perch. Youngsters learn to tell pectoral from dorsal fins and about other features of fish anatomy, using a dead fish as a model. The fish is then used to teach some biology, with educators dissecting it and even pulling bits of clam and other creatures from its stomach to show what fish eat.

Every child under 14 who hooks a fish receives a certificate authenticating his or her catch. Rods, reels, bait, and instruction are provided. The event is often coupled with musical entertainment and children's crafts, which usually begin at noon; so if you want a quiet fishing experience, arrive early. An inviting lawn behind the seawall is great for relaxing; and a café and restaurant sell snacks and beverages.

Big City Fishing

(All ages, but recommended for 5 and Older)

**Hudson River Park
212-791-2530**
www.hudsonriverpark.org

Three locations—Pier 25, at North Moore Street; Pier 45, at West 10th Street; Pier 66a, at West 26th Street. July–August, Tuesday–Sunday, 11 AM–5 PM. Closed Monday. Free.

Try a little saltwater fishing along the Hudson River.

the river was once a working waterfront. This pier also hosts free walk-up kayaking on weekends (see chapter 5, Paddling with Kids), so consider combining the two experiences.

The area around Pier 45 is designed for passive recreation, so there are no cyclists or roller skaters zooming by. There's a perfect lawn for picnicking, as well as clean restrooms and a refreshments concession. Young kids will love the water-themed playground at nearby Pier 51.

There are plans to rebuild Pier 25, but for now it has a sandy area for beach volleyball, a snack bar, a small sprinkler play area for children, a miniature golf course open from May to October, and one of the last surviving Ellis Island ferries, the *Yankee Ferry*. If you fish late on a summer Friday, hang around for one of the pier's free movies at dusk, which in the past have included such kids' favorites as *Chitty Chitty Bang Bang* and *Harry Potter and the Chamber of Secrets*.

While this fishing program doesn't have the bells and whistles of the Go Fish Program, it does offer consistency—it's available all summer long—and it supplies the essential equipment: rods, reels, and bait. The rods come in 8-foot and 6-foot lengths, the latter best for younger kids. Personnel usually scoop up some creatures from the river so kids can see and touch them, including hermit crabs, glass shrimp, and baby fish. Baby blue-claw crabs are especially fun to watch because as soon as you pass a hand over their container, they raise their pincers, all set to defend themselves.

Fishing on one of these piers is like stepping out onto a peninsula with nothing but the water and wide-open space in front of you and the city tucked away someplace behind you. Each of the piers juts out into the Hudson River, so all the fish are the same, but each pier also has its own attraction and you'll probably favor one over the others.

Pier 66a is a restored historic float bridge used from 1954 to 1973 to transfer railroad cars from the Baltimore & Ohio Railroad (B&O) warehouse at 11th Avenue and 26th Street to barges along the river and ultimately to the B&O rails in New Jersey. Remind your children that

Old Fishing Line

Discarded fishing line is a great hazard to shore birds. A bird that gets tangled in line is not able to fly and feed itself and may die. One thing you can do to help is pick up any fishing line you happen to find while fishing. A good children's book that illustrates how one little boy rescues a shy gull is *Kiya the Gull*, by Fen H. Lasell. (Look for it in your local library, because it is out of print.)

Go Fish (East River)

(Ages 5 and Older)

East 96 Street and Robert Wagner Jr. Esplanade, East River
212-427-3956
www.eastrivercrew.org

Various dates in June, July, and August. Free.

Like the Hudson River, the East River has advocates committed to improving it and bringing people to its shores. In this case, it's East River CREW (Community Recreation and Education on the Water), which has its own Go Fish program providing children with rods, bait, and fish traps so they can learn about the creatures that live in the river.

The fish traps often corral small creatures like baby flounders, crabs, and even sea squirts—clear, grape-sized filter feeders that spurt water when gently squeezed, a real kid pleaser. Small fish and other creatures are kept in aquariums, so youngsters can observe them, and are then returned to the river. Once bigger fish are caught, kids may pose for photos with them before releasing the catch back to the water. There are also interactive science activities related to watersheds and estuaries (which the East River is) and art projects, including gyotaku, the Japanese art of printing with real fish.

East River CREW hopes to include rowing in its programming in the near future, using 25-foot Whitehall gigs that families with older children can try out during free rowing days on the East River.

Queens

Family Fishing Clinics

(Ages 16 and Younger)

Bayside Anglers Group
718-631-4394
www.baysideanglers.com

Family Fishing Festival, last Saturday in June, at Kissena Lake; Children's Snapper Derby, late August or early September, at Bayside Marina; and Children's Fishing Clinic, held annually at Gantry State Park. Free.

This Queens-based, nonprofit organization and fishing club, established by a few fishing buddies in 1994, defies the image of the solitary fisherman gone fishing to get away from it all. The members are eager to share their knowledge of and enthusiasm for fishing, particularly with kids, providing them not only with fishing fundamentals but with the principles of responsible fishing to boot.

The club does so through its public events, which are usually held in cooperation with the New York State Department of Environmental Conservation (DEC) and the New York City Department of Parks & Recreation. Most of the events include a raffle to win a rod and reel and giveaways like kids' tackle boxes and other fishing equipment.

At the Kissena Park event, the DEC teaches kids and their parents about freshwater fishing, fish anatomy, species identification, and fishing ethics. Youngsters catching their first fish receive their own photograph to take home. The Snapper Derby at Bayside Marina exposes kids to saltwater fishing. While most children will probably catch snappers, they may also hook a flounder or a weakfish. Index cards that the kids wear around their necks get punched each time they hook a fish. Trophies are also awarded to the top three fisher-kids, with club members are on hand to help them hook the big one. Gantry State Plaza is also a saltwater venue with instruction, free loaner rods and reels, and bait.

Gateway Striper Club

(Ages 9 and Older)

Fort Tilden, Gateway National Recreation Area
718-768-9794
www.nps.gov/gate

Several times in summer. Free.

There's nothing like standing on the shore, casting a fishing line into the water and out, into the water and out, trying to attract a fish with your lure. It's even better when you wade out into the water to be a little closer to nature, facing the waves and the breeze, all the while working the line and achieving a rhythm.

If your children are bored by just dropping a line into the water, and they're big enough to handle an 8- to 11-foot rod (which the club provides), try surf fishing together at the annual workshops offered by the Gateway Striper Club, a bunch of angler volunteers eager to teach. Granted, they run the workshops in summer, when there's not much biting (that's why they're not fishing themselves); but even still, your children may be lucky enough to catch something, or at least learn proper technique so you can take them out on their own one day.

Surfcasters generally fish from the shore or in the water, casting their line and lure just beyond the break in the surf to catch big saltwater fish. One club member likens casting to "chopping wood with an ax. It's the same basic motion. You cast out and you reel in." Of course, there's more to it than that—anglers are constantly trying to perfect their techniques, taking into account changing conditions like wind, waves, and currents. But for now, just cast out your lines and see what happens.

Gyotaku (Fish Prints)

Back in the 1800s and 1900s, when a Japanese fisherman caught fish he would make a record of his catch by brushing ink onto the fish and pressing it onto paper or cloth. Sometimes, these prints would adorn a fisherman's home. Kids can do this at home today by purchasing fish at a local fish market or frozen in the supermarket, perhaps choosing a flat fish like a flounder and a streamlined fish like a striped bass in order to study how their different body designs are related to their lives in the water. For example, flounders are flat because they are bottom dwellers, while striped bass are streamlined because they are fast swimmers. The process will also reveal the different shapes and sizes of scales, which are big in blackfish and tiny in eels, for example. You'll also need rice paper and water-soluble ink or an acrylic paint. If touching slimy fish is unpleasant for you, you can buy rubber fish replicas designed to be used for gyotaku at www.enasco.com (enter "gyotaku" in the keyword search box), or by calling 1-800-558-9595.

Once you are done printing with either real or artificial fish, help your child label the parts of the fish for a little lesson in anatomy.

MUSEUMS, ZOOS, AND FARMS

Although it usually involves going outside, often getting dirty, touching things, breathing fresh air, and guiding your kids along, enjoying nature with your children doesn't have to be a strictly outdoor adventure. The city has some of the finest museums anywhere, many of them with exhibits and programs focusing on insects, animals, plants, and other living things, as well as programs that instruct families on particular species or groups of animals, with some specific to New York City. The city's zoos also offer educational family programs, in which youngsters sometimes meet unusual creatures up close, as well as plenty of indoor animal exhibits for families to explore even on the rainiest or coldest of days. Barnyard animals also call New York City home, with several venues providing a feel for the old days, when plants and animals were part of daily life on the farm.

So if you want to leave the nature lesson to someone else or take a break from going out in the field, pack up the kids and take advantage of the many structured nature experiences that abound around town and witness how they too can inspire and instruct us all.

Museums

Brooklyn

Brooklyn Children's Museum
(All ages)

145 Brooklyn Avenue
718-735-4400
www.bchildmus.org

Exhibits; greenhouse; outdoor garden; live animals; family and public programs; summer rooftop concerts; library; gift shop; restrooms.

In addition to cultural and art programs and exhibits, the Brooklyn Children's Museum offers various nature programs and exhibits, including a "please touch me" greenhouse, outdoor garden, live animals, and a permanent collection of 27,000 objects, many of which are natural-history specimens.

When visiting the greenhouse, encourage your kids to wear the special aprons marked "biologist," grab a magnifying glass, and look for nuances in the greenhouse plants—fuzzy leaves, juicy stems, distinctive markings, and so on. A kids' favorite is the African spear plant, with its extremely long and hard, dagger-like leaves. There are also carnivorous plants, such as Venus flytraps, Cape sundews, and pitcher plants. Youngsters may also use their sense of smell to distinguish between Cuban oregano and lemon eucalyptus.

Children are invited to dig into some compost for worms and pick up shells in the hermit crab tank to see if one of those squatters is living inside. Explain to your kids that just as they need new clothes as they grow, hermit crabs seek out new shells when they outgrow the old ones. There are also bullfrogs and snails to see.

Behind the greenhouse is an outdoor garden, the newest feature being a Japanese-style hill-and-pond garden, complete with Japanese maples, wooden chimes, and white, sparkling sand that children can rake to achieve a bit of kiddy bliss. The garden is planted with butterfly-attracting flowers, so bring a field guide and see how many winged gems you and your kids can identify. In spring, dogwood, magnolia, and weeping cherry trees are in full regalia. In summer, raspberry and blackberry canes are in full fruit. There's also an herb garden and a bench where you and your children can sit under a beautiful dawn redwood tree.

If you're lucky, the museum's iguana may be out sunning himself; but most of the museum's 30 animals, mainly reptiles, are kept inside, including the huge, 17-foot Burmese python. There are also box turtles, a Payaso parrot, and basilisk lizards. A nifty video depicts the birth of basilisk babies at the museum.

Be sure to check out Collections Central, a rotating exhibit featuring objects from the museum's permanent collection, one of the few in a children's museum. Natural specimens include rocks, minerals, fossils, mounted birds, mammals, insects, and skeletons—and even the complete skeleton of an Asian elephant, not to mention dinosaur footprints and a whale rib. Items not on exhibit may be viewed on computer monitors. The library has plenty of nature books that youngsters are free to peruse.

The museum will soon be even closer to nature. It's planning an expansion that will double its size to 102,000 square feet, a facility that will rely on sustainable, renewable and/or recyclable materials and systems to operate.

Open—September-June: Wednesday-Friday, 1-6 PM; weekends, 11 am-6 pm (closed Monday and Tuesday). July and August: Tuesday-Friday, 1-6 PM; weekends, 11 AM-6 PM (closed Monday). Fee, free for kids under 1.

Manhattan

American Museum of Natural History (Manhattan) *(All ages)*

**Central Park West, at 79th Street
212-769-5100
www.amnh.org**

Natural history exhibits; space exhibits and planetarium; live-animal presentations and exhibits; films; family programs and events; restaurants; gift shops; restrooms.

The American Museum of Natural History is every kid's dream; but it can also be overwhelming, because there are just so many wonderful things to see. Beyond the museum's archaeological, anthropological, and cultural record of life on earth is its core of natural science. And there are many must-see exhibits for students of nature—from small children to inquisitive teenagers. But keep in mind as you and your chil-

dren wander the 42 exhibition halls on four floors: you can't do it all in one day.

So plan a course of action before visiting the museum, perhaps exploring the museum's "Resources for Learning" Web site, at www.amnh.org/education/resources, for some ideas and activities. The museum also has knowledgeable "explainers," museum volunteers wearing special buttons that indicate their area of expertise. Encourage your kids to ask questions of these experts, who will be thrilled to provide answers.

Open—Daily 10 AM-5:45 PM. Rose Center for Earth and Space remains open until 8:45 PM on Friday. Closed Thanksgiving and Christmas. Some individual exhibits have different hours. Fee.

Discovery Room *(Toddlers-12)*

Seen enough of T-Rex and the blue whale for 10 lifetimes? If you and your children are craving a natural history experience that's a little more intimate, a little more hands on, the museum offers the Discovery Room, a kid-centric nature center.

The Discovery Room encourages youngsters, especially those between 4 and 12—but younger children are welcomed—to behave like little scientists, both in the lab and the field, by using microscopes and telescopes, mock archaeological sites, and actual specimens to learn about life on Earth.

The first floor is devoted to biodiversity, anthropology, and paleontology. Kids are immediately drawn to a two-story replica of an African baobab tree. Tucked inside and on the tree are creatures ranging from a dung beetle to a dwarf mongoose. Pick up a clipboard and together with your children find as many animals, birds, and insects as possible. Nearby, youngsters can piece together their own 14-foot Prestosuchus skeleton, a reptile from the Triassic Period, or dust the dirt off an Oviraptor nest site.

Young children have trouble using microscopes, but here they can study slide specimens on an eye-level monitor that projects the images suitably large, so that kids can see the hairs on a house fly and the tiny legs on a tick. They can also learn the science of specimen categorization by studying everything from brain coral and a lotus seedpod to a trilobite skull and petrified wood—all kept in accessible child-level cabinets. There are also models of local favorites like the red-tailed hawk, flicker, and garter snake. And the center has a wonderful collection of nature books.

The second floor is the laboratory area, a serious place for kids about 8 and older, complete with microscopes, seismographs, and astronomy labs. Check out up-to-the-minute data on recent earthquakes around the world, courtesy of the U.S. Geological Survey.

A limited number of 40-minute passes (free with museum admission) are given out on a first-come, first-serve basis. Sunday mornings and Mondays are the best days to visit. Purchase admission passes as soon as you arrive at the museum, then mosey through the museum's other exhibits until your appointed time. If it's not crowded, you and your children may stay for a second, or even a third, 40-minute spot and soak up more science.

Open–July 1-Labor Day: Monday-Sunday, 10:30 AM-5:15 PM. Labor Day-June 30: Monday-Friday, 1:30 PM-5:15 PM; Saturday-Sunday and public holidays, 10:30 AM-5:15 PM. Closed for lunch 1:30-2:15 PM. Story time (ages 2 and older)–Monday, 10:30-11:15 AM and 11:15 AM-noon), as well as monthly visits by a scientist. These programs are not held during July and August. Free with museum admission.

The Butterfly Conservatory
(All ages)
When city skies are too cold for butterflies, more than 500 winged gems make their winter home inside a self-contained, climate-controlled, 1,315-square-foot vivarium. Here it's always summer—about 80 degrees and with high humidity, just like a rainforest—perfect conditions for these tropical inhabitants and the flowers and plants they thrive on.

While waiting in line, you and your kids can check out wall exhibits illustrating everything from the life cycle of butterflies to efforts at preserving their fragile habitats.

Once inside, you'll hear howler monkeys and tropical birds, recordings that make you feel that you're thousands of miles from home. Indeed, most of the butterflies here are not locals, but have been raised on farms in Costa Rica, Texas, and Florida, arriving at the museum in the pupal stage.

Follow the curved path flanked by nectar feeding stations and lush tropical plants, and look around for butterflies like the blue morpho, zebra longwing, and gulf fritillary. Point out the butterflies' colorful scales and designs and the curling proboscis ("tongue") that they use to sip nectar. Some of the butterflies may even mistake you and your children for flowers and come in for a landing. A display case filled with chrysalises (moths develop inside cocoons) allows you and the youngsters to witness the birth and flight of new butterflies, whose short lifespan is only about two or three weeks.

Although visits are timed, you won't be rushed out of the exhibit if you choose to linger. But after 20 minutes or so, the heat and humidity will feel worse than a New York City summer.

Open–Early October-late May: daily, 10 AM-5:45 PM; last timed entry at 5 PM. Fee includes admission to the Rose Center for Earth and Space. Tickets may be purchased in advance online at www.amnh.org.

Hall of Biodiversity
(Ages 3 and Older)
This high-tech exhibit introduces kids to nine different ecosystems and the creatures that live in them, the ecological importance of these

habitats, how we depend on them for our survival, and what can be done to minimize degradation of these vital systems of life.

The 100-foot-long, jaw-dropping Spectrum of Life Wall shows kids just how many different kinds of creatures make the world go 'round. There's everything from algae to amphibians and mosses to mammals, with models of some creatures hanging from the ceiling and jutting out from the wall. Arranged as a kind of evolutionary family tree and with computer stations designed to help youngsters delve deeper into species specifics, this exhibit reveals how all life is related.

A walk-through diorama depicts how species diversity is played out in the rain forest—although it is important to point out to your children that biodiversity exists beyond the rain forest. It's right in our own backyards and parks.

Hall of Ocean Life (Ages 3 and Older)

Here kids learn about marine environments—from estuaries to polar seas—as well as species that live within these unique ecosystems, including seaweed and jellyfish, striped bass and sharks.

The exhibit focuses on how well adapted marine life is to the sea, explaining, for example, how fish breathe, eat, and move through water. The hall's lighting and sound effects make kids feel like they're part of the ocean, while high-definition videos project humongous moving images of spawning horseshoe crabs, fish in barrier reefs and other marine species, making kids feel as if they're encountering them up close.

For delving even deeper, computer stations provide children with information and fun facts on vertebrates and invertebrates and plant life; models of these species are showcased in the Tree of Life wall displays on either side of the exhibit's main entrance. There are also 14 dioramas and the beloved 94-foot blue whale model suspended from the ceiling.

Hall of Planet Earth
(Ages 3 and Older)

This is where kids learn that the earth is alive and that it has been for 4.5 billion years. They also learn what natural processes went into making the earth what it is today. The exhibit addresses such complicated geological questions as how the earth came to be, what it's made of, and why it's habitable—as well as the forces behind mountains and valleys, weather and climate change, and natural disasters. Younger children will gravitate toward the huge rock specimens—168 to be exact—mounted like fine sculptures around the exhibit space. Best of all, they can all be touched!

Hall of Minerals and Hall of Gems (Ages 3 and Older)

These halls are dark, giving the impression that you have delved deep into the earth to discover some of the 5,000 minerals and gems known to exist. Many are displayed here—chunks of olivine, serpentine, gypsum, and garnet, among them—all different in structure and color. Scattered throughout the exhibit on pedestals are huge specimens, including psychedelic-looking petrified wood, icy quartz, and golden topaz, to name only a few. There's also a large stalagmite and beautiful purple amethyst geode (a far cry from those little eggs you get in rock shops) to touch. And don't forget to peer into the recreated tourmaline gem pocket, a huge cavity dazzling with blue-green crystals with touches of pink.

Rose Center for Earth and Space (Ages 4 and Older)

While some of the Rose Center for Earth and Space exhibits may be difficult for very young children, and even—dare I say—some adults to grasp, your visit here can be as in depth or as cursory as you want it to be. It may involve only a simple walk through the Hall of Meteorites, where young kids may be satisfied enough to touch the nooks and crannies of billion-year-old space rocks, while older youngsters may wish to explore just what these meteorites can tell us about the formation of our own solar system.

If your children are ready to go one step further, they may want to visit the Hall of the Universe, where they'll really feel like specks of dust in the scheme of things. And kids of all ages love the space shows projected with high-definition equipment on the domed ceiling and walls of the Hayden Planetarium Space Theater.

There are also less obvious places in the Museum of Natural History where you and your children can explore nature, places that perhaps you've whizzed by en route to the dinosaurs, blue whale, or butterflies. Many of these exhibits highlight specimens of local interest that are perhaps too difficult to see in the wild. And because they're frozen in time, families can take the time to study them—they won't run away.

Mollusks of New York
(Ages 3 and Older)

You won't even find this exhibit on the museum's official map, but it' on the first floor, tucked between Northwest Coast Indians and Café Caribe. In this wonderful display of marine and freshwater bivalves and snails, with some international specimens for comparison, you and your children can see what a perfect channel whelk, slipper shell, moon snail, and periwinkle look like—before going beach-combing yourselves.

Hall of North American Forests
(Ages 3 and Older)

The huge cross section of a giant sequoia displayed here is worth seeing, not only because it is simply amazing in and of itself, but also because it prompts discussion about local trees. This specimen has 1,342 annual rings, which means it lived from 550 to 1891 C.E. This sequoia was also huge—16.5 feet in diameter.

Why not go out and measure the diameters of some of the biggest trees you and your children can find in parks and neighborhoods throughout the five boroughs, then record your findings in a journal, along with photos of the trees.

Another great exhibit here is the microenvironment of a forest floor magnified 24 times. Just look for the diorama with the giant acorn, millipede, daddy long legs, and earthworm. This is a good time to talk about how every day is recycling day in the forest, with insects and other tiny critters always hard at work breaking down old leaves and rotting wood to create new soil for the earth. Everything in nature has its use.

Hall of North American Birds
(Ages 2 and Older)

If you plan to go bird watching with your children, first visit this hall's dioramas, which feature stuffed birds in recreated environments. Just be prepared to answer your children's inevitable question: "Are those birds dead?"

The duck diorama contains plenty of quackers that you and your kids will see in New York City, from northern shovelers and snow geese to common mergansers and buffleheads. The shore bird diorama has black skimmers, common terns, ruddy turnstones, and laughing gulls.

Other dioramas feature a long-legged wader colony, a peregrine falcon and chicks, and young and adult bald eagles in different stages of plumage (the young don't achieve the signature white head until they're about 4 years old). Owls and hawks are displayed perching, so that you and your children can see how species differ in size.

Note: You may wish to skip the nearby New York City Birds exhibit, because it may be creepy to kids. The specimens are not taxidermal, but are rather stretched-out study skins, sometimes with empty eye sockets, used by researchers to measure and examine.

Public Programs and Contests
(All ages)

The museum offers numerous family-friendly programs, including geological tours of New York City, nature walks in Central Park, and live-animal presentations, the latter of which are often paired with hands-on workshops for parents and kids ages 4–9. The presentations themselves, which in the past have featured live raptors and predators, such as a black bear cub, a lion cub, and bats—including one with a 6-foot wingspan—are for all ages.

There are also astronomy programs, including "Astronomy for Young Adults," which welcomes children as young as 10 who wish to learn about the moon and its phases, constellations, and other objects and workings of the universe. There are astronomy classes for kids as young as 4, including one that explores what it's like to be an astronaut.

Programs are always changing or being refined, so check the museum's Web site for the latest. And if you have a budding naturalist in grades 7 through 12, encourage him or her to enter the museum's annual Young Naturalist Awards competition by exploring a topic in biology, Earth science, or astronomy. For information, go to www.amnh.org/youngnaturalist awards or call 212-533-0222.

Identification Day (All ages)

Mark your calendar for this annual event, then round up any strange rocks, bones, or feathers you have at home but know nothing about, and see if the museum's experts are able to tell you what they are. For the date of the next Identification Day, usually in March, call 212-769-5176.

Science and Nature Program for Families (Ages 3-7)

Parents can learn about nature alongside their children by attending a four-week program held during the school year. Each class starts out in the museum's learning center, home to creatures like box turtles and tadpoles kept in kid-level aquariums. There are also visits from museum scientists and specialists. There is a different focus each week, using children's nature literature, specimens, and artifacts to create a world of discovery. Emphasis is placed on hands-on activities that parents and youngsters can enjoy together. Kids also get special safari vests and flashlights to create a sense of adventure as they head out with their grownups to explore the museum.

Classes are small, at 10–12 child-adult pairs, so enrollment is limited. A personal interview with the program staff is required of child applicants and their parents, with interviews usually taking place in May and June preceding the next school year. Classes for younger kids begin before the museum opens to the public, while older kids attend after school. The program is also open to youngsters aged 8–10 without the company of their parents. There is a program fee.

Queens

The New York Hall of Science
(Ages 3 and Older)

47-01 111th Street
718-699-0005
www.nyhallsci.org

Nature exhibits, activities, and public programs; indoor play place for kids 6 and younger; outdoor science playground; Magic School Bus activity area; biochemistry lab; astronomy discovery lab; audio tours; science clubs; science shop; restrooms.

The newly expanded New York Hall of Science, on the grounds of Flushing Meadow–Corona Park, is mostly focused on science and technology, but does offer—among its 400 exhibits—some nature and astronomy exhibits, as well as hands-on programs. In the Preschool Discovery Place, kids 6 and younger—using puppets, a tree habitat, and ethnic produce—

explore ways in which the natural and man-made environments are interconnected. Youngsters 7 and older are best suited for the hands-on experiments in the new Pfizer Foundation Biochemistry Discovery Lab—they can choose from among 12 experiments, including the extraction of colors from flowers. By using high-powered microscopes in the Hidden Kingdoms exhibit, kids may explore the otherwise invisible world of microbes, tiny creatures such as bacteria, fungi, and viruses that live not only all around us but also on and in us.

Weekend workshops for families explore topics as varied as the scale of the solar system, the world of tiny protozoa and algae, the classification of insects, and the doings of sea creatures. Outside is a 30,000-square-foot science playground (open from March 31 through December 31; separate fee), where youngsters of all ages may hang on a giant spider web, scamper around a Climbing Space Net, and check out the Energy Wave—among other fun undertakings.

Open—January 1-June 30 and September 1-December 31: Monday-Thursday, 9:30 AM-5 PM; weekends, 10 AM-6 PM; weekday holidays, 9:30 AM-5 PM. July and August: Monday, 9:30 AM-5 PM; weekends, 10 AM-6 PM.

Preschool Discovery Place

Every weekend, noon-4:45 PM. Free with general admission.

Pfizer Foundation Biochemical Discovery Lab

Saturday-Sunday, noon-4:45 PM; Fee. July-August: Tuesday-Friday, 2-4:45 PM. September-June: Friday, 2-2:45 PM; Free with general admission.

Staten Island

Staten Island Children's Museum

(All ages)

**At Snug Harbor Cultural Center
1000 Richmond Terrace
718-273-2060
www.silive.com/sites/si_childrensmuseum**

Insect and animal feedings; story time; summer musical performances; toddler programs; summer bug camp (ages 4 and older); restaurant; picnic area; gift shop; restrooms.

The Staten Island Children's Museum's "Bugs and Other Insects" exhibit is already a fun place to explore with budding entomologists; but it's slated to get even better, with an expansion that will include a new beehive, possibly a live ant colony, and components focusing on insect survival, adaptations, and communities.

For now, kids can crawl through a replica anthill and watch live butterflies in every stage—from chrysalis to flying adults—inside a huge clear cube. The "Arthropod Zoo" is particularly fascinating, with live hermit crabs, crickets, a tarantula, a scorpion, huge cockroaches, millipedes, and praying mantises—all in their own glass homes, so that youngsters can watch them go about their day. The praying mantis habitat even has foamy-looking egg cases attached to twigs, so you may encounter hundreds of baby mantises being born.

Little children will enjoy doing rubbings of all kinds of insects engraved on metal plates scattered throughout the exhibit. Older kids can consider the array of insect specimens displayed in the art corner and sit down for a while to sketch and color their favorites. The "Take a Closer Look" station features magnified insect specimens that kids can study from every direction by turning a wheel that flips the specimens over and onto their sides, and then identify the various body parts by using charts on display.

In addition to non–nature-related exhibits —like "Great Explorations" where kids can explore a rainforest, drive a dogsled, and go virtual scuba diving; and the outdoor Sea of Boats play space—the museum explores animal pets in "It's a Dog's Life." Youngsters learn how different animals smell, hear, and see, while taking in a live animal show or visiting the live guinea pigs, birds, and fish that reside here.

Open–Summer: Tuesday-Sunday, 11 AM-5 PM. During the school year: Tuesday-Sunday, noon-5 PM. Closed Memorial Day, Independence Day, Thanksgiving, and Christmas. Fee.

Staten Island Museum of the Staten Island Institute of Arts & Sciences *(Ages 5 and Older)*

75 Stuyvesant Place
718-727-1135
www.statenislandmuseum.org

Natural history exhibits; family programs and events; summer Earth camp (ages 8-2); Saturday science club (ages 8-13); nature walks; gift shop; restrooms.

While the Staten Island Museum of the Staten Island Institute of Arts & Sciences may appear stuffily serious, it's a relaxed place where children can learn about local natural history and wild places. In addition to historical, artistic, genealogical, and cultural resources, the museum has more than 500,000 entomological specimens, 25,000 plant specimens, 10,000 shells, and 15,000 stone, bone, and, clay artifacts—as well as marine invertebrates and ornithological specimens—all periodically showcased in institute exhibits.

In the past, this small museum has had to be satisfied with featuring some of its specimens in revolving exhibits, but there are plans to enlarge the institute by opening a satellite at the Snug Harbor Cultural Center. This will allow the institute to devote the entire Stuyvesant Place building to natural history, with reptile specimens, bird's nests and eggs, rocks, bones, and other examples of nature on permanent exhibit. Past shows have focused on the bedrock of New York City, the lifespan of the 17-year cicada, and minerals—including large chunks of phosphorescent minerals that look like ordinary rocks to the naked eye but radiate like hot charcoal briquettes or neon beacons when viewed under various short- and long-wave lights.

Permanent exhibits that appeal to kids include "Wall of Insects," featuring 162 specimens of butterflies, moths, cicadas, and beetles from around the world, and "Lenape: The First Staten Islanders," which explores 10,000 years of Native American habitation on Staten Island, and how these indigenous people coexisted with nature. On view are many artifacts—projectiles, mortar and pestles, pipes, drills, and other tools that the Lenni Lenape fashioned from Staten Island rock and which were excavated thousands of years later.

Speaking of rocks, kids who collect rocks, shells, and other earthly delights will love "Stump the Curator," a program held at 4 PM on the third Wednesday of every month. Every youngster who successfully stumps Ed Johnson, the Curator of Science, wins a free family membership to the museum. Families can also participate in the museum's naturalist-led ecology walks, which explore the borough's natural areas. On Thursday evenings, from 6:30 to 8 PM, everyone can enjoy science games and activities at Family Science Thursdays.

Open–Tuesday-Saturday, 9 AM-5 PM; Sunday 1-5 PM; Monday by appointment only. Closed Christmas, New Year's Day, Fourth of July, and Thanksgiving. Fee; kids under 12 free.

Zoos and Aquariums

For most city kids, getting close to animals means visiting a zoo or aquarium, and New York's are among the best, with everything from gorillas and grizzly bears to pink flamingoes and tufted puffins. Most of these creatures are not city natives but come from someplace else and are frequently exotic species that really "wow" kids. Visiting the city's zoos and aquariums can have benefits locally as well, however. By watching animal behaviors, learning about the animals' home environments and habits, or sitting in on programs that study specific animals or ecosystems in depth, kids may better appreciate all living things, including those in their own backyards and parks. The beautiful, endangered snow leopard is not that far removed from the neighborhood alley cat, but sometimes it takes a visit to a zoo to see that.

Note: The city's zoos and aquarium (except for the Staten Island Zoo) are managed and maintained by the Wildlife Conservation Society (WCS). In 2003, the city drastically reduced funding to WCS and threatened to close the Prospect Park and Queens Zoos. Public pressure kept the zoos open, but public programming has ceased at those two zoos and has been decreased at other institutions, except the venerable Bronx Zoo. Find out more about the Wildlife Conservation Society by visiting www.wcs.org.

Bronx Zoo *(All ages)*

2300 Southern Boulevard, Bronx
718-220-5100
www.wcs.org

Extensive animal exhibits, animal feedings and demonstrations; public events; family programs; junior zoo-guide program; children's zoo (ages 6 and under, seasonal); restaurants and cafés; gift shops; stroller and wheelchair rentals; restrooms.

This is truly the greatest zoo on earth, where kids can romp through the Congo Gorilla Forest with nothing but a pane of glass between them and these huge primates, then visit the big cats of Tiger Mountain. There's Jungle World's Asian rainforest, cool and wet and occupied by red river hogs, huge pythons, mandrills, and okapi—which looks like a part-zebra, part-giraffe kind of animal. And don't forget the lions, bears, rhinos, elephants, giraffes, and other big mammals. In fact, there are 4,000 creatures to see within this 265-acre complex.

And when it comes to local nature, the zoo's grounds are simply fabulous, with colorful native wildflowers and lush trees shading the pathways and butterflies and hummingbirds, chipmunks and rabbits flitting and darting in and out of foliage. And there are animals native to the United States on exhibit as well, from bats in the World of Darkness and familiar rodents in the Mouse House to snowy owls and American pelicans. The zoo also offers some exhibits and public programs that focus

Climbing on a termite hill at the Bronx Zoo.

on local nature and its importance. To avoid crowds, the zoo suggests visiting on nonholiday Mondays, on Saturday and Sunday mornings, and on most weekdays after 1 PM, when most school groups are gone.

Riverwalk *(Ages 3 and Older)*

Most people will probably rush by the entrance to this new .04-mile path that parallels the Bronx River, because once they've parked their cars or entered the grounds, they head straight into the zoo proper to see all the animals.

The Bronx Zoo's new Riverwalk trail guides visitors along a portion of the Bronx River.

This path, however, is a gorgeous place to walk with even your youngest children, fringed as it is with lovely wildflowers such as black-eyed Susans, goldenrod, and little blue-stem grass and visited by chipmunks, cottontails, and other animals. Best of all, it runs along the Bronx River and feels far removed from what most people think of as the Bronx. What a great way to show your kids that nature exists right in the city.

To find the path, look for the huge totem pole near the Bronx River Parkway entrance to the zoo. This healing totem depicts various animals fitted together like a puzzle and was carved into a hallowed Alaskan cedar log by some California youths and given to the city after 9/11. Keep the totem on your left to find the path into the woods.

At the fork, bear left (you'll see a northern red oak on your left) and listen for the soothing sound of the river. Along the way, you and your kids will find many of the trees and plants identified by markers, so this is a good way to learn about some tree species. Interpretive signs along the way describe various animals, fish, insects, reptiles, amphibians, and birds found along the Bronx River—from spotted salamanders to wild turkeys. Informative panels also illustrate how the river and its inhabitants cannot survive alone, but are interdependent.

The Riverwalk brings you to a spot high above the river where you and your children will see two dams. A sign explains just what the dams are doing there and how they affect the river, the only freshwater river in the City of New York. Native Americans called it *Aquehung*, or the "River of High

Bluffs." It starts in southern Westchester County and meanders through the Bronx before emptying into the East River. Industrialization along the river almost killed it; but in recent decades both government and local communities have worked together to revitalize the river and its shoreline and improve public access, so that today people can walk or bike along its banks and kayak and canoe its waters.

At the "T," go left and continue until you reach an area with benches overlooking the river. This is a great place just to sit awhile and let the sound of the river wash over you and your family. Ask the kids how cold they think the water is, then get up and check the digital readout on the display panel—which, in addition to the present water temperature, notes the animals that are probably in the river at that time of year. In summer, brilliant purple loosestrife blooms around the river. The plant is invasive, meaning it doesn't really belong here and could take over the area, edging out native plants.

The path soon descends and leads you to a flowery area that has a sandy spot along the river reserved for nesting snapping turtles, which dig down 4 to 7 inches to deposit their eggs.

When you reach trail's end, walk down to the river. There are two large pin oaks here. Look for ducks, swallows, egrets, and other birds; and if you look across the river, you may see (or at least smell) the zoo's bison.

Open—During zoo hours. Free, with admission.

The Butterfly Garden (All ages)

Until recently, the zoo's popular Butterfly Zone was a seasonal exhibit, open from memorial Day through early October. But a brand-new, permanent home for more than 1,000 North American butterflies, many of them New York City natives, has opened across from the Reptile House.

The centerpiece of the one-acre site is a 5,000-foot greenhouse and indoor butterfly habitat as lush as a summer's day, with monarchs, painted ladies, and even luna moths sipping nectar from tons of gorgeous flowers. Outside is yet another butterfly garden and meadow, planted with butterfly favorites, including lantana, purple coneflower, butterfly bush, and milkweed, and dotted with whimsical sculptures and caterpillar benches. Exhibits teach everything from monarch migration and plant pollination to the butterfly's role in the food chain and its importance to biodiversity and ecological health. There's even a video that depicts a butterfly emerging from its chrysalis.

Next to the garden and greenhouse is a new 76-seat insect carousel, where kids can ride on the backs of grasshoppers, praying mantises, fireflies, and other insects.

Open during zoo hours. Fee, with separate cost for carousel ride.

Family Programs (Toddlers and Older)

The Bronx Zoo's menu of family programs is immense and impressive. Most of the programs feature live-animal presentations, require advanced registration, and are often age specific. For example, many programs do not allow very young children. There are also fees. Past programs have included "Native New Yorkers," which focused on New York City's own wildlife, from black rat snakes and red-tailed hawks to screech owls and diamond back terrapins. The zoo's "Fall Frolic" is for kids 3–6, with an adult, and, with visits from some local animals, explores how animals and plants prepare for the winter. Every year, 4- to 8-year-olds may join their parents for a "Mommy and Me" program that explores the mothering skills of other animals, with special animal guests, and a "Daddy and Me" program that introduces kids to animal daddies who do a lot of hands-on parenting. And when birds are migrating through the City, the zoo leads "Migratory Bird Weekend" walks that are open to kids.

Open–April-October: Monday-Friday, 10 AM-5 PM; weekends and holidays, 10 AM-5:30 PM. November-March: Monday-Sunday, 10 AM-4:30 PM. Fee; kids under 2 free. Admission is by donation on Wednesday.

New York Aquarium *(All ages)*

**West 8th Street and Surf Avenue
Brooklyn
718-265-3474**
www.wcs.org

Animal exhibits and feedings; live animal shows; family programs and events; gift shop; restaurant; picnic tables; restrooms.

Situated a stone's throw from the Coney Island boardwalk, the New York Aquarium features more than 10,000 maritime animals and fish. A new exhibit (opened in 2005) with floor-to-ceiling tanks showcases the biodiversity and fragility of coral reefs. Called Glover's Reef (named for the atoll and research station the Wildlife Conservation Society has operated off the coast of Belize since 1997), the exhibit features many colorful species of fish and invertebrates, including spiny lobsters, triggerfish, and others.

After walking through Conservation Hall and checking out the piranhas, clownfish, and other kids' favorites, pop back outside to Sea Cliffs, complete with penguins, seals, and walruses, which can also be viewed via an underwater gallery where youngsters are able to watch them all swim through the water. En route to the gallery, you'll pass through a rocky passageway with a few nooks in it. Have your kids look around for two eggs. They're not real eggs, but they do illustrate penguins' nesting technique.

Inside the Sea Cliffs building are some kids' favorites, including a tall coral reef tank filled with such colorful creatures as tangs, angelfish, and a variety of seahorses that are really neat, especially since the fathers are the ones swim-

ming around with babies in their belly pouches. Youngsters also love the sharks, in a tank that holds the submerged safe from the ill-fated *Andrea Doria* luxury liner, salvaged and donated by a trustee in 1981.

The beluga whales are in a huge outside tank, where a baby beluga was born in 1991, the first in an aquarium. And don't forget the live dolphin and sea lion shows in the outdoor Aquatheater.

Explore the Shore teaches kids how sea creatures breathe, move, reproduce, see, hear, and eat. There's also a touch tank with horseshoe crabs and sea stars to pet and a recreated 400-gallon wave that crashes while you stand dry underneath.

Alien Stingers features many varieties of sea jellies, corals, and anemones—all of them sea creatures that sting. A Sting-O-Meter shows which jellies pack the least painful stings and which are the deadliest. Thankfully the local moon jellies score low on the pain meter. Also on exhibit are lots of "Little Nemos," clown fish with the ability to swim unscathed into and out of the long, stinging tentacles of sea anemones. This benefits both creatures. The colorful clown fish leave the safety of the tentacles to attract larger fish, which are then stung and devoured by the anemone, which in turn leaves enough remains for the tiny clown fish to eat.

In addition to "Breakfast with the Animals" and other programs, the aquarium offers some great hands-on programs during which families can explore ocean creatures by land and by sea. There is a fee for these programs.

Beach Bonanza *(Ages 6 and Older)*
Families explore the Coney Island shoreline (just outside the aquarium's doors) for shells and creatures that have yet to leave their homes behind, then help drag a seining net through the surf to pull up animals swimming nearby, all the while learning how ocean life adapts and survives in this ever-changing environment of tides, breaking waves, sun, salt, and sand. The

City zoos offer kids the chance to bring out their inner animal.

program includes making fish prints and pressing seaweeds.

Science at Sea *(Ages 5 and Older)*

This annual 3-hour boat excursion out of Sheepshead Bay is a great way for families to learn about local ocean life. During what is much more than just a boat ride, participants rotate among five education stations: plankton, native fish, signal flags, food chain, and bottom dredge—the latter featuring animals lifted from the bay, including hermit crabs, moon snails, barnacles, limpets, mussels, and various fish. Kids love playing the roles of various creatures along the food chain, with the bigger animals like orca whales at the top of the chain and tiny beings like krill and plankton at the bottom.

Open—Every day. Memorial Day-Labor Day—weekdays, 10 AM-6 PM; weekends and holidays, until 7 PM; April 1-Memorial Day and Labor Day-October 31—weekdays, 10 AM-5 PM; weekends and holidays, until 5:30 PM; November 1-March 31—10 AM-4 PM daily.

Prospect Park Zoo *(All ages)*

**450 Flatbush Avenue
Brooklyn
718-399-7339**
www.wcs.org

Animal exhibits and feedings; drop-in programs; self-serve cafeteria with automated machines; picnic area; souvenirs; restrooms.

This is a great, small zoo for young kids, one of its nicest attractions the mulch path of the Discovery Trail, with various animal stops along the route. A huge hit is the black-tailed prairie dogs that live atop a big, dusty hill in the World of Animals. Youngsters experience a real face-to-face with the dogs by entering a tunnel beneath the exhibit and popping their heads up into clear bubbles overlooking the hill.

In summer, the path is colored with black-eyed Susans, Queen Anne's lace, and viburnum berries frequently visited by local birds, including cardinals and catbirds. In the pond area, bullfrogs peek out from between lily pads in a *Where's Waldo?* kind of way. See if you and your kids can spot clumps of frog eggs among the pond plants. Turtles—mostly red-eared sliders and painted turtles, line up like soldiers along partially submerged branches to catch some rays. Children can walk out onto sculpted lily pads for a closer look.

Two other favorite exhibits are "Animals in Our Lives" and "Animal Lifestyles," the latter featuring hamadryas baboons that are intimately viewed through a huge window. Some folks sit for hours observing the baboons, which is extremely entertaining—especially to kids, who like to see mother baboons nursing their babies and individuals of all ages scratching their itches and grooming one another.

Animals in Our Lives features farm animals in a beautiful green space with trees, wildflowers, and a pond. Kids can feed the animals—Agatha the Cow is a favorite with her big eyes and wet, black nose—or pet a llama. The llamas' thick coats are shorn during even years, turning these fluffy ruminants into goofy-looking creatures that resemble the animal in Bill Peet's book, *The Wingdingdilly.*

The Animals in Our Lives exhibit also includes an indoor component, at the entrance to the barnyard, that exhibits other animals, including saw-whet owls (which migrate to New York City), poison-dart frogs, and a big-headed turtle.

Open—April-October: Monday-Friday, 10 AM-5 PM; weekends and holidays, 10 AM-5:30 PM. November-March: Monday-Sunday, 10 AM-4:30 PM. Fee; kids under 3 free.

Central Park Zoo *(All ages)*

830 Fifth Avenue
New York
212-439-6500
www.wcs.org

Animal exhibits and feedings; children's zoo (ages 6 and under); family programs and events; café; picnicking in nearby Central Park; gift shop; restrooms.

The Central Park Zoo is another small zoo with the usual penguins, sea lions, and barnyard animals, as well as not-so-common polar bears; but a particularly wonderful exhibit is its indoor rain forest, a tropical paradise where bats and colorful birds fly free and deadly piranhas swim. Don't worry though; the bats pretty much stay high up in the canopy and the piranhas stay in the water—but a bird may land on your head.

Kids will love the leaf-cutter ants marching around with little green blades held high above them like umbrellas and marvel at the cotton candy-colored scarlet ibises and Victoria crowned pigeons, both somewhat fancier and more vividly attired than our local ibises and pigeons.

The noises here are wonderful too, with squawking macaws and other tropical birds calling out to each other. The zoo also hosts family programs, where parents can learn right alongside their children, from toddlers on up.

Open—April 1-October 31: weekdays, 10 AM-5 PM; weekends and holidays, 10 AM-5:30 PM. November 1-March 31: 10 AM-4 PM.

Queens Zoo *(All ages)*

53-51 111th Street
Flushing
718-271-1500
www.wcs.org

Animal exhibits and feedings; walk-in programs; cafeteria with automated machines; gift shop; picnicking in nearby Flushing Meadows–Corona Park; restrooms.

Like the Prospect Park Zoo, this small wildlife center is perfect for young visitors, who can easily stroll the tree-lined pathway leading to various habitats, from the Great Plains to a northeastern forest. In fact, all of the animals here are North American species, except the spectacled bears, an endangered animal from South America's Andes Mountains. Some of these animals—coyotes and bald eagles, for example—have even been seen in the wilds of New York City. The zoo also has a farm with domesticated animals.

The Staten Island Zoo offers some terrific hands-on programs, including an annual dinosaur festival.

At the start of the path is a waterfowl marsh, a pleasant spot to sit with your children to watch and talk about ducks. Explain to your kids that ducks have flight feathers only on their wings and tail, with a separate muscle controlling each feather independently so that the wing's shape may be tailored for efficient flying. Fluffy down feathers are tucked under the outer feathers and keep the ducks warm.

Along the path, you'll encounter alligators, sandhill cranes, a lynx, a puma, barred owls (an eastern species), Roosevelt elk, and five coyotes, one of them rescued from Central Park in 1999. There are also sea lions, a bird aviary shaped like a geodesic dome, American bison, two bald eagles, and—in the newest exhibit—noisy, brightly colored, thick-billed parrots, a Mexican endangered species whose natural range once included the southwestern United States.

Open–Every day. April 1–October 31: weekdays, 10 AM–5 PM; weekends and holidays, 10 AM–5:30 PM. November 1–March 31: 10 AM–4 PM daily.

Staten Island Zoo *(All ages)*

614 Broadway
Staten Island
718-442-3100
www.statenislandzoo.org

Animal exhibits and feedings; family programs and events; pony rides; café; gift shop; restrooms.

Traditionally a zoo with a variety of farm animals, pony rides, other small animals and a renowned serpentarium—with one of the largest collections of North American rattlesnakes—the Staten Island Zoo has in recent years gotten much more elaborate with the creation of a small Tropical Forest and

African Savannah exhibits that feature more exotic animals, such as two-toed sloths, spider monkeys, mandrills, and leopards. (There are plans to move the leopards to a brand-new, naturalistic outdoor space.) These exhibits are entirely indoors and seem artificial and confined, but they give kids a chance to see animals they wouldn't see in the city's other small zoos.

For children who love snakes, nothing beats the Serpentarium, where a volunteer walks around with a large boa around his neck. There are dozens of reptiles and amphibians here, including some local species—such as diamondback terrapins, wood frogs, and eastern box turtles—and the extensive collection of North American rattlesnakes previously mentioned. The building is soon to be upgraded and modernized.

The zoo's aquarium is also lovely, with sea creatures from around the world, including tropical coral-reef fish, spotted puffer fish, clown fish, two huge green moray eels, seahorses, and even fish that frequent New York City waters.

The Staten Island Zoo is the only city zoo not affiliated with the Wildlife Conservation Society. It is operated by the Staten Island Zoological Society.

One of the zoo's most popular programs—among several—is its own annual Groundhog Day, when Staten Island Chuck, New York City's only weather forecasting groundhog, predicts a long winter or early spring. A fee is charged for this breakfast-with-Chuck event and it's open to kids of all ages.

Another big event is Hug a Bug Day, devoted to everything buggy. In addition to presentations and live insects, insect crafts occupy the youngsters involved. The event is free with zoo admission. And don't miss the annual Dinosaur Festival, at which children see tons of bone and skull specimens, speak to experts about these ancient creatures, and make dinosaur crafts.

There's also a breakfast feeding program for kids 5–10 (accompanied by an adult), who help zookeepers prepare meals and feed the animals.

Open—Monday–Sunday, 10 AM–4:45 PM, except Thanksgiving, Christmas, and New Years day. Fee; free for children 2 and younger; donation day Wednesday after 2 PM.

Farms

Green Meadows Farm *(All ages)*

**73-50 Little Neck Parkway
Floral Park
1-800-336-6233 or 718-470-0224
www.visitgreenmeadowsfarm.com**

Seasonal, traveling farm, with pony rides, hayrides, gift shop, picnic area, and restrooms.

Green Meadows Farm isn't really a farm; it's a company that brings a taste of farm life to city kids across the country. For several weeks in spring and autumn, Green Meadows Farm sets up in Queens, on land next to the Queens County Farm Museum, which sponsors the program. The animals—everything from cows to chickens and pigs to ponies—arrive via trailers from various breeders and farms. Visitors pay $9 per person for a 90-minute guided walk around the farm.

If you're expecting to learn about farm life, husbandry, and animal life, however, you'll be disappointed. But if you want to expose your kids to animals not often seen in the city, and give them the opportunity to touch these critters, you'll be pleased. The tour consists of tugging on the udder of an 80-pound Holstein. (The milk is not collected in a pail.) Then it's off for a quick pony ride, followed by a 7-minute hayride, which is a lot of fun. Everyone sits on homey hay bales as the tractor speeds through bumpy farmland and woods, with kids giggling nervously every time they're thrown into the air.

Then it's off to mama pig and her cute, pink, suckling babies, which squeal when awakened by the farm guide. There's no mud here; the porker family is cozy in a crib just low enough for little ones to see. There are also fluffy Japanese suki chickens, ducklings and chicks to hold, and sheep and goats to feed. The guide constantly moves the group along, careful not to linger too long. There's also a pot-bellied pig, bunnies, and geese—and then it's on to the next group. In spring, kids leave with a souvenir drinking cup and in autumn, a pumpkin.

Ted Keyes—whose parents started the first Green Meadows Farm in 1964, in Waterford, Wisconsin, while he was growing up—owns the farm, which also operates in California, Florida, Illinois, Maryland, and Texas. The farm's seasonal dates vary from year to year, so it's best to get on their mailing list to learn when they'll be in New York. The Farm is open to the public only on Saturdays; weekdays are reserved for school groups. There are restrooms, snacks, and souvenirs available.

Open—Call or check out the Web site for dates.

Queens County Farm Museum

73-50 Little Neck Parkway
Floral Park
718-347-3276
www.queensfarm.org

Seasonal festivals; hayrides (fee); farm stand; greenhouse; self-guided farm tours; weekend tours of historic farmhouse; gift shop; restrooms.

If you've ever wondered what a real farm looks like and how it operates, visit the Queens County Farm Museum, where work hasn't stopped since 1697, when Elbert Adriance started the family homestead. Today, it's a working historic farm with 7.5 acres of croplands and orchards used to demonstrate the history of agriculture in New York City. It also

City kids can milk a cow at Green Meadows Farm.

has the city's first vineyard, a pilot project begun in 2004. There's also an old farmhouse with barn and tractors—and turkeys, ducks, roosters, lambs, and an old farm dog that roam the 47-acre grounds. And there are cows, laying hens, and goats to see, too. Volunteers, including two older men with graying ponytails and feathers in their hats, look like the real thing . . . with an urban touch.

Youngsters may enjoy hayrides or, with their parents, take self-guided tours of the farm and visit the colonial farmhouse that dates to 1772. Crops such as tomatoes, eggplant, and corn are harvested and sold at an on-site produce stand from August through October,

Wednesday–Sunday, 10 AM–4 PM. You can even buy eggs and honey produced by the farm's hens and bees.

Executive Director Amy Fischetti suggests that first-time visitors attend one of their seasonal festivals to get acquainted with the farm. These include a strawberry festival in spring, an apple festival in October—featuring the largest apple cobbler in the country—and an official Queens County Fair in September, complete with blue-ribbon competitions in livestock, crafts, produce, and more, with entry open to residents of New York City and Nassau and Suffolk counties. There's also a pie-eating contest, a corn-husking contest, scarecrow making, lumberjack shows, and a petting zoo. The farm also hosts an annual Native American Pow-Wow featuring dancing, music, and other Native American traditions. In mid-September, a maze is carved into a 2.5-acre tract of corn, and kids are invited to follow clues as they wander through the tall stalks.

Open–Monday-Friday, 9 AM–5 PM (outdoor visiting only); Saturday and Sunday, 10 AM–5 PM, when tours of the historic farmhouse and hayrides (weather permitting) are available. Free, except on special event days and for group visits.

City farms offer kids a chance to join the flock.

Wyckoff Farmhouse Museum and Education Center

**5816 Clarendon Road, corner of Ralph Avenue
Brooklyn
718-629-5400**
www.wyckoffassociation.org

Small farm; historic farmhouse; children's and family programs; tours; gift shop; restrooms.

An organic farm grows in Brooklyn, and it's a place where families are encouraged to help plant, tend, and harvest the crops, which are then sold on site on Sunday afternoons. The 4,000-square-foot farm—technically called the Wyckoff Farmhouse Community Demonstration Garden—grows eggplants, tomatoes, onions, chard, cabbages, corn, squash, cucumbers, okra, herbs, flowers, and more, and is the centerpiece of M. Fidler–Wyckoff House Park.

The 1.5-acre triangular site is a green oasis in a neighborhood fringed with auto-repair shops and car washes. Yet it's worth the trip for families who live in other neighborhoods, because inside this compact tract is such a beautiful, manageable place where kids can get close to a working farm, see how things grow, and discover that farming is part of Brooklyn's not-too-distant past.

Families are encouraged to stop by during regular hours to help out at the farm or attend one of the public programs, which include gardening with kids, learning all about herbs, Canarsie Native's Day (which focuses on the area's Native American history and traditions and features open-hearth cooking), an annual apple festival, canning workshops, and other farm-related activities.

Future plans for the farm include adding an apple orchard and an extensive herb garden with a clamshell path system (as used in colonial times), and augmenting the present blackberry bushes with raspberries, currents, and strawberries. A real 19th-century Dutch timber-frame barn that stood on the New Jersey farm of a Wyckoff descendant was recently donated to the Brooklyn farm and will soon be raised near the crop fields, where it should feel right at home.

The park also features the city's oldest house, the Pieter Claesen Wyckoff homestead, a Dutch farmhouse built in 1652. Wyckoff descendents lived in the house for 250 years, sold it, then bought it back in the 1960s, and eventually donated it to the city as a museum, with the city naming it its first landmark in 1965. It is also a national historic landmark. During the house tours, youngsters learn how nature was such an integral part of farm life, with shearing sheep, then spinning and dying wool, harvesting apples and making cider with an apple press, hauling water from the well, and sleeping on hay-filled pallets on beds whose primitive "springs" were made of rope.

Open—Tuesday-Sunday, 10 AM-4 PM; closed Monday. Nominal fee for museum tour.

GETTING THERE

NOTE: For all MTA bus schedules, go to www.mta.nyc.ny.us/mta/bus/schedules, or call 718-330-1234. For additional bus and subway information, as well as service advisories, go to www.mta.nyc.ny.us or call 718-330-1234.

Bronx

Bronx Zoo

Subway—2 or 5 train to East Tremont Avenue station. Exit left after turnstile. Walk straight ahead on Boston Road to Zoo.

Express Bus from Manhattan—BXM11 express bus directly to Zoo.

Car—Grand Central Parkway, Van Wyck Expressway, or Cross Island Expressway to Whitestone Bridge, to Hutchinson River Parkway North. Exit at Pelham Parkway West. After 2 miles, left onto Boston Road, then right at 1st traffic light. Zoo is directly ahead, after underpass. Parking (fee).

Or: F.D.R. Drive North to Triborough Bridge, to Bruckner Expressway East (I-278), to Bronx River Parkway North, to Exit 6, to Zoo. For parking, see above.

Or: Henry Hudson Parkway North to Cross Bronx Expressway East (I-95). Exit 4B, to Bronx River Parkway North (bear left after exit ramp), to Exit 6, to Zoo. For parking, see above.

City Island Bridge

Subway—6 train to last stop, Pelham Bay Park. Transfer to Bx29 bus for City Island.

Trolley—Bronx Tour Trolley from Metro-North's Fordham Plaza station to Zoo (weekends only). For schedule and more information, go to www.ilovethebronx.com and click on Bronx Tour Trolley, or call 718-590-3518.

Car—Triborough Bridge to Bruckner Expressway East, to I-95 North (also Bruckner Expressway), to Exit 8B (City Island/Orchard Beach). At 1st traffic light, right onto City Island Road. Follow traffic circle to City Island Bridge. For parking, cross the bridge onto City Island and look for street parking.

Crotona Park Nature Center

Subway—2 or 5 train to East 174th Street station. Walk 1 block north to Crotona Park East. Turn left. At top of hill, bear right onto Crotona Park North, to the park.

Car—Cross Bronx Expressway East to Exit 2B/Webster Avenue. Right onto Webster Avenue, left onto 173rd Street, left onto Park Avenue, then right onto Cross Bronx Expressway service road, to Crotona Park North. Street parking.

Or: Cross Bronx Expressway West to Exit 3/Third Avenue. Left onto Third Avenue, left onto Cross Bronx Expressway service road, to Crotona Park North. Stay right. Right on Crotona Avenue. For parking, see above.

New York Botanical Garden

Subway—D or 4 train to Bedford Park Boulevard station. Walk southeast on Bedford Park Boulevard to Garden, or take Bx26 bus to Garden gate.

Metro North Railroad—Harlem Local Line from Grand Central Terminal to Botanical Garden Station.

Trolley—Bronx Tour Trolley from Metro-North's Fordham Plaza station to Garden (weekends only). For a schedule and more information, go to www.ilovethebronx.com and click on the Bronx Tour Trolley, or call 718-590-3518.

Car—Bruckner Expressway East (I-278) to Bronx River Parkway North, to Exit 7W/Fordham Road. Stay right, keeping Garden on right. To Southern (Kazimiroff) Boulevard. Right at next traffic light, into Garden's Conservatory Gate. Right into parking lot (fee).

Pelham Bay Park

Including Twin Island, Orchard Beach Nature Center, and Orchard Beach Canoe Launch

Subway—6 train to last stop, Pelham Bay Park. In summer, transfer to Bx12 bus for Orchard Beach. Off season, Bx29 bus to Rodman's Neck (inform driver) and walk north about 1 mile on park road to Orchard Beach parking lot. Nature center and Twin Island are to left of beach. Canoe launch is at northwest corner of parking lot.

Car—Hutchinson River Parkway (I-678) to City Island/Orchard Beach exit. Follow signs to Orchard Beach parking lot. See above. Parking fee, Memorial Day–Labor Day, otherwise free.

Pelham Bay Park Ranger Station

Including Thomas Pell Wildlife Sanctuary

Subway—6 train to last stop, Pelham Bay Park. Take walkway over I-95, then left into Park. Red-brick ranger station is about 100 yards farther on. Thomas Pell Wildlife Sanctuary, north of ranger station, may be reached from the Split Rock Trail.

Car—Bruckner Expressway North (I-95) to Pelham Bay Park exit. Stay on service road until Middletown Road. Turn right. Continue to end, then left into parking lot (free). Walk north through Park to reach ranger station.

Van Cortlandt Park

Including the Van Cortlandt Nature Center and Van Cortlandt Lake

Subway—1 or 9 train to last stop, 242nd Street/Van Cortlandt Park. Walk north on Broadway. Enter Park at West 244th driveway. Nature center (with orange door) is straight ahead, behind Van Cortlandt House Museum. The lake is just east of nature center.

Car—Major Deegan Expressway North (I-87) to Exit 11, Van Cortlandt Park South. Keep to right on exit ramp. Turn right onto Van Cortlandt Park South. Next right onto Review Place, which leads into Broadway. Follow Broadway through 2 traffic lights and look for street parking. Enter Park at the West 244th Street entrance. See above.

Wave Hill

Subway/Bus—1 or 9 train to 231st Street station. Transfer to Bx7 or Bx10 bus for 252nd Street. Walk across parkway bridge and turn left. Walk to 249th Street and turn right. Continue to garden gate.

Metro-North Railroad—Grand Central Station to Riverdale Station. Walk for 5 blocks along 254th Street to Independence Avenue and turn right to garden. Wave Hill operates a free weekend shuttle between Riverdale Station and garden. For schedule, call 212-532-4900.

Bus—Bx7 and Bx10 buses run from East and West Sides of Manhattan, respectively, to 252nd Street. Call 718-330-1234 or 718-330-3322 for schedule.

Car—Major Deegan Expressway North to Exit 12/Henry Hudson Parkway. First right onto Henry Hudson Parkway South, to Exit 22/West 254th Street. Left at stop sign, then left at 1st traffic light. Right onto 249th Street, to garden gate. Limited parking; but from mid-April through mid-October, free parking at nearby Riverdale Country School. Shuttle bus between school lot and garden. Also street parking.

Or: Henry Hudson Parkway North to Exit 21/West 246th–250th Streets. Left onto 252nd Street. Next left onto service road, then right onto 249th Street, to garden. For parking, see above.

Brooklyn

Brooklyn Botanic Garden

Subway—Q train or local Franklin Avenue Shuttle (S) to Prospect Park station. Enter Garden at Flatbush Avenue and Empire Boulevard.

Or: 2 or 3 train to Eastern Parkway–Brooklyn Museum station. Walk east along Eastern Parkway to the Eastern Parkway Gate, next to the Brooklyn Museum.

Car—From Brooklyn Bridge, straight through 6 traffic lights. Left onto Atlantic Avenue. After 1 mile, right onto Flatbush Avenue. Continue to Grand Army Plaza. Proceed around traffic circle to Eastern Parkway. Drive 1 block and turn right onto Washington Avenue, then right into parking lot (fee). Also street parking.

Or: Brooklyn–Queens Expressway West (I-278) to Kent Avenue exit. Follow service road (Park Avenue) for 5 blocks. Left onto Washington Avenue. Approximately 2 miles to Garden. For parking, see above.

Or: Jackie Robinson Parkway to Bushwick Avenue exit. At 3rd traffic light, left onto Eastern Parkway extension, which becomes Eastern Parkway. After 3 miles, left onto Washington Avenue, then right into parking lot. For parking, see above.

Brooklyn Bridge Park

Subway—A or C train to High Street station. Exit to Cadman Plaza West. Walk west, toward Brooklyn–Queens Expressway and down the hill. Cadman Plaza West becomes Old Fulton Street. Right onto Front Street, then left onto Main Street. Walk 1 block to Park.

Or: 3 train to Clark Street station. Walk west on Henry Street, turn right onto Middagh Street, then left onto Cadman Plaza West/Old Fulton Street. Proceed as above.

Or: F train to York Street station. Walk toward water on Washington Street, to Park.

Car—Brooklyn Bridge to Cadman Plaza West (1st exit). Stay in right lane. Drive down hill on Old Fulton Street, toward water. Turn right onto Front Street, then left onto Main Street. Park is along waterfront. Street and garage parking.

Or: Brooklyn–Queens Expressway West (I-278) to Exit 28A/Cadman Plaza West. Exit quickly to right and make U-turn at traffic light. Drive down Cadman Plaza West/Old Fulton Street. Proceed as above.

Or: Brooklyn–Queens Expressway East (I-278) to Exit 28B/Brooklyn Bridge. Stay right (do not get on bridge) and turn right onto Cadman Plaza West/Old Fulton Street. Proceed as above.

Brooklyn Center for the Urban Environment

Subway—F train to 7th Avenue station. Walk east 2 blocks along 9th Street to the park at Prospect Park West, continue straight on park path, crossing main drive. Tennis House, the Center's headquarters, is to the left of the path.

Car—After Brooklyn Bridge, continue straight, to Atlantic Avenue. Turn left. After slightly less than 1 mile, right onto 3rd Avenue. Left onto Union Street, then right onto Prospect Park West. The Center is inside the park at 9th Street and Prospect Park West. Street parking only.

Or: Triborough Bridge, to Grand Central Parkway East, to Brooklyn–Queens Expressway West (I-278), to Atlantic Avenue exit. Turn left. Proceed as above.

Or: Belt Parkway West, to Brooklyn–Queens Expressway East (I-278), to Atlantic Avenue exit. Proceed as above.

Or: Verrazano-Narrows Bridge to Gowanus Expressway, to Brooklyn–Queens Expressway East (I-278), to Atlantic Avenue exit. Proceed as above.

Brooklyn Children's Museum

Subway—3 train to Kingston Avenue station. Cross Eastern Parkway and walk north 6 blocks on Kingston Avenue to St. Mark's Avenue; turn right. Walk 1 block to Museum.

Or: A train to Nostrand Avenue station and walk south on Nostrand 6 blocks. Left onto St. Mark's Avenue, and 2 blocks to Museum.

Or: C train to Kingston–Throop Avenues station and walk south on Kingston to St. Mark's Avenue. Turn right and continue to Museum.

Car—Brooklyn–Queens Expressway West (I-278), to Tillary Street. Turn right on Flatbush Avenue, then left onto Atlantic Avenue. Go 3 miles. Right onto Brooklyn Avenue, and proceed 4 blocks to Museum. Street parking.

Or: Brooklyn Bridge to Atlantic Avenue. Left onto Atlantic. Proceed as above.

Or: Grand Central Parkway West, to Jackie Robinson Parkway West, to Bushwick Avenue exit. Exit onto Bushwick. After 3rd traffic light, left onto Eastern Parkway Extension, which becomes Eastern Parkway. Right onto New York Avenue, and 6 blocks to St. Mark's Avenue. Turn right. One block to Museum. Street parking.

Or: Verrazano-Narrows Bridge to Gowanus Expressway, to Brooklyn–Queens Expressway East (I-278), to Atlantic Avenue exit. East on Atlantic. Proceed as above.

Canarsie Pier

Subway—L train to last station, Canarsie/Rockaway Parkway. Walk southwest on Rockaway Parkway about .5 mile to Pier. Or take B42 bus from subway station.

Car—Belt Parkway to Exit 13/Rockaway Parkway. If traveling east, bear right to Pier. If traveling west, exit then turn left onto Raockaway Parkway to the pier. Free parking.

Floyd Bennett Field

Including seaplane ramp, North Forty Nature Trail, Gateway Marina, and Deadhorse Bay

Subway—2 train (5 train during weekday rush hours) to last stop, Flatbush Avenue/Brooklyn College. Transfer to Q35 Greenline bus South on Flatbush Avenue, to Park—just before Marine Parkway Bridge. Seaplane ramp is left of greenhouse, on Jamaica Bay. North Forty Nature Trail is in northern section of park, next to model airplane field. Deadhorse Bay is across Flatbush Avenue from Floyd Bennett Field. Gateway Marina is also on west side of Flatbush Avenue, north of Deadhorse Bay trailhead and entrance to Floyd Bennett Field.

Car—Belt Parkway to Exit 11S. Flatbush Avenue South about 1 mile and, at traffic light just before Marine Parkway Bridge toll plaza, left into Floyd Bennett Field. See above. Parking (free).

Gowanus Dredgers Launch Site

Subway—M or R train to Union Street station; or 2, 3, 4, 5, B, or Q train to Atlantic Avenue station. Walk south along 4th Avenue to 3rd Street; turn right. (Or walk to 3rd Avenue and take B37 bus to 3rd Street.) Then walk to Bond Street and turn right. Walk 1 block to 2nd Street and turn right. Launch site is at end of 2nd Street.

Car—Brooklyn–Queens Expressway West (I-278) to Tillary Street exit. Stay in 2 left lanes. At 2nd traffic light, left onto Flatbush Avenue. After less than 1 mile, right onto 3rd Avenue. At Hoyt Street, right again. After 2 blocks, right onto 1st Street. Right onto Bond Street, and then right onto 2nd Street. Launch site is at end of street. Street parking.

Or: Brooklyn Bridge to Atlantic Avenue. Left onto Atlantic, then right onto Hoyt Avenue. Proceed as above.

The Green-Wood Cemetery

Subway—R train (during rush hours, M train) to 25th Street station. Walk 1 block east to the Cemetery entrance.

Car—Brooklyn–Queens Expressway West (I-278), to 38th Street exit. After exit, continue straight to 5th Avenue; turn left. Cemetery entrance is at corner of 5th Avenue and 25th Street. Parking (free). Also street parking.

Or: Brooklyn–Battery Tunnel, bearing right to Hamilton Avenue exit. Continue on Hamilton, which becomes 3rd Avenue. Left at 25th Street. 2 blocks to 5th Avenue and Cemetery entrance. For parking, see above.

Louis J. Valentino Pier and Park

Including the Coffey Street Boat Launch

Public Transportation—A, C, or F train to Jay Street/Borough Hall station. Transfer to B61 bus for Red Hook. Get off at Van Brunt and Coffey Streets. Walk northwest on Coffey Street to Park and Launch.

Car—Brooklyn–Queens Expressway West (I-278) to Atlantic Avenue exit, and turn left onto Columbia Street, then right onto DeGraw Street, which becomes Van Brunt Street. Right onto Van Dyke Street. Right onto Conover Street, then right onto Coffey Street; to end. Street parking.

Or: Brooklyn–Battery Tunnel, bearing right to Hamilton Avenue exit. Stay right. Turn right onto Henry Street, then right again onto West 9th Street. Left onto Columbia Street and right onto Lorraine Street, which becomes Wolcott Street. Left onto Conover Street. Right onto Coffey Street; to end. See above.

Or: Verrazano-Narrows Bridge to Gowanus Expressway, to Brooklyn–Queens Expressway East (I-278), to Atlantic Avenue exit. Proceed as above.

Magnolia Tree Earth Center

Subway—G train to Bedford–Nostrand Avenues station. Walk west on Lafayette Avenue a block and a half. Center is directly across from Herbert Von King Park, between Marcy and Tompkins Avenues.

Car—Triborough Bridge to Grand Central Parkway, to Brooklyn–Queens Expressway West (I-278), to Humboldt Street Exit. South on Humboldt to Metropolitan Avenue; then quick right; then directly left onto Bushwick Avenue South. Right onto Flushing Avenue; left onto Dr. Gardner C. Taylor Boulevard (Marcy Avenue); then left onto Lafayette Street. Street parking.

Or: Williamsburg Bridge to Broadway. Right on Roebling Street; left on Lee Street; right on Nostrand Avenue; then left on Lafayette Avenue. Street parking.

Or: Manhattan Bridge to Jay Street, and right onto Sands Street. Merge onto Brooklyn–Queens Expressway East (I-278), to Exit 30/Flushing Avenue. Left onto Classon Avenue; right onto Flushing Avenue; right onto Nostrand Avenue; then left onto Lafayette Avenue. Street parking.

Or: Verrazano-Narrows Bridge to Gowanus Expressway, to Brooklyn–Queens Expressway East (I-278), to Atlantic Avenue. Right onto Atlantic; right onto Nostrand Avenue; then left onto Lafayette Avenue. Street parking.

New York Aquarium

Subway—D, F, or Q train to West 8th Street/New York Aquarium station. Walk south to aquarium entrance.

Car—Belt Parkway West to Exit 7B/Ocean Parkway South. Left onto Ocean Parkway; continue to Surf Avenue. Aquarium is on the left. Park in Aquarium lot (fee) or on street (2-hour meters).

New York Aquarium continued on next page.

Or: Triborough Bridge to Grand Central Parkway West, to Brooklyn–Queens Expressway West (I-278), to Belt Parkway East, to Exit 7/Ocean Parkway. Right onto Ocean Parkway; continue to Surf Avenue and Aquarium. For parking, see previous page.

Or: Brooklyn Battery Tunnel (I-478), Brooklyn Bridge, or Manhattan Bridge to Brooklyn–Queens Expressway West (I-278), to Belt Parkway East, to Exit 7/Ocean Parkway. Right onto Ocean Parkway; continue to Surf Avenue and Aquarium. For parking, see previous page.

Owl's Head Park

Subway—R train to Bay Ridge Avenue station. Walk 3 blocks northwest (toward the water) to Colonial Road; turn right to the park.

Car—Triborough Bridge to Grand Central Parkway East, to Brooklyn–Queens Expressway West (I-278), to Belt Parkway East, to 65th/67th Streets exit. Continue on Shore Road Drive to ramp for Ridge Boulevard. Right onto Ridge Boulevard, then right onto 67th Street. Right onto Colonial Road. Continue to Park entrance. Bicycle path begins at Wakeman Place and Colonial Road. Street parking.

Plum Beach

Car—Belt Parkway East or West to exit 9B/Knapp Street. Turn right or left, respectively, off the parkway into the Plum Beach parking lot (free).

Prospect Park

Including Prospect Park Audubon Center, and the Nethermead

Subway—Q train or local Franklin Avenue Shuttle (S) to Prospect Park station. Enter Park at Lincoln Road and Ocean Avenue. Cross park drive and continue on path to Cleft Ridge Span

Bridge. Walk under bridge. Boathouse is on right. The Nethermead is west of boathouse.

Or: F train to 7th Avenue station. Walk east 2 blocks to Prospect Park West and enter Park. Follow pathway through Park and across drive. Tennis House is on left and baseball fields on right. Proceed through Ravine (at Dog Beach) and follow path that leads to Nethermead and nature center. Signs throughout Park guide you.

Car—From Brooklyn Bridge, continue straight to Atlantic Avenue and turn left. After 1 mile, right onto Flatbush Avenue. Proceed 0.5 mile to Grand Army Plaza traffic circle. Halfway around traffic circle, continue on Flatbush Avenue. Right onto Ocean Avenue, to the Lincoln Road entrance to Park. Look for street parking and continue as above.

Or: Brooklyn–Queens Expressway to Atlantic Avenue exit. Left onto Atlantic Avenue. After just over 1 mile, turn right onto Flatbush Avenue and proceed as above.

Prospect Park Zoo

Subway—Q train or local Franklin Avenue Shuttle (S) to Prospect Park Station. Take Flatbush Avenue/Ocean Avenue exit and walk north on Flatbush Avenue to Zoo.

Car—From Brooklyn Bridge, continue straight to Atlantic Avenue and turn left. After 1 mile, right onto Flatbush Avenue. Proceed 0.5 mile to Grand Army Plaza traffic circle. Halfway around traffic circle, continue on Flatbush Avenue. Zoo entrance is on Flatbush Avenue, just north of Empire Boulevard. Street parking.

Or: Grand Central Parkway to the Jackie Robinson Parkway, to Bushwick Avenue exit. Through 3 traffic lights to Eastern Parkway Extension, which becomes Eastern Parkway. Approximately 3.5 miles to Grand Army Plaza, go around traffic circle, and right onto Flatbush Avenue. Continue to Zoo entrance on right. Street parking.

Or: Bronx Whitestone Bridge to Whitestone Parkway south (I-678), to Van

Wyck Expressway, to Jackie Robinson Parkway. Proceed as above.

Or: Brooklyn–Queens Expressway to Tillary Street exit. At 2nd traffic light, left onto Flatbush Avenue. At Grand Army Plaza, go around traffic circle, and right onto Flatbush Avenue. Zoo entrance is on right. Street parking.

Salt Marsh Nature Center

Subway—F or N train to Avenue U station. Transfer to eastbound B3 bus, to East 33rd Street. Nature Center is on south side of Avenue U, at East 33rd Street.

Car—Belt Parkway to Exit 11N/Flatbush Avenue North. Left on Avenue U. Nature Center is on south side of Avenue U at East 33rd Street. Parking available across street in Marine Park (free).

Sebago Canoe Club

Subway—L train to last station, Canarsie/Rockaway Parkway. Transfer to B6 bus traveling southwest along Flatlands Avenue. Get off at East 76th Street. Walk southeast (away from South Shore High School) on East 76th Street and continue as it changes to Paerdegat Avenue North (about 12 blocks). Club entrance is before intersection with 13th Street, between Diamond Point Yacht Club and Paerdegat Athletic Club.

Or: 2 or 5 train to last station, Flatbush Avenue/Brooklyn College. Transfer to B6 bus for Flatlands and Ralph Avenues. Walk northeast 1 block on Flatlands to East 76th Street, which becomes Paerdegat Avenue North. Continue as above.

Or: Local Q train to Ave J and transfer to B6 bus, as above.

Car—Belt Parkway to Exit 13/Rockaway Parkway. Follow Rockaway Parkway northwest (perpendicular to Belt Parkway) .5 mile. Left on Avenue M and continue to end, at Paerdegat Avenue North. Turn left. Parking (free).

69th Street Pier

Subway—R train to Bay Ridge Avenue station. Walk toward 3rd Avenue, continuing about 5 blocks to Pier.

Car—Brooklyn–Queens Expressway West (I-278) to Belt Parkway East, to 65th/67th Streets exit. Exit onto Shore Road and continue to the park at the corner of Colonial Road and Wakeman Place. Street parking.

Or: Belt Parkway West to 65th/67th Streets exit. Exit onto Shore Road, to Colonial Road and Wakeman Place. See above.

Steeplechase Pier, Coney Island

Subway—D, F or Q train to Stillwell Avenue/Coney Island station. Walk south toward water, and right onto the boardwalk. Pier is at West 19th Street, behind Keyspan Park.

Car—Brooklyn–Battery Tunnel to Brooklyn–Queens Expressway West (I-278) to Belt (Shore) Parkway East, to Exit 7S/Ocean Parkway. Right onto Ocean Parkway. After several blocks, Ocean Parkway ends and Surf Avenue begins, paralleling Coney Island Beach. Pass the Cyclone and Nathan's. At Keyspan Park look for street parking or park in a lot. Pier is on boardwalk at West 19th Street, behind Keyspan Park.

Wyckoff Farmhouse Museum and Education Center

Subway/Bus—2 or 5 train to Newkirk Avenue station. Transfer to B8 bus, east. Get off at Beverly Road and East 59th Street. Walk 1 block south to Clarendon Road. The Farmhouse is between East 59th Street and Ralph Avenue, within M. Fidler–Wyckoff House Park.

Or: A train to Utica Avenue station. Transfer to B46 bus to Clarendon Road. Proceed as above.

Or: D or Q trains to Newkirk Avenue station. Transfer to B8 bus eastbound on Foster

Avenue, and get off at Beverly Road and East 59th Street. Walk 1 block south to Clarendon Road. Proceed as above.

Car—Manhattan Bridge to Flatbush Avenue. South on Flatbush Avenue 4 miles, to Clarendon Road. Turn left. Continue 2 miles to Farmhouse. See above. Street parking.

Or: Belt Parkway to Exit 13/Rockaway Parkway. Northwest on Rockaway Parkway to Ditmas Avenue; turn left. Continue to East 59th Street. Farmhouse is within M. Fidler–Wyckoff House Park. Street parking.

Manhattan

American Museum of Natural History

Subway—B (weekdays only) or C train to 81st Street/Museum of Natural History station. Museum entrance is at street level, although a subway entrance is sometimes open.

Or: 1 train (also 9 train during rush hours) to 79th Street station. Walk 2 blocks north, then 2 1/2 blocks west. Museum entrance is on West 81st Street, between Columbus Avenue and Central Park West.

Car—Henry Hudson Parkway to West 79th Street exit. East on West 79th to Museum. Entrance is on West 81st Street, between Columbus Avenue and Central Park West. Parking available in Museum's garage (enter from West 81st Street); expensive. Street parking may be difficult to find; time-limited meters.

Or: F.D.R. Drive to East 61st Street exit. West on East 61st, left onto 2nd Avenue, then right onto East 60th Street. Right onto Park Avenue. Left onto East 79th Street, and through Central Park. At Central Park West, you'll see Museum. For parking, see above.

Central Park

Including Charles A. Dana Discovery Center, Harlem Meer, North Woods, and East Meadow

Subway—2 or 3 train to 110th Street/Central Park North station. Walk west on Central Park North and enter Park at Farmer's Gate (110th Street and Lenox Avenue). Nature center and Harlem Meer are straight ahead. North Woods are southwest of nature center.

Or: B or C train to Cathedral Parkway station. Walk east on Central Park North to Farmer's Gate (110th Street and Lenox Avenue). See above.

Or: 6 train to 110th Street/Lexington Avenue station. Walk west to Fifth Avenue and enter Park at Pioneer's Gate, at corner of East 110th Street and Fifth Avenue. Nature center is just southeast of entrance.

Or: For East Meadow, at 97th Street and Fifth Avenue, take 6 train to East 96th Street and walk 1 block north on Fifth Avenue.

Car—F.D.R. Drive to East 96th Street exit. Left onto East 96th Street, then right onto Park Avenue. Left onto East 109th Street and right onto Madison Avenue. Left onto East 110th Street and look for street or garage parking. Enter Park at Pioneer's Gate, at corner of East 110th and Fifth Avenue. Discovery Center is just southeast of entrance. North Woods are southwest of nature center.

Or: Triborough Bridge to 125th Street/Second Avenue exit. Bear right onto East 125th Street, left onto Second Avenue, and continue to East 110th Street (Central Park North). Turn right and continue to Fifth Avenue. See above.

Or: Henry Hudson Parkway to West 96th Street exit. East on West 96th, through Park, and left onto Madison Avenue. Then right onto East 110th Street. Park entrance is at 110th Street and Lenox Avenue. See above.

Or: For East Meadow—F.D.R. Drive to East 96th Street. Left onto East 96th Street, to Fifth

Avenue. Street or garage parking. East Meadow is at Fifth Avenue and East 97th Street.

Or: Triborough Bridge to 125th Street/Second Avenue exit. Bear right onto 125th Street, left onto Park Avenue, then right onto East 110th Street and continue to 5th Avenue. See above.

Central Park

Including Henry Luce Nature Observatory at Belvedere Castle, Loeb Boathouse, Conservatory Water, and Jacqueline Kennedy Onassis Reservoir

Subway—B (weekdays only) or C train to 81st Street station/Museum of Natural History. Enter Park at 81st Street and Central Park West, following path across West Drive toward Delacorte Theater. Castle is just to right. Loeb Boathouse is southeast of nature center, at East 75th Street and East Drive. Conservatory Water is east of boathouse, between 72nd and 75th Streets. Reservoir is north of Great Lawn, about mid-park, between 86th and 96th Streets.

Or: 6 train to 77th Street station. Walk north 2 blocks to East 79th Street, then east to Fifth Avenue. Follow path into Park and pass Great Lawn. Nature center is at southwest corner of Great Lawn. For additional sites, see above.

Car—Brooklyn–Battery Tunnel to West Side Highway, to 79th Street exit. East on West 79th to Central Park West. Street and garage parking. Enter Park at West 81st Street and Central Park West. Follow path across West Drive toward Delacorte Theater. Castle is just to right.

Or: Henry Hudson Parkway to West 79th Street. Proceed as above.

Or F.D.R. Drive to East 61st Street exit. Drive straight onto East 61st Street. Left onto Second Avenue, then right onto East 60th Street. Right onto Park Avenue, then left onto East 79th Street. Street or garage parking. Enter Park at Miner's Gate (Fifth Avenue and East 79th) and walk west to Castle.

Or: 59th Street (Queensborough) Bridge to Second Avenue. Right on Second Avenue. Left onto East 60th Street, then right onto Park Avenue. Left onto East 81st Street, to Fifth Avenue. See above.

Or: Bronx River Parkway South to Bruckner Expressway West (I-278), to Triborough Bridge. After Triborough Bridge, exit at East 125th Street/Second Avenue. Bear right onto East 125th Street, then left onto Park Avenue. Right onto East 79th Street. See above.

Central Park Zoo

Subway—F train to Lexington Avenue/63rd Street station. Walk west to Park. Zoo is inside Park at East 64th Street.

Or: N or R train to Fifth Avenue/59th Street station. Walk north along Fifth Avenue to East 64th Street. See above.

Or: 6 train to Hunter College/68th Street station. Walk west to Fifth Avenue and south to East 64th Street. See above.

Car—59th Street (Queensborough) Bridge to Second Avenue. Turn right. Left onto East 60th Street, then right onto Park Avenue. Left onto East 66th Street, then left onto Fifth Avenue. Street and garage parking. Zoo is inside Park at East 64th Street.

Or: Brooklyn Bridge or Brooklyn Battery Tunnel to F.D.R. Drive North. Exit at East 61st Street. West on East 61st, then right onto First Avenue. Left onto East 66th Street, left onto Fifth Avenue. See above.

Or: Bruckner Expressway West (I-278) to Triborough Bridge. After bridge, merge onto F.D.R. Drive South, to East 63rd Street exit. Right onto East 63rd, right onto First Avenue, then left onto East 66th Street. Continue as above.

Or: Henry Hudson Parkway to West 79th Street exit. East on West 79th, through Central Park to Fifth Avenue. Turn right. Continue to West 64th Street. See above.

Downtown Boathouse Kayak Launch Sites

Pier 26 (See Hudson River Park)
Pier 66a (see Hudson River Park)
72nd Street Dock

Subway—1, 2 or 3 train (also 9 train during rush hours) to 72nd Street station. Walk west 2 blocks to Riverside Park. Take 72nd Street stairs into park and follow walkway all the way to the river.

Car—West Side Highway or Henry Hudson Parkway to 72nd Street exit. No auto access to river. Best to park on Riverside Drive, any nearby side street, or in parking garage. Proceed as above.

Or: 59th Street (Queensborough) Bridge to East 57th Street ramp. West on East 57th Street, across town to Riverside Drive. Turn right and continue to West 72nd Street. See above.

Or: Cross Bronx Expressway West, to Henry Hudson Parkway South, to West 79th Street exit. Right onto West 79th Street, and right onto Riverside Drive, to West 72nd Street. Continue as above.

Hudson River Park

Piers 25 and 26

Subway—1 train (also 9 train during rush hours) to Franklin Street station. Walk west to the water.

Or: 2 or 3 train to Chambers Street station. Walk west to river and then north 6 blocks.

Or: A, C, or E train to Canal Street station. Walk west to river and then south 5 blocks.

Car—Brooklyn–Battery Tunnel to West Side Highway North (or Henry Hudson Parkway South to West Side Highway South) to North Moore Street. Street or garage parking. Piers are along river on West Street (also called West Side Highway) at North Moore Street.

Or: 59th Street (Queensborough) Bridge to 2nd Avenue South exit. Drive about 3 miles to East Houston Street; turn right. Left onto West Broadway, then right onto Broome Street. Continue across Avenue of the Americas onto Watts Street, then turn left onto Varick Street. Right onto North Moore Street to West Street. See above.

Pier 45

Subway—1 train (also 9 train during rush hours) to Christopher Street station. Walk west to Pier.

Or: A, C, D, E, or F train (also B or V train on weekdays) to West 4th Street station. Walk north to Christopher Street, then west to the pier.

Car—Brooklyn–Battery Tunnel to West Side Highway North (or Henry Hudson Parkway South to West Side Highway South), to Christopher Street. Street or garage parking. Pier is west of West Street at Christopher Street.

Or: 59th Street (Queensborough) Bridge to Second Avenue South exit. Drive about 3 miles to East Houston Street and turn right. Right on West Street to Christopher Street. See above.

Pier 63 (at West 23rd Street) and Pier 66a (at West 26 Street)

Subway—C, E, or 1 train (also 9 train during rush hours) to West 23rd Street. Either walk approximately 4 blocks west on West 23rd Street or transfer to M23 cross-town bus to Chelsea Piers bus/taxi loop. Walk north of horseback-riding arena, through parking area, and then turn left to Pier 63. Pier 66a is a few blocks north.

Car—Brooklyn–Battery Tunnel to West Side Highway North (or Henry Hudson Parkway South to West Side Highway South) to West 23rd St. Turn into Chelsea Piers. Parking area (fee); or street parking. Pier 63 is right there; Pier 66a is just to the north.

Or: Queens–Midtown Tunnel to Downtown/34th Street exit. Left onto East 34th Street and west, across town, to West Street

(West Side Highway). Turn left. Proceed to West 23rd Street and continue as above.

Pier 84 (at West 44th Street)

Subway—A, C, or E train to West 42nd Street. Walk approximately 4 blocks west, or transfer to M42 bus on 42nd Street, to river and walk 2 blocks north to Pier.

Or: 1, 2, 3, or 9 train to Times Square/42nd Street. Walk approximately 5 long blocks west, or proceed as above.

Car—Brooklyn–Battery Tunnel (or Cross Bronx Expressway West (I-95) to Henry Hudson Parkway South) to West Side Highway, to West 44th Street exit. Street or garage parking.

Or: Queens–Midtown Tunnel to Downtown/34th Street exit. Left onto East 34th Street and west, across town, to West Street (West Side Highway). Right onto West Street, to West 44th Street. Continue as above.

Hudson River Greenway at West 79th Street

Subway—1 train (also 9 train during rush hours) to West 79th Street. Walk west 2 blocks. Enter Riverside Park, then follow any path to river.

Car—Brooklyn–Battery Tunnel to West Side Highway North, to 79th Street exit. No auto access to river. Park on Riverside Drive or any side street, or in a garage. Enter Riverside Park and follow any path to river.

Or: Cross Bronx Expressway West (I-95) to Henry Hudson Parkway South, to West Side Highway South, to West 79th Street exit. Proceed as above.

Or: 59th Street (Queensborough) Bridge to Second Avenue South exit. Left onto Second Avenue, then right onto East 57 Street. Across town to Henry Hudson Parkway North. Exit at West 79th Street/Boat Basin exit and look for parking around Riverside Drive. Follow any path through Riverside Park to river.

Under George Washington Bridge at West 179 Street

Subway—A train to West 181st Street/Fort Washington Avenue station. Walk about 4 blocks west to river.

Car—Brooklyn–Battery Tunnel to West Side Highway North to Henry Hudson Parkway North to Exit 14 (Cross Bronx Expressway/West 178th Street/George Washington Bridge). After exit, turn left onto Wadsworth Avenue. Then left onto West 179th Street, to river. Street parking.

Or: Triborough Bridge to Harlem River Drive North toward Uptown and George Washington Bridge. Get off at Exit 24, toward 179th Street. Right onto Amsterdam Avenue, and then left onto West 179th Street, to river.

Inwood Canoe Club

Subway—A train to Dyckman Street/Broadway station. Walk approximately 4 blocks west to river. Walk under Henry Hudson Parkway overpass. Turn left through open fence, and walk several yards farther on trail leading to boathouse, on the right.

Car—Henry Hudson Parkway to Exit 17/Dyckman Street. After exit, take 1st left. Go to end of block and left onto Dyckman Street. Drive to end of street and into Dyckman Street Marina. Limited parking (free). Also street parking. Walk through open fence at marina, and continue several yards on trail leading to boathouse, on the right.

Or: Harlem River Drive North to very end. At traffic light, turn left onto Dyckman Street. Drive to end of street and continue as above.

Inwood Hill Park Nature Center

Subway—1 train to West 215th Street/Tenth Avenue station. Walk north to 218th Street and turn left. Follow hill to end of street and into Park. Nature Center is straight ahead.

Or: A train to last stop, Inwood/207th Street. Walk west 2 blocks to Seaman Avenue. Then north along park path (parallel to Seaman Avenue) to Indian Road and Nature Center.

Car—Henry Hudson Parkway North to Exit 17/Dyckman Street. Merge onto Broadway. North on Broadway, left onto West 218th Street. Entrance to Park is at end of street. Nature Center is straight ahead. Street parking.

Or: Fordham Road West to University Heights Bridge, to West 207th Street. Turn right onto Seaman Avenue, then left onto West 215th Street, to Indian Road and entrance to Park.

Or: Bronx–Whitestone Bridge (I-678 North) to Cross Bronx Expressway West (I-95), to Alexander Hamilton Bridge, to Henry Hudson Parkway North. Continue as above.

Manhattan Kayak Company

Subway—C, E, or 1 train (also 9 train during rush hours) to West 23rd Street station. Walk approximately 4 long blocks west—or transfer to M23 cross-town bus—to Chelsea Piers bus/taxi loop. Walk north of horseback-riding arena, through parking area, and turn left. Manhattan Kayak Company is on Pier 63, directly ahead. Office is at top of wooden stairs on left.

Car—Brooklyn–Battery Tunnel to West Side Highway North (or Henry Hudson Parkway South to West Side Highway South) to West 23rd Street exit. From south, turn left into Chelsea Piers. From north, turn right into Chelsea Piers. Parking in lot (fee). Also street parking. Continue as above.

Or: Queens–Midtown Tunnel to Downtown/34th Street exit. Left onto East 34th Street and west, across town, to West Street (West Side Highway). Left onto West Street, to West 23rd Street. Proceed as above.

96th Street, Robert Wagner Jr. Esplanade

Subway—6 train to East 96th Street station. Walk east, eventually passing under F.D.R. Drive and East 96th Street exit ramp, to East River Esplanade, also called Bobby Wagner Walk.

Car—F.D.R. Drive to East 96th Street exit. After exit, look for street parking or garage. Walk to Esplanade, as above.

Or: Triborough Bridge to Harlem River Drive/125th Street/Second Avenue exit. Left onto Second Avenue, then right onto East 96th Street. Continue as above.

Riverside Park Boat Launch, The River Project Estuarium

See Hudson River Park, Pier 26

Subway—A, C, or D train (also B train on weekdays) to 145th Street/Saint Nicholas Avenue station. Walk about 4 blocks west to river.

Car—Henry Hudson Parkway North to West 125th Street exit. Turn right directly from exit onto St. Clair's Place. After about 5 blocks, left onto Dr. Martin Luther King Boulevard. Left onto Broadway, left onto West 139th Street, and right onto Riverside Drive. Launch is at 140th Street and the Hudson River. Parking available (free).

Or: Triborough Bridge North, toward the Bronx, to Major Deegan Expressway North (I-87), for approximately 1.5 miles to Exit 4 and 145th Street Bridge. Cross bridge to West 145th Street, then left onto Riverside Drive, to West 140th Street. See above.

261 • Getting There

Robert F. Wagner Jr. Park, Battery Park City

Subway—4 or 5 train to Bowling Green station. Walk about 4 blocks west to river. Park is just south of Jewish Heritage Museum in Battery Park City, not in Battery Park.

Or: 1 or 9 train to South Ferry station. Walk northwest through Battery Park to Battery Place and turn left. At river, turn right and walk north to the Park.

Car—Brooklyn–Battery Tunnel to West Side Highway—or Henry Hudson Parkway South to West Side Highway (West Street). If driving north, turn left onto Liberty Street, then left onto South End Avenue. If driving south, turn right onto Liberty Street, then left onto South End Avenue. Park in a garage. Walk toward river. Park is just south of Jewish Heritage Museum.

Or: Queens–Midtown Tunnel to Downtown/34th Street exit. Left onto East 34th Street, then right onto Second Avenue. Right onto East Houston Street, then left onto West Broadway. At Battery Place, turn right, then quickly left onto West Street, then quickly right again back onto Battery Place. At West Thames Street, turn left. Street or garage parking.

Or: F.D.R. Drive all the way south until it becomes South Street (just past Brooklyn Bridge/Civic Center exit). South Street then becomes West Street. Left onto West Thames Street and continue as above.

Roosevelt Island

Including Lighthouse Park

Subway—F train to Roosevelt Avenue station. Walk north to Lighthouse Park. Or take tram from Second Avenue and East 59th Street to Island, and continue as above.

Car—59th Street (Queensborough) Bridge (Upper Level, toward Queens) to 21st Street North, left onto 36th Avenue, to Roosevelt Island Bridge, to the island. Park in Motorgate Garage and explore on foot or bicycle.

Or: Brooklyn–Queens Expressway to Long Island Expressway West, to Van Dam Street exit, the exit before Queens–Midtown Tunnel. Follow service road to Vernon Boulevard and turn left, then left onto 36th Avenue. Continue as above.

Sara Delano Roosevelt Park

Subway—B or D train to Grand Street station. Park is up the stairs from subway, on Grand Street, between Chrystie and Forsythe Streets. Bird garden is on Forsythe Street side.

Car—Manhattan Bridge to Chrystie Street. Right onto Grand Street and look for street parking (difficult) or garage. Bird garden is at Forsythe and Grand Streets.

Or: Long Island Expressway West to Queens–Midtown Tunnel, to Downtown/34th Street exit. Left onto East 34th Street, then right onto Second Avenue, which becomes Chrystie Street. Right onto Grand Street. Continue as above.

Or: Cross Bronx Expressway (I-95) to Bruckner Expressway West (I-278), Triborough Bridge (toward Manhattan), to F.D.R. Drive South. Continue to Grand Street/Williamsburg Bridge exit. After exit, right onto Grand Street and west to Forsythe Street. Continue as above.

Stuyvesant Cove Park

Subway—6 train to 23rd Street station. Walk east approximately 4 long blocks to river. Or transfer to M23 cross-town bus. Get off just before it turns at Avenue C. Park is on East River, between 23rd and 18th Streets.

Car—Manhattan Bridge or Brooklyn Bridge to F.D.R. Drive North, to 23rd Street exit. Or Triborough Bridge to F.D.R. Drive South to 20th Street exit. Street or garage parking. Walk toward East River. See above.

Swindler Cove Park

Subway—1 or A train to Dyckman Street station. Walk east to Tenth Avenue and turn left. Then right into driveway next to Public School No. 5 and walk behind school to Park.

Car—F.D.R. Drive North to Harlem River Drive North, to Dyckman Street exit, straight onto Tenth Avenue. You'll very quickly come to driveway of Public School No. 5; turn right into driveway and follow to back of school and Park entrance. Limited free parking.

Or: Henry Hudson Parkway to Dyckman Street. East on Dyckman Street, then left onto Tenth Avenue. You'll very quickly come to driveway of Public School No. 5. Continue as above.

Or: Bronx–Pelham Parkway West to Fordham Road West, to University Heights Bridge, to West 207th Street. Left onto Tenth Avenue. Just past West 201st Street, Public School No. 5 is on left. Turn into driveway. Continue as above.

Queens

Alley Pond Park

Including Alley Pond Environmental Center, Little Neck Bay, and Oakland Lake

Subway—7 train to last station, Main Street/Flushing. Transfer to Q12 bus for Northern Boulevard East. Bus stops outside the center. Little Neck Bay is on opposite side of Northern Boulevard, and is accessible from Joe Michael's Mile bicycle path. For Oakland Lake, take Q12 bus on Northern Boulevard as far as 223rd Street, then walk south to Park.

Car—Queens–Midtown Tunnel to Long Island Expressway East, to Clearview Expressway North (toward Throgs Neck Bridge). At Northern Boulevard, exit right onto Northern Boulevard. Drive approximately 3 miles. Center is just past Cross Island Parkway,

on right. Free parking. Little Neck Bay is on opposite side of Northern Boulevard, accessible from Joe Michael's Mile bicycle path. For Oakland Lake, exit Clearview Expressway and drive along Northern Boulevard, then right onto Springfield Boulevard. Then left onto 46th Avenue, which leads to lake. Street parking.

Or: Throgs Neck Bridge (I-295) South to Clearview Expressway, to Exit 5/Northern Boulevard. Left onto Northern Boulevard and continue as above.

Urban Park Ranger Adventure Center, Alley Pond Park

Subway—E or F train to Kew Gardens/Union Turnpike station. Transfer to eastbound Q46 bus and get off at Winchester Boulevard. Walk north on Winchester toward highway overpass. Park entrance is on left, underneath Grand Central Parkway. Walk across parking lot and soccer field to the Center.

Car—Triborough Bridge to Grand Central Parkway East, to Exit 23 (Cross Island Parkway/Alley Pond Park). Bear right off exit ramp. At stop sign, left onto Winchester Boulevard. First left, under highway, into Park and parking lot (free). Adventure Center is across soccer field.

Or: Grand Central Parkway West to Exit 23 (Cross Island Parkway/Alley Pond Park). Follow signs for Union Turnpike, and then left onto Union Turnpike. Left onto Winchester Boulevard. Continue as above.

Baisley Pond Park

Subway—E or J train (also Z during rush hours; peak direction) to last station, Jamaica Center. Transfer to Q111 bus on Guy R. Brewer Boulevard and get off at Baisley Boulevard. Walk southwest along Baisley Boulevard to Park and pond.

Car—Long Island Expressway East, or Grand Central Parkway East, to Van Wyck

Expressway South, to Exit 2/Rockaway Boulevard. Left onto Rockaway Boulevard. At Baisley Boulevard, left into Park entrance. Parking (free).

Or: Belt Parkway East to Van Wyck Expressway North, to Exit 2/Rockaway Boulevard. Right onto Rockaway Boulevard and right onto Baisley Boulevard. Continue as above.

Bayside Marina

Public Transportation—Long Island Railroad from Penn Station, Manhattan, to Bayside. Transfer to northbound Q13 or Q31 bus on Bell Boulevard. Get off at 28th Avenue. Right onto 28th Avenue and walk approximately 4 blocks. Right onto 26th Street, then right onto 28th Road, to the pedestrian overpass to Marina.

Car—Long Island Expressway East or Grand Central Parkway East to Clearview Expressway North, to Northern Boulevard exit. Right onto Northern Boulevard, then left onto Bell Boulevard. Right onto 28th Avenue, to Little Neck Boulevard. Park on street and walk over pedestrian bridge at 28th Road to Marina.

Or: Bronx–Whitestone Bridge or Throgs Neck Bridge to Clearview Expressway South, to Exit 6B/26th Avenue. Left onto 26th Avenue, to Little Neck Boulevard. Right to the pedestrian overpass at 28th Avenue. Park on street. Walk across overpass to Marina.

Or: Cross Island Parkway North directly to Marina parking lot, which is between exits 31 and 32.

Breezy Point

Car—Van Wyck Expressway South or Brooklyn–Queens Expressway East to Belt Parkway East, to Exit 11S/Flatbush Avenue South. South on Flatbush Avenue. Cross Marine Parkway Bridge and take exit for Breezy Point. On left at Beach 169th Street, you'll see Fort Tilden. If visiting April 15–September 15, you must stop here for a day permit for Breezy Point. Otherwise continue about 2 miles until you reach gate of private community at Breezy Point. Drive left of guardhouse and follow road to end of peninsula. Parking for nonanglers without permit at 222nd Street lot, dawn to dusk, September 1–March 14. Fishing parking permit required at all times, March 15–August 31. Entry to sand access road and beach driving are permitted only to fishermen bearing off-road fishing parking permit. One-day birding pass free of charge, 9 am–4 pm daily, at Fort Tilden Visitor Contact Station—valid only at 222nd Street parking lot. Walk along sandy path behind parking lot to beach.

Flushing Meadows-Corona Park

Including Meadow Lake, Passarelle, and New York Hall of Science

Subway—7 train to Shea Stadium/Willets Point station. Passarelle is straight ahead, near tennis center and Shea Stadium. New York Hall of Science is short walk southwest of station. To reach Meadow Lake, walk southeast through Park (about 25 minutes).

Car—To Meadow Lake: Belt Parkway East to Van Wyck Expressway North, to Exit 12A/Long Island Expressway East. Stay left on exit road. Look for sign on left to Meadow Lake. Make immediate 1st left turn, then right into Park. Park in large parking lot (free).

Or: Queens–Midtown Tunnel to Long Island Expressway East, to Exit 22. Follow signs to Van Wyck Expressway South, to Jewel Avenue exit. Follow signs into Park, and into parking lot. See above.

Or: Throgs Neck Bridge or Bronx-Whitestone Bridge to Van Wyck Expressway South. Continue as above.

To New York Hall of Science: Brooklyn–Queens Expressway East (or Queens–Midtown Tunnel) to Long Island Expressway East. Exit at 108th Street, and left onto 108th Street. Right onto 52nd Avenue, then left onto 111th Street. Right at 49th Avenue and into Hall's entrance drive. Parking (fee).

Or: Whitestone Bridge or Triborough Bridges to Grand Central Parkway East, to Exit 10. Bear right, following Queens–Midtown Tunnel signs. Right onto Corona Avenue, then right onto 111th Street. At 49th Avenue, turn into Hall entrance drive.

To Passarelle: Grand Central Parkway East to Exit 9 (Northern Boulevard/Shea Stadium). Bear right at bottom of ramp. Continue right to Park.

Or: Grand Central Parkway West to Exit 9. Right into Park. Passarelle is near tennis center and Shea Stadium.

Forest Park Nature and Visitor Center

Including park-drive bicycle path

Subway—J train (also Z train during rush hours, peak direction) to Woodhaven Boulevard station. Walk north on Woodhaven Boulevard to Center, on left (between Forest Park Drive and Myrtle Avenue). Bicycle path begins at eastern intersection of Forest Park Drive and Woodhaven Boulevard.

Car—Jackie Robinson Parkway East to Forest Park Drive exit. Right off exit and proceed down hill. Left onto Park Lane South. At Woodhaven Boulevard, turn left and look for street parking. If Park drive is open, free parking in band shell parking lot on Park's west side. Nature center is also on west side of Woodhaven Boulevard, between Forest Park Drive and Myrtle Avenue. Bicycle path begins at eastern intersection of Forest Park Drive and Woodhaven Boulevard.

Or: Long Island Expressway East to Wood-haven Boulevard. Right onto Woodhaven Boulevard and continue to Myrtle Avenue. Nature center is on right, just beyond Myrtle Avenue. See above for parking and bicycle path.

Or: Belt Parkway East to Exit 17N/Crossbay Boulevard. Left onto Crossbay Boulevard and continue as it intersects with Rock-away Parkway. Crossbay Boulevard becomes Woodhaven Boulevard. Continue past Jamaica Avenue. At Forest Park Drive, look for parking. See above.

Fort Tilden and Jacob Riis Park

Subway—2 train to last station, Flatbush Avenue/Brooklyn College. Transfer to Q35 bus southbound to either Fort Tilden or Jacob Riis Park.

Car—Belt Parkway, either direction, to Exit 11S. South on Flatbush Avenue and across Marine Parkway Bridge. For Jacob Riis Park, stay left after bridge and proceed to parking lot. For Fort Tilden, turn right after bridge and then left into Fort Tilden. From June 15 through September 14, parking restricted to fishermen with permits. Many parking areas have additional restrictions, although parking is permitted for anyone attending a public pro-gram—usually in the lot in front of the visitor center. Parking also available in nearby Jacob Riis Park lot (fee in summer), a short walk from Fort Tilden.

Or: Long Island Expressway East to Woodhaven Boulevard exit. Right onto Woodhaven Boulevard, which—after approxi-mately 4 miles, becomes Crossbay Boulevard. Continue 6 miles and cross 2 bridges. After 2nd bridge, follow signs to either Jacob Riis Park or Fort Tilden. See above.

Gantry Plaza State Park

Subway—7 train to Vernon Boulevard/Jackson Avenue station. Walk 2 blocks west on 48th Avenue to Park.

Or: G train to 21st Street/Jackson Avenue station. Walk 3 blocks west.

Car—Long Island Expressway West to Exit 15/Van Dam Street. Right onto Van Dam Street, then left onto 49th Avenue. Continue to the end. Street parking.

Or: Queens–Midtown Tunnel to Long Island Expressway East, to Borden Avenue exit. Right onto Borden Avenue, right onto Vernon Boulevard, and left onto 49th Avenue, to the end. Or: 59th Street (Queensborough) Bridge to 21st Street. Turn right. Then right onto Jackson Avenue, and right onto 48th Avenue. Left at corner by City Lights Building and then right onto 49th Avenue, to the end.

Green Meadows Farm and Queens County Farm Museum

Subway/Bus—E or F train to Kew Gardens/Union Turnpike station. Transfer to northbound Q46 bus, which runs along Union Turnpike. Get off at Little Neck Parkway. Walk north 3 blocks to Farm and Museum.

Car—Grand Central Parkway East to Exit 24/Little Neck Parkway. Turn right, 3 blocks south to Farm and Museum. Parking (free).

Or: Long Island Expressway to Exit 32/Little Neck Parkway. Turn left, south 1 1/2 miles to Farm and Museum.

Jamaica Bay Wildlife Refuge

Subway—A train (marked "Far Rockaway") to Broad Channel station. Walk west on Noel Road, and right onto Cross Bay Boulevard. Walk approximately 0.75 mile to Refuge.

Car—Belt Parkway East to Exit 17S/Cross Bay Boulevard. After exit, right at traffic light onto Crossbay Boulevard. After crossing Joseph P. Addabbo Bridge, continue about 1 mile to traffic light and turn right to visitors center. Parking (free).

Or: Long Island Expressway East (I-495) to Exit 19/Woodhaven Boulevard. After exit, right at traffic light onto Woodhaven, which—after approximately 4 miles becomes Cross Bay Boulevard. Stay on Crossbay about 4 more

miles, cross Joseph P. Addabbo Bridge, and continue as above.

Joseph P. Addabbo Bridge

Subway—A train (marked "Far Rockaway") to Howard Beach/159th Avenue station. Walk south to Bridge.

Car—Belt Parkway East to Exit 17S/Cross Bay Boulevard. Right at traffic light onto Cross Bay Boulevard, to 165th Avenue, just before Bridge. Lot parking (free) and street parking.

Or: Long Island Expressway East (I-495) to Exit 19/Woodhaven Boulevard. After exit, right at traffic light onto Woodhaven, which—after approximately 4 miles—becomes Cross Bay Boulevard. Continue as above.

Kissena Park

Including Kissena Lake

Subway—7 train to last station, Flushing/Main Street. Transfer to eastbound Q26 bus and get off at 46th Avenue and 164th Street. Walk south to Park entrance and Lake.

Car—Van Wyck Expressway (I-678) to Long Island Expressway East (I-495), to Exit 24/Kissena Boulevard. After exit, continue on service road and left on 164th Street. Continue 1 block to Booth Memorial Avenue and Park entrance. Lake is just north of entrance. Street parking.

Queens Botanical Garden

Subway—7 train to last station, Flushing/Main Street. Transfer to southbound Q44 bus, or walk south on Main Street 8 blocks, to Garden.

Trolley—For information on the free Queens Culture Loop Trolley, which operates on weekends, call 718-886-3800.

Car—Long Island Expressway (I-495) to Exit 23/Main Street. North on Main Street for

.75 mile. Left onto Dahlia Avenue, to Garden. Parking (fee) in Dahlia Avenue lot, weekends through September and weekdays during July and August.

Or: Van Wyck Expressway (I-678) to Exit 12A/College Point Boulevard. North on College Point; right onto Blossom Avenue; then right again onto Crommelin Avenue, which becomes Dahlia Avenue. Continue as above.

Queens Zoo

Subway—7 train to 111th Street/Roosevelt Avenue station. Walk south on 111th Street to Flushing Meadows–Corona Park, then bear right through New York Hall of Science parking lot to Zoo.

Car—Long Island Expressway East (I-495) to 108th Street exit. Left onto 108th Street, right onto 52nd Avenue, then right onto 111th Street. Zoo parking lot (free) is on left side of 111th Street, between 54th and 55th Avenues.

Or: Bronx–Whitestone Bridge to Whitestone (Clearview) Expressway, to Grand Central Parkway East, to Exit 10 (Long Island Expressway/Queens–Midtown Tunnel). Take 1st right off exit ramp, then right onto 111th Street. See above for parking.

Staten Island

Blue Heron Nature Center

Public Transportation—Staten Island Ferry to S78 bus (Ramp D), to Poillon Avenue. Right onto Poillon and walk 0.2 mile to Center.

Or: Staten Island Ferry to Staten Island Rapid Transit train, to Annadale station. Walk southeast to Poillon Avenue, turn left, and walk to Center.

Car—Verrazano-Narrows Bridge to Staten Island Expressway West (I-278), to Hylan Boulevard West exit. Left at traffic light, then

right at 3rd traffic light onto Hylan Boulevard. After approximately 5.5 miles, right onto Poillon Avenue and continue 1.5 miles to Center. Parking lot (free) is on left.

Clay Pit Ponds State Park Preserve

Public Transportation—Staten Island Ferry to S74 bus (Ramp B), to Sharrott Road. Cross Arthur Kill Road and walk down Sharrott Road approximately 0.25 mile to Carlin Street. Turn right to Park.

Car—Verrazano-Narrows Bridge to Staten Island Expressway West (I-278), then approximately 6 miles to Route 440 South exit. Proceed 5 miles to Exit 3/Bloomingdale Road. Left onto Bloomingdale Road, right onto Sharrott Road., then right again onto Carlin Street, which leads to Park. Parking (free).

Clove Lakes Park

Public Transportation—Staten Island Ferry to S61 or S62 bus (Ramp A), to Clove Road.

Or: From ferry, S48 (Ramp C), to Clove Road and Forest Avenue. Enter Park at Clove Road and Forest Avenue or at Clove Road and Victory Boulevard.

Bus—S53 bus from Bay Ridge, Brooklyn (4th Avenue and 86th Street) to Park.

Car—Verrazano-Narrows Bridge to Staten Island Expressway West (I-278), to Exit 13/Clove Road. Right onto Clove Road. Park entrance is just beyond intersection of Clove Road and Victory Boulevard, on left. Free parking, but lot is small.

Conference House Park

Public Transportation—Staten Island Ferry to S78 bus (Ramp D), to Park.

Car—Verrazano-Narrows Bridge to Staten Island Expressway West (I-278), to Hylan Boulevard exit. Left at traffic light, then right at

3rd traffic light onto Hylan Boulevard. Approximately 12 miles to end of Hylan Boulevard and right onto Saterlee Street. Park is on left. Parking lot (free) at end of Hylan Boulevard.

Goethals Pond

Public Transportation—Staten Island Ferry to S40 bus (Ramp D), to Forest Avenue. Walk west on Forest to Home Depot store. At far left entrance to Home Depot parking lot are viewing platforms along Pond.

Car—Verrazano-Narrows Bridge to Staten Island Expressway West (I-278), to South Avenue exit. Continue on service road (Goethals Road North) to Forest Avenue, then right into Home Depot parking lot. See above.

Great Kills Park

Including boat launch and Crooke's Point

Public Transportation—Staten Island Ferry to S78 bus (Ramp D), to Buffalo Avenue. Park entrance is across the street. Boat launch is about mid-park; Crooke's Point is at very end of peninsula.

Bus—S79 bus from Bay Ridge, Brooklyn (95th Street and 4th Avenue) to Park entrance (R train stops at 86th Street and 4th Avenue). See above.

Car—Verrazano-Narrows Bridge to Staten Island Expressway West (I-278), to Hylan Boulevard exit. Left at traffic light, then left at 3rd traffic light onto Hylan Boulevard. After approximately 2.5 miles, left onto Buffalo Avenue and into Park. Parking (free). See above.

Greenbelt Nature Center

Public Transportation—Staten Island Ferry to S74 bus (Ramp B), to Rockland Avenue. Transfer to S54 or S57 bus to Brielle Avenue. Nature Center entrance is across street.

Car—Verrazano-Narrows Bridge to Staten Island Expressway West (I-278), to Exit 11/Bradley Avenue. Stay on service road to traffic light, then left onto Bradley Avenue. Right onto Brielle Avenue, and go to end of road and into Nature Center parking lot (free).

High Rock Park

Including High Rock Park Environmental Education Center and High Rock Park Nature Center

Public Transportation—Staten Island Ferry to S61, S62, or S66 bus (Ramp A), to Victory Boulevard and Manor Road. Transfer to S54 bus to Nevada Avenue. Walk up hill on Nevada Avenue to Park entrance.

Car—Verrazano-Narrows Bridge to Staten Island Expressway West (I-278), to Bradley Avenue exit. Continue along service road, turn left on Bradley Avenue, then right onto Brielle Avenue. Continue for 0.75 mile to the end of street and Nature Center. Parking lot (free).

Lemon Creek Pier

Public Transportation—Staten Island Ferry to S78 bus (Ramp D) to Sharrott Avenue and Hylan Boulevard. Cross Hylan and walk toward water. Pier is straight ahead.

Car—Verrazano-Narrows Bridge to Staten Island Expressway West (I-278), to Hylan Boulevard exit. Left at traffic light, then right at 3rd traffic light onto Hylan Boulevard. After approximately 9.5 miles, left onto Sharrott Avenue and into Pier parking lot (free).

Or: Verrazano-Narrows Bridge to Staten Island Expressway West (I-278), to Route 440 South (toward Outerbridge Crossing), to Exit 3/Bloomingdale Road. Stay straight onto Veterans Road West, then right onto Bloomingdale Road, which—after crossing Amboy Road—becomes Sharrott Avenue. Stay on Sharrott into Pier parking lot. See above.

Mariners Marsh Preserve

Public Transportation—Staten Island Ferry to S48 bus (Ramp C), to Holland Avenue and Richmond Terrace. Preserve is across the street.

Car—Verrazano-Narrows Bridge to Staten Island Expressway West, to South Avenue exit. Right onto South Avenue, then left onto Richmond Terrace. Preserve is on left. Parking on street or in dirt lot across from Preserve.

Midland Beach, Ocean Breeze Pier

Public Transportation—Staten Island Ferry to S51 bus (Ramp B), to Seaview Avenue and Father Capodanno Boulevard. Walk across boulevard to beach.

Bus—S79 bus from Bay Ridge, Brooklyn (86th Street and 4th Avenue; R train stops here), to Hylan Boulevard and Midland Avenue. Walk east to beach.

Car—Verrazano-Narrows Bridge to South Beach exit. South on Lily Pond Avenue, which becomes Father Capodanno Boulevard, to Midland Avenue. There are parking lots (free) along the beach.

Miller Field Ranger Station

Public Transportation—Staten Island Ferry to S76 bus (Ramp B), to New Dorp Lane and Hylan Boulevard. Cross Hylan and walk down New Dorp Lane to Cedar Grove. Park entrance is on left.

Bus—S79 bus from Bay Ridge, Brooklyn (86th Street and 4th Avenue; R train stops here) to New Dorp Lane and Hylan Boulevard. Proceed as above.

Car—Verrazano-Narrows Bridge to Staten Island Expressway (I-278), to Hylan Boulevard exit. Left at traffic light, then right at 3rd traffic light onto Hylan Boulevard. After approximately 2.5 miles, left onto New Dorp Lane. At Cedar Grove, left into Park entrance. Parking (free).

Mount Loretto Unique Area

Public Transportation—Staten Island Ferry to S78 bus (Ramp D), to Hylan Boulevard and Richard Avenue. Walk east on Hylan, right onto Cunningham Road, and into Area.

Car—Verrazano-Narrows Bridge to Staten Island Expressway West to Hylan Boulevard exit. At traffic light, turn left and then at the 3rd traffic light, turn right onto Hylan Boulevard. Drive approximately 11 miles to Cunningham Road and left into parking lot (free) inside gate.

Silver Lake Park

Public Transportation—Staten Island Ferry to S61 bus (Ramp A), to Victory Boulevard and Forest Avenue, in front of Park entrance.

Car—Verrazano-Narrows Bridge to Staten Island Expressway West (I-278), to Clove Road exit. Right at 1st traffic light onto Clove Road, then right at 3rd traffic light onto Victory Boulevard. Continue to Forest Avenue. Park is on left. Street parking.

Snug Harbor Cultural Center and Staten Island Botanical Garden

Public Transportation—Staten Island Ferry to S40 bus (Ramp D), which stops in front of Snug Harbor.

Car—Verrazano-Narrows Bridge to Staten Island Expressway West (I-278), to Exit 13 (Clove Road/Richmond Road). At 3rd intersection, right onto Clove Road. Then right onto Bement Avenue and right onto Richmond Terrace. Then make quick right at Snug Harbor sign and quick left at brick gatehouse. Parking (free).

Staten Island Museum of the Staten Island Institute of Arts and Sciences

Public Transportation—From Staten Island Ferry Terminal follow sign "To Streets." Turn left onto Richmond Terrace, then left onto Wall Street. Institute is at Wall Street and Stuyvesant Place.

Car—Verrazano-Narrows Bridge to Staten Island Expressway West (I-278), to Bay Street exit. Right onto Schoolhouse Road; then left onto Bay Street, which becomes Richmond Terrace; then left onto Stuyvesant Place. Institute is at Stuyvesant Place and Wall Street. Parking across street at Allied Parking. $2 charge for museum visitors on weekdays. Be sure to obtain voucher at museum and present it to parking attendant upon your return. Parking free on weekends.

Staten Island Zoo

Public Transportation—Staten Island Ferry to S48 bus (Ramp C), to Broadway and Richmond Terrace. Walk 3 blocks on Broadway to Zoo entrance.

Bus—S53 bus from Bay Ridge, Brooklyn (R train at 86th Street and 4th Avenue) to Zoo.

Car—Verrazano-Narrows Bridge to Staten Island Expressway West (I-278), to Slosson Avenue exit. Right onto Slosson Avenue, then right onto Martling Avenue. Free parking on right side of Martling Avenue, just before Zoo entrance.

Willowbrook Park

Public Transportation—Staten Island Ferry to S44 bus (Ramp A), to Richmond Avenue and Eton Place, and Park entrance.

Car—Verrazano-Narrows Bridge to Staten Island Expressway West (I-278), to Victory Boulevard exit. Left onto Victory Boulevard (west), then left onto Richmond Avenue. Left at next traffic light, onto Eton Place, which leads into Park. Several parking lots (free).

Wolfe's Pond Park

Public Transportation—Staten Island Ferry to S78 bus (Ramp D), to Hylan Boulevard and Cornelia Avenue. Cross Hylan to Park entrance.

Car—Verrazano-Narrows Bridge to Staten Island Expressway West (I-278), to Hylan Boulevard exit. Left at traffic light, then right at 3rd traffic light onto Hyland Boulevard. After approximately 8 miles, right onto Cornelia Avenue, which leads into Park. Several parking lots (free).

Additional Resources

Picture Books

Allen, Judy. *Are You A Bee?* Kingfisher, 2004. Also seven additional books in the "Backyard Books" series.

Arnosky, Jim. *Crinkleroot's Nature Almanac.* Simon & Schuster, 1999.

Bash, Barbara. *Urban Roosts: Where Birds Nest in the City.* Sierra Club Books, 1990. Paperback: Little, Brown, 1992.

Byrd Baylor. *Everybody Needs a Rock.* Atheneum, 1974. Paperback: Aladdin, 1985.

Carle, Eric. *Little Cloud.* Philomel Books, 1996. Paperback: Putnam, 2001.

Cooney, Barbara. *Miss Rumphius.* Viking, 1982. Paperback: Puffin Books, 1985.

Fife, H. Dale & Arnosky, Jim. *The Empty Lot.* Sierra Club Books, 1996.

Fleischman, Paul. *Weslandia.* Candlewick Press, 1999. Paperback: 2002.

Ginsburg, Mirra. *Mushroom in the Rain.* Macmillan, 1974. Paperback: Aladdin, 1997.

Honey, Elizabeth. *Not a Nibble.* Allen & Unwin (Australia), 1997. Paperback: 1997.

James, Simon, *The Birdwatchers.* Candlewick Press, 2002.

Johnson, D. B. *Henry Hikes to Fitchburg.* Houghton Mifflin, 2000.

McDonald, Megan and Johnson, Paul Brett. *Insects are My Life.* Scholastic, 1995. Paperback: 1997.

Napoli, Donna Jo. Albert. *Silver Whistle,* 2001. Paperback: Voyager, 2005.

Torres, Leyla. *The Subway Sparrow.* Sunburst Books, 1997. Paperback: Farrar, Straus and Giroux, 1997.

Wallace, Nancy Elizabeth. *The Paperwhite.* Houghton Mifflin, 2000.

Williams, Vera. B. *Three Days on the River in a Red Canoe.* Greenwillow, 1981. Paperback: HarperTrophy, 1984.

Yolen, Jane. *Owl Moon.* Philomel Books, 1987.

Zolotow, Charlotte. *When the Wind Stops.* HarperCollins, 1995 (revised). Paperback: HarperTrophy, 1997.

Field Guides

Brown, Tom. *Tom Brown's Field Guide to Nature Observation and Tracking.* Paperback: Berkley, 1988.

Docekal, Eileen M. *Nature Detective, How to Solve Outdoor Mysteries.* Sterling, 1989. Paperback: 1991.

Fowle, Marcia T. & Kerlinger, Paul. *The New York City Audubon Society Guide to Finding Birds in the Metropolitan Area.* Comstock Publishing, 2001.

Hansen, Judith et al. *Seashells in My Pocket: AMC Family Guide to Exploring the Atlantic Coast from Maine to Florida,* 3rd edition. Appalachian Mountain Club, 2005.

Hatchett, Clint. *The Glow-in-the-Dark Night Sky Book.* Random House, 1988.

Hickman, Pamela. *The Night Book: Exploring Nature After Dark with Activities, Experiments and Information.* Kids Can Press, 1996. Paperback: 1996.

Kochanoff, Peggy. *Beachcombing the Atlantic Coast.* Paperback: Mountain Press, 1997.

Laubach, Christyna, Laubach, Rene, & Smith, Charles W. G. *Raptor! A Kid's Guide to Birds of Prey.* Storey Publishing, 2002. Paperback: 2002.

Matsen, Brad. *Go Wild in New York City.* National Geographic Children's Books, 2005.

Stokes, Donald. *Stokes Guide to Observing Insect Lives.* Little, Brown, 1983. Paperback: 1984.

Recommended Field Guide Series

Kaufman Focus Guides. Houghton Mifflin.
National Audubon Society First Field Guides. Scholastic.
National Geographic My First Pocket Guides. National Geographic.
Peterson First Guides. Houghton Mifflin.
Smithsonian Kids' Field Guides. DK Publishing.

Activities

Day, Marlena (illustrator). *Trails, Tails & Tidepools in Pails: Over 100 Nature Activities for Families with Babies and Young Children.* Paperback: Nursery Nature Walks, 1992.

Drake, Jane et al. *The Kids Campfire Book.* Kids Can Press, 1998. Paperback: 1998.

Evert, Laura et al. *More Fun with Nature.* NorthWord Press, 2002.

Milford, Susan. *The Kids Nature Book, 365 Indoor/Outdoor Activities and Experiences.* Revised edition. Williamson Publishing, 1996.

Martin, Laura C. & Cain, David. *Nature's Art Box: From T-shirts to Twig Baskets, 65 Cool Projects for Crafty Kids to Make with Natural Materials You Can Find Anywhere.* Storey Publishing, 2003. Paperback: 2003.

Books for Parents

Barnard, Edward Sibey. *New York City Trees.* Columbia University Press, 2002.

Bosselaar, Laure-Anne, editor. *Urban Nature: Poems about Wildlife in the City.* Paperback: Milkweed Editions, 2000.

Caduto, Michael J., Fadden, David Kanietakeron, & Bruchac, Joseph. *Keepers of the Night: Native American Stories and Nocturnal Activities for Children.* Paperback: Fulcrum Publishing, 1994.

Carson, Rachel. *The Sense of Wonder.* HarperCollins, 1998 (reprint). Paperback: 1987.

Cornell, Joseph. *Sharing Nature with Children.* Dawn Publications, 1998 (anniversary edition).

Cornell, Joseph. *Sharing Nature with Children II.* Dawn Publications, 1989.

La Rocco, Barbara. *Going Coastal New York City.* Paperback: Going Coastal Productions, 2004.

Lawrence, Gale. *The Beginning Naturalist: Weekly Encounters with the Natural World.* Paperback: New England Press, 1980.

Lovejoy, Sharon. *Roots, Shoots, Buckets & Boots: Gardening Together with Children.* Workman Publishing, 1999. Paperback: 1999.

Mikula, Rick. *The Family Butterfly Book.* Storey Books, 2000. Paperback: 2000.

Morey, Shaun & Smith, Elwood H. *Kids' Incredible Fishing Stories.* Workman Publishing Co., 1996. Paperback: 1996.

Perrone, Joe & Luftglass, Manny. *Gone Fishin' with Kids: How to Take Your Kid Fishing and Still be Friends.* Gone Fishin' Enterprises, 1997.

Roberts, Janet Wier & Huelbig, Carole. *City Kids and City Critters: Activities for Urban Explorers.* Learning Triangle Press, 1996.

Rosen, Michael J. *The Kids Book of Fishing and Tackle Box.* Paperback: Workman Publishing, 1991.

Sanders, Jack. *The Secrets of Wildflowers: A Delightful Feast of Little-Known Facts, Folklore, and History.* Lyons Press, 2003.

Shaffer, Carolyn, & Fielder, Erica. *City Safaris: A Sierra Club Explorer's Guide to Urban Adventures for Grownups and Kids.* Sierra Club Books, 1987.

Silverman, Goldie. *Backpacking with Babies and Small Children: A Guide to Taking the Kids along on Day Hikes, Overnighters and Long Trail Trips.* 3rd Edition. Wilderness Press, 1998.

Web Sites for Children

www.backyardjungle.org—Nature-loving kids from close to home and around the world showcase and share discoveries made in their own backyards, from sighting a luna moth to the goings-on in a home aquarium.

www.dnr.state.wi.us/org/caer/ce/eek—The Wisconsin Department of Natural Resources' Environmental Education for Kids Web site, for kids in grades 4–8, has tips on stargazing and animal tracking and leads youngsters in such unusual crafts as making winter ice wreaths and preserving snowflakes.

www.enature.com—Among other riches, this site provides online field guides to thousands of creatures, a Native Gardening and Invasive Plants Guide, and bird calls that you can really listen to.

www.enchantedlearning.com—A great site with craft ideas, printouts, coloring pages, and more, covering everything from astronomy to zoology.

www.epa.gov/kids—This United States Environmental Protection Agency Web site for youngsters—Environmental Kids Club—provides information on the nation's endangered plants and animals as well as on big-picture topics and issues, such as global warming and pollution, the latter written as a kid's adventure story.

www.gowildnyc.org—In addition to fun facts about urban nature, this site offers cool activities, including bug and geology quizzes and an ant-farm game, as well as links to other great sites.

www.insects.org—Bugbios presents everything children might want to know about insects, including wonderful macrophotography.

www.mesc.usgs.gov/resources/education/butterfly/bfly_intro.asp—The USGS Children's Butterfly Site—from the United States Geological Survey—explores the life cycle of butterflies and moths and includes coloring pages and answers to frequently asked questions.

www.nationalgeographic.com/kids—Games, activities and experiments, "creature features," cartoons, coloring pages, challenges, maps, bookmarks, and more—all for kids, and all from National Geographic.

www.nefsc.noaa.gov/faq—FishFAQ (from the Woods Hole Science Aquarium and Northeast Fisheries Science Center) answers tons of strange and not-so-strange questions: Can fish swim backwards? and Do fish sleep? and Do fish chew their food? for example.

www.nwf.org/kids—Divided into four age-appropriate groups, this National Wildlife Federation Kidzone site explores different habitats and animals, recommends nature books, sponsors contests, and has animal-themed crafts and games. There's even a kid's guide to animals that's great for helping with homework and class projects.

www.ology.amnh.org—The American Museum of Natural History's nature and science Web site for kids, with helpful information for parents as well.

www.urbanext.uiuc.edu/kids/index.html—The University of Illinois Extension's Just for Kids Web site has kid-friendly graphics and easy-to-follow information on worms, insects, trees and other plants, and other topics—all just perfect for very young children.

Web Sites for Parents

www.acornnaturalists.com—This online store offers plenty of educational resources—field guides, literature, and curricula—as well as practical resources—activities, kits, and games—to help guide your children along the path of nature.

www.americanbirding.org—The American Birding Association offers conservation and education programs, workshops, tours, and an online store of bird-related books, optics, multimedia, and more.

www.audubon.org—The National Audubon Society's main focus is on birds (and everything having to do with them), but its Web site also includes information on conservation issues and campaigns.

www.carolina.com—Carolina Biological Supply Company is a source for all kinds of scientific and educational equipment, services, and resources.

www.cs.gc.cuny.edu/~nature/about.htm—Developed by the City University of New York, this Web site (Exploring the Nature of New York) explores the relationship between nature and urban living, and also offers an annual course—open to the public—entitled "Nature of New York: Its Natural History and Environment."

investigate.conservation.org/xp/IB—This is Conservation International's Investigate Biodiversity Web site, with a wealth of ideas for protecting the environment as part of our everyday lives.

www.kidsgardening.com—A guide for parents and educators who want to engage children in gardens—even in small spaces—through activities, designs, and other projects. Check out the great grants, awards, and resources page.

www.milkweedcafe.com—Everything butterfly, including live insect kits, information on how to plant your own butterfly garden, and Club Caterpillar activities for kids of all ages.

www.naba.org—The not-for-profit North American Butterfly Association is dedicated to increasing public enjoyment of butterflies and their conservation. The Web site is a treasury of information and images.

www.nationalgeographic.com—One of the oldest, most esteemed organizations offers loads of information on animals and nature, including photographs, news stories, conservation guidelines, and a comprehensive Animals Index.

www.natureserve.org—This conservation-minded nonprofit features an online encyclopedia of more than 60,000 plants, animals, and ecosystems.

www.nnyn.org—Through programs, publications, Web sites, books, and art, this nonprofit is dedicated to promoting awareness of urban nature and its importance to all city residents.

www.thenaturestore.com—The Web site of the well-known retail chain is chock full of all kinds of things to help make nature part of your family's life, from insect-rearing kits and binoculars to nature books and cool T-shirts.

www.treebranch.com—A resource for anyone interested in environmental and urban quality-of-life issues in New York City; includes a monthly newsletter. Also includes numerous links to other resource sites.

www.wildmetro.org—This organization has a global perspective on environmental understanding and protection in metropolitan areas, with a new Manhattan-based portal. They conduct research outings and field trips for adults and kids.

INDEX

A

Abraham's Pond, 73
Albert (Napoli), 77
Alley Creek, 59, 87
Alley Pond Park: bicycling, 198–200; birding, 87, 103, 108; camping out, 116; freshwater fishing, 218; getting there, 262; horseshoe crabs, 157; nature and environmental center, 16–18; nature walks, 57–59, 68; programs and festivals, 127
Alley Pond Wetlands Trail, 57–59
Amateur Astronomers Association of New York, 114, 127
American bald eagle, 104
American beach grass, 161
American black duck, 80
American Canoe Association, 141
American coot, 80–81
American crow, 97
American elm tree, 60
American goldfinch, 97
American kestrel, 104
American Littoral Society, 89, 108, 151, 157, 163
American Museum of Natural History, 127, 230–34, 256
American oystercatcher, 88
American robin, 97
American Small Craft Association, 135
American sycamore tree, 60
American toad, 46
American widgeon, 81
Andre (video), 123
Annual Fishing Jamboree, 228
Arthur Kill, 84
Arverne, 85
Atlantic bay scallop, 154
Atlantic Flyway, 109

Atlantic jackknife clam, 154
Atlantic menhaden (bunker), 159
Atlantic mole crab, 158
Atlantic silversides, 159
Atlantic slipper shell, 155
Atlantic surf clam, 154
Audubon Cooperative Sanctuary System, 100
Audubon Society, 8, 9, 106, 107
Audubon Video Guide to the Birds of North America (National Audubon Society), 77
Autumn olive, 162
Azalea Way, 173

B

Back Fort Trail, 18, 100, 106, 201–3
Baird, Jack and Lois, 24–25
Baisley Pond Park, 218, 262–63
Bald cypress, 51, 54
Baltimore oriole, 97
Barn owl, 102
Barnacles, 158
Bartow-Pell Mansion, 6
Bats, 128–29
Battery Harris East, 18, 106, 202
Battery Park City Parks Conservancy, 107
Battery Weed, 193
Bayberry, 162
Bayside Anglers, 199, 226–27
Bayside Historical Society, 200
Bayside Marina, 147, 199, 200, 263
Beach heather, 161
Beach pea, 161
Beach plum, 161
Beachcombing, 150
Belvedere Castle, 13–15, 105, 257

Bette Midler's New York Restoration Project (NYRP), 108, 195
Big City Fishing, 224–25
Big John's Pond, 21
Bird feeders, 90–91
Birdathon, 89
Bird-feeding stations, 93–94
Bird-watching field kit, 80
Bittersweet nightshade, 66
Black cherry tree, 162
Black crappie, 216
Black oak tree, 61
Black skimmer, 88
Black squirrel, 39
Black-capped chickadee, 91
Black-crowned night heron, 86
Bladder campion, 66
Bladder wrack seaweed, 160, 161
Blue Heron Park: bat viewing, 129; birding, 93, 103; camping out, 116–17; getting there, 266; nature and environmental center, 24–25
Blue Heron Pond, 25, 117
Blue jay, 91
Blue Trail, Forest Park, 68
Blue-claw crab, 158
Bluefish, 219–20
Bluegill, 216
Bow Bridge, 87, 102
Brant goose, 81
Breeze Hill, 93, 100
Breezy Point, 18–19, 84, 85, 263
Broad-winged hawk, 104
Bronx: bat viewing, 129; beachcombing, seining and tidal pools, 152; bicycling, 191–92; birding, 83–84, 100, 103, 105; camping at the zoo, 120–21; camping out, 113; canoe and kayak

launch sites, 146; canoeing, 138; freshwater fishing, 217; gardens, 167–74; nature and environmental centers, 4–8; nature walks, 32–38; saltwater fishing, 221; zoos, 237–40
Bronx River, 107, 121, 138–39, 172
Bronx River Alliance, 138–39
Bronx River Flotilla, 139
Bronx Victory Memorial, 192
Bronx Zoo, 107, 120–21, 129, 237–40, 249
Brooklyn: aquariums, 240–41; bat viewing, 129; beach-coming, seining and tidal pools, 152; bicycle tours and events, 210; bicycling, 192–93, 201–3; birding, 84, 87, 89, 93, 100, 103, 105, 106–7, 108; boating, 134; campfires, 128; camping out, 113, 118–20, 123–24; canoe and kayak launch sites, 147; canoeing, 138, 140–41; family fishing programs and contests, 223; farms, 246–47; freshwater fishing, 218; gardens, 176–79; museums, 229–30; nature and environmental centers, 8–12; nature walks, 40–48; night walks, 105, 125; programs and festivals, 127; saltwater fishing, 221; stargazing, 127; zoos, 241–42
Brooklyn Bird Club, 95, 129
Brooklyn Botanic Garden, 103, 176–79, 251
Brooklyn Bridge Park, 84, 251
Brooklyn Center for the Urban Environment, 10, 251
Brooklyn Children's Museum, 229–30, 252
Brooklyn N-Trak, 120
Brooks Pond, 84
Bruchac, Joseph, 124
Buegler, Dick, 75
Bufflehead duck, 82

Bullfrog, 46
Burke, Dr. Russell, 64
Burnett, Frances Hodgson, 182
Burr, Antonio, 144
Busse, Paul G., 174
Butter-and-eggs flower, 66
Butterflyweed, 64
Buzz-a-Rama, 174

C
Caduto, Michael J., 124
Calico crab, 159
Camp Goldenrod, 118–19
Camp Tamarack, 118–19
Camperdown Elm, 9
Campfires, 128
Canada goose, 81
Canarsie Pier, 221, 252
Canoeing, 136–43, 145–47
Canvasback duck, 82
Carl Schurz Park, 127
Carolina Biological Supply Company, 101
Carthan, Hattie, 10, 11
Cass Gallagher Trail, 113
Cattail Pond, 57, 87
Cedar waxing, 97
Central Park: bat viewing, 129; bicycle tours and events, 210–11; bicycling, 208; bicycling by moon-light, 126; bike rentals, 208–9; birding, 84, 87, 93, 100, 103, 105, 106, 107; boating, 134–35; camping, 114, 122–23; family fishing programs and contests, 224; freshwater fishing, 218; getting there, 256–57; nature and environment centers, 12–13; nature walks, 48–51; programs and festivals, 127
Central Park Conservancy, 13
Central Park Zoo, 122–23, 242, 257
Century Bike Tour, 211
Chain pickerel, 216
Channel catfish, 216–17
Charles A. Dana Discovery

Center, 12–13, 256–57
Chenille weed, 160
Cherry Walk, 194
Chicory, 66
Children's Fishing Clinic, 226
Children's Garden 177
Children's Snapper Derby, 226
Chinese Scholar's Garden, 182, 183
Cinnamon fern, 178
City Island Bridge, 191, 221, 249
Clay mining, 25–26
Clay Pit Ponds State Park Preserve, 25–27, 71–75, 128, 266
Clove Lakes Park: birding, 84, 100; boating, 136; freshwater fishing, 219; getting there, 266
Coffey Street Boat Launch, 253
Cohen, Barbara, 163
Cohen, Mickey, 151
Common carp, 217
Common garter snake, 47
Common goldeneye, 82
Common tern, 88
Common yarrow, 66
Community Farm, 188
Community gardens: Clinton Community Garden, 188; Community Farm, 188; Crotona Park Nature Center, 4; Floyd Bennett Field Garden, 188; history, 189; information, 188; Liz Christy Garden, 188; Magnolia Tree Earth Center, 10; Miller Field Ranger Station, 28; organizations, 188–89; Ryan Visitor Center, 10–11
Compost, 175
Concrete Plant Bark, 139
Coney Island Light Station, 28
Conference House Park, 84, 152, 157, 266–67
Conservatory Water, 135, 257
Cooper's hawk, 104

Cornell Lab of Ornithology, 90, 94, 95
Cornell University, 93–94
Corona Park, 135, 209–10, 218
Crabbing, 220
Cretaceous Period, 71
Crooke, John Jeremy, 27, 204–5
Crooke's Point, 27, 84, 203–5, 267
Croton Woods, 8, 38
Crotona Park, 4–5, 138, 217, 249
Cullen, Tom, 106

D
Dark-eyed junco, 91–92
Deadhorse Bay, 139, 152–53, 252
Diamondback terrapin turtle, 21
Discovery Garden, 176–77, 179
Dorosh, Peter, 95
Double-crested cormorant, 82–83
Douglass Mackay Wetland Nature Trail, 59
Douglaston Windmill, 16, 17, 59
Downtown Boathouse Kayak Launch Site, 143–44, 258
Downy woodpecker, 92
Dragonfly, 14, 47
Drey (squirrel nest), 4
Dulles seaweed, 160
Dutch Elm Disease, 60
Dwarf tree, 162
Dyckman Street Boat Basin, 144–45

E
Eagles, 103–6
Earth Celebrations, 189
East Meadow, 106, 256–57
East Pond, 20–21, 89
East River, 138, 197
Eastern bluebird, 97
Eastern box turtle, 46
Eastern chipmunk, 39

Eastern cottontail, 39
Eastern gray squirrel, 39
Eastern mud snail, 155
Eastern oyster, 154
Eastern painted turtle, 47
Eastern red cedar tree, 162
Eastern screech owl, 102
Eastern towhee, 97–98
Eastern white pine tree, 60
Ellis Swamp, 26, 72, 73
Enid A. Haupt Conservatory, 167–68, 172, 173
European starling, 92
Evening primrose, 66
Everett Children's Adventure Garden, 168–70, 171
Evodia Field, 93

F
Falconry Extravaganza, 106
Falcons, 103–6
Family Field Guide to the Natural Areas of Great Kills Park, 28
Family Fishing Clinics, 226–27
Family Fishing Festival, 226
Family Nature Trail, 176, 177
Family Overnight Safari at the Bronx Zoo, 120–21
Farmer's Market, 173
Fiddler crab, 158–59
15 Easy Folktale Fingerplays (audio cassette), 126
Fishing: freshwater, 216–19; saltwater, 219–22
Floyd Bennett Field: beach-combing, seining and tidal pools, 152; bicycling, 203; birding, 84, 87, 106–7; campfires, 128; camping out, 118–20; canoe and kayak launch sites, 147; getting there, 252; horse-shoe crabs, 157; nature and environmental centers, 10–11; nature walks, 40–43; programs and festivals, 127; stargazing, 127
Flushing Meadow-Corona Park, 135–36, 209–10, 218, 263–64

Fordham gneiss (rock), 4
Forest Edge Trail, 173
Forest Park: bicycling, 208; birding, 100; getting there, 264; nature and environmental center, 19–20; nature walks, 68
Fort Tilden: beachcombing, seining and tidal pools, 152; bicycling, 201–3; birding, 89, 100, 106; family fishing programs and contests, 227; getting there, 264; nature and environmental center, 18–19
Fort Totten, 198–200
Fort Wadsworth, 28, 193
Fort Washington Park, 116, 194, 195
Fowler's toad, 46
Freilich, Mark, 127
Friends of Blue Heron, 24
Friends of Crotona Park, 4
Frog, 46
Furnicolla, Joe, 26–27

G
Gadwall duck, 79
Gantry Plaza State Park, 221, 264–65
Gardener's Resource Center, 179
Gardening with children, 183–87
Gateway National Recreation Area: bicycle tours and events, 210; birding, 108; campfires, 128; canoe and kayak launch sites, 147; canoeing, 139; family fishing programs and contests, 227; Fort Tilden Ranger Contact Station and Breezy Point, 18–19; Great Kills Park Field Station, 27–28; Jamaica Bay Wildlife Refuge Visitor Center, 20–21; night walks, 125; overview, 3–4; Ryan Visitor Center, 10–11; seining programs, 151

Gateway Striper Club, 227

George Washington Bridge, 116, 194, 195, 259

Gericke Farm Trail, 74

Gerritsen Creek: bat viewing, 129; birding, 84, 87; camping out, 113; canoeing, 138; nature and environmental center, 11–12; nature walks, 43–45

Ghost crab, 159

Gil Hodges/Marine Parkway Bridge, 119

Gingko tree, 60

Glen Span Arch, 49

Glossy ibis, 86

Go Fish (East River), 226

Go Fish (Hudson River), 224

Goethals Pond, 89, 267

Golden shiner, 217

Goldenrod, 66

Gowanus Dredgers Canoe Club, The, 140–41, 252

Graffiti, 34

Grand Central Terminal, 33

Grasslands Trail, 69

Gray catbird, 98

Gray squirrel, 39

Great black-backed gull, 95

Great blue heron, 86

Great egret, 86

Great Hill, 48, 51, 114

Great horned owl, 102

Great Kills Harbor, 27, 84, 204

Great Kills Park: beachcombing, seining and tidal pools, 152; bicycling, 203–5; birding, 84, 89; campfires, 128; canoe and kayak launch sites, 152; getting there, 267; horseshoe crabs, 157; programs and festivals, 127; stargazing, 127

Greater yellowleg, 88, 89

Green Guerrillas, 188

Green heron, 86–87

Green Meadows Farm, 244–45, 265

Green Thumb, 188

Greenbelt Conservancy, 22

Greenbelt Native Plant Propogation Garden, 22

Greenbelt Nature Center, 21–22, 267

Green-Wood Cemetery, 100, 253

Guiliani, Mayor Rudolph, 189

Gulls, 95

Gully, The, 68

H

Hagen, Cliff, 129

Harbor seal, 39

Hard-shell clam, 154

Harlem Meer: birding, 84; camping out, 114; family fishing programs and contests, 224; freshwater fishing, 218; getting there, 256–57; nature and environmental center, 12–13

Harlem River, 52, 108, 195–97

Harlem River Ship Canal, 15, 56

Harry by the Sea (Zion), 160

Hart Island, 83

Hartland schist (rock), 38

Harvest Fair, 193

Hawk Family Weekend, 106

Hawks, 103–6

Henry Hudson Bridge, 56

Henry Luce Nature Observatory at Belvedere Castle, 13–16, 257

Hermit crab, 159

Heron Island, 107

Herring gull, 95

High Bridge, 196

High Rock Park: birding, 106, 108; camping out, 117–18; getting there, 267; nature and environmental center, 22–24; nature walks, 75

High Rock Park getting there, 267

Highbridge Park, 57, 108, 196

Historic Aircraft Restoration Project, 119

Holiday Train Show, 173

Hooded merganser, 83

Horseshoe crab, 156–57

House finch, 92

Howard Beach, 62, 221

Huddlestone Park, 51, 114

Hudson River, 16, 116, 143–45, 147, 193–95

Hudson River Greenway, 193–94, 259

Hudson River Park, 209, 224–25, 258

Hunter Island, 6–7, 38, 192

I

I Fish NY, 222–23

Ibis: A True Whale Story (Himmelman), 123

Indian Lake, 4, 217

Indian pipe, 73

Indiana limestone, 33

Inwood Canoe Club, 144–45, 259

Inwood Hill Park: birding, 93, 100, 103, 105–6; camping out, 114–15; canoe and kayak launch sites, 147; canoeing, 138; getting there, 260; nature and environmental center, 15–16; nature walks, 52–56

Irish moss seaweed, 160

J

Jacob Riis Park, 85, 89, 119, 264

Jamaica Bay, 12, 43, 119, 203

Jamaica Bay Wildlife Refuge: bat viewing, 129; birding, 84, 87, 89, 93, 100, 103; getting there, 265; horseshoe crabs, 157; nature and environmental center, 20–21; nature walks, 62–65

Japanese black pine, 162

Japanese Hill-and-Pond Garden, 179

Jaqueline Kennedy Onassis Reservoir, 49, 84, 257

Jellyfish, 159

Jewelweed, 52

Jingle shell, 154

Joe Michael's Mile, 198
Joe Two Trees, 37
John Kieran Nature Trail, 32–35
John Muir Nature Trail, 38
Johnson, Herbert, 20
Joseph P. Addabbo Bridge, 221, 265

K
Karim, Lincoln, 106
Kayaking, 143–47
Kazimiroff, Dr. Theodore, 6, 7, 37
Kazimiroff Nature Trail, 6–7, 38, 103
Keepers of the Night (Caduto, Bruchac), 124
Keim, Paul, 129
Kelp, 160
Kieran, John, 32
Kingsbridge Burial Grounds, 35
Kissena Park, 218, 226, 265
Kiya the Gull (Lasell), 225

L
Lady crab, 159
Lake, The, 84, 87
Largemouth bass, 217
Lasker Pool, 51
Last Algonquin, The (Kazimiroff), 37
Laughing gull, 95
Least tern, 85
Lemon Creek Park, 147, 221, 267
Lenapes, Lenni, 117, 172
Lightning bugs, 130
Limpet, 155
Linnaean Society of New York, 108
Lion Rock, 38
Little Alley Pond, 201
Little Bay Park, 198–200
Little Neck Bay, 84, 157, 198, 262
Little Neck Bridge, 199
Little Red Lighthouse, 115–16, 193–95
Little Red Lighthouse and the Great

Gray Bridge, The (Swift), 115, 116, 193, 195
Little Red Lighthouse Festival, 116
Loch, The, 49, 51, 114
Loeb Boathouse, 84, 134–35, 208, 257
London plane tree, 60
Long Island City Community Boathouse, 141
Long Island Motor Parkway, 18
Long Island Sound, 37, 58
Long-eared owl, 102
Look Around New York City (NYC Audubon), 107
Lookout Hill, 9, 45, 100
Loosestrife Swamp, 117
Louis J. Valentino Pier and Park, getting there, 147, 253
Lullwater Nature Trail, 9, 48, 93

M
Macy's Annual Fishing Contest, 223
Magnolia Tree Earth Center, 10, 253
Mallard, 81
Mammals, 39
Manhattan: bat viewing, 129; bicycle tours and events, 210, 211; bicycling, 193–98; bike rentals, 208–9; birding, 84, 87, 93, 100, 103, 105–6, 107, 108; boating, 134–35; camping, 114–16, 122–23; canoe and kayak launch sites, 147; canoeing, 138; family fishing programs and contests, 224–26; freshwater fishing, 218; kayaking, 143–45; museums, 230–34; nature and environmental centers, 12–16; nature walks, 48–57; programs and festivals, 127; saltwater fishing, 221; zoos, 242
Manhattan Kayak Company, 145, 260

Manhattan schist, 15, 52, 55, 114
Maple trees, 60–61
Maps: Alley Pond Park to Fort Totten to Little Bay Pond, 199; Alley Ponds Wetland Trail, Alley Pond Park, 58; Back Fort Trail, Fort Tilden & Floyd Bennett Field, 202; Five Boroughs, vi; Inwood Hill Nature Trail, 53; John Kieran Trail, Van Cortlandt Park, 33; Mount Loretto Nature Walk, Staten Island, 69; North Forty Nature Trail, Floyd Bennett Field, 40; Orchard Beach & Pelham Bay Park, 5; Roosevelt Island, 187; 79th Street Boat Basin to the Little Red Lighthouse, 146; Snug Harbor Cultural Center and Silver Lake Park, 205; Swindler Cove Park along the Harlem River, 196; Vanderbilt Motor Parkway, 199
Marine Park, 11–12, 119
Marine Parkway-Gil Hodges Memorial Bridge, 203
Mariners Marsh Park, 74, 75, 87, 268
Marsh snail, 155
Martling Lake, 84
Meadow Lake, 218, 263–64
Merlin, 104
Middle Reef, 83
Midland Beach, Ocean Breeze Pier, 221, 268
Milanese, Ed, 26–27
Milkweed, 45
Miller, Captain James Ely, 28
Miller Field Ranger Station, 28, 128, 268
Mishow (glacial erratic), 6
Mitsubishi Wild Wetland Trail, 169
Model Boat Pond, birding, 106
Monk parakeet, 98
Moon snail, 155

Moses, Robert, 7, 20, 22
Moses Mountain, 22, 75, 106
Mount Loretto Unique Area, 68–71, 268
Mourning dove, 92
Muir, John, 38
Mullein plant, 63
Muskrat, 39
Mussel, 154
Mute swan, 81–82

N

Narrows Botanical Garden, 193
National Estuaries Day, 145
Native Americans, 6, 48, 141
Native Flora Garden, 177–79
Native Plant Demonstration Garden, 22
Natural History of New York City (Kieran), 32
Neighborhood Open Space Coalition, 188
Nethermead, 105, 254
New England aster, 72
New York Aquarium, 123, 240–41, 253–54
New York Botanical Garden: birding, 107; exploring the forest, 171–73; farmers' market, 173; gardens for children, 167–74; getting there, 249; Holiday Train Show, 173–74; rock garden, 173
New York Central Railroad, 32
New York City Department of Environmental Protection, 25
New York City Department of Parks & Recreation, 3, 48, 138, 145
New York Hall of Science, 135, 234–35, 263–64
New York Invasive Plants Council, 57
New York Restoration Project, 189
New York State Department of Conservation's Division of Fish, Wildlife and Marine Resources, 99
New York State Department of Environmental Conservation, 68, 222–23
New York State Office of Parks, Recreation and Historic Preservation, 4
New York State Wildlife Rehabilitation Council, 99
North Forty Nature Trail, 40–43, 252
North Garden, 65, 100
North Woods, Central Park, 13, 48–51, 100, 114, 256–57
Northern cardinal, 92
Northern Forest, 19
Northern harrier, 104
Northern mockingbird, 92
Northern pipefish, 159
Northern quahog, 154
Northern saw-whet owl, 102–3
Northern shoveler, 81
Northern water snake, 47
Novick, Andy, 142
Nunez, Steve, 4

O

Oak trees, 61
Oakland Lake, 108, 138, 218, 262
Old Croton Aqueduct Trail, 38, 57
Old Place Creek, 147
Old Putnam Trail, 32
Olmsted, Frederick Law, 9, 14, 208
Orchard Beach Nature Center, 6–7, 146, 192, 250
Osprey, 105
Owls, 101–3
Owls Head Park, 192–93, 254

P

Paerdegat Basin, 142
Paper birch tree, 61
Participation in Project Feederwatch, 90
Pelham Bay Park: beachcombing, seining and tidal pools, 152; bicycling, 191–92; birding, 83, 100, 103, 105; canoe and kayak launce sites, 146; getting there, 250; horseshoe crabs, 157; nature and environmental center, 5–7; nature walks, 35–38; tidal pools, 152
Peregrine falcon, 105
Perennial Garden, 182–83
Periwinkle, 155
Peter Jay Sharpe Boathouse, 196
Phragmites, 59
Pie-billed grebe, 83
Pier 26, 16, 143–44
Pier 45, 224, 258–59
Pier 84, 259
Pigeons, 94
Pin oak tree, 61
Pink lady's slipper, 167
Piping plover, 85
Plankton, 159
Plough, Richard, 92
Plum Beach, 157, 254
Poison ivy, 52
Pokeweed, 67
Pond Trail, 202
Pool, Central Park, 48–49, 51
Pratt, Frederick B., 45
Prickly pear cacti, 178
Princes Bay Lighthouse, 70–71
Project Pigeon Watch, 94
Prospect Park: bat viewing, 129; bicycling, 208; bicycling by moonlight, 126; birding, 84, 93, 100, 103, 105; boating, 134; family fishing programs and contests, 223; freshwater fishing, 218; getting there, 254; nature and environmental centers, 8–9, 10; nature walks, 48
Prospect Park Alliance, 8, 48
Prospect Park Audubon Center, 8–9, 48, 106, 107, 254
Prospect Park Zoo, 241–42, 254–55

Protectors of Pine Oak Woods, 27, 68, 75, 106, 125–26
Public gardens, 165–83
Pugsley Creek Park, 146
Pumpkin Smash, 188
Pumpkinseed fish, 217
Purple martin, 98

Q

Quaking aspen tree, 61
Queen Anne's lace, 67
Queens: bat viewing, 129; beachcombing, seining and tidal pools, 152; bicycle tours and events, 210; bicycling, 198–203, 208; bike rentals, 209–10; birding, 84, 87, 89, 93, 100, 103, 106, 108; camping out, 116; canoe and kayak launch sites, 147; canoeing, 138; family fishing programs and contests, 226–27; farms, 244–46; freshwater fishing, 218; gardens, 181; museums, 234–35; nature and environmental centers, 16–21; nature walks, 57–68; night walks, 125; saltwater fishing, 221; zoos, 243
Queens Bicycle Path, 200
Queens Botanical Garden, 181, 265–66
Queens County Bird Club, 108
Queens County Farm Museum, 245–46, 265
Queens Museum of Art, 135
Queens Zoo, 243, 266

R

Raccoon, 39
Ramble, 13–14, 93, 100
Raptors, 100–107
Raritan Bay, 68, 70, 71, 84
Ravine, 49, 51, 100, 114
Red maple tree, 61
Red Oak Trail, 68
Red oak tree, 61

Red Trail, Mariners Marsh Park, 75
Red-backed salamander, 46
Red-eared slider, 47
Red-shouldered hawk, 105
Red-tailed hawk, 105
Red-winged blackbird, 98
Renwick, James, 198
Return-A-Gift Pond, 42, 87
Ringed-billed gull, 95
River Project, 16, 261
Riverbank State Park, 194–95
Riverside Park, 126, 147, 194, 195, 260
Robert F. Wagner Jr. Park, 107, 224, 260, 261
Rock Garden, 173
Rockaway Peninsula, 18, 85
Romer Shoal Light, 28
Roosevelt Island, 197–98, 261
Rose-breasted grosbeak, 98
Ruby-throated hummingbird, 92
Ruddy duck, 83
Ruth Rea Howell Family Garden, 170–71
Ryan Visitor Center, 10–11, 84, 120

S

Salamander, 46
Salt Marsh Nature Center: bat viewing, 129; beachcombing, seining and tidal pools, 152; birding, 84, 87, 89; camping out, 113; getting there, 255; nature and environmental center, 11–12; nature walks, 43–45
Salt-spray rose, 161
Sand, 153
Sand dunes, 205
Sanderling, 88
Sandpiper, 88
Sandy Hook Light, 28
Sara Delano Roosevelt Park, 93, 261
Sassafras tree, 61
Scarlet tanager, 98
Sea beach amaranth, 85, 161
Sea lettuce, 160

Sea rocket, 161–62
Sea star, 160
Seahorse, 159
Seaside goldenrod, 162
Seaweed, 160
Sebago Canoe Club, 141–43, 255
Secret Garden, 182
Seining, 150–51
Sensitive fern, 178
Serpentinite (rock), 22
Seuffert Bandshell, 20
Shadbush, 162–63
Shakespeare Garden, 14, 209
Sharing the Wonder of Birds with Kids (Erickson), 77
Sharrotts Pond, 26, 74
Sheep Meadow, 127
Shorakkopoch Rock, 54, 56, 93
Shore Road Bike Path, 193
Silver Lake Park, 205–7, 219, 268
Silver-maple tree, 61
69th Street Pier, 193, 221, 255
Skate egg case, 160
Skunk cabbage, 66
Sleep in the Deep and Bedtime with Belugas at the New York Aquarium, 123
Smallmouth bass, 217
Snapper, 219
Snapping turtle, 46
Snooze at the Central Park Zoo, 122–23
Snow goose, 82
Snowy egret, 87
Snug Harbor Cultural Center, 182, 205, 207, 268
Solomon's seal, 67
Some Plants Have Funny Names (Harding), 166
Southpoint Park, 198
Sparrow, 92
Sphinx, The, 38
Sphinx Boulder (glacial erratic), 6
Spider crab, 159
Split Rock, 173
Split Rock Trail, 6, 38
Sponge, 160

Spotted salamander, 46
Spring beauty, 67
Spring peeper, 46
Spring Pond, 25, 117, 127, 129
Spuyten Duyvil Creek, 15, 32
Stargazing, 126–27
Staten Island: bat viewing, 129; beachcombing, seining and tidal pools, 152; bicycling, 203–7, 208; birding, 84, 87, 89, 93, 100, 103, 106; boating, 136; campfires, 128; camping out, 116–18; canoe and kayak launch sites, 147; canoeing, 138; freshwater fishing, 219; museums, 235–36; nature and environmental centers, 21–28; nature walks, 68–75; night walks, 125–26; programs and festivals, 127; saltwater fishing, 221; stargazing, 127; zoos, 243–44
Staten Island Botanical Garden, 182–83, 268
Staten Island Children's Museum, 235–36
Staten Island Museum of the Staten Island Institute of Arts & Sciences, 236, 269
Staten Island Zoo, 74, 243–44, 260
Steeplechase Pier, 221, 255
Strack Memorial Pond, 68
Sugar maple tree, 60–61
Sweet gum tree, 61
Swindler Cove Park, 108, 195–97, 262

T
Tackle box, 218
Thomas Pell Wildlife Refuge Sanctuary, 6, 38, 105, 250
Tibbetts Brook, 8, 32, 34–35
Tidal pools, 152
Tides, 149
Toad, 46
Transit Authority, 20–21
Tree swallow, 98

Trees, 60–61
Trees New York, 10
Trout lily, 67
Trust for Public Land, 68, 189
Tufted titmouse, 92–93
Tulip tree, 61
Tulip Tree Trail, 18
Turtle, 46
Turtle Cove, 192
Turtle Pond, 13–14, 100, 168
Twin Island: birding, 83; getting there, 250; nature and environment center, 6, 7; nature walks, 35–38
Two Trees Island, 37

U
United Wildlife Rehabilitation and Education Center, 99
Urban Park Ranger Adventure Center, 17–18, 262
Urban Park Rangers: bicycle tours and events, 210; camping, 111–18; canoeing, 137–38; family fishing programs and contests, 222; night walks, 125; programs and festivals, 128
Urban Starfest, 127

V
Van Cortlandt, Jacobus, 8
Van Cortlandt Mansion, 8
Van Cortlandt Park: birding, 84, 100, 103; camping out, 113; freshwater fishing, 217; getting there, 250; nature and environmental center, 7–8; nature walks, 32–35
Vanderbilt, William K., Jr., 18, 200
Vanderbilt Motor Parkway, 200–201
Vaux, Calvert, 9, 208
Vernal pond, 69, 117
Verrazano-Narrows Bridge, 22, 192–93
Virginia creeper, 163
Vista Rock, 13, 14

W/X
Water lily, 134
Water strider, 47
Wave Hill, 174, 250
West Pond, 20–21, 64–65, 87
West 79th Boat Basin, 147, 193–95
Whelk, 155
Whirligig beetle, 47
White, Alfred T., 45
White ash tree, 61
White Island, 45
White oak tree, 61
White water lily, 67
White wood aster, 67
White-breasted nuthatch, 93
Why the Moon Gets Smaller (Gordh), 126
Wild Birds Unlimited, 93–94
Wildflower Meadow, 13, 50–51
Wildflowers, 66–67
Wildlife Conservation Society, The, 120
Willowbrook Park, 118, 219, 269
Windmill Pond, 59
Winged Migration (documentary), 109
Winged sumac, 162
Wolfe's Pond Park, 219, 269
Wood duck, 82
Woodchuck (groundhogs), 39
Woodcock, 89
Woodlands Trails, 68
World's Fair Marina, 147
Wyckoff Farmhouse Museum and Education Center, 246–47, 255–56

Y/Z
Yellow and Blue Trails, Clay Pit Ponds State Park, 71–75
Yellow Dot Trail, 68
Yellow perch, 217